High, Wide,
and Handsome

High, Wide, and Handsome
The River Journals of Norman D. Nevills

Edited by
Roy Webb

With a foreword by Brad Dimock

Utah State University Press
Logan, Utah

Copyright © 2005 Utah State University Press
All rights reserved

Utah State University Press
Logan, Utah 84322–7800
www.usu.edu/usupress

All photographs courtesy of the Special Collections Department, Marriott Library,
University of Utah, Salt Lake City

Cover design by Brad Dimock

Manufactured in the United States of America by Sheridan Books
Printed on acid-free, recycled paper

Library of Congress Cataloging-in-Publication Data

Nevills, Norman D., 1908-1949.
    High, wide, and handsome : the river journals of Norman D. Nev-
ills / edited by Roy Webb ; with a foreword by Brad Dimock.
        p. cm.
    Includes bibliographical references and index.
    ISBN 0-87421-602-8 (case-bound : alk. paper) – ISBN 0-87421-603-6
(pbk. : alk. paper)
    1. White-water canoeing–West (U.S.) 2. Rivers–West (U.S.) 3. Nev-
ills, Norman D.–Diaries. I. Webb, Roy. II. Title.
    GV776.W3N48 2005
    797.122'092–dc22

2004029562

Contents

for Sarah,
river girl

Foreword

On September 19, 1949, Norman Davies Nevills was at the top of his runway and the top of his game. He adjusted his twin-pitch propeller for climb, pushed the throttle of his new high-powered engine to full and accelerated down the crude gravel incline toward the gulch that separated him from his tiny settlement of Mexican Hat, Utah. His wife, Doris—beautiful, devoted mother of their two young daughters—sat beside him. They planned to land in Grand Junction in two hours. Doris would catch a flight to the West Coast; Norman would return to Mexican Hat and attend to his burgeoning river business.

Life was good. In the last two decades, Nevills had invented the commercial river business—the idea of taking passengers down extreme whitewater may have occurred to others, but Nevills made it real. Beginning in the 1930s he carried explorers, then tourists down the rollicking San Juan. In 1938 he began trips on the Colorado through Cataract and Grand Canyons, navigating America's biggest whitewater for pay. Although he scaled back to solely San Juan trips for three years during World War II, Nevills pushed his business hard, by reaching for publicity wherever and whenever he could, trying new rivers—the upper Green, Idaho's Salmon and Snake—and always making bigger and better plans for the future.

By 1949 he had spawned his own competition. Friend Harry Aleson had teamed up with disgruntled former passenger Charles Larabee to siphon off Glen Canyon business. Former boatman Don Harris was running private river trips with Bert Loper and would soon begin commercial operations with passenger-turned-partner Jack Brennan. Boatman Kent Frost had guided a group of Salt Lake City Boy Scouts and Scout leaders through Glen Canyon, some of whom would spawn several new river companies in years to come. Former boatman and devoted booster Dock Marston had broken off and begun powerboating rapid rivers and, for reasons unclear, disparaging Nevills to anyone who would listen. But Nevills was a good hundred paces ahead of any of them in terms of reputation, momentum, experience, and publicity. No one before him had ever made more than two transits of Grand Canyon. Nevills had logged seven. He was called the Fast Water Man.

Detractors criticized Nevills's boating as being too conservative. But to be honest, conservative boatmen in those days ran flat water. Even showing up on a whitewater river bordered on insanity in most minds. To do it successfully was almost unheard of. Most river expeditions that preceded Nevills were rife with wrecks, flips, and worse. Yet Nevills never flipped a boat, never lost a passenger, and never aborted a trip. Conservative, perhaps, but a conservative wild man—flirting with the edge of possibility, but poised to pull things back into control at a moment's notice.

***

Nevills hit take-off speed and eased back on the stick. The clattering and bouncing along the runway quieted once the plane rose from the earth. A broad, jagged gulch opened up ahead and below. Airborne again, he began a low, banked turn over the Nevills Lodge, preparing to buzz a farewell before climbing out toward Blanding and up over the high country toward Colorado. A kaleidoscope of colored, bent, desert stone rotated beneath them.

Lord, did that man love to fly. He could not drive by an airport without stopping to rent a plane for a quick zoom around the terrain. Nevills bought his first plane in 1946 and quickly mastered the art of flying. Some called him reckless, but by a crop duster's standards, he knew his craft and flew it bravely, cleanly, and well. He worked as a bush pilot for geologists—dropping into likely spots in the desert and then clearing enough of a runway to take off again. That is edgy work, and it takes a sure and quick hand on the control stick. Yet in all his cavalier moves he only banged things up once, snapping a prop on a bad desert landing due to, he claimed, a lack of concentration from a bulging bladder. The plane itself was unharmed. Today, bush pilots in Alaska and Idaho fly like Nevills did. They have to. And they are very, very good.

But pilots and boatmen operate near the edge, and there is a reason it is called the edge. Things happen out there with little margin. On the river it can end up in a boat wreck or a flip, though rarely much worse. Water is soft and slow and almost always forgiving. It's different in an airplane. Things can happen way too fast, and gravity is relentless. Pilots practice stalls, simulated power failures at altitude, and power-off landings to be ready for ill fortune. But there is one situation practicing pilots cannot duplicate, and it is one of the worst things that can happen: a power failure immediately after takeoff. The plane has barely enough speed to fly, is scarcely above the ground, and the runway is never close enough. There are few options and no time.

That day, it happened. The *Cherry II*'s souped-up engine sputtered and quit. Some later spoke of a known fuel problem, of Nevills's recklessness, of the inevitability of disaster. They said every pilot knows you can't get back to the runway in this case; simple physics—dictates that you have to land somewhere else. But not one of them really knows what happened. Not one of them was at the stick that day. Nevills had a fraction of a second to pick a likely place to set it down. He made his decision and tried to hold enough altitude to clear the cliff edge as he headed for the end of the runway. That's when all his good fortune, good luck, and fine skills came to an end. He was three feet too low. The *Cherry II* exploded on impact.

The river world was shocked, his family devastated. Three boatmen, Frank Wright, Jim Rigg, and his younger brother, Bob, picked up what remained of Nevills Expedition. They renamed it Mexican Hat Expeditions and ran trips into the 1960s. By then, his daughter, Joan, was married, and she and her husband, Gaylord Staveley, had taken over the company. But the river business had changed.

***

On July 30, 1947, Nevills sat along the Colorado at Diamond Creek and wrote, "This will never be a 'milk run,' it will always be a trip filled with unexpected thrills, surprises, some hardships, and above all, a feeling of having pitted oneself against dangerous and trying conditions—and winning out." What he could not foresee was the introduction of far more economical inflatable boats—boats that never had to be lined, that could carry more people per boatman, that could bounce off rocks and cliffs with impunity, that could take the biggest waves in Grand Canyon head-on. Nor could he predict the large, motorized rafts that took anywhere from a dozen to twenty or more passengers through the Canyon in a week. He could not know that in a mere twenty years the hardships, dangers, and trying conditions he experienced would be minimized on the river and denied in advertising—that Grand Canyon, for many, would indeed become a milk run.

By 1969 the Staveleys realized they could no longer compete in the small, cramped cataract boats. Pricing was too high, lining boats around rapids was increasingly impractical and unpopular, and the public was shopping for more of a tour and less of an expedition. Mexican Hat Expeditions organized one last trip for the Nevills cataract boats to commemorate the centennial of John Wesley Powell's "voyage of discovery" down the Green and Colorado. They launched the expedition in Green River, Wyoming, portaged around the new reservoirs at Flaming Gorge and Glen Canyon, and finished near the foot of Grand Canyon. At the end of that trip, the cataract boats went into storage and Mexican Hat Expeditions threw in the towel. They emerged the following year as Canyoneers, Inc., running seven-day tours from Lees Ferry to Lake Mead in large, motorized, pontoon boats.

In 1973 Canyoneers hired a gangly, pallid teenager from upstate New York to work as a swamper on river trips—cooking meals, washing dishes, managing the portable toilet, driving the boat in flatwater—a grunt. His first day on the job, trying to impress the rest of the crew, he fell down the ramp off the truck with an outboard motor in each hand. No one was all that impressed. That was me. That was my entry into commercial river guiding. I spent the next two summers swamping for Canyoneers, training under Nevills's grandson, Cam Staveley, slowly learning the art of managing sunburned tourists and running huge boats through whitewater. All the while I was absorbing bits of the Nevills legacy. During my second summer, Joan let me live in a spare bedroom of her house, and more Nevills lore and tradition seeped into my pores as river runners came, went, and, always, told stories. In 1975, on my nineteenth trip through Grand Canyon, I rose to lead pilot, operating trips myself. I felt young, green, and inept, with much to learn. Yet Nevills, who had invented the trade and led it for more than a decade, had not lived to see his eighth run through Grand Canyon.

I was one of several dozen new guides who swarmed into the river business as it exploded in the early 1970s. Together we learned—or I should say, relearned—much of what Nevills had pioneered. We came to know each rapid's personality, and how that changed with each stage of river flow. We hammered out menus, found good camping spots, devised sensible schedules; we learned stories to entertain our clients, pioneered hikes to quench their thirst for beauty and adventure, and yes, we, too, engaged in ego wars within the river trade. Like Marston, Aleson, and Reilly, we too, bandied bile among and between ourselves. But we had the liberty Nevills did not: we got to outlast it and realize we were all—every last one of us—in the same boat, on the same river, in the bottom of the same very great yet very tiny Grand Canyon. By and large, the arrogance and ill will faded into a river-wide camaraderie.

In 1978 I moved on to row rafts for Ken Sleight—who had gotten his start on the Scout trips from Salt Lake—who, in turn, had learned from Kent Frost, who was trained by Nevills. I changed jobs again to row wooden dories for Martin Litton, who had learned from Pat Reilly, who was trained by Nevills. There was no escaping it. By the 1990s the river lore began to bubble out of me, and I began to write river history.

It was not just on the river that I kept running into Nevills's ghost. In the 1990s I learned to fly an airplane and gained intimate knowledge of the hazards and exigencies of flight. I learned that in spite of the best-laid and most careful plans, things can go suddenly and drastically awry. I had just flown over the San Juan River west of Mexican Hat and was heading home to Flagstaff, Arizona. I planned to buy gas in Page, Arizona. Although the forecast was clear, in the minutes before arriving at Page, a fierce squall line formed and was about to engulf the airport. I had little gas and less time. In gale force crosswinds, I forced a landing and was blown off the runway three times in the attempt. When I stopped, I was right side up and at the end of the runway. I had been lucky that time, luckier than Nevills. I called a good friend in Page and, although it was still mid-morning, booked a couch for the night. My friend was Norm Nevills's daughter, Joan.

In May of 1991 I led a forty-seven-day dory expedition from Green River, Wyoming. I was to hire the interpretive staff, and for the upper half, picked historian Roy Webb. In addition to his *If We Had a Boat: Green River Explorers, Adventurers and Runners*, Webb had written *Riverman, The Story of Bus Hatch*, and recently processed the Norman Nevills Collection in his job as archivist at Marriott Library at the University of Utah. Thus began a long friendship, a shared interest in the Nevills story, and a series of peculiar river trips down the Green and Colorado.

Two years later I led a canoe trip down the Lower Green, switching to rafts for the rapids of Cataract Canyon. Picking up where we had left off, Webb accompanied us in his folding kayak and each night around the campfire, told stories of river history. Finally, in September of 1994, both Webb and I were invited on a Bureau of Reclamation "old-timers" trip organized by geologist Bob Webb to mine the memories of pre-dam river runners for details of the evolution of the river environment. Among the historic river runners on the trip were Norman Nevills's daughters, Joan and Sandy, and Mexican Hat Expeditions boatman, Bob Rigg. I had the honor of running a Nevills cataract boat replica, Jack Treece's *Bonnie Ann*, and had as passengers not only Rigg, who shared with me much of the art of running a cataract boat, but often the Nevills sisters as well. At Tanner Rapid, a "nothing" in many boatmen's minds, I took Joan and Sandy into the biggest hole in the rapid. I was used to dories, which cut the big waves with their high, pointed prows and burst out the far side. The *Bonnie Ann* hit the wave hard. The wave collapsed over the deck as it stalled, filling and nearly flipping the boat. Laughing and shrieking, we wallowed out the far end, but I had learned a cheap lesson.

The following day, Bob Rigg and I hit the wrong place in Sockdolager Rapid at precisely the wrong time. The *Bonnie Ann* was over before we could grab a breath, and we swam the rest of the rapid. Another lesson, this one not so cheap. What I had learned was that these boats, the state of the art of their day, were still not evolved far enough to take on the biggest waves of the Colorado. That step would come later with the introduction of Oregon driftboat hulls. The cataract boat was designed to take on the small to medium-sized waves and slip off to the side of the truly big stuff.

The next day we stopped to take a look at Granite Falls, one of the biggest on the Colorado. I found myself alone. Rigg was in another boat, and the few folks nearby all chose other vessels. That's when Roy Webb walked by. I asked him if he'd like to take a spin in the old Nevills boat. He jumped at the chance. We are both big men, and we know which way to lean in huge waves. We made it through Granite just fine. Half an hour later we drifted toward the head of Hermit Rapid, the great roller coaster of Grand Canyon. The water level was perfect to make the biggest, crashing-est waves imaginable—waves said by many to be the biggest on the Colorado. This was a stage Nevills, and many before and after him, chose to avoid, as the odds of flipping were high and rescue was chancy. With resignation they had roped the boats laboriously down the shore.

Humbled by my spankings the previous day, I told Webb I thought we should sneak off to the side of the biggest stuff. He understood but seemed disappointed. As we drifted closer to the lip, a gusting wind was tearing the caps off the breakers below. It looked utterly horrid. That's when the ghost of Nevills, knowing we had safety boats waiting below to pluck us out should this go sour—a liberty he never had—took over my brain. We turned and pushed straight down the tongue. I told Roy to hold on and try to keep me in my seat. And we hit them—dead on, over, under, airborne, and through them. Drenched, howling, awash, but upright, the cataract boat and its passengers flew out the far end—as Nevills would say—high, wide, and handsome.

—Brad Dimock

Introduction

In 1988, I started getting to know Norman Davies Nevills, even though he died three years before I was born. One of the facets of the archival profession is the ability to do this kind of time traveling through whatever kind of record people leave behind. In the case of Norman Nevills, it was surprisingly comprehensive, and I spent almost two years arranging and describing his records, and preparing an index to the collection. I read his diaries, pored over thousands of his letters, went through his tax records, and scanned his scrapbooks; I read of his hopes, his plans, his frustrations, and his dreams. In short, I got to know him and know him well. As I did so, a portrait at times subtle and at times transparent began to emerge. He was an intense, even driven man, but one who loved his family and friends with a deep loyalty. At times he seemed almost Machiavellian, with his desire to dominate the small world of river running. Yet at other times he seemed like a big kid, romping around the outdoors with his shirt off, having a great time. He craved the spotlight and resented others who took its focus away from him, but he was generous with his time and his labors to those who needed it.

As I delved deeper into his papers I began to realize that here was a complex individual who deserved a biography because of his impact on the world of river running and the calumny that was heaped on his name after his sudden death.

Yet try as I might, many attempts at starting on a biography died a-borning, almost as if Nevills himself didn't want me to write about him. In 1994, I went along on a Grand Canyon river trip sponsored by the Bureau of Reclamation that brought together a remarkable group of former river runners, boatmen, and owners of river companies, including Joan and Sandra Nevills. One of our tasks was to conduct oral history interviews with the participants, and so I interviewed Joan and Sandy in a camp at Nevills Rapid. We talked long about their father and tears were shed. After the interview, I talked with one of the boatmen and the cameraman for a while, and then started toward my camp. As I walked through the darkness, I couldn't shake the feeling that somehow we had invoked Nevills's ghost that night, and I lay in my sleeping bag like a child—with the bag pulled up to my eyes—expecting at any moment that his shade was going to step out from behind a bush and confront me for not writing about him.

1

Nevills Lodge at Mexican Hat

During that trip, and others, I've had the opportunity to ride and row cataract boats like the ones that Nevills used, so I got a feel for what a trip with Nevills Expedition would have been like. But still Nevills's ghost followed me—like Hamlet's father—expecting me to give him his historical due.

Then one day I traveled to southern Utah to give a talk for a local history group about Nevills, and on the way home drove through Mexican Hat, the tiny town on the border of the state where he had lived and made his mark on history. There is not much evidence of the Nevills family left in Mexican Hat; the Mexican Hat Lodge was bulldozed in the 1960s, and there was no one in that sleepy town who could remember, or would talk about, Norman Nevills.

On the way home, I drove north on the highway toward Cedar Mesa, and something caused me to stop just outside of town. On the west side of the road was a flat section of land, a rarity in that curved and humped landscape. I pulled off the road and drove over, and suddenly realized that I was driving on Nevills's old airstrip, the one that he had carved out of the dirt with his own hands. Sure enough, there was the outline of the hanger he had built, and it was obvious that here was where he had stored and serviced his beloved airplane. I drove to the upper end of the airstrip and let my truck roll downhill, hearing in my mind the roar of the engine as the light airplane made its takeoff roll. As I came to the end of the strip, I got out and walked to the edge of a small cliff. Suddenly, with a chill of recognition, I realized that I had stumbled onto the site of the 1949 crash that claimed the life of Nevills and his wife, Doris. Still visible were the scorch marks of the fire that consumed them almost fifty years before.

After paying my respects, I started home, driving north from Mexican Hat past Valley of the Gods, up onto the Grand Gulch Plateau. I couldn't stop thinking about the man and his life; I felt I owed Norman and his family an obligation to somehow bring him and his world back to life. As I climbed the dirt road over the edge of the plateau, with its view back over the landscape that Nevills knew so intimately, it struck me: the journals! Nevills was a prolific journal writer. Edit and publish his journals, I thought, and let him tell his own story. The more I thought about it, the more it seemed the perfect solution. He never liked sharing center stage, and this way he wouldn't have to; he could tell his own tale in his own way. Even though it has taken a few years from that moment to this, now, at last, Nevills has the chance that posterity never gave him: the chance to tell his own story.

Norman Davies Nevills was born in Chico, California, on April 9, 1908, the only child of William Eugene Nevills and Mary Davies Nevills.[1] Norman's paternal grandfather, William Alexander Nevills—known as "Captain Nevills" —was a successful miner and promoter in the California goldfields. He had amassed a considerable fortune by the time of the San Francisco earthquake of 1906, but died penniless and estranged from his son, William E. Nevills, in 1912. William E. Nevills, Norman's father, prospected in Alaska during the Klondike gold rush, and there, according to Norman, designed and built boats that were used in running the rapids of the Yukon River.[2] In 1903 or 1904, he married Mary Davies, ten years younger than he was, and immediately went prospecting for the next three years. By 1908, he had settled down in Chico, California, long enough for Norman Davies Nevills to be born.

Norman's mother, who went by "Mae" until her granddaughters changed it to "Moe," was seriously ill at the time of his birth, and as a result, Norman was a sickly, undernourished child. In 1912, after his father's death, W. E. Nevills moved his wife and child to Oakland, California. In 1920 William left for Goodridge, Utah, to work on an oil claim owned by a family friend. By 1927 William decided to strike out on his own in the oil business and began drilling his own wells. In the meantime, Norman was finishing high school and starting college at the College of the Pacific in Stockton, California. He first saw Goodridge—later re-named Mexican Hat—in 1925 when he went to visit his father. Further academic study was not in Norman's future, however, and he and his mother joined William in Mexican Hat in 1928.

The hoped-for gusher never materialized—although Norman drilled for oil off and on until his death—and the Nevills family was forced to turn to other means of making a living. They built a tourist lodge above the San Juan River, which flowed just south of the town, and Norman began guiding parties of visitors by car through Monument Valley, Valley of the Gods, and other nearby attractions. He supplemented the family income by doing whatever odd jobs he could find. In 1932, a miner asked Norman

Norman Nevills in 1938 with father, William E. Nevills (center), and mother, Mae Nevills (right)

to haul a load of supplies to a placer mine a few miles downriver. A couple of years before, his father had taken a boat sixteen miles down river, a feat which "both chilled and thrilled" young Norman. He quickly accepted the offer, even though the locals warned him about the dangers of the river. The Navajos, in fact, called the San Juan *To-husskay,* "river that is mad." Then in the summer of 1933, Norman participated in the Rainbow Bridge-Monument Valley expedition, a survey of the area around the Colorado and San Juan Rivers for a proposed national park. The surveyors brought along several Wilson Fold-Flat canvas boats to get around on the water, and Norman had a chance to paddle them.

On October 18 of that same year, after a short but fervent courtship, Norman married Doris Drown, a native of Portland, Oregon, whom he had met at a dance in Monticello, Utah. In December 1933, Norman, Doris, and his friend, Jack Frost, of Farmington, New Mexico, set off down the San Juan, intending to go to Copper Canyon, about seventy miles downstream. They were going to use one of the Wilson Fold-Flat boats left from the RBMV expedition, but the ten-foot boat was too small for the three of them, so Nevills built a boat out of scrap lumber that was caulked with old rags jammed into the cracks. In the low water of December, the rocks soon tore out the caulking, which caused the boat to leak.

It was obvious the boat would never make it to Copper Canyon, so they pulled the boat to shore at the Honaker Trail, some twenty miles from

NEVILLS HOUSE   MEXICAN HAT

Nevills home in Mexican Hat

Mexican Hat, and hiked overland back to town. Undaunted, Nevills and Frost decided to try again, this time in two boats. That winter Nevills built another boat, and in March of 1934, he and Doris, along with his mother and father, floated to the foot of the Honaker Trail, where they met Frost and his wife. They repaired the old boat and successfully floated to Copper Canyon. During this trip, a realization dawned on him: that the scenery alone could bring people to Mexican Hat to float the San Juan River.

For the next two years, Nevills floated the San Juan when he could. Then in 1936, Ernest "Husky" Hunt, whom he had met during the Rainbow Bridge survey, contacted him and asked him to guide a party down the San Juan and Colorado Rivers, so Hunt could visit Rainbow Bridge. Although, as it turned out, they knew nearly as much about outfitting and guiding a river trip as Nevills did, he was never one to let something like that stand in his way and threw himself into it with characteristic enthusiasm. The boat Nevills built for this trip became known in the family as the "horse trough boat." According to legend, it was built from boards salvaged from an old horse trough and an outhouse. Despite some snags, the trip was a success, and save for a short period during World War II, from that year to the end of his life, Nevills led excursions down the San Juan. These trips became his main source of income, and helped to finance his other trips on the Green, the Snake and Salmon Rivers, and through the Grand Canyon.

Nevills's first major expedition and the beginnings of his subsequent fame as the number one whitewater man in America came in 1938. In

Nevills's first "San Juan punt"

the summer of that year he led a sometimes reluctant crew of two other boatmen and six passengers—including two women—from Green River, Utah, through Cataract Canyon and the Grand Canyon, in three boats of his own design. Although internal dissensions threatened to end the expedition at Lees Ferry—the beginning of the Grand Canyon—Nevills and Elzada Clover, the co-organizer of the trip, were able to keep the party together and complete the trip. Nevills and Dr. Clover had planned to write a book about their experiences on the river, but this never materialized, and each went on to other things.

Nevills's second major trip was in 1940. This time he ran almost the entire length of the Green River, from Green River, Wyoming, through the Grand Canyon. The crew included his wife, Doris, and a woman from New York named Mildred Baker. Barry Goldwater, later to become a powerful Western politician, traveled with the party to Lake Mead. Again, low water caused the trip to be slow and at times, arduous, and as Nevills came to realize, a thousand miles of river was just too much.

In 1941 and 1942, Nevills conducted private charter trips through the Grand Canyon, giving him a permanent place in Colorado River history as the first person to go through the Grand Canyon more than twice. On the later trip, Otis Marston was one of the passengers. Marston and Nevills were at first close friends, and Marston helped attract passengers with showings of his films and ran a boat for Nevills on the river. Nevills called Marston "Oty," while Marston in turn referred to Nevills as "Admiral." But personality conflicts drove them apart, and after Norman's death, Marston became one of Nevills's most vocal detractors.

By the time the 1942 trip was over, the US was involved in World War II, and Nevills's nascent river outfitting business was considerably curtailed.

A Nevills Expedition San Juan River trip, Norman standing second from left

Although he did conduct a few parties down the San Juan during the war years, most of his time was spent working for the US Geological Survey, whom he joined as resident engineer at Mexican Hat in 1943, working around the Nevills Lodge, and drilling for oil and water.

In 1945, with the war almost over, Nevills took a party that included Otis Marston and Ed Hudson (who had also been on the 1942 Grand Canyon trip); Marston's daughters, Loel and Maradel; wife, Margaret; and others, down Cataract Canyon. This marked the resumption of a pattern that Nevills held throughout the rest of his life: spring and early summer trips on the San Juan, then a major expedition on another river later in the summer, followed by more San Juan trips on the monsoon rise in late summer and autumn.

In 1946, it was the Snake and Salmon Rivers in Idaho. In 1947, a shorter trip on the Green River and the Grand Canyon, a pattern he followed in 1949. In 1948, he only ran the Grand Canyon besides his San Juan trips. These were expeditions in the true sense of the word: lengthy, arduous, using specially designed equipment and a select crew. These trips were also expensive. One of his Grand Canyon trips, for instance, could cost as much as $1,500 per person, a princely sum in the 1930s and 1940s. There were very few people that could afford that kind of money during the Depression and the post-war years, and those that did tended to come from the upper classes, while his San Juan trips were filled with teachers, photographers, secretaries, and others who could afford the $75 weekly rate. But it was his longer trips that were widely reported, and the journals he kept then form the basis of the rest of this book.

How did people find out about Nevills Expedition? Nevills himself promoted the trips tirelessly, writing hundreds of letters to prospective clients, and produced a mimeographed brochure called "Canyon Wonderland" by the hundreds. And Nevills could be very persuasive; in a letter to a prospect he explained why one should go down the San Juan:

> It's the thrill of going where few have ever gone, or will, it's the thrill of seeing cliff walls too sheer and stupendous to describe—in myriads of colors—to be around a campfire at night and talk over the days adventures—and those of the past voyagers—Rainbow Bridge, Outlaw Cave, Mystery Canyon. And the River is absolutely unique. The boating itself is fascinating.[3]

Personal contacts were also a good source of passengers; on at least two separate occasions, women he met at Rainbow Bridge, who had hiked in overland, were persuaded to sign up for a Nevills trip later. As his fame grew, a number of articles appeared in national magazines such as *National Geographic, Atlantic Monthly, Saturday Evening Post,* and *Arizona Highways.* He ran ads in a number of regional magazines such as *Desert Magazine,* and his name spread by word of mouth among outdoor-oriented groups such as the Sierra Club and the Appalachian Club. Late in his career, newsreels, travel lecture films, and a short film called *Facing Your Danger*—which won an Academy Award in 1946—were seen by thousands. Nevills also toured Utah and the West showing slides and films and giving lectures wherever he could, and never missed any chance for publicity, no matter how fleeting.

People went on a Nevills Expedition river trip for many different reasons: a sense of adventure or artistic vision, to make films or take photos for profit, or as a graduation gift. One friend of Nevills asked him to hire his son as a boatman to try to cure the son's drinking problem. Nevills always encouraged anyone who was interested in his major expeditions to take the San Juan trip first, to get some river experience before attempting the "big'un," as he called the Grand Canyon. Unlike other outfitters of his time, Nevills took many women, children, and older people on the river; he often commented that he preferred taking women, as they "made the best men." He also took older people—ages over seventy were not uncommon—and the disabled, such as a man with severe arthritis who had to run all the rapids on the San Juan River, as he was unable to walk around them.

Nevills had many repeat customers and got many passengers for his Grand Canyon trips based on experiences on the San Juan. Many who were bitten by the river bug with Nevills went on to start their own river outfitting companies, or at least kept running rivers for the rest of their lives. Familiar figures in Colorado River history such as Otis Marston, Frank Wright, Kent Frost, P.T. Reilly, the Rigg brothers, and Don Harris all got their start with Nevills Expedition.

Many of Nevills's guests found themselves thinking about their river experience long after the trip was over, and it remained a central part of their memories the rest of their lives. Alice Bates, months after her return to her home in Los Angeles, wrote:

> I longed to be back on the rivers again—for the huge boulders, the sand waves, the sand bars and even the rapids. Most of all I longed for those long calm stretches through Glen Canyon where we floated down the river without a thought or care, feasting our eyes on the beauty all around us— often so close together that our voices joined the three musical instruments and we sang, "It's moonlight on the Colorado."[4]

Many wrote detailed, amusing accounts of their trip, or even composed songs, such as "Two Little Flies," by 1948 passenger Tro Anspach, and sent copies to Nevills. Others wrote him long letters extolling the ever-changing beauty of the canyon, the excitement of the rapids, the thrill of exploring hidden side canyons, or the tranquility of a riverside camp. Few failed to note, however, what had really made the trip live in their memories: Norman Nevills himself. Evelyn Box, a 1941 passenger, summed it up in one sentence better than all the accolades Nevills received throughout his career on the river: "Never was anything so heavenly as this trip."[5]

But the number of trips and miles on a river are one thing; and anyone who runs a tourist-based business has to have a public face. So what was Norman Nevills—the man—like? P.T. Reilly, who got to know Nevills well in the years just before his death, looked at Nevills with the cold eye of an engineer and left this portrait in words:

> Norman Nevills was small in stature yet impressive physically. He was not taller than five feet seven inches, weighed less than 140 pounds, but he had the arms and torso of a man thirty pounds heavier. He had unusually large forearms and beefy, horny, capable hands. He was quick as a cat and was aware of it. He was affable but impersonal. One had to know him before realizing that his amiable exterior was a facade that disguised a shy but highly competitive person with unresolved doubts about many things. He had no use for alcohol, barred it on his trips, but was a heavy smoker. His wife and children adored him—a claim that not all men can make. [6]

Nevills had a high forehead, a "contagious smile," a booming voice— what guests called his "river voice"—and pale blue eyes. He was a man of enormous energy He not only went on every expedition and San Juan trip, he helped manage the Nevills Lodge, conducted guests on tours of Monument Valley, picked up passengers coming to Mexican Hat for river trips, drilled for oil and later for water, built a water system for the house and lodge, prospected for uranium, and learned to fly and built his own airstrip and hangar, measured the San Juan three times daily (starting in 1943) for

Nevills performing his duties as USGS water-gauger, Mexican Hat, 1944

the US Geological Survey, helped Doris with two small children, dealt with an ailing father and difficult mother, and did any and all odd jobs he could find to help support his family. In the winters he composed lengthy, detailed letters to a wide assortment of friends, acquaintances, and prospects; single-spaced, typed letters of six- or seven pages are not uncommon among his papers. In addition, he typed and edited the journals that he kept on all his major expeditions, and wrote and updated his brochure about the river trips and the Nevills Lodge. Nevills also had a sense of history; he read widely and deeply, devouring books on the Colorado River and his favorite hobbies, such as archeology, geology, and history.

Throughout his career guiding parties on the rivers of the West, his beloved wife, Doris, supported him. Indeed, many who knew them say that Doris was a very real reason for his success. Doris organized all the menus, shuttles, and other logistical details that are absolutely essential for a successful commercial river trip. In addition, she smoothed over disputes and ruffled feelings among passengers and boatmen that were sometimes caused by Norman's intense personality. Doris was by all accounts completely devoted to Norman, and endured with good spirit the nagging by Norman's mother, Mae Nevills. Doris' support of Norman's chosen career extended to pawning her jewelry during the lean early years before Norman became famous, and caring for their two daughters, Joan, born in 1936, and Sandra, born in 1941. The one thing that Doris reportedly did not share was Norman's passion for flying, even though the light airplane that Norman bought in 1946 was a great convenience, given their isolated home and the atrocious roads that they had to use. It was in Norman's beloved *Cherry II*,

The Nevillses as home: (left to right) Harry Aleson, Pres Walker, Mae Nevills, Norm Nevills, Doris Nevills

as he called his airplane, that they met their deaths together in September 1949.

But there is an epilogue to the story of Norman and Doris Nevills, or rather two epilogues. The first is tangible: Nevills's boats and business were taken over by some of his former boatmen, Frank Wright and Jim and Bob Rigg, who continued to offer river trips under Mexican Hat Expeditions. Later, Norman and Doris's oldest daughter, Joan, also carried on the family business; after she married her husband, Gaylord Staveley, she ran the office while Staveley, who also had heard the call of the river, guided trips. In time, Mexican Hat Expeditions became Canyoneers, one of the prominent river outfitters in the Grand Canyon. Today a third Nevills generation, grandsons Cameron Staveley and Gregg Reiff, have continued the family tradition of "facing your danger."

The other epilogue is nothing so concrete. Indeed, it reaches into that realm of historical indulgence called "What If?" It has to do with a trip that Nevills had been planning a year before his death. Dr. Andrew Chamberlain, a passenger on a 1948 trip, was also a member of the California Sierra Club. Through Chamberlain, Nevills signed a contract to take seventy-five members of the San Francisco chapter of the Club down the San Juan in June of 1950. To get that many people down the river he planned to purchase a number of inflatable, rubber life rafts and tow them behind his San Juan boats, each of which would be equipped with an outboard motor. The cost was to be $42 each. The nineteen boats would have been an unwieldy flotilla, but no doubt Nevills would have pulled it off had he lived.

Now it just so happened that the planning for Glen Canyon Dam was going on right at this time. In fact, the legislation authorizing the Colorado River Storage Project (including the dam) was still in Congress. Nevills was aware of the project and of what it might do to his river business, although he was realistic and as always, looked at the possibilities for his own interests. In response to a letter from a former passenger in 1948, he wrote:

> Like you, I hate to see the dams go in, as it will spoil a lot of things for a lot of people. Fortunately, tho, there is very little chance in our lifetime of seeing a dam on the lower San Juan. One at Lees Ferry won't hurt us too much tho it will make easier travel in that area and see some tin can tourists on the resulting Lake.[7]

Now it also happened that the San Francisco chapter of the Sierra Club was just then beginning to feel the first stirrings of environmental consciousness since the death of John Muir in 1914. By 1955 the Sierra Club would transform itself from a hiking club concerned with strictly local issues to a nationally focused, activist environmental group. Together with other environmental organizations and a wide range of citizens, the Club would lead the successful fight against the Echo Park Dam—the "centerpiece" of the Colorado River Storage Project—just a few years after Nevills's death.

So here's the *What If?* What if Nevills *had* taken those seventy-five articulate, energetic and politically active men and women down the San Juan and into Glen Canyon? What if those Sierra Club members—the doctors, lawyers, businessmen, writers, the very ones who were to mobilize and defeat the Bureau of Reclamation for the first time in its history—had seen the beauties about to be lost to Lake Powell and decided to oppose the construction of Glen Canyon Dam, just as they did a few years later in Dinosaur National Monument? Could history have taken a different course? Could Glen Canyon Dam have been stopped before it was built?

"Ah Well," as Major Powell said, "we may conjecture many things." For better or worse, the river gods ruled otherwise. Nevills died in the wreckage of his beloved plane, and the Sierra Club trip was canceled. The attention of the Sierra Club members was soon diverted to the threat to canyons of the Green and Yampa Rivers, where they led the campaign against the Echo Park Dam. Glen Canyon Dam was built, flooding forever the places that Nevills had worked so hard to make known: Zahn's Camp, Paiute Farms, Redbud Canyon, Thirteen-Foot Rapid, Hidden Passage, Mystery Canyon, Music Temple. The name of Norman D. Nevills, once so preeminent among those who love the wild rivers of the West, was reduced to a footnote of history, and Glen Canyon became, ironically, the Place No One Knew. The

Nevills the tour guide, Monument Valley

rest, as they say, is history.

In today's high-tech and big-business world of commercial river running, where thousands of paying passengers are taken downriver annually, and hundreds of thousands of dollars are spent on equipment and permits by outfitters, Nevills Expedition, with its wooden boats and slim margin of profit, seems quaint, like something out of a distant past. Indeed, after his death, Nevills's reputation suffered at the hands of later rivermen, who said he was too cautious, too much of a showman, and so on.[8] Undeniably, Nevills was a showman and was concerned with his own reputation. He was not above manipulating facts to make himself look good; he irritated later river runners by changing the names of features along the river so he could claim credit for "discovering" them and for always seeking the spotlight.

Undeniably, however, Norman Nevills must be given credit for a number of firsts (so important to boatmen!) on the Colorado. He was the first to run the Colorado through the Grand Canyon more than twice, the first to run a strictly commercial river trip (in the modern sense) through the Grand Canyon, the first to take women on commercial river trips, the first to take women through the Grand Canyon, which was unheard of at the time, and the first to take children through the Grand Canyon. Nevills never denied being a cautious boatman, and was proud of the fact that he never flipped a boat on all the rivers he ran, a safety record hardly matched today. His boat design—the cataract boat—remained one of the standard river craft until well after the end of World War II; those who continued to use his style of boat did so long after others had converted to inflatable rubber boats. Nevills's principle of "face your danger" (i.e., the boatman faces the obstacle and rows away from it) is still the way rapids are run today, and although others had used the technique before him, he popularized the idea. Before Nevills began running the San Juan and Colorado, river running was looked upon as either a necessary evil to reach a scientific end such as surveying or collecting specimens, or a risky adventure indulged in by thrill-seekers. When he started, there were few others on the river; only men such as Bus Hatch and his brothers, and the Smith brothers in Idaho dared the rapids and isolated canyons. Their trips, though often reported in the local newspapers, did not garner the publicity that Nevills Expedition did. Norman Nevills made river running a household phrase, and opened the lonely canyons and rapids of the Green, the San Juan, and the Colorado to thousands of people who would not otherwise have ever heard of Flaming Gorge, Cataract Canyon, or Lava Falls.

Norman Nevills was a pioneer, indeed, one of *the* pioneers of commercial river running, and there are still companies operating today that can trace their roots directly back to Nevills Expedition. It would not be exaggerating to say that virtually everyone on the river today is there because Norman and Doris Nevills were willing to "face their danger."

Cataract and Grand Canyons,
June 20 to August 1, 1938

By 1937 Nevills sensed that he was on the verge of that big strike that had eluded his father and so far, eluded him; he might be able to make a good living taking paying passengers down the wild San Juan and Colorado Rivers. The key was publicity: people wouldn't sign up for what they didn't know about, and he knew he needed a lot more publicity than was it was possible to obtain living in remote southeastern Utah.

The chance for something bigger came along in the form of Elzada Clover, a small, unassuming botanist from the University of Michigan, who drove into Mexican Hat in August of that year looking for cacti. A plan that had been bubbling in Nevills's head for a while surfaced, and he quickly found a willing ally in Clover. Over the table at the Mexican Hat Lodge, they hatched a plan to traverse the rugged canyons of the Colorado. Clover headed back to Michigan to recruit crew and obtain funding from the university, while Nevills, along with USGS engineer Don Harris, spent the winter of 1937–38 building three boats to Nevills's design, that he called cataract boats. Harris agreed to go along as a boatman, as long as he did not jeopardize his job with the USGS (this being the Depression), and he was promised one of the boats in return for his labor. Nevills also recruited a San Francisco artist, Bill Gibson. Clover, meanwhile, brought back her lab assistant, Lois Jotter, and a graduate student in zoology, Gene Atkinson.

The party departed in high spirits from Green River, Utah, on June 20, 1938, for the first leg of the trip that would take them through Labyrinth and Stillwater Canyons on the Green River to the confluence with the Colorado, through the dangerous rapids of Cataract Canyon, then through Glen Canyon to Lees Ferry, Arizona. The water was near its peak flow, at 17,400 cubic feet per second (cfs). In the words of historian David Lavender, "It was not a good trip. Nevills had never been in charge of a group before, and he barked orders instead of giving suggestions."[1] The journey through Cataract Canyon was a learning experience for all of them, Nevills included, and learning experiences are almost by definition unpleasant. After joining the Colorado at the head of Cataract Canyon, the volume of water more than doubled, to almost 50,000 cfs, a daunting level in Cataract even for modern boatmen. Perhaps because of his experiences on the 1938 journey, Nevills only ran Cataract Canyon twice more, in 1940 and 1945. By the end of this section of the trip there was quite a bit of tension between the crew, and Nevills and Clover. Although after Nevills's death, historians

The first three cataract boats under construction at Mexican Hat, 1938—Norman Nevills on left, Don Harris on right

made much of this, the same tensions can easily break out on a modern river trip, which does not have the element of facing the unknown that the 1938 journey had. Cameramen and reporters were waiting at Lees Ferry and the journey made national headlines. Nevills was delighted to learn that the party had been feared lost, as the resulting publicity was more than he could have paid for.

At any rate, when they reached Lees Ferry on July 8, there were some personnel changes. Don Harris, concerned that they would not finish the Grand Canyon before he had to report for a new job in August, dropped out, to his everlasting regret. Nevills told Gene Atkinson that his continued participation was not wanted, at which Atkinson created "a great to do about going on." Nevills was not impressed, and instead recruited two men he knew locally, Lorin Bell and Del Reed, to be boatmen. The Cataract Canyon leg proved to a shakedown cruise, and the Grand Canyon journey went much smoother. Nevills had settled into his role as leader, the new members were more accommodating, and all had a wonderful journey. There were no upsets, no bad feelings between members of the crew (although Nevills still resented Jotter siding with the "whisperers" on the first leg of the trip), and the water levels and the weather held fair. At the end of the journey, Nevills was poised to take the fame generated by this pioneering voyage and turn Nevills Expedition into the first real river-outfitting business.

JUNE 20

Shoved off at 9:10 AM. Various passengers rode to below the Geyser.[2] I shoved off with Elzada[3] in my boat, and as we got nearly to highway bridge the second boat with Lois[4] and Harris[5] shoved off. Next in order came Bill[6] and Gene,[7] with Gene at the oars and having trouble handling the boat. We landed below the railroad bridge and some of Harris' folks got in the boat with him. Off again.

At the Geyser said "Good-bye" to Doris[8] and Joan,[9] and Dan Hayes and wife got in boat to ride the next mile or so. At this point 11 visitors were left and the expedition was really under way.

Lunch at 12:00 Noon 11 miles downstream. In afternoon bucked heavy upstream wind. Extremely hard to make headway. Once on the west wall, about 75' high, with a dune at its top, the wind caused a literal waterfall of sand.

Mouth of San Rafael at 3:15 P.M. 22 miles covered!

Lois loses hat in wind—hat recovered.

Camp at 6:05 P.M. Mile 84. 33 ½ miles for the day.

Tried to rain during night, with sky heavily overcast, and considerable lightening. Mosquitoes very bad.[10]

June 21

All boatmen have blistered hands from rowing. In loading the boats a bucket is lost while being tossed to a boat from shore. I lecture on the need and necessity for caution in handling equipment and to toss no more equipment.[11]

River has dropped 2" during night in 350' section.[12] The sky still heavily overcast and the day starts delightfully cool. A very slight upstream wind.

Shove off at 7:35 A.M. We are just drifting, as the current is around 4 mph, and we make good headway.

Gene and Bill have gone ahead in hopes of sneaking up on game. They are to time themselves so we will catch them at 10:00. Lois and Harris are 100 yds ahead of us. Gene shot a goose yesterday and it got away.

Mile 75 ½. On east wall, top of talus slope we spy names of previous parties. I put NEVILLS EXPEDITION on the wall [with] those of the Hydes,[13] Eddys,[14] and others.[15] On again at 10:40.

Eat lunch a short distance below.

Mile 68. Upper end of BOWKNOT BEND. Elzada, Lois, and myself leave the boats and start climbing for the top of the saddle in order to get pictures of the boats round the loop. I get Lois up alright on the trail I pick but have to rescue Elzada.

The boats make the seven mile loop in 1 hr. 40 min. They could have made it lots faster but a duck hunt delayed the party, but resulted in shooting fat duck.—On again at 4:30 PM.

June 22

No change in river during night. Mosquitos very bad, and all but the women complained much about biting. The two women slept on huge rock used as dinner table. Another big rock was likewise employed by Bill and Gene. Harris and I slept on sand at foot of talus slope 75' from river.

Yesterday Bill and Gene dropped an oar and had to unship a spare to catch up with it.

Arose this morning at 5:00 AM, but it is 8:10 AM when we shove off.

Elzada rows until noon while I mount hatch cover bolts. Harris does likewise while Lois rows, or rather guides the boat. We also put in screws that were not in when the boat left Mexican Hat.

Last night Elzada and Don played duets on their harmonicas.

Arriving at mile 21 (Yokeys Flat?) explored around to see cabin, old boat, and oars.[16] Took pictures, on at 3:30 PM. It is threatening rain, and there's an upstream wind.

Stopped to see little P[ueblo]2 dwelling east bank. It had been much visited. Gene and Bill leave a life-preserver on the deck of their boat, and when we return to shove off again at 4:55 PM the wind has taken it away. We now have no spare life-preserver!

Camp on right bank. A fine natural landing spot with rock ledge. I wish to run boat fifty feet upstream into a cove so have Elzada use a stick to hold boat away from shore while I pull. The stick breaks and I look around to see Elzada endeavoring to climb out on shore. At this moment the other boats pull in and much merriment ensues, enhanced by the fact that I snatch up my camera and take a picture. While dinner was being prepared, wishing to check our position, I decided to climb the low cliffs in back of camp so as to see if the river made a close bend as I thought. Accompanied by Gene we went to the top and crossed some ½ mile to the other side. Followed a deer track to this point. I walked out on an abutment and saw a yearling buck—8 points—some 125 yds below. He stood just away from the foot of the cliff, between the cliff and grove of trees that always fringe the sandbars. Motioning to Gene brought him quickly, and he down[ed] the deer with one shot from his 22 pistol. We climbed down and spent some little time in skinning and cleaning the carcass. In climbing back up the cliffs we fell and Gene got a mild bruise on his wrist that was to bother him for several days. Reaching the top we were nearly to the other side when we met Harris and Bill looking for us. The help was needed and welcome. The deer was shot at mile 20.

Harris went swimming, but water was very cold. I washed out my bloody clothes.

JUNE 23

Shove off at 9:00 AM. On left wall is inscription as follows:

U.S.G.S.
21-m-Col. Riv.
S. Hargen
H.T. Yokey 10–09
E. Bitzer 19[17]

Mile #3 is coming! It's a weird feeling to realize that the Colorado River and Cataract Canyon are almost here. All the members are looking forward to Cataract Canyon with the proper respect. I have done my best to impress the seriousness of this undertaking on them. It's good to know that the folks at home are thinking of us. They needn't worry, I'll get the party through. Am in the best shape of my life and feel most confident. Have kept us located every inch of the way, on the Green. Here she is!

Colorado River—2:25 PM

We row across to the other side and make a precarious landing on quicksand to look over a little riffle directly downstream. A cursory examination is all we give and on we go on a mighty big river that is in full flood.

MILE 213. Here we stop ¼ mile from Cataract Canyon. We are looking for a large rock with inscriptions left by the Powell party.[18] They are found and photographed. Leaving the women to make more detailed photographs, the men and myself walk along the rocky ban[k] to the foot of rapid #1. After coming off relatively smooth water this short rapid with about fifteen foot waves looks quite impressive. The rapid terminates in a huge eddy. Then directly below is a double channel rapid, #2. It is now 5:30 PM. Gibson turns, looks upstream, and lets out a cry—"My God! There's the MEXICAN HAT!" We all looked to see the MEXICAN HAT riding the waves of #1. I couldn't help but remark at how beautifully the boat rode! Stern first and in perfect alignment! Never doubting but what the boat would stop in the huge eddy below, I sent Harris the ½ mile back to our mooring spot with orders to bring down my boat and pick me up so we could bring in the truant craft. I told him to come alone.

Gene, Bill and I scrambled over the rocks nearly an eighth of a mile to discover the MEXICAN HAT[19] already through the eddy and headed for rapid #2! I then sent Gene and Bill back to get the BOTANY[20] and bring it down to the head of #2, telling them to have the women walk down. At this moment the WEN[21] hove into sight with LOIS in the passenger cockpit! As the boys turned back I scrambled on down to meet the boat—but it too went on into rapid #2! With a sinking feeling I ran on as fast as I could. Not far to the reportedly bad #4, and worse than a greenhorn at the oars!

With much difficulty I got to where I could just make out the head of rapid #4. No boat in sight! I turned back to retrace my trail, and over me came the feeling that I surely must be tackling too big a job. Words can't tell the allgone feeling I experienced. This surely must be a warning to turn back! Yet I knew that I was qualified to carry on.

Not far above #2 I came upon Elzada, Gene and Bill in a small draw at the river's edge. They struck me as feeling quite low, so I tried to not show the despondency I felt. I believe I succeeded, as am sure they felt I displayed little concern over this catastrophe. Got things ready to eat and were making shift with pieces of wood for spoons (the mess kit was in the WEN) and were about to eat when a call reached us from across the river. It was true! MEXICAN HAT OK was all we could decipher, plus "COME OVER." Fearful of the true conditions, and dreading the trip, we loaded our supplies into the boat, and with three passengers, a twenty mile current, and very little light—crossed the river. It was an eerie feeling. We landed in good shape and learned that Harris and Lois ran to the head of rapid #7, at MILE 208 ½. Looking down at the next rapid, they saw the MEXICAN HAT lodged in an eddy at the foot. They rushed down to secure the boat. Returning then to their own boat, they decided upon Lois remaining, while Don would walk back up if possible and advise us of their fortune. Surely few rapids have had such a flaunting of disregard and not answered back!

After giving Harris a bit to eat we decided that it would be best for he and Gene to return to camp by flashlight to Lois' camp.

In the morning I will take the BOTANY down with Bill and Elzada as passengers.

We make our beds just at the edge of the river on some sand. There is little bedding and it promises to be a rather uncomfortable night. The river is roaring and sounds threatening. This is a terrifically powerful river. It's really impressive in its fury. I can see this is going to be a big job, but I still feel confident, tho mighty respectful.

JUNE 24

What an experience last night! Elzada, Bill and I went to sleep side by side trying to make up for inadequate covering. We slept feet towards the river, and some four feet back from the edge.

1:00 AM I awoke yelling, with the sensation of the river taking me! The others awoke at the same time and we all made a backward leap. The river had risen and cut the bank out from under us until our legs were actually dangling out over the water! To sleep again.

The day dawns coolish. The river is in full flood and is a dreadful sight with the enormous big trees rushing past. I decide to take Elzada and Bill with me on the run to Lois' camp spot.

Shove off at 7:15 AM without breakfast. Ran to head of #7, 3 ½ miles in 10 minutes! Twenty-one miles per hour! In #4, on the right side we saw our first really big hole. It was huge and looked bottomless. In #5, Harris reported skirting the big waves. They were over twenty feet high. I decided to try our boat out properly, so went through the middle of them. The sensation is indescribable! And how the boat rode! upon landing found that the boat had only 5" of water in it. I can't understand why these boats seem to keep from filling. The first breaking wave or two had me gasping in the cold water.

We all get together to have breakfast and talk over the nights experience. Lois moved her bed three times because of rising water.

And the boys had just preceded us into camp. It seems that after leaving us they made a precarious way for something over a mile. Between dodging and jumping around rattlesnakes, and taking nasty spills over unseen boulders, they finally gave up as impractical proceeding any further, and decided to await break of day. Gene was fully clothed, but Harris had on only trousers and shoes. When his shoulders would get chilly he'd remove his pants and wrap up the upper part of his body. Then back on with the trousers. And thus passed the night!

After breakfast I go to my boat and find the stern hatch cover missing! We institute an immediate search which finally discloses the errant cover float[ing] upstream some fifty yards in an eddy! Someone had been careless again! We certainly seemed to have a guardian angel along! But rather than place too much responsibility on the guardian angel I again lecture everyone on the need for extreme caution at all times. It wasn't until several days later that Harris admitted tying his boat to a tiny bush at the head of rapid #1.

Have decided to coach the boys in rapid running technique, so we will run down through #7 with Harris coaching Bill in the BOTANY, going first to the head of #8, to the eddy where the MEXICAN HAT is moored. I will follow Gene at the oars.

We're off. This experiment works nicely and we are able to give valuable pointers. We then look over #9.

We all ride through #9 and then drop down to the head of the much talked about MILE[-long] RAPID. It's a hair-raiser and will prove a terrific undertaking to line. Yet we must play safe and line the worst drops. The MILE[-long] is more than a mile long! We climbed over rocks most of the afternoon trying to get along it to the foot.

Have returned to the boats and are dropping them down to the very head of MILE[-long] RAPID, and are going into camp on the left bank at 5:20 PM. We're dead tired and going to take a swim to freshen up.

June 25

I still am determined to line this rapid. All the party are in favor of running, but I won't let my judgement be swayed by incompetent opinions. After all I am the one that is to get this party through.

At 7:55 we start to line the very first drop. We line in order: MEXICAN HAT, WEN, BOTANY. Drop down through an eddy and at 10:50 AM we are but barely started. The WEN tilted when being run through and filled the cockpit level with the seat.

The task of lining this whole rapid, at least two miles long, seems hopeless. So I determine to take one more look and see if I can't figure some safe way in which to run it. Leaving the women in camp the men and myself start out. About a mile down, after summing up the possibilities in my mind I decided to run. The looks on all faces was far from assuring. I leave Don and Gene about ½ mile down, at one of the worst drops, and Bill and I return towards the boats. Bill grabbed a bite to eat at the boats then hastened to get back to an advantageous position to get some movies. I ate just a light lunch so as to not get cramps if I went in. Also dumped out the water from the canteens so they would give an added buoyancy in case of an upset. At time drew close to shove off I indulged in prayer. This looked like it might be the "last mile."

Instructed the women to stay with the boats until they heard from me and off I went. The next nine minutes were filled with thrills galore. I was getting the fastest, most dangerous ride of my career. At times thirty miles an hour, and twenty-five foot waves combined to make an unforgettable ride. I rode the Mile[-long] and three others, landing on the left at 202 ¾ with 6" of water in the boat! I had to work my boat back upstream about fifty feet into a better anchoring eddy. Was just finished bailing out when Gene and Don came into camp. I left Gene with my boat, and Harris and I went to bring the other two boats down. Met Bill and the two women half way back. They appeared relieved at seeing the run was successful. They establish themselves in strategic positions to photograph the next run.

Arriving at the boats, I shove off at 5:20, and Harris follows at 5:25 PM. This ride proved to be a 100% more thrilling one than the other. On the second drop, a furious combination of waves took my left oar and bent it straight down! I moved about the fastest in my life in getting my weight on this oar so as to bend the lock back. Going down the second wave I succeeded. At one spot a mushroom wave developed that forced me to climb out on the deck and give my added weight on the boat so it wouldn't turn a backflip.

I land in the same spot again, and look back to see Harris coming along. Instead of following my course he picks one for himself and is almost upset by a freakish big wave. His repeated not following of instructions is going to bring him to grief. He can't seem to stay in line.

Camp left bank Mile 202 ¾.

The women are standing up beautifully so far.

Atkinson is getting some of the sneer out of him and beginning to realize what really big water can do.

Harris seems to be OK but is going to have to follow orders better.

Bill is frankly in a blue funk over the whole business.

All members are high in their praise of the way the boats handle and ride the big water. From the top of a twenty foot wave a hole seems enormous. The biggest waves in the San Juan are infants alongside these big fellows. The secret in riding these big backlashing waves is in loading everything in the stern and thus holding the boat down when it tries to back-flip. Have had one or two close calls from going over sideways—but not too bad. Rocks so far are simple to dodge, likewise the holes. Harris seems to tire easily. After I first shoved off to-day, Bill told the women "Well, if Norm cracks up we'd better walk." He really meant it! Have a swell camp stop again to-night. I like the settled river water, tho the others speak longingly of fresh spring water. No portages so far, and two rapids ahead of the Eddy party!

JUNE 26

Didn't break camp until 9:00 AM. Don, Bill and I walked about a mile and a half below to look over the situation. 1st rapid OK, 2nd, OK, but 3rd, a terror, and the 4th a wicked looking maelstrom of water.[22] #3 could be

run, tho dangerous and tricky, but it drives headlong into #4 with a series of big waves. Hitting the left side of #4 would be deadly as there are several tremendous big holes. Only chance would be to work to the left coming through #3 and thus hit the right-hand and runnable portion of #4. The only course is to line.[23]

Got back to camp at noon and had lunch.

I then got in the WEN and going through #1, whistling and enjoying the ride, I was careless enough to get caught by a tricky lateral wave and thrown off the seat and down into the cockpit. Bent an oarlock, so headed for shore. Barely made it at head of #2 just above a big pour.

Harris made it through alright and ran #2, pulling out at foot of #2 into an eddy on the left. I assured myself that Harris was alright then went on through after bailing out.

Harris went after the BOTANY to run it through, but we decided to line the boat through #2 as chances for getting caught in main drag are considerable. Lined all boats to head of #3, then took the BOTANY (line) through #3, on down to head of #4. Pulled the BOTANY up high and dry ready to portage overland.

Returning to the other boats, we found a heavy shore swell battering the boats against the rocks shore. We wearily worked the boats out of the river and some two feet above. Had dinner literally hanging onto the steep rock bank. A goodly sized Hackberry tree offered fine anchorage.

Only available camp spot some ¼ mile back upstream in the bed of a small lateral canyon. In the dark, and with much stumbling and falling we finally work our way to our camp site. A hard day.

We haven't enough man-power for this trip. The women are doing more heavy work than they should, especially Elzada. Bill is just useless as he doesn't know how to work. Gene is worse than nobody at all. Harris is good at lining and is my mainstay. I do think that Don and Bill would like to quit. I'm disgusted too as we haven't the personnel for this heavier work. Have to get more manpower. Will see what can do at Lees Ferry.

JUNE 27

To work! Lined the MEXICAN HAT a few hundred yards to the first series of holes. Lined by, then dropped on down to the point of portage.

Gathered logs and laid them for skids, then dragged the BOTANY up a forty-five or fifty degree slope for about sixty feet, turning sharp right and resting boat there. Then cleared a roadway by moving and removing boulders etc. Moved the BOTANY a few feet further on. Then moved or dragged the MEXICAN HAT up the slope and then stopped.

After lunch went after the WEN. After getting the WEN down to the point of portage, and out some ways from the water, decided to call it a day.

It's now 7:30 PM and we've just finished eating. It's been a mighty hard day. I measured out ½ jigger of whiskey to everyone but myself.[24] I think it was wise as they are all so tired. We've bit a big job off on this portage. We should be able to get back into the water and under way tomorrow. A few miles more will end the steepest part of Cataract Canyon. We have yet to hit a rock with a boat, though in lining and anchoring for the night they take a terrible beating.

Bill feels sort of sick, and I think he will want to pull out at Lees Ferry. I intend to see that he goes through. Don would be only too glad to stop at Lees Ferry. Gene and Don have both been sick today, likewise Lois. I feel fine, though have a sort of infection in my forefinger of my right hand. Am wearing a pair of Lois's shoes. For lining I wear an old pair of Elzada's. The river is dropping. Looks like a storm for tonight. A high clay bank or wall behind us studded with all sizes of rocks makes this a very dangerous camp spot. I have concluded we will be safe unless it gets to raining hard. We've had some trouble getting suitable bed spots.

JUNE 28

Last night was tough. Very light rain worried us for fear of falling rocks from the clay bank. I got up about 11:00 PM to check the WEN in its berth close to the water, and almost stepped on a rattlesnake that evidently was just crawling from past my bed. Finding the WEN OK, I took my bed down and spent the rest of the night on a big sloping rock with Bill. We took turns having nightmares etc. Lois was sick in the night to her apparent shame. To date Elzada and I are the only ones left that aren't sick. They all think it's the water. I really think it's the nervous strain, heat, and hard work.

This morning we dragged the WEN to the top of the slope, and incidentally killed the rattlesnake that I went the rounds with last night.

Captured the snake alive and he was kept in the sun some twelve minutes which proved fatal to him.

Then dragged the BOTANY across country some hundred yards, then downhill back to the river. The shore lash makes it necessary to hold the boats high and dry until ready to leave. It's an awkward launching spot but could be worse.

Brought the MEXICAN HAT down. It's hard work, and needing a rest, we stop a while. Gene and I walked about a mile to look over the river. O.K. Bill and Don slept on a rock. On our return we worked the WEN to the launching spot and then had lunch.

It is now 12:50 PM, and in a few minutes we will start relaying our supplies to the boats.

Boats loaded—and I shove off, followed in turn by the MEXICAN HAT, BOTANY, with Gene at the oars. Bill is in a dead funk about handling a boat. We will run two or three rapids before pulling in—we hope.

It's clouding up and looks a bit like rain. We really have been fortunate in the weather.

I am determined if at all possible to run home for a day when we land at Lees Ferry. Am worried about Dad and would like to see Cherry[25] and Joan, and Mother. It seems like we have been out a long time.

Mile 200 ¾. Camp. Left bank, beautifully sandy. Plenty of wood, and all spirits high though it is beginning to rain.

JUNE 29

Up at 7:00 AM. Started to sprinkle last night as dinner was being prepared, so the canvas I have was made into a flat roofed tent under which to eat. Barely got into bed when it began to rain in earnest. Finally got drowned out, so I got up and refueled the two big fires. Took down the kitchen shelter, put food under cover, then constructed a sort of pup tent. In the meantime I ate a big meal of raisins, candy, beef-stew, and coffee, thus proving that I am the iron stomached man of the trip. The two women and myself shared the tent all night and slept after a fashion. This morning my two arms are so cramped I can hardly use them.

Bill and Harris rigged up a shelter too, but Gene slept on, getting somewhat damp, though he has much more equipment than the rest.

The river is really COLORADO this morning, though not appreciably higher. We have finally gotten clothes, beds etc. dried out and now shove off at 11:15 AM.

Ran ½ mile and walked down along rapid extending to MILE 200. Run: WEN, BOTANY, MEXICAN HAT. Landed in eddy on right bank at MILE 200 for lunch.

River is plenty fast. Pulled in just above Gypsum Creek on left, thinking was at mouth of canyon. Water smooth and decided to run on to mouth about ½ mile below, at MILE 196 ½.

We proceeded in order: WEN, BOTANY, MEXICAN HAT. Approaching the [Gypsum] Canyon mouth I decided against stopping and to go on to Clearwater. It was just 1:20 PM. Just then I noticed I couldn't see the river below! Standing on the deck didn't help! Directly ahead of us was smooth looking water and a suggestion of a hump. Maybe a hole! I saw I couldn't make shore so decided to run to the right where the current dashed against a low cliff, also forming a hole. Yelled at Elzada as we went for the drop "this is the biggest drop of the trip." I scooted just to one side of the big mushroom and got into a mess of other big fellows, but we took them beautifully. In about a hundred yards I looked back to see the BOTANY on top of the mushroom and as it started off turned a front flip to go end for end. I immediately pulled towards an eddy on the left, then looked to see the BOTANY bottom side up, with one man clinging close to the prow rope, and the other man drifting close to the right hand shore. I finally got to an eddy so as to hold up to catch the BOTANY as it went by. In the meantime the MEXICAN HAT came through alright and made for the drifting man. This proved to be Bill, and he was played out when picked up I learned later. When he came to the surface after being thrown out of the boat, the first thing I saw was the peak of a comical black hat he wore appear.

By now the BOTANY was close upon us so I set out in the current to intercept it. Saw Gene hanging on grinning from ear to ear. He had well be grinning as he had a mighty close call. Barely got ahold of the BOTANY when he swept through the next rapid, a mild one. Gene then got aboard, with Elzada holding the BOTANY in tow. My arms were tired thanks to last night. I fought to tow in the boat, but the current was strong. Once when we were almost out of the main current the BOTANY swung around and pinned my left oar. I stood up to row, facing the prow. I had Gene take an oar, and between us we got within six feet of the shore. Directly below was a really nasty rapid, and on our side two holes! I took the stern rope and dived for shore. Got to shore as rope began to pull through my fingers. Couldn't hold it! The boats were off! I swam again as never before and just barely made it to the bank at the head of the drop. I hardly touched the bank in my haste to get out and see what had happened. Saw the WEN, still towing the BOTANY just leaving the second hole! I started running as best I could along the rocky shore, and after five or ten minutes thought I saw the two boats on the left bank just below the next rapid. I ran on, but no boats. Kept on going until the sheer wall on my left stopped me at MILE 194.

I started back as fast as I could as was afraid the MEXICAN HAT would come rolling by without seeing me, and there'd be. I dashed back over the rocks to the head of the 3rd rapid below Gypsum Creek.

I finally attracted the attention of Bill, Gene and Lois. I motioned them to run this rapid, then pick me up on the left bank at the foot. This they did. I ran the empty boat through the rapid at MILE 193 ½. Thus got to Clearwater at 5:30 PM. Smooth water just below the rapid at the mouth of Clearwater—but no boats! Debated on camping but decided to go at least around the next bend. I decided to line even this simple rapid as no chances whatsoever could be taken now. We rounded the bend ½ mile below and there on the left bank was Elzada and Gene, and both boats! The relief was more than words can describe. One oar lost, and food and clothing soaked. We quickly righted the BOTANY and started unloading it. After dinner we played hearts around a campfire.

The worry of this trip is hard, and the responsibility is tremendous. I sometimes wish I had never taken this trip as expedition leader. Elzada and Bill are a bit bunged up.

June 30

Up at 7:00 this morning, and are drying out equipment. My appetite is and has been enormous, so my nerves must be O.K. We will shove off at about 1:00 PM and try to reach Dark Canyon to camp. I have put my spare oar in the BOTANY.

July 1

We laid around yesterday afternoon. All but Bill and I slept. Bill and I worked on his movie camera. It seems to be alright now, tho must be looked after at Lees Ferry. Played a game of hearts in the evening.

Time going by will mean August 10–20 when we actually reach Boulder Dam, unless we get more and *better* manpower. Gene has to go to Texas by Aug. 5, Bill must be in San Francisco by Aug. 1. Don in Salt Lake by July 28th. Lois is good 'till Aug. 20th. I should be at the Hat not later than Aug. 10th. Elzada has no time limit. She wants to go on in the WEN if all the others leave. I consider it too dangerous with all my responsibilities to take such a long shot gamble. We'll see what Lees Ferry brings. I certainly am going to Mexican Hat for at least a day when we get to Lees Ferry. Grand Canyon with its tough portages is going to be a long hard job, and would take until probably Aug. 20th with our present personnel.

We are about eight miles from Dark Canyon this morning, with 9 rapids between, some at this stage of water should be hair-raisers.

It is now 7:10 and we should be off in a few minutes.

Shove off.

Dropped down little over a quarter of a mile to left hand bend and rapid at MILE 190 ½. Anchored on left, walked along rapid, it OK for all passengers. had quite a time crossing the lateral canyon at the head of the rapid as the water was backed way in.

Land left and lunch at head of rapid MILE 184. Have decided to line this one as the current hits the right bank on a left turn with such velocity that several big side lashing waves are more than liable to upset us. It's an easy lining job.

Line: MEXICAN HAT—20 min. BOTANY—12 min. WEN—10 min.

On again at 1:45 PM. Next rapid simple.

Mouth of Dark Canyon. Left.

First look suggests a lining job on this rapid.[26]

At MILE 184, after hitting the right bank, the current swung sharply to the left and in 150 yds. impinged against left cliff wall. Between the right and left impingements was a big eddy, flowing upstream some 10 miles an hour following the left bank. We'd set out and almost get into the current and a lateral wave would force us back into the eddy and around again. We kept circling, and Gene broke through, and I came up on third lap and got free, followed by Harris. It was hard work and tiring.

The boys are off up Dark Canyon looking for ruins. By the signs I feel sure they will have a fruitless search without going way up. Before leaving, Gene, without even a good look informed me that this rapid would be easy to run. He would soon wreck everybody if he were directing navigation.

The two women are lying in the shade just a ways up the canyon. I am looking over the rapid. Wish Dad could see the fine pickings here for driftwood. Closer inspection proves this rapid a dangerous proposition at the prevailing stage. The current drives against the right wall as at MILE 184, setting up some terrific sidelashing waves. The current also swings to the left directly below with an eddy that promises to be trick to get out of.

Am looking for a rock for Cherry, and a cactus for Mother. Well! Just found Cherry's rock, and glancing up on the cliff wall see some names: Pathe-Bray[27], Holmstrom,[28] Frazier,[29] this is 1/8 mile below mouth of Dark Canyon.

The boys returned without seeing any signs of ruins. They found, just around first bend on right, the inscription:

Andy Delaney-Gold Prospector 8-2-27

There's a fine camping spot just upstream from Dark Canyon. Go to make camp. After dinner a game of hearts determines that Lois is to do dishes in the morning.

Elzada found a beautiful spring, enclosed by ferns, about 200 yds on right up Dark Canyon. The water as Eddy says, is very metallic tasting. Probably aluminum in it.

Spirits are high and discussion trends to "pot hunting" in Lake Canyon. Will probably lay over there a few days and try our luck.

I have our lining route picked out and it should not take long or be difficult.

JULY 2

Hope to get the boats lined down by noon or shortly after, tho we are starting late. We've really had wonderful weather so far, tho to-day the sky is cloudless and bright, and we may get a real taste of heat.

I hope to send mail out at Hite if possible. And if we're going after pots in Lake Canyon we'll have to pick up some flour etc. Our food has been great and very ample. There's no question but what we've had real meals. Tho stopping over at Lake Canyon will not be figured on our schedule and would run us short. To date good cheer and fine feelings have prevailed, tho I look for a reaction to set in after reaching the easy water in Glen Canyon. Wonders will never cease, but I have never even partially blown up. Was complimented on the cool way I took things when the MEXICAN HAT got loose. River rose and dropped a few inches during the night.

Start lining: 8:45 AM. Finish and start on: 1:50 PM.

At noon today we were 100 yards from main channel. Harris was inclined to be contrary about the eating of lunch. It was the logical time and place and his querulousness was uncalled for. The boats were lined to this point with the loads in them. Don, Bill and I did the lining, while Atkinson painted the expeditions name on the wall with the others. After lunch, with more difficult and tricky water to line, I had the loads taken out which the omen portaged, while we lined again, all finishing about together.

Atkinson has lost the paintbrush tho denies it!

We are better prepared this time and take off from the eddy and get into and stay in the main drag alright.

3:00 PM. Mile 177, Mille Crag Bend. Water is slowing down, and as we start into Narrow Canyon begin watching left hand wall for names of Eddy's expedition and others.

Mile 173, left, and at top of talus slope are the names. We stop and inscribe our names with the rest. Eddy's has worn off a lot.[30] On again at 4:50 PM.

Mouth of Dirty Devil and camp. Just below Dirty Devil is a good level rock ledge on which we make camp. We all bathe. I washed my clothes and hair.

We're sitting around the campfire talking and joking. We had planned on going on to Hite, but I thought it wiser to pull in here and bathe and shave as we are all really tired.

JULY 3

What a night. Bill and I were careless enough to make our beds by a pissant hill and we took turns waking each other up in the night fighting the ants.

River an inch or so lower. Sky brilliantly clear. Cool upstream wind. River 250' wide.

Off at 7:50 AM.

MILE 162 ½, almost at the abandoned town site of Hite we see on the right bank a man. He turns out to be a Mr. Saltz, recently of Prescott, Arizona, here prospecting. He was through the Hat about a month ago. He directs us to Chaffins.[31]

We land on the north bank of Trachyte Creek at 9:25 AM.

After beating through the willows we find a crossing on Trachyte Creek, and then proceed through some cornfields to the Chaffin House some ¼ mile south. the green things look good to us, and we all have visions of an invitation to a home cooked meal. We find the Chaffins very pleasant and hospitable people and spend much time talking with them.

Mr. Chaffin wants to see our boats, and as we should have landed some ¼ mile below where we did, Chaffin, Harris and I go to run the boats down. Chaffin leads, Harris follows, and I bring up the rear down through the little riffle at mouth of Trachyte Creek to the willows just downstream from the house and approached by a very good trail and road.

Returning to the house we take pictures, learn of things to look for downriver. Mr. Saltz returns for lunch, and I try to get him to go along for man-power, but thoughts of the Grand Canyon are obviously spooky to him. If Chaffin were younger I believe he would go. Have a swell lunch and we all gorged.

We get a box of matches, and I left 50¢ in payment as they wouldn't accept pay for anything.

3:00 PM all hands down to see us off. They predict we will make 10 miles, but when we go into camp at 6:00 PM we are at MILE 142 ½, almost 20 miles.

Mile 155 at 4:00 PM Ticaboo Creek 5:00 Mile 148 ½.

Our camp was the best I could find, and although requiring about 50 yds steep climbing it is good. There was considerable complaining on lugging things up. I do not like the attitude all but Elzada has taken. Lois is obviously a trouble maker, and Don is weak enough to be led. He will quit at Lees Ferry tho won't admit it yet.

Am anxious to reach Lees Ferry and reorganize or something. The pot hunt tomorrow won't amount to anything. Going to get up at 4:00 or so and take off so as to reach Moqui Canyon early.

July 4

Up at 4:00 AM. Breakfast and shove off at 5:40 AM. 17 miles to Moqui Canyon. We make good time even drifting. Seem to average 6 MPH. Was interested in some maps Chaffin had that Holmstrom had used then sent him. With his hard rowing over this same section he only made 4 ½ MPH.

My plan now is to try and get Del Reed and one man from the Hall Expedition to go on with us from Lees Ferry, so we will have enough man-power for portages.

MILE 134 ½. Knowles Canyon. Just above here saw an old mining claim with a broken down water wheel.

It just occurred to me that not one single leak has appeared in any of the boats, they are wonderfully constructed.

MILE 132. Smith Fork.

We start looking here for three Japanese miners that Chaffin told us about.

Right bank. MILE 130 ½. We see a placer workings and look for the Japs. Elzada and I stop, look over the pump etc., see they have been used but recently, but decide the Japs have gone out for the Fourth. We drift on about 100 yds. when an excited hailing discloses the three Japs. We land, just as the other boats hove into sight. We all stop, get out and look over their workings, visit their camp etc. They heard over the radio we were coming. They have a wonderfully neat camp, tho their gold looks awfully fine.

Taking a break during portage in Cataract Canyon, 1938

Lois Jotter in Glen Canyon, 1938

The California Bar is opposite, and repeated hailing fails to attract the attention of one Jake for whom we have a package sent by the Chaffins. This we leave with the Japs.

MILE 125. MOQUI CANYON. Landing here we attempt to go up canyon but the river backwater makes it to difficult. After much work in crossing or trying to cross one dangerously boggy spot I decide to let it go and sail on to Lake Canyon.

MILE 122 ½. We see a row of wooden pegs driven into the sandstone cliff wall and stop to investigate. Across the river is an old engine and other machinery. After much speculation I decide it's an old power line. We see some pictographs. The pegs are some 12" apart, six to eight feet above the ground, and spaced about 150'. See the name: Loren Taylor. Jan 9, 1903.

MILE 121 ½. What appeared to be a pile of drift lodged on a rock about 100' from shore turned out to be an old dredge.[32]

MILE 117 ¼. Old placer camp on left. Stop and take a picture. Quite a large dump. Been abandoned good many years.

MILE 113 ¼. LAKE CANYON. Terribly hot. First real heat we've had. The other boats had gone ahead. I went to sleep at the oars, and woke when the light roar of waves came to me. Lake Canyon. We drifted on past the mouth and found the two boats, with only Gene occupying them. The others had gone pot-hunting. Gene was one of the most eager to go. Elzada went to seek shade, but she finally came down to share the shelter I rigged up on the WEN, with Gene and I occupying it.

The others finally return to find us sleeping. They found a little dwelling rather well preserved some ways up the canyon.

Want to reach MILE 100 tonight for camp.

MILE 108. Just below here on left is Chaffins mine, which we pass at 5:45 PM.

High on cliffs to let we see a large natural bridge. We toy with the idea of visiting it but I can see it would involve a lot of time.

Mile 100. We pull into camp on left bank and anchor behind some great large rocks. It is growing dusky and I am about to light a fire to signal our camp stop to the boats lagging behind when they show up.

Sat around the lantern until after 10:00 PM. Elzada made fudge, with KLIM, sugar, and Chocolate. Gene has infection in his leg, which he seems to foster, but so far doesn't look bad. Except for Elzada the rest act like a bunch of kids, whispering amongst themselves and trying to work up a good excuse to quit at Lees Ferry. I came out flatfooted and told them that I was getting two more men at Lees Ferry. Lois says she's going on. Gene isn't enthused, but *says* he's going on. I don't know as I will let him. He's a poor sport and shirks his work. I don't trust Don, but he says he'll go on as far as Grand Canyon. Bill says he'll go on, tho any excuse at all to save his face and he'll quit. They hate to admit that the water is too much for them. I am worried about getting more men on such short notice. Feel sure of Del Reed and that's all. I can't go on without more manpower. Something will turn up.

JULY 5

Swell nights sleep and the sun is poring down. We have an easy run of 32 miles to Rainbow Bridge.

Shove off.

We're just drifting this morning. After much cross questioning it *seems* as if all the party will continue from Lees Ferry except Gene. Am sorry to say that he is a terrible griper and the Colorado is no place for him.

Escalante River. It is pretty tho looks like the other side canyons. It is mainly distinguished by a small discharge of water. These maps are really fine. I know exactly where we are every minute.

Hole in the Rock. MILE 84 ½. Elzada and I stop right at mouth of canyon, and as there is no sign of others proceed to eat. Other two boats drifted in as we were finished. So we take off after others started to eat. As I go to jump in the boat the amber colored glasses Mother gave me fell off into the river from my pocket! I hate it as wanted to return them intact.

A ways below we just saw a stretch of the Old Mormon Road out of the Hole in the Rock.[33]

MILE 83 ½. Stopped on left bank to look at remains of old road. It's quite washed out and almost impossible to discern. Across the river it seems in good shape.

MILE 83. We land in dense brush and start to look over the road. Other boats no come and we find shade along shore and wait. None of the

Camp at mouth of Forbidden Canyon, 1938

rest shown any interest in either scenery or historical points of interest. Found a board off of one of their boxes. Although gone in places, much of the road in is good shape. We were interested in seeing little bridges they had made from cottonwood drift. They were quite sturdy.

The latest trick is for everyone to pile in Harris' boat, he rowing and towing the BOTANY. His lack of observance of orders to hold position is provoking and disgusting.

Can first see Navajo Mountain.

The good old San Juan! It looks pretty small and apparently is quite low.[34]

Forgot to look up Music Temple![35] Will look it up on my next San Juan trip. Think it lies at MILE 2 or 3 below San Juan, on right. It's a very narrow walled canyon.

FORBIDDEN CANYON![36]

It is now 7:15 PM. At the island at MILE 69 ½ I took the left channel expecting the boats to follow. I was looking for pictographs. Instead, Harris led the other boats to the right, and almost opposite Forbidden Canyon we came upon them holding the boats in an eddy against the right cliff wall. Fast water begins here at the riffle opposite Forbidden Canyon and it's a hard pull to land above the canyon at the regular anchoring spot. I started across and looked to see the other two boats swept on down. They landed in the trees some ¼ mile below. I immediately went after them after my landing above the canyon. Harris looked properly chagrined, and all stuff was portaged back up to the camp we now occupy under the ledge just up the canyon on the left. Just had a swell swim here at camp. The women went above, and are eagerly awaiting dinner. It's nice here, neither too hot nor too cold. Been quite hot during the day. The others, excepting Elzada are worn out. It's from their lying on the decks of the boat in the hot sun. They can't seem to take advice.

July 6

Slept on the lower ledge, with the exception of boys, who parked up on the upper ledge.

And off for the Bridge. Set a fair pace and arrive at Bridge at 10:30 AM. All except Atkinson seemed quite impressed. We wrote our names in the visitor book. We were numbers 2641–2646 incl.

Then walked up to Wilson's Camp, and broke into the cache and enjoyed hot biscuits until we were ready to burst.

All except Atkinson was grateful for the feed. I explained I would probably pack the stuff up the canyon from my next San Juan River trip. Yet Atkinson kept insisting on more and more and was disagreeable about not being given a free hand with the cache. Even Harris was disgusted with him and hinted that Gene filched an extra can or so.

Don and I are now on top of Rainbow Bridge, while Elzada and Bill are setting up for pictures. We are having a good time, almost back to normal. I believe some of the effects of Cataract Canyon are wearing off.

Picked up some little round pebbles as souvenirs. Lost my helmet just as leaving bridge top.

6:00 PM and another big feed, mostly of biscuits. Gene and Lois spent the time sleeping. Lois seems to tire easily and always wants to sleep. Anemic, probably, tho she looks big and husky. Lois has been mighty rude and short with Elzada. I would never want to take Lois on another trip. Would like to drop her off at Lees Ferry.

The party, jolly in spirits, started off and began to get dark at Forbidden Canyon. We stumbled on without serious spills and made camp and welcome beds. About two miles up I nearly stepped on a rattlesnake. Never did see him, just heard the warning.

Don is sort of considering going on. I don't believe he is sincere. Although he says that if it means wrecking the expedition he will go on as far as Bright Angel 'till I break in the new boatmen. This will help a lot and I am planning on it. Elzada is sure that Don will go on, but her judgement of human nature seems to be worse than poor. Bill wants to go on. Poor Bill, he's scared to death, but he's man enough to say so, and may turn out the best yet.

Want to try to pick up some air mattresses. The best bet or stunt for this trip in good weather is an air mattress and blanket.

July 7

A big transport plane just flew over us not very high, traveling from east to west.[37]

Shove off. We have all the equipment and will take it a ways then give it to the boats it belongs to.

MILE 66 ½. Stop and wait for the other boats and give them their load.

On again and we see three steps cut into cliff on right hand wall. A trail from the placer diggings just below evidently.

MILE 49. Right bank. Lunch. A distinctly unfriendly attitude prevails against Elzada and myself. I'm disgusted with the whole outfit. I think Elzada is the best man in the bunch. We take a siesta.

MILE 40 ½. Crossing of the Fathers.[38]

MILE 25 ½. NAVAJO CREEK. We land lower side of canyon, and find mosquitos so bad that we decide to just eat, then drift on down to some spot free of mosquitoes.

Dinner barely started when a plane came over us and commenced circling and dropping notes. Harris and I go for one that has landed downstream and up high on the talus slope. Notes continue to fall, mostly in the river. Bill has gone across Navajo Creek after one. Elzada also. Gene staid in camp, also Lois. And they got one that landed a few yards away. Lois and Gene signal as the note indicates, assuring everyone we are safe. This is our first real sign that the outside world is concerned for our safety. We all return to camp empty handed, and eat a hurried, unpleasant meal. The mosquitoes are terrific.

Shove off. It is dusk with a moon getting higher. Beautiful out. We all sing Moonlight on the Colorado.

Wahweap Creek. Stop a few minutes to try to get a moonlight shot. Impossible and so on.

MILE 15 ¼. Left Bank. Camp. Elzada makes some chocolate in lieu of fudge.

July 8

First chilly night. I couldn't find my pajamas and was cold. Bill's bed was wet. We all were uncomfortably cool. Got up at 4:00 AM and put on a shirt.

Shove off.

Feel a bit excited tho not very. We're at MILE 9. Am dying to get to Mexican Hat.

MILE 3. I order formation to be *held*.

And there's the cable!

I mistake a cabin and we land too far upstream. Drift under gov't cable and Anderson directs us on down.

LEES FERRY!

As we pull up to the right bank I see reporters sprawled around sleeping. As the WEN touches shore I call out "Church is out, we're here!" We get a frantic reception, then in order to give them a landing picture we drift upstream in an eddy and come in again. We enjoy some watermelon and other goodies.

Lunch break for
(left to right)
Gene Atkinson,
Elzada Clover,
Lois Jotter

Things finally quiet down and I start the equipment up to the gov't garage some hundred yards away for storage. We also turn the boats over for painting.

Then, as we received an invitation from Hubbels[39] to dinner etc. we are hauled to the Marble Canyon Lodge by the gov't boys in two cars. Anderson and Manson. Get about a mile and meet a Ford sedan which disgorges a very excited fat man. He proves to be a Pathe News cameraman, who tells us a sad story of missent film. I promise to return after lunch and put the outfit through still another arrival.

It seems that our invitation was for dinner, but the Hubbels make us welcome and serve lunch. We eat to the clicking of cameras. Lois gets jittery and drops things.

Leaving the table we go in the reception room and I run into Ada, her mother and father. She gives me the news from the Hat, and I see I must get back immediately. More pictures taken, then we all go back to the boats, right them, launching them, and reenact our arrival. When this is done to everybody's satisfaction, the camera man leaves. He promised to get me to Mexican Hat.

We sort over our stuff, Harris takes his, and I take things back we won't be using from here down.

Get back to the Lodge late and find the Pathe man gone and no car ready. I have talked to a Jack Stockwell about going on to supply man-power, and I find he will drive us to Mexican Hat.

The car is a decrepit affair and I am afraid it won't stand the trip so we decided to inquire enroute for a better car!

Load and get away at 10:00 PM. Have instructed Bill to go to Kolbs[40] and have his camera overhauled.

Stop at both Warrens and O'Farrels but have no luck in raising a car.

We are about three miles below Tuba City when I think of Kerleys and announce that this will see us through if Ed is around.

I pound on the door and raise Ed. He is leaving early for Gallup, but says he will drive us to Kayenta where we can pick up a truck-pick-up, he says Lorin Bell[41] is asleep and would I like to say "hello." I reply in the affirmative and we go to awaken him. I finally succeed, and Ed asks him "Want to go down the Colorado?" "Sure," answers Lorin, "when?"

I go on to tell him my dilemma and he is keen to go. I give him our sailing date and equipment he must have. He says he will be ready, and while Ed is dressing he goes out in his singlet to meet the other and inform Jack he can start back. Ed is out in a few minutes with his new Chev. coupe, and we soon transfer our luggage and take off. It is now 12:00 PM. Don and I curled up in the turtleback. It was cold.

July 9

Arrive Kayenta. On the way over Harris has assured me he will consider going on. I don't believe him. I ask him to keep the promise he made about going as far as Bright Angel if necessary. All he replies is "I'll think about it."!

We soon have the Kerley pick-up gassed and leaving Ed to drive back to Tuba we take off again. I ride in back.

At the State Line Harris comes in back and I drive.

Arrive Mexican Hat.

Harris and Atkinson go right to bed. I see Jenny Barton and the folks. Elzada also sees them then goes to bed.

I go to my house, wake up Cherry and Joan. After eating I turn in then sleep 'til 10:00.

Then see Harris and with a hangdog air he says goodbye.[42]

Return to the house and Doris goes over and has Gene come over to see me. He is going to Lees Ferry in his car. His going on seems to be problematical in his mind. Wants to save his face. I will not take him.

Then Del Reed[43] comes over and I ask him to go. He is ready!

Decide to go to Monticello and look up Elwyn Blake, a boatman with the '23 gov't expedition.[44]

Eat dinner in Blanding. Three malted milks which I have trouble keeping down along with the big steak.

Find in Monticello that Blake is in Colorado, so give up the ghost and return, with the idea of maybe getting another man at Halls camp.

Midnight. Arrive Mexican Hat.

JULY 10

Elzada, Del, and I leave at 10:00 for Grand Canyon where I want to get some data from Emery Kolb.

Stop and see Weatherills in Kayenta.

About 1:30 I reach Halls camp and have lunch. Prof. Winning hasn't any more crew for us.

Stopped at Kerleys in Tuba. Ed and Lorin not back yet from Gallup, but left word they would meet us at Lees Ferry tomorrow night. Got some added food supplies, to be taken down for us at Bright Angel trail.

Arrive South Rim. Visit with Tillotsons, and the reporter, Franz comes in to interview us. Finally leave after arranging certain signals to be made when we reach Tanner Trail.

Get to Kolbs[45] too late for the show, and Tillotsons, Elzada, Del, Edith, and others visit 'till 10:30. I get data from Emery on where to find water. Also promise to see he gets to ride from Bright Angel to Hermit.

Manage to get a sandwich at Bright Angel Lodge. So to bed on a partially empty stomach.

JULY 11

Emery and I visit and go over data again. Gives me book.

Arrange for packing down of supplies.

Leave in an anxious hurry to reach Lees Ferry. We will be glad to see how the other members have gotten along and get shoved off.

Arrive Lees Ferry about noon and have lunch. I win a bet from Elzada that the boats will be unpainted.[46] The others had gone to Flagstaff for fun and [?] in at 6:00 AM tomorrow.

We go down to the boats, and Del, Elzada, and I paint the boats.

River is under 30,000 and dropping fast. Several thousand per day.

Return to the Lodge for dinner. I arrange for the Pathe man, Jack McFarlane to go with us as far as Badger Creek to get pictures.

Lorin and Ed came in time for dinner. Ed's going right back, but will be here in the morning or during the night again. Going to take him as far as Badger Creek too.

After dinner we finally get a ride through the kindness of Jack Stockwell, who I just told I couldn't take because of load. I have good men now and we'll get by.

Ed and Miles Kendricks arrive during the night. We all drive up to the Lodge for breakfast.

Lorin Bell, Bill Gibson, Norman Nevills, Del Reed

The others have gotten in. We find that Bill, Gene, and Lois are circulating unpleasant rumors. I tell off Atkinson who makes a great todo about going on. I write him a letter to save his face and wire Calif. for money for him to get home. We're mighty lucky to be rid of him.

Quick work is made of the packing by the women, and in the meantime we have the boats launched to go. A small crowd is on hand. It's terrifically hot and I can hardly wait to get started again.

Much fumbling by the Pathe man delays us.

We shove off.

Drift a short distance and pull in on left to await Bill and McFarlane who were taking pictures of the take-off. Here they finally come.

We're finally off, Elzada, Mac. and I lead in the WEN, then Lois, Ed, and Lorin in the MEXICAN HAT, the Del and Bill in the BOTANY. Del is fumbling a bit with the oars.

Pass under the Navajo Bridge. Lined with people and cars. The bridge is a breathtaking sight. It's such a graceful delicate span. And so high!

MILE 8. BADGER CREEK. Land just above on left and prepare for lunch. It's a lining job as the tongue cuts off abruptly just over the drop between two bad looking holes. If a straight course was made it would be simple, but the least slip to left or right, and into one of the holes!

Mac. was scared coming this far! Thought we were done for in the second little riffle above. Wait 'till he sees us in action at the bottom of this first drop.

Had lunch, then lined the WEN to the bottom of the first drop. Then I ran the WEN with Ed Kerley as passenger to the foot of left. It was a fast and enjoyable ride.

We've all had a swim.

The Pathe man has gotten good pictures.

Stuff all portaged to eddy here just past first drop.

This is a swell gang and we're going to town!

Wonderful moonlight effects tonight.

Stayed up late talking, then gave Mac. my air mattress, and Lorin contributed a blanket—and so to sleep.

July 14

Lined the MEXICAN HAT, then with Lorin as passenger, ran on through to the WEN.

Next brought the BOTANY down. Mac., tho in fear of his life, decided to go with me to get pictures. I decided to really thrill him and in pulling out got slapped by a big wave and knocked off the seat and turned a perfect back-flip, landing in Mac. He gave me a shove and groaned: "God!"

At the foot he was greatly enthused and longed for another ride! This is real sport and this is the type of rapid water I like.

I write a letter to Cherry to send off with Mac. and Ed.

We finally wave farewell and shove off. Seems like we're really started now as we've broken our last contact with the outside world—and Marble Canyon stretches before us.

Arrive SOAP CREEK.

Have looked it over and decided to run. It's wild looking.

I made it! Thank God.

MEXICAN HAT by Lorin.

Then BOTANY by Bill. I tried my form of psychology on Bill and told him he was to run. He nearly fainted, but too his orders like a man. He came through mostly out of control and made one of the wildest rides I've ever seen. At the foot he yelled: "By God, Norm, you're right! I've got my nerve back!"

We're off to find a bit of shade.

Ran the much talked of SHEER WALL RAPID. Just looked it over from the boat!

MILE 16 ½. Fine camp on left.

July 15

This is a swell camp spot. Last night Elzada made some penuche that was slightly off breeded—but we ate it. Spirits are fine. Lorin is a natural born boatman and river shooter. Del is not getting on to handling a boat too well, but hope today will see him getting on to things better. The rapids from SOAP CREEK to here were just fun to run. Nothing to them if you ride the tongue out and keep alert. Several fast drops, but good going. At lunch yesterday repaired rings on BOTANY oars. They caused Bill to go out of control in Soap Creek. Good ship WEN still going beautifully.

Shove off.

MILE 17 HOUSE ROCK RAPID. Land on left to look over. Will run it will passengers, while Bill takes pictures. Wheww! Damn rough! All boats through at 9:26. Del came second and got his baptismal fire in a real rapid. Then Lorin and Lois.

NORTH CANYON RAPID. A bit tricky.

TWENTY-ONE MILE RAPIDS. Dangerous and tricky.

MILE 24½ and MILE 25. Two dangerous rapids with false tongues.

This was really a wild day. The House Rock Rapid was one that was plenty risky. Also at Twenty-one Mile. At 21 Mile Rapids had to pull out of the main drag just right to miss a deadly hole. The rapid seems more dangerous than Soap Creek at this stage of water. Bill and Del were terribly scared of running it and asked me to let them off. Lorin offered to run it the 2nd time, but I decided to. The river raised a few inches during last night be is back to near normal again this evening.

Tried to rain when we first go in tonight, but soon cleared up. We are having beautiful weather, tho in midday the siestas are welcome.

July 16

Ran 11 rapids yesterday, several of them really tough. It's good practice for the bad ones to come.

At MILE 24½ and 25, just by chance, I felt an urge to look over what appeared to be a very simple rapids. They had straight shots, a nice tongue, and perfect waves. Only at the end of the tongue and over the first wave was a big hole! It is the most deadly trap I have ever seen.

This canyon is most beautiful, and doesn't at all ever seem gloomy. The crew is fit for the job. Whereas Del is no riverman, so far, and Bill gets scared, they all pitch in and help things to go well. Even if Lois tries to agitate again am sure she will get a poor reaction from this present outfit.

Finally loaded and off.

Found two undeveloped films from Cataract Canyon in the boat. I will send them out from the South Rim.

MILE 30. We land on left to look over this one. It's OK for all hands. In landing, Jotter, when the boat touched an unsuspected rock, made a perfect back-flip into about two feet of water.

Vasey's Paradise—and lunch. Rounding the left bend we saw ahead on the right our objective. It was expected to be a difficult landing in this fast water, but we made a dash across a little riffle, then pulled in sharp into an eddy almost opposite the spring.

It's gorgeous. The cliff is covered with ferns and other plants, watered by several springs, the principal one gushing out some 100' above us, and shooting out like a fire hydrant. The water is very cold and excellent drinking.

We're going to eat lunch here. Quite a few clouds in the sky and a few drops of rain have fallen. The day is fairly cool.

Rapids this morning a bit snorty, but not dangerous if handled right. Bill is still scared silly of rapids, but think he may come out of it. Del is pretty booed too. Hope Ed Kerley can join us at the Canyon to handle a boat.

MILE 43 ¾. President Harding Rapid. Left [bank] CAMP.

Fine camp. We landed at head of rapid, but were in such a humor for rapid running that couldn't resist running it first. This is the one where the gov't party lost a boat. A big rock in the middle is also in the center of the tongue. Have to slip down about 100' on left side of tongue, then pull sharp left, and into an eddy.

The scenery in the canyon is simply beyond description, and the coloring gorgeous.

Water slow, so far, between rapids. 17 miles today. The little rapids are lots of fun. The medium sized ones are usually fun, but the big ones, tho thrilling, are usually spooky.

JULY 17

Shove off.

MILE 52. Nankoweep. Just back from look them over. They're simple to run and nothing much. The water in Nankoweep is very clear and fine drinking. Saw some cliff dwellings high up on wall just south of the canyon. Found some mounds with sherds close to mouth of Nankoweep and just below. Found an arrowhead (white) for the baby. Am taking a few sherds. Saw a toad with red spots. We are all assembled except Jotter, and we find she has been sleeping again!

MILE 56. Lunch. Right. Mouth of Kwagunt Creek, head of rapid. After lunch I run the WEN through, followed by Del and Lorin. Ploughed over several rocks in this one. First time hit rocks on trip.

LITTLE COLORADO RIVER!

I won two bets. One that there'd be water in L.C., and the other that this *is* the L.C. It is not a very impressive sight, and a poor place to camp, so on we go. We first drift in left close to the L.C. and have to buck the main river current back a ways in order to get far enough back to run down through the water to the left of the island caused by the junction here. It's a hard pull and we finally make it.

MILE 65 ½ RAPID #1 Grand Canyon. Can see Watchtower on Hopi Point![47]

MILE 68 ½. Head of TANNER CANYON RAPIDS, left, and in sight of the watchtower.

Twenty-five mile run today.

We go down along the rapids, and see they are a cinch. Find lots of driftwood and build a huge pile up some ½ mile from camp. Returning to the boats we run them on down to a cove at the mouth of Tanner Canyon. Find a pile of drift just around the corner from us and decided to save walking by lighting it.

Perfectly beautiful here, tho stormy and looks like rain.

After dinner touch off the fire and spend some time in watching the rim for an answering light. We think several times we see one, tho not entirely sure.

JULY 18

Had fudge last night. No change in River. Del is not feeling too well, but rest of us fine. Threatened rain, but none fell. It's very cloudy this morning, and promises rain. This again is a swell place to camp.

Marble Canyon has the best camp spots we've seen.

Wore my new shoes last night around camp. Have had a bit of sinus cold and feel sure it's because I haven't changed from wet clothes in the evening.

Shove off.

MILE 72. UNKAR CREEK RAPIDS. Wide and easy.

MILE 75. SEVENTY-FIVE MILE RAPIDS.[48] Wide, fast, and easy

MILE 76. Land left. HANCE RAPIDS![49]

Wheww! and these are enough to chill one's blood! Had thought to line here, but by following an intricate route through the upper half of the rapid I believe it can be run alright.

I am in my boat and ready to run Hance. Have a funny feeling in the pit of my stomach and will be glad to see this one behind.

Made it! Elzada takes my picture after running. What a ride!

Other two boats through alright. On to Sockdologer!

MILE 78 ½. Left. SOCKDOLOGER!

It's a corker and isn't a case of following the tongue down the middle. The tongue goes about a hundred yards in a fast drop and delivers right into a hole. Another hole on the left at the take off means riding the tongue a ways then pulling sharp left to miss the hole in the center. That's as far as we can see. This looks to be a mighty spooky ride. And to think we were talking about running Sockdologer without looking it over!

We're off. Elzada so rattled she forgot to strap on life preserver. We were started when a call from shore warned her.

MILE 78 ¾. TWO THIRDS WAY THROUGH SOCKDOLOGER. Left.

All boats anchored in line to mine. I pulled in here to get a picture, and we're going to have lunch. I bet last night that I could find an eddy in Sockdologer where I could stop a boat. Sure enough, after passing the big center hole we found the big easy 10–12 foot waves. I saw a ledge jutting out from the left and dived in behind. I had Elzada hold the boat while I climbed up on a point to signal the other boats. Poor Bill and Del when they saw me thought we were wrecked and was warning them of impending trouble. They barely made it in as were afraid of a hole! Lorin made it in without similar qualms.

From the takeoff on this baby, and the way it acts I have a feeling that the GRAPEVINE is going to be mighty tough, ugly, customer.

We're restless to know the worst about Grapevine. The hour is up and we're off!

MILE 81 ½. LEFT—GRAPEVINE!

We pull in on the left barely above the head of the rapid. The roar is terrific and impressive. It takes but a few minutes to see that if

Sockdologer was bad, this is tough beyond description. Under different circumstances this would be considered un-runnable. But lining would be exceedingly dangerous, if at all possible. And of course portaging is out of the question. The complications of big holes and lashing waves doesn't look good.

But it has to be run, and here we go! Wicked ride. I pull in on the right below so as to get pictures of the other boats. They come a-tossing! And all safe at 3:20 PM.

Pull into right hand cove just above Bright Angel Creek, and just below the suspension bridge. Three photographers on hand, who convey the invitation from Bright Angel lodge for dinner. We gratefully accept, then took showers and shaved at the Forest Service camp. Had nice dinner at Phantom Ranch. Spent the evening talking, and played some pool. Bill, Elzada, and I.

We were watched through a telescope running Hance Rapid.

19 miles today, ran 11 rapids, four of them major.

If Ed Kerley doesn't join us there's a man here from the Forest Service[50] who will be willing to pay to go.

However I feel I have crew enough. I have good men now, and we work well together.

Back to boats. All but me help in "killing" the last of our Four Roses.

July 19

We're up, cooking breakfast and going up the Bright Angel trail. Del is staying to watch the boats. The Forest Service is taking us across the tramway which will save a couple miles or so of walking.

11 ½ MILES! It's all up. Elzada played out at 2 ½ miles from the top. We arrive Kolbs studio, tired, hot, and dirty. Emery turns us loose on the shower, which precedes a fine luncheon with great quantities of iced tea. I put on the brand new shoes to start out and my feet are extremely sore. Oh, Well, they'll be worse before we get back.

The others lodge at Bright Angel, I stay as Kolbs guest.

Spend the rest of the day going over maps, visiting, writing, and in the evening see Kolbs pictures again. We are besieged by autograph hounds.

After talking it over, Emery has decided to accept my invitation to go on with us as my guest.

Meet a Karl Lehnert, asst. supt. at Boulder, Kolbs son-in-law, and expects to meet us himself in a gov't boat. He will fly over us and keep track of our progress down the canyon.

July 20

Should have started back today, but have to arrange for some leather to repair our oar leathers. Time flies. And now we are asked to broadcast over NBC tomorrow at 3:15 PM. I accept. Dinner will follow at Tillotsons.

We take in shows at Kolbs, make speeches, etc.

Grand Canyon, 1938

JULY 21
Broadcast at 3:15 PM.
    Tillotsons for a very nice dinner.

JULY 22
Out late last night and up late today. We spend most of our time at Kolbs.
Finally, after singing together for over an hour around the piano, we take
formal departure from park officials, then arrive at head of Kaibab trail and
start down at 5:15 PM.
    I have arranged, mostly with Mrs. Tillotson, to reach Granite Falls
about noon, and run about one o'clock. A big crowd will watch us from the
rim.
    Sonny, Emery's grandson is going down the trail with us to see us off.
I lent my support to his pleas, and here he is.
    Bill and I reach the boats, followed by Sonny, then somewhat later, the
rest. My feet are so sore I can barely walk.
    We go up to the gov't cabin where our supplies were sent, and have
dinner. Then sleep out on cots. It sprinkles a bit but soon passes over. Bill
and I have great time sharing one canvas.

JULY 23
Up early, eat breakfast, then pack our stuff down to the boats, almost ¼
mile away.

Last night Del told us of taking people around in the big eddy on excursion trips while we were gone. He had a fine time.

Am taking Emery in my boat, so his stuff is with us. The other two boats are loaded, and after positioning ourselves and the boats for pictures we are ready.

We're off on the last lap!

Quite a crowd is congregated at mouth of Pipe Creek, presumably to see us run that rapid. At the present stage of water it seems but a piddling riffle to us.

Been told that Horn Creek would be simple at this stage, so we expect to get to Granite Falls in short order.

HORN CREEK. And what a rapid! To the left of the tongue is a series of offset holes. To the right, more holes. The tongue dives right into a hole! At this stage it's a might dangerous rapid. Could easily be turned down for lining. And half way down on the right side a lava ledge projects that is dashed madly at by the speeding current. Look it over closely from all angles and decided to run it by cutting through the right hand side of the hole in the middle of the river, then pulling sharply left to the middle of the river and down through the simpler water below.

I make it alright and pull in below on right. Lorin starts out and breaks an oarlock, right, just at the hole. He barely manages to keep from being swept on to the right into the holes and dike.

Del makes it alright. He pulls a strong oar, and when danger looms ahead he fairly makes the boat fly!

LUNCH at MILE 92 ¾ LEFT, foot of Salt Creek Rapids.

Approaching Granite Falls a sudden heavy rain made us take shelter in a little cove on the left for a few minutes.

As we approach Granite Falls we see a boat high up on the left bank. This proves to be a canvas boat built by Emery in 1927 to search for some bodies of two rangers killed in Horn Creek when their boat entered the rapid as they tried to cross the river above.[51] One man managed to get on the projecting ledge. The bodies not recovered.

MILE ¼ GRANITE FALLS. Land left. And this promises to be a big 'un and a good 'un. The main drag dashes into the right hand wall, follows it with big waves for several hundred yards, then swings sharply left and right around an island. Must go to the left below and it's going to be hard.

That's that! I took off in good shape, and was about half way down along the cliff, got on top of a twenty foot wave, pulled on my left oar, it slipped through the ring, and before I really knew what happened saw the granite rushing to meet me as I slid off the right hand side of the wave, turning end for end (not over) and coming in sideways at the wall at a wonderful speed. I flattened my left oar and stood up to fend off a bit. But a caprice of the current stopped the boat as if with brakes. The left oar pushed against the wall and my stomach, bending it considerably. I finally worked loose from the oar, and saw directly below me about fifty feet a jagged projecting ledge. It was the lower enclosure for the cove like eddy I was in. I decided to try to pull out into the trough of two waves prow first fast enough to clear the ledge. I got out alright, and the oar slipped through again. I pulled it back in time and sailed on! As I mounted the crest of the last big wave just past the right wall I remember stories of a huge whirlpool I glanced down to see a whirlpool with a hole close to five feet in diameter.

Water some six inches deep in the boat made it hard to handle, and I had quite a struggle getting to the left of the island. This it did however, and soon pulled in to the left below.

Elzada had been walking down, and she joined me just in time to see Del swept around the right of the island. I didn't worry as I knew he could land alright, bail his boat then work it back to

Emery Kolb

where he could round the island. In the meantime Lorin came through, and soon Del joined us.

MILE 94 ¾. HERMIT FALLS. We pull in on the left just downstream from Hermit Creek and camp at the mouth of the canyon.

I look over the rapid roughly, and am inclined to think I will line. This comment causes good natured complaints, and I say I will withhold my final decision until morning and looking it over more closely.

This has been a full day and we are all tired and ready for bed.

July 23

Fine camp last night. Good stream of clear water from Hermit Creek. This morning looked over the situation again am definitely decided to line. There is no way to avoid going through the big explosion wave, and it builds from twenty-five to thirty feet in height. It is further complicated by the wave ahead being a good twenty feet in height and steep.

WEN 45 min.   MEXICAN HAT 45 min.   BOTANY 28 [min.]

All boats are lined and we have had lunch. Am letting Del take off first as to get a picture. He's off! From the eddy some 200 yds down to where we lined, and just about the big waves, was fairly good going. Del left the dead

Lining Hermit Rapid, Grand Canyon

water of the eddy and hit the 20 mile current so fast that he seemed to fly. I have never seen a boat take off so fast.

MEXICAN HAT takes off, we follow, then assume the lead again just below.

BOUCHER RAPIDS! At this stage, about 20,000 [second-]feet, it's a fast, tho not overly dangerous rapid.

The water is fast in the rapids down to Serpentine, but we've run through it all just looking the rapids over from the boat, then plunging through. It's great sport.

MILE 106. SERPENTINE CANYON RAPIDS. This looked to be too big a proposition to run without looking over so I pulled in on the left, just above the take-off. Main drag way over on right, and ugly looking holes just below us. Del following me closely made the landing alright, but Lorin and Lois, keeping further out, got sucked in! Had a queer feeling as they went over. Lorin looked plenty scared. I stood up in my boat and see that they make it through the real bad hole below. Partly in relief, partly disgust, I give the order for us to follow, tho swinging across to the other side.

What a ride! I kept in the main drag and we bumped into the biggest waves we've encountered since Cataract Canyon. Emery was riding the deck and got knocked down. Went up on a big mushroom wave, and we all had to scramble around to keep the boat balanced and right side up. Del kept to the left and avoided the bad ones.

MILE 107 ¾. Right. CAMP. We are now on the right side above Bass's trail. Lorin kind of knocked out from a rupture, and the let down after his ride. Gave him a jigger of Four Roses. Also gave him a minute dose of opium, which was ineffectual, and he spent little of the night sleeping.

Lois is a dangerous one to have on a trip as she has no judgement whatsoever and doesn't seem to care what she does.

The canyon is beautiful and certainly is far from a gloomy looking place. Of course our cool weather and green growth adds much. Another thing, I believe, owing to the descriptions in other books, we were prepared to encounter gloomy depths and forbidding walls.

JULY 24

Shove off. Lorin not so well, so have Lois in Del's boat, and Bill handling the MEXICAN HAT with Lorin as passenger.

MILE 112. Land left. Walthenberg Rapids. We've been looking for trouble here, but at the prevailing stage they can be run with certain success. Current runs to the right. Although I have given orders for no passengers, I take Emery in the boat with me and we have a swell ride. Others come through in good shape.

MILE 116 ½. LEFT. Elves Chasm. It's hot and quite climb up to the cave. It's beautiful here. We see on the walls, inscribed in charcoal, the following names:

N. Galloway 1897
Frank Dodge—23
Eddy's name written twice—again!

I put:

NEVILLS EXPEDITION '38.

On again. Leaving the cave we get a blast of heat that seems furnace-like in its intensity. But once upon the water and under way we don't notice it.

MILE 125 ½. Left. CAMP. Fine camp. As Lois gets dinner, Elzada and I go in search of cactus, which is beginning to grow as high as 3'. Returning for dinner, we eat, then I beat Del at a game of checkers on a board he picked up at the Forest Service camp.

This has been a great stretch of river for fast going. Only really wild rapid was Walthenberg. At a different stage of water it could be exceedingly dangerous.

Made 17 ½ miles today! Dubendorff tomorrow! We all discuss what our thoughts of Dubie are. I have a peculiar feeling that I may run it, tho if it's like I interpreted Eddy's picture, no thanks![52]

JULY 25

Made fudge last night, then sat around while Elzada and Emery played the harmonica. Emery is a master on the harmonica. Threatened rain, but nothing came of it. It's really hot already this morning. We are all anticipating the sight of Dubendorff. I suspect it will really be a lining job—and how we hate them! We've already run three rapids in the canyon that Eddy lined.

Emery has ropes rigged up on the deck so he can *stand up*, riding the big waves. I tried it too, yesterday, and it's great sport.

In Conquistador Aisle, yesterday, we all jumped overboard and swam around in our life preservers. It's sport and real refreshing.

The cactus are certainly getting thick. I want to get some around Las Vegas to take home.

Only rapid we looked over yesterday was Walthenberg. Didn't even look over Fossil, just above camp. There are some ahead that will need looking over! Lorin is still knocked out, so Bill will continue to handle a boat as far as Dubendorff.

Shove off.

MILE 130 ½. BEDROCK RAPIDS. These are tough. The current drops fast straight into a huge rock which splits the channel. The left is deadly and impassable. If it's run will have to start down the tongue, then pull to the right in order to get away from the rock. And this is a tough place to get around for passengers. They all set out. I give a great deal of thought to this one as it is really tough.—Here goes!

Made it.

Everybody through OK, and on again!

MILE 131 ½. RIGHT. DEUBENDORFF RAPIDS!

We all approached properly humble, but after one look I decided to run. Took off, dropped through one hole on right, then jumped up on deck, and holding Emery's ropes rode the rest of the way standing up! Others through OK, tho Del almost got too far to the left. Del came 2nd, then Lorin. No passengers, of course.

At the foot of BEDROCK RAPIDS I had to have help to get my boat back upstream to pick up passengers. Bill jumped in with Del and I had to reprimand Del. We dropped on down to a cave and ate lunch, anxious to see Dubendorff.

MILE 133 ¾. TAPEATS RAPIDS. My hat blew off half way through, and we spotted it and recovered it in an eddy on the left at foot!

Mile 136 ½. DEER CREEK FALLS. RIGHT. Back about 100 yds from river is this beautiful falls, about 125' high. Water icy cold. Get several pictures.

MILE 137. We see cliff dwellings top of talus on left. We stop a few minutes, but there is nothing to see. All eroded away. It looks like this was on a trail, and that at one time the cliff dwellers must have forded the river here.

5:20 PM. MILE 143 ¼. CAMP, LEFT. This too is a fine camp, across the river, and just below us is historic Kanab Canyon, where Powell's second expedition left the river. It is an interesting Canyon, and enters the river between high, narrow, sheer walls.

July 26

Shove off.

MILE 149 ½. UPSET RAPIDS.

These are tough, and have had a lot of trouble deciding my course. Change my mind several times. Can't start out on the tongue as it will surely pull me over into some bad holes. This is one of the trickiest rapids we've hit on the trip. I finally am decided to keep to the rocks on the right for a ways, then drop back into the main drag some 200 yds. below. I take off and drop through the rocks as planned. Am pleased to see how well I can handle the big boat in rock filled channel.

Upon landing Emery suggests I had better run the other two boats through too, so I set out, and find Del on his way. He makes it through, likewise Lorin, tho both boats got pulled further out than I deem safe.

MILE 156 ¾ LEFT. HAVASU CANYON. This is a tricky landing as the current is fast and we have to pull quick to the left, in behind a canyon wall, into the very mouth of Havasu Canyon. We anchor our boats on the ledge at the downstream side of Havasu Canyon. Lorin, Bill, and Lois decide to wade, swim, and work their way up the canyon bed to the falls above some ¼ mile. After they start Elzada tries to follow suit, but in shoulder deep water loses her feet, gets panicky, and is hauled back in by Emery and I. We then load up, and after a short walk arrive with the others at a series of pools and falls. The water is an unbelievable shade of turquoise blue. It's color was the inspiration for the noted song: "Land of the Sky Blue Waters." We swim, then walk up the canyon a ways. The scenery is breathtaking, and the water is an incredible contrast to that which we've been boating on.

Elzada and Emery return to the boats overland, and I join the others in returning via the canyon. The current is deep and swift at one point, and it's great sport to shoot between the walls. Del has watched the boats.

Shove off. We circle back upstream, then drive hard right so as to get through the little rapid below us in good shape.

At MILE 162 it commences to sprinkle, and by MILE 163 we are in a terrific downpour. It's colder than hell, and visibility is bad. We can't see any shelter so keep going. It's terribly cold and we're all shivering. Back upstream, coming over the walls 6000' above pours the rain in a veritable waterfall. It's a beautiful sight. It resembles a dust storm, the rain is so dense. To cap it all, a double rainbow formed, from wall to wall. One of the most spectacular and beautiful sights I've ever seen.

We drift on to the bend, and pull in through the rocks to a worse than poor anchoring spot. We hastily tie the boats, then wade through the muck to the shelter of the east wall of 164 Mile Canyon. I am concerned about the boats as the river already appears to be rising. A rapid lies in front of us. We are loath to leave our shelter, but I take off, with Del and Lorin following and we drop through the rapid and pull in to a good anchoring spot on the right. It has a high talus in case of flood.

We are anchored, and the rain has let up, and a couple of hundred yards upstream is a fine camping spot. We can sleep under the shelter of the cliff wall. Bill and Del and Emery go up to canyon to look for a better camp but return after some time with nothing in the way of camps, but did find a cache of miners supplies. They return with the remains of a folding boat which we use as kindling. Soon all is in order and we have a delightful evening. Emery is bitten by a scorpion, I doctor it and watch for swelling, but nothing serious develops, so we all go off to bed.

High on top of the cliff wall is a natural bridge, above us.

July 27

Delightfully cool during the night. River fluctuated a very little from the storm. All local stuff. Quite cloudy this morning.

After breakfast I go up the canyon to see the cache, and after much hunting finally locate it high up on the left, first bench.

Location notices indicate that in 1902, men working under a Mr. Clapp, filed here. I collect to bring home the following:

Sulphur matches that still light
Gold pan
Knife, fork, and spoon
Bill got a prospectors pick.

Remaining in the cache are:

60' lariat rope, weathered until weak
matches in with baking powder
forks and spoons
1 butcher knife, badly nicked
cooking kettles
1 rock pick
beans, tea, salt, sugar
can condensed milk—dried up
can corn—Iowa 1902.

All in order and shove off.

MILE 174 ½. Red Slide Canyon. Right. Evidences here show old silver prospects of early days.

MILE 179 ¼. LAVA FALLS. Land Left. Made an awful fast run this morning. Lorin was way behind us, and as he approached the Falls we were out of sight on the left. He couldn't see how we could have run this water, and was ready to pull ashore as he spotted us, landed, and learned this was the famous Lava Falls.

We eat lunch crowded around the meager shade of a hackberry tree.

The rapid could be run, tho at this stage with very little safety, so we shall line. All members would like to run, of course.

If run it would have to be on the right hand side.

Hate not to run this rapid, but the chances of turning over are too strong. Another trip and I will run every rapid on the river.

We look over the rapid for lining and find a route that isn't too tricky. Can keep the boats in the water all the ways.

I go back upstream some hundred yds. and bring each boat down to the very takeoff. It's quite tricky to do without being swept over, and I breathe a sigh of relief when it's over.

We lined the WEN first, while others portaged the loads. Half way through my trick knee went out and made it awkward. At the foot, about 150 yds, we loaded the stuff back in the WEN and Emery and I took off to the camp spot. It's nearly a quarter mile below, on the left, in a cove. Nice camp. Just below the river bangs into the left cliff wall, and it's a bit tricky getting into this cove. We start back, having much difficulty working our way through the reeds.

MEXICAN HAT next. This too is then reloaded, and to the camp again. I take the women this trip so they can get camp started. The walk back is mighty painful.

Then the BOTANY. Half way down, as Lorin is holding the boat, ready to let me swing out at the ropes ends, I hear a yell for shore, and glancing to my left, *downstream.* He had gotten swept loose and sucked in between and under two large rocks. He does it twice more for pictures.

We finish lining, load up, and with the male members embark.

At camp, [Mile] 179 ¾. this is a good enough camp. The water, quite limey and a bit too mineralized tasting, gushes out for some ways along the bank just upstream from us. Emery rigs up a sort of bathtub, which Elzada and I share.

July 28

Soon after getting into bed last night my knee began to ache. Finally got some Absorbine Jr. and rubbed it again. But spent an almost sleepless night.

Shove off.

MILE 204 ¼. RIGHT. Was going to camp here, but wood too scarce. Fill our canteens with best water since Vasey's Paradise.

MILE 205 ¼. RIGHT. Swell place to camp, tho have to grub a bit for wood.

25 ½ mile run today!

Today has been one of the most painful in my life. Knee hurt and ached continuously.

None of the rapids were major. Just nice going.

I found wearing my life preserver without a shirt is quite cool as it seems to insulate against the sun. And the days are getting hot now. Going to be a bearcat around Lake Mead.

July 29

Party spirits are great. This is a good gang. I had my dinner served reclining on my air mattress, while Elzada bathed my knee. She bathed it 'till late, and we talked over plans for writing a book.

Spent a pretty good night, wind when downstream quite warm, but upstream cool, in fact cold.

Just changed to PACIFIC TIME. It is now 6:30 AM.

Norman Nevills, Lois Jotter, Gene Atkinson, Elzada Clover, Bill Gibson

At 6:00 AM a monoplane circled over us a number of times so we know that word is on its way of our safety this far!

The way we're traveling we should be at Pierces Ferry the 31st or 1st. I'm afraid of getting in ahead of Doris.

The knee is damn sore this morning, tho not near like it was yesterday.

A tricky looking rapid is roaring below camp. We will get a nice bath to start the day with.

This country we've been passing through is relatively uninteresting. Opens up quite a bit. Mostly limestone terracing back, with occasional breaks of lava.

I frankly have been surprised at the rapids of Grand Canyon. Expected much severer rapids. Guess am used to them. If it hadn't been that I want a sure thing in getting through perfectly OK, and no upsets, I would have run Lava Falls. It isn't so much.

We are planning a trip from Green River Wyoming, next year.[53]

I will probably leave Bill out, though he's a pretty good egg, tho no good for work. He just doesn't know how to work.

Lois is not mature enough and is too reckless, so wouldn't consider her in any way.

Just put on an initiation into the river rat fraternity. Emery was director, with Elzada helping. I was first victim, then served as initiator proper for the rest. Took movies of Bills.

Kneeling, the proselyte, with head deeply bowed, repeated after Elzada the following:

"I know I'm weak, I know I'm blind, I swear that I extend behind . . ."

With the word "behind," I came down with a life preserver on the exposed rear section and thus sealed the vows.[54]

Shove off.

MILE 209. We barely halt here, and determine the right channel the best. It's easy to run.

MILE 217 ¼. Land left. Looking for trouble here, but it looks OK.

MILE 219 ⅞. Just downstream from TWO HUNDRED AND TWENTY MILE CANYON. RIGHT. Walk over to the shade of a big cottonwood tree for lunch. It's hot. Everybody gratefully lies in the shade and sleeps. It's only ⁵⁄₁₂ miles to Diamond Creek, where we'll camp, and I'm not too anxious to hurry as want to arrive Boulder not sooner than the first.

MILE 223 ½, left, just above 224 MILE CANYON, we see a boat. We stop to look it over and it proves to be 14'x 4', made of masonite. Emery is of the opinion that it belongs to someone in Peach Springs who comes down occasionally to trap.

MILE 225. LEFT. Just upriver from DIAMOND CREEK. It's a swell place to camp. Boys go upstream ¼ mile on Diamond Creek to some tumbled down cabins and bring boards for tables, etc. Everybody washes, shaves, etc.

We're all ready to sleep after such a hot day. Made 18 ½ miles today, tho could have made way more if had wanted to.

Knee is some better, tho stiff and aches some.

Saw wild burros on both sides of the canyon today, mostly on the right. They don't seem wild, and are sleek looking. Saw a mountain sheep on the left. Lorin popped at it, but it didn't impede the sheep's progress any.

Quite hot this evening, tho shows signs of cooling off.

Rapids today just wide splashy affairs.

JULY 30

Shove off and run the splashy, tho unusually long DIAMOND CREEK RAPIDS. The rapid is fully a half mile or so long.

MILE 230. TRAVERTINE FALLS. The canyon is narrow again and we're in the Lower Granite Gorge. This is a wild looking affair, but can be run alright.

MILE 232. LEFT. The shade looks good and we stop here for lunch. A rapid is booming below. After lunch Lorin swims across the river, landing a few hundred yards below. He is on the sunny side, and his walk back upstream to get high enough for crossing is funny to watch. The rocks and sand literally blister his feet. We're all dopey from the heat, and reluctantly go on.

MILE 239. SEPARATION CANYON! We land on right, expecting to camp, but it's a poor spot and decide to go on. I am sure I see back water below!

Shove off into Separation Rapid.

We're on the LAKE! Back waters of Lake Mead at foot of Separation Rapid.

MILE 243. RIGHT. CAMP. The current even here is down to not more than one mile an hour. This camp spot is right where MILE 243 RAPIDS USED TO BE!

All spirits are high and we make plans for our arrival. Old clothes are discarded, washing shaving, etc. We all sign each others hats. Wood is scarce, but mesquite saves the day.

JULY 31

We're off to a good start. Anxious to see where the famous Lava Cliff Rapid was.

We're at Lava Cliff. We row up Spencer Canyon to get fresh water for our canteens.

MILE 249. Current about gone, and going slow. It's terribly hot, and everyone takes a spell at the oars. Even Elzada, but she is absolutely hopeless with oars.

MILE 252. Opposite REFERENCE POINT CREEK. This is tough going, and it also hard to locate points in the widening channel.

We pull in on the left and gain a scanty shade . . . We're all enervated by the heat. Pierces Ferry looks a long ways off. We hope that a boat will come above to meet us.

On again. Our pace grows steadily slower. It's all a question of rowing now, and these boats are not built for rowing.

MILE 255. LEFT. Pull in to some good shade to sleep a while. Thought we heard a powerboat. No such luck.

MILE 259. We pull in on left, and Emery gets out to explore for a camp spot. He walks over and sees a channel up a side canyon that looks good.

We are up the side canyon about ¼ mile. Land on a point at right. Not much place for beds, but we can make out. Wood is scarce, so Del rows me across the pond, and we go for wood. All of a sudden Del manages to convey a warning and I leap without pause. A three foot white rattlesnake was about to hit me. Lorin comes over, and after some trouble catches him alive. He is put in an empty bacon can, holes punched in the lid, then weighed down with a rock. We become apprehensive of more snakes.

A waterfall is about 150 yds from us, but brush, water, are not conducive to further exploring so we let it go, tho signs indicate a possible cave entrance close by the falls.

I clear off a place for the girls to sleep, and Emery and I together clear one for us. Bill elects to sleep on the boat!

Emery and I use my air mattress and make a fine bed. We have a tarp that he had on his famous first trip in 1911. Clouding up a bit.

AUGUST 1

We shove off. And the going is mighty slow.

MILE 264 Left. Here we stop to photograph the rattlesnake in action. He's a vicious fellow and provides plenty of excitement.

On again. Getting tired.

MILE 265. We're all tired, and are going to pull in on left, have lunch, and then siesta, if the shade holds out. I can barely make it in to land I'm so tired with the heat. Didn't think I'd make the last hundred yards.

We get lunch ready and are just starting to eat when we distinctly hear a motor! What a thrill! I dash out to the point 220' away and wave and yell. They see us! And at 10:20 AM in rolls a power boat with Buzz Holmstrom at the wheel.

Although we hadn't finished eating, we hurriedly gather up our luncheon paraphernalia and embarked on the powerboat.

At 6:30 this morning, just as we left what we now learn was QUARTERMASTER CANYON, we saw a plane overhead looking us over. We had figured that the plane would get word to Pierces Landing, and thus get a boat to around 10:00 AM. But we weren't sure that they would come on up from Pierces Landing, so on we rowed.

We row down lake a few miles and turned in to EMORY FALLS. Here we again got cold, fresh water, and took a swim.

Just above QUARTERMASTER CANYON, ½ mile we came upon the blue, clear waters of the lake.

Next we went a mile or so below to visit the sloth caves. They were a hard climb in the heat, lie 500' above the river. We came back down to the lake, and were just back at Emery Falls when the big boat with officials, reporters, etc. showed up. Much photographing, then, with the three boats being towed in line we started for Boulder Dam.

Iced drinks, (pop), box lunches, and unlimited ice water was ours! We gave interviews etc. Bill's wife, mother, and dad were on the boat.

Towards late afternoon Emery and I laid out on a hatch and fell fast asleep.

Awakened by a powerboat meeting us. I have a sudden hunch that it is Doris! Sure enough! And a wire from Harbor Plywood offering to buy all three boats!

Doris has had a dangerous and painful experience with a felon on her left thumb.[55] Must go to the hospital immediately upon landing.

We reach the landing and Doris and I are first off and push through the crowd to our car. Drive in to the Boulder Doctor who whisks us to Las Vegas, leaving my car in Boulder. An operation is necessary in the morning.

I consume a number of hambergers, then return to a sound sleep at Boulder.

Temperature of water at Boulder day of our arrival—92!

Temperature in shade—139.

Green River through the Grand Canyon, June 17 to August 22, 1940

After the success of his 1938 expedition, Nevills hoped to repeat the trip the next year but work and family intervened. He conducted several parties down the San Juan River, but plans for another "big trip" fell through. By 1940, he was ready to put together another long river expedition. This one would be longer than the first, and would follow the route of the famous explorer, John Wesley Powell, from Green River, Wyoming, through the Grand Canyon, a distance of some 1,200 miles.

For this journey, Nevills brought along his wife, Doris, as well as Mildred Baker, an adventurous woman from Buffalo, New York, who would become the first women to float the entire length of the river. As usual, Nevills was full of plans for movies, photo spreads, and publicity for his nascent river business. He asked Art Runkle, a freelance newsreel cameraman, to accompany the journey, but at the last minute, Runkle had medical problems and was not able to go, and no feature film was ever made. Charles Larabee of Kansas City, Kansas, came along to handle still photography, and he took away from the trip not only photographs but an everlasting enmity for Nevills.

Nevills lined up a powerful radio transmitter to take along, but that too fell through. In fact the greatest publicity for the trip came from one of the most ancient of forms of communication: the homing pigeon. The Salt Lake Tribune-Telegram provided homing pigeons to send news stories and negatives so that its readers could track the progress of the expedition. Doris, having "monkeyed around with birds," in Norman's words, was placed in charge of the pigeons; she also wrote the daily dispatches that were sent off via the birds. Another publicity angle was to be the "discovery" of a large natural bridge up the Escalante River in Glen Canyon. Never mind that the Herbert Gregory Bridge had long been known to prospectors and Indians; Nevills planned to "discover" and name it.

Not everyone went the entire length, and there were personnel changes at Green River, Utah, and at Phantom Ranch. For those who went the entire length, the cost was $650, somewhat less for the others. For the journey Nevills built two new cataract boats: the Mexican Hat II *and the* Joan, *the latter named for his baby daughter. Both boats were identical to the original trio. Besides Nevills, the boatmen were Del Reed, who had been on the 1938 Grand Canyon traverse; and Hugh Cutler, a botanist from St. Louis, Missouri, who, as it turned out, didn't care very much for the job of boatman.*

61

The trip left Green River, Wyoming, on low water in the middle of June. The water was much lower than in 1938; the peak flow on the Green during the entire year was only 4,340 cfs, and that had occurred at the end of May. The low water would cause some delays and problems throughout the trip. Some tensions were evident from the start, tensions that would only grow after too many long hot days on the river. Nevills's tendency to snap out orders had only grown since the success of the previous expedition, and by the end of the 1940 trip, he was barely on speaking terms with Larabee and Baker. Some members of the party only went part way: B. W. Deason went from Green River, Wyoming to Green River, Utah, and came back at the Bright Angel Trail for the completion of the voyage. Barry Goldwater went from Green River, Utah, through the Grand Canyon, fulfilling a lifetime ambition. Anne Rosner, a schoolteacher from Chicago, went from Green River, Utah, and had to leave at the Bright Angel Trail because Nevills felt the boats were overloaded. Besides Norman and Doris, only John Southworth, Larabee, Reed, Cutler, and Baker went all the way.

Although several parties had made the same continuous journey from Wyoming to the end of the Grand Canyon, in the years since John Wesley Powell's exploration of the river canyons, the 1940 Nevills expedition was the first to include women as members. The trip was well over two months long, and along the way they passed through a slice of America coming out of the Great Depression.

Nevills and his party met by design or accident some of the best-known river runners of their day, people like Bert Loper, Don Harris, Bus Hatch, Harry Aleson, and Buzz Holmstrom. The river-running world was a small one in those pre-regulation days, and even though Nevills was always aware of the business aspects of what he was doing and didn't show any jealousy in his journal, he knew that some of them could become competitors in the future. By the end of this trip, despite the tensions, Nevills was on the cutting edge of commercial river running, and Nevills Expedition had become, in adventurous circles through the United States, a household name.

GREEN RIVER, WYOMING, TO GREEN RIVER, UTAH, JUNE 17 TO JULY 11, 1940

JUNE 17TH
Loaded the three boats on the Lyman truck driven by Ray Lyman. Left Mexican Hat at 4:00 PM. with Doris, Reed,[1] Larabee[2] and Cutler[3] aboard. Had to fix the loading rack in Bluff as it wasn't properly designed.[4] Reached Blanding at 8:30 PM. where we showed the '38 trip pictures along with some of Larabee's of Grand Canyon, Zion, etc. Doris and I stayed at Hattie Barton's,[5] and were to meet the truck at 4:30 AM. next morning. To bed at 12:30 AM.

JUNE 18TH
Leave Blanding 5:00 AM. Breakfast in Monticello at 6:00. Held over in Moab visiting doctor. Lunch at Green River, Utah, 1:30 PM. Reach Price at 6:00

PM. Dinner at Roosevelt 9:30 PM. Got to Vernal at 11:00 PM and looked up Bus Hatch.[6] Our extra oars did not come in to Green River, Utah, so we're after some from Bus. Dig up a pair of light eight footers and pay $3.00. On at midnight. Drive all night. Its cold,[7] and we are lying in the top boat, middle boat, and three in the cab.

JUNE 19TH

Arrive at Green River, Wyoming precisely at 6:00 AM. Park the truck and hurry to get breakfast. Return to truck and run into Adrian Reynolds,[8] newspaper man and chairman of Green River committee to see us off. He welcomes us, puts his car at our disposal, and does much to smooth things for us. Drive down to the river where a railroad section gang unload the boats for us. Ray Lyman leaves immediately. Then to the blacksmith shop to forge out some oarlocks, the steel for which we drive to Rock Springs to get. Meet M. Baker[9] at the Mohawk Hotel where we're staying. Soon J. Southworth[10] shows up. Late in day B. W. Deason,[11] accompanied by Ethel Farrel and Marie Crane[12] put in appearance. Package with huge supply of flashlight batteries[13] shows up. We trade off many of the batteries around town, keeping the extra bulbs and 15 flashlights. These were a gift of the National Carbon Co. Telegrams of best wishes arrive from Rosner,[14] Clover,[15] and Goldwater.[16] A wire advises me that oars were missent to San Francisco, and will meet us in Green River, Utah. We are badly in need of oars, but pick up another old home carved paddle to take along. At 5:15 PM Al Tannehil of Station KDVR, Rock Springs has Doris, Reed and I put on a 15 minute broadcast from that station. We get back to Green River just in time for a banquet given us by the Green River Community Club. Then on to a hall to show pictures. We're tired by now. Sheriff Danowsky gave me a deputy sheriff to watch the boats during the banquet. To bed at midnight.

JUNE 20TH

Up early and stow all luggage in boats. The time for departure was set for 10:00 AM., and right on the dot we shove off!

WEN—Nevills-Baker-Southworth
MEXICAN HAT II[17]—Cutler-Deason
JOAN[18]—Reed-Doris Nevills-Larabee

A large crowd were on hand to see us off, and the general atmosphere was most cheerful. Much unlike that of the '38 take-off. The pigeons,[19] which were taken over early in the morning from the freight office were lashed in the JOAN.

Green River, Wyoming is 386 miles from Green River, Utah, by river, thus, is MILE 386 on the map. Elevation is 6088'. Towards noon wind comes up, and get a brief shower.[20]

Launch from Green River, Wyoming, 1940

LUNCH. MILE 377. Old Logan Ranch, operated by the Kincaid Cattle Co. A rather bedraggled woman and two very shy children hold the place down, prominent for its collection of filth, [wildcats?], and goats. We eat sitting in the boats, nonetheless one goat moves in and has to be driven off. DO NOT STOP HERE IN FUTURE[21]

CAMP #1. MILE 366.

JUNE 21TH

Doris and Dell up first, then Baker and Nevills. Story written for pigeons to take, and pigeons sent off at 6:45 AM. Camp pretty efficient. Shove off at 8:00 AM.

MILE 356. Shot two big Canadian geese. Chased and chased them, finally bagging them at mouth of BLACKS CREEK[22] at 11:45 AM. It was aggravating to chase them, and Baker was very indignant over their being shot. I hope her temperish spells don't presage trouble with her below.

MILE 353. LUNCH. Tough going, high winds. Hard rowing. Clean the ducks *[sic]* and put in bucket ready for tonight. Current Creek just across river from us. Very little current in river. Very low. Hardly 2000'. Looks bad for below.

MILE 351½. HOLMES RANCH.[23] Get canteen water here. Two elderly people who have seen and met all the river parties to date starting with Kolbs. Nice couple. Leave here with awfully hard upstream wind.

MILE 350. Old Ferry across river.

CAMP #2. MILE 340. Been old farm here. It is still inhabited by millions of ants and plenty of mosquitoes. Everyone tired, but the geese certainly hit the spot. Beautiful setting.

JUNE 22

Up early. Larabee got out film with change bag to send off in a pigeon capsule. Wrote a report of days events. Pigeons released at 6:45 AM.

Shove off at 7:15 AM.

MILE 338. A ferry here with a car crossing on it.[24]

MILE 335. Ferry indicated on map. NO FERRY.

MILE 333. Abandoned Krause [Crouse?] Ranch

[MILE] 331. Just above DEAD MANS ISLAND.

MILE 329 ½. LUNCH.

MILE 324. Having trouble here keeping bearings.

MILE 321. WYOMING-UTAH Line. Many Canadian geese. Water low and have to be careful in finding channel. Southworth is best of party in locating channels.

MILE 319 ½. SMITH FERRY. Just above here two cowboys flapping their horses with sacks to beat off mosquitoes. Just below a truck is being ferried across the river. We gladly keep going as the mosquitoes are particularly voracious.

MILE 318. Entrance to FLAMING GORGE.[25]

MILE 317 ½. Fight a terrific headwind here for fifteen minutes. Kept the WEN bow first to the upstream wind and row hard to keep it going straight. Cutler's oars play out and he is driven to shore, while Reed is almost upset. Wind suddenly abates and we go on looking for a camp.

MILE 316 ½. CAMP #3. Looked over two sites before taking this uninviting spot, but this looks the lesser of many evils, tho the mosquitoes here are frightfully thick. After much unpleasant battling with the mosquitoes we get dinner stowed away. Fortunately a light wind comes up and sleep is possible more or less free from the pests. This camp is just between FLAMING GORGE and HORSESHOE CANYON. The rowing was hard to-day and we earned all our miles.

JUNE 23TH

Shove off 7:25 AM. Unhandy place to load and unload.

MILE 316 ¼. HORSESHOE CANYON.

MILE 314. Two deer on the right bank (just a spot big enough to hold them due to low water) jumped in the river and swam across the other shore.

MILE 310 ½. Stopped here to visit with a young couple, a man and wife who were irrigating a potato field with a small pumping plant. Plenty of mosquitoes. A road here goes a bit over a mile to join the main Sheep Creek Road, also another fork goes back upstream about a mile to the old Flaming Gorge Damsite camp. The people are from Denver. We take off, entering Kingfisher Canyon.

MILE 309 ¼. SHEEP CREEK.[26] Here we are to meet a party headed by Adrian Reynolds, our rendezvous set for this date NOON. So we figured our sailing to the dot. Its pretty here, and we welcome the chance to get some washing done. Good road by here that goes out to the Vernal-Manila Highway. From here downstream it goes to a picnic ground at MILE 307. After LUNCH Doris, Baker and myself did washing while the rest of the sturdy crew slept. We had our stuff put in the boats and were just going to take a nap along with the rest when the expected party showed up. They were preceded by a pickup with two men apparently bound fishing. We took off right away, with five of the party in the boats, while Mr. Deason drove Reynolds car.

MILE 308 ½. BEEHIVE POINT[27] and first rapid. Nothing but a riffle as well as the next two. This occurs at 2:10 P.M.

MILE 307. HIDEOUT CAMP GROUND.[28] Fine water here. Even a regular tap to draw it from. Fill all canteens which were lugged by small boys of the party. Want to get started, so invite the whole outfit to ride a ways with us. After some hesitancy they climb aboard, and our normal crew of eight is now increased by eleven women, men and children to 19. I find the next two rapids open enough to go right thru even with this big load. This we go to head of #3 at MILE 305 ½.

MILE 305 ½. Final farewells are said and we take off for our real start into Red Canyon. The following rapids are merely splashy little fellows but with plenty of rocks showing. Reed surprises me by not being able to dodge better.

MILE 305 CARTER CREEK. Stop here to look around and possible camp, but decided to slip on down a ways. MILE 299. SKULL CREEK. CAMP #4. A bit tired, tho was a lot of sport running this afternoon. Was a great and welcome relief from the awful open stretches. There's water here, but finding a snake skin on the beach above behooves me to spend a great amount of effort in making a sort of rock perch to sleep on. Doris is most efficient in getting meals, and Mildred pitches right in. Wish the river were higher. These rapids so far are a joke, tho could be interesting with plenty of water. Deason is fishing and lands one or two.

JUNE 24TH

Shove off 7:15 AM. We look forward to the thrill of the famous Ashley Falls to-day.

MILE 292 ½. ASHLEY FALLS. After some study I decided to run thru on the left, with passengers. Its a bit tricky, tho not dangerous. With the landing of the WEN, look across river and see names of various parties on wall. Decide to cross over and put our names up too. Signal the MH II thru, then the JOAN. Doris and Larabee rode with me thru this rapid. Was quite a job to get the names up on a huge rock on the left bank. Had to work from a sling. Saw a good many names, including those of the Stone party. Our names, written under: NEVILLS EXPEDITION 1940, are about 75' above the river, in white paint.[29]

MILE 290. LUNCH. Found some meager shade here and took a brief lunch period.

MILE 290, just below Cart Creek, Reed hits a rock pretty hard. He seems to have little judgement of rocks in this white water. This is about 12:30 P.M.

MILE 282 LITTLE DAVENPORT CREEK. This last mile was thru area designated as Little Hole.

MILE 280 ½. Talk a bit with Orson Burton and son who dashed down to see us, having heard about us and the pigeons over the radio.

MILE 279. RED CREEK RAPID. Had a hard time picking a channel, which I did however without landing, but finally decided to run close to the right wall. We all made it, tho took some pretty good blows from the rocks that were terribly thick. Holmstrom lined this one first trip, and others have lined here too. A movie actress, Lorraine Day, with a party up on the rim watching us with glasses run the rapid.[30]

MILE 275. We have left the current behind it seems and comes now plenty of rowing. Here we run into a peculiar action of the river which I finally identify as a homemade dam of great boulders from bank to bank. A narrow passage or spillway in one spot lets us thru.

MILE 274. This is the Jarvie Ranch.[31] A number of people here, and we get some news of outside conditions. Are told where we can get eggs etc. further on [at] Charlie Taylor's [ranch]. Also are advised that a rowboat got away this spring and to please look for it. Opinion is strong against camping so close to civilization, so we decided to push on to an island just ahead.

MILE 273. CAMP #5. Not a bad place to camp. Deer are around and we chase one all over the island. Look forward to getting eggs and milk tomorrow. This trip is funny in a way. Don't believe a day has gone by so far that we haven't run across someone.

JUNE 25TH

Shove off at 7:30 AM. Going to try to make time by rowing regular shifts.

MILE 272 ½. OLD BRIDGEPORT[32]

MILE 270. We see a house here and signs of life so decided it might be Charlie Taylor's. The bunch decide to relax, so Doris and I go up to the house. We meet Mrs. Jess Taylor, whose husband is the son-in-law of the Charlie Taylor we are looking for. The other Taylor is downstream a ways and on the other side of the river. We get some more war news here.

MILE 268 TAYLOR RANCH. Here the genial Charlie Taylor and his wife welcome us and we have a fine visit with them. Fill canteens in their spring house. Get eggs and milk from them. Reed gets some coffee which he is very close in buying. He and Larabee swill coffee every meal. I suspect Reed of having ulcers no doubt brought on by his usual meals and great quantities of coffee. Quite a collection of animals here. Principal of which are some Buffalo which we all go down to see.

Take a reluctant start as it is pleasant here.

MILE 265. ENTRANCE to SWALLOW CANYON.

MILE 263. MOUTH of SWALLOW CANYON. LUNCH right.

MILE 261. This is really tough and slow going here.

MILE 253. Stop here a few minutes to stretch.

Downstream wind shows up so we try rigging a man-held sail. Erractic spurts of wind do help a bit, tho steady rowing gets more mileage in the long run. Pass a man this afternoon who greets us with a 30-30 rifle. No words are spoken, but as we drift slowly by he seemed to recognize us as being harmless, and gave a sort of sheepish grin.[33]

MILE 244 ¼. CAMP #6. Left. Not too bad camp, at least there aren't too many mosquitoes. Take baths, tho the water is quite chilly. At last! The entrance to Lodore Canyon is seen ahead.

JUNE 26TH.

Shove off 7:05 AM

MILE 244. Pass a place with two outboard powered boats that we learn is the site of a dude ranch.[34]

MILE 243 ½. Head OF LODORE CANYON.[35]

MILE 240. First riffles

Mile 240 ¼. Short fast one. Dell doesn't do so well, as this one you have to turn quick on. We briefly look at a boat the "Illinois Girl," which shows effects of pretty bad battering. Later learn that a chap from Illinois came out to try the Colorado but just below at Lower Disaster Falls he got trapped under a ledge.[36] It seem the dude ranch outfit towed the boat up here so as to show it to their dudes!

MILE 237. UPPER DISASTER FALLS.[37] On approaching this one it doesn't look so much and I see that by quickly slipping to rock in middle of narrow channel that we can go thru in slick shape. The WEN and MEXICAN HAT II go thru beautifully, but Reed in JOAN gets balled up and tries to go the wrong side, and he and Baker and Deason are caught up high and nearly dry on the rock. Continual rocking doesn't loosen boat, so Cutler and I go over in the WEN to other side to render aid. We get a line from the JOAN, and I try to go up the line to the JOAN but the terrific current shoves the water right down my throat and choked me. For several days my throat bothered me. Finally, taking the rope and bracing ourselves, combined with the lurching of the JOAN passengers the boat was brought free. Close call.

MILE 237. Look this over fairly close, and all boats land at the foot by 11:05 A.M.

MILE 236 ½. LOWER DISASTER FALLS. Pick out the channel which goes under ledge on the right and go thru with no trouble. This is the first rapid we haven't taken passengers on. After running my boat was going back up to give high sign when nearly lost my breakfast. Thot it must be nerves, but finally decided it was the swallowing of so much water.

LUNCH. Foot of Lower Disaster.

MILE 235 ½ Just above POT CREEK. Couple of fellows here have a prospect up the hill a ways next to a dike. They have great hopes, and Deason takes samples. The reports later on show that the "mine" wouldn't pay to work.

MILE 234. Just below here a small rapid I look at. OK.

MILE 232. Head of TRIPLET FALLS.[38] No passengers. Nice to run and quite zippy. Bottom left side a wonderful place to camp. French Trio stopped here along with many more. Clyde Cox wrecked a boat here, also Frank Swain. The remains of a boat is leaned up against the wall. Been a good boat, tho shows it had a bad wreck. This is such a delightful spot we decide to camp here early as it is. I build a table and get ready for a campfire. Reed, nervous over Hell's Half Mile below goes down to see it. He's always getting the jitters.

CAMP #7. Plenty of deer tracks. Sit around fire and sing after dinner. Good camp. 12 miles to-day.

JUNE 27TH.

Leave CAMP #7 at 7:25 AM. I feel anxious to get to this rapid as its only been run successfully once or twice. It has a bad reputation, and is part of the biggest drop on the whole Green-Colorado series.

MILE 231. Hell's Half Mile.[39] This baby has a real back on it. Takes a minor drop, then plunges between two closely spaced rocks directly into another rock. The trick is to slide off to one side of the center rock. Below is a complicated rock filled channel, but no killing water. I finally get my technique worked out and take off. Make the first part smoothly, but get hung up a bit below and wiggle around to get to the bottom of the last drop. Have to take my oars back up to Cutler as his are too frail to stand up. Cutler comes thru OK, likewise Reed. Walking alongside of rapid is tough, and we all get bunged up a bit due to spills and slipping.

MILE 230. RIPPLING BROOK.

MILE 226. We can see the slick high wall on the right that forms STEAMBOAT ROCK.

MILE 225 ¼ YAMPA RIVER. Larabee wanted to go up the YAMPA with an outboard motor. The few second feet discharge was enough to squelch this idea. We decided to get some fresh water for our canteens.[40]

MILE 224 ½. PATS HOLE.[41] CAMP #8. Looked to meet Buzz Holmstrom[42] here, and sure enough I spotted him on shore building a boat.

He ran down to meet us and we had a nice reunion. Had lunch with Buzz, then the afternoon was spent making some minor repairs to our boats. Had to fix the side molding in the rain.

So late when we got thru that accepted Buzz's invitation to stay overnight and go on in the morning. So we had dinner together, then sat up half the night swapping yarns. Met rest of the crew with Buzz and all were most pleasant. This is a crew of diamond drillers testing for possible dam site just below here. Deason caught some fish. 8 miles to-day.

June 28th

Shove off 7:55 A.M.

MILE 223. Stopped here on right to get water from a spring that Buzz told us of. Fine water, tho a bit hard to get to.

MILE 221. Stopped here on right to look over the drill site. They were just dismantling one test hole so we didn't get to see much. They have big barge to move their outfit on.[43]

MILE 221 ½. Water plenty slow and promises to get slower, tho we have the promise of Split Mountain before us.

MILE 219. UTAH-COLORADO LINE.

MILE 216 ¼. Run this quarter mile long rapid in two minutes flat.

MILE 213. RUPLE RANCH.[44] We see a stick on the right bank at this point with a bottle tied to it. Obviously a note for us tho some members ridicule the idea. The note is an invitation to us to go to visit the Evans, Mrs. Evans formerly being a Ruple. We find them very nice and we have a marvelous dinner. Canned venison even. We learn much of interest about the country and here by the ranch house is a huge cottonwood tree that is one of the biggest in the world. After lunch, we go to the river and ferry a load of eight persons in the WEN across and slightly upstream to the neck of the loop from where there is a grand view. Most of the party continued on down to the river on the other side, while I returned the Evans back to their shore. Then with Reed and Cutler in their respective boats we started on around the loop.

MILE 210 ¼. Briefly pause to pick up the party. Muddy all around and they have trouble getting to the boats. On we go lured by the promise of Split Mountain Canyon and fast water ahead.[45]

MILE 206 ⅘. ENTRANCE SPLIT MOUNTAIN CANYON. This bearing using a cottonwood tree on right bank.

MILE 204. Rapid #7, Split Mountain. Whew! I got rapid fever and we've been hitting the high spots. Passed several along that we were strongly warned against by Holmstrom and others. Its been real sport, and we've really been traveling. Off again! Just stopped here more or less a formality.

Head of rapid #9 CAMP #9. We first land on left side in wonderful spot to camp, but the very high sheer wall doesn't look good to me overhead. The gang kid me for my fears, but we suddenly get a small bombardment of rocks from overhead and everyone seems most willing to follow my orders

Below Split Mountain Canyon, 1940: Charles Larabee (standing, center), Doris
Nevills (second from right), Norman Nevills (far right)

to break camp and move across the river. We finished our dinner first on
the right side. The pleasant fellowship and good will marking our travel on
the upper river was cropping out later in the evening in a game involving
spotting a flashlight beam for our flashlights across the canyon to the
opposite wall, then another person trying to superimpose his light spot on
mine while they traveled quickly around the wall face. A very fine camp.[46]
20 ½ miles to-day. .

JUNE 29TH.
Shove off 7:25 AM
    MILE 199. END SPLIT MOUNTAIN.
    MILE 199. LUNCH. Right bank. We see two people gesticulating and
land to meet Mr. and Mrs. Ashael Bush, Associated Press, Salt Lake City.[47]
Nice couple and we get to be good friends in short order. Leaving Ace's
wife in camp with Dell, Ace loaded us all into his car and took us over to the
Dinosaur National Monument.[48] Had a grand trip, and when we got back
to river had a big lunch, also took on a lot of supplies that Ace and wife
insisted on giving us. Charley L. and John took Ace's car to go overland to
Jensen, while rest of us took off via river. Ace in my boat and did most of the
rowing. Had plenty of what it takes to buck stiff rowing.
    MILE 195 ½. Placer mine operating.
    MILE 188. Right bank. Brief stop. Brick house. Powell camped under
cottonwood tree here. Going slow and hard all along here.

MILE 184 ½. Left. Meet Charlie, John and Bus Hatch. Also bottle of whiskey. Bus takes my place in WEN and all leave the boats to Bus, Dell, and Ace and his wife. I drive the Packard overland to Jensen, and we wait on the bridge to see them come in. Don Harris, his brother, and Bert Loper arrive with our boats, their having a 4.6 [horsepower] Johnson outboard. We invite them to the high school auditorium, where our river trip '38 pictures will be shown at 8:00. Reed stays with the boats while all the rest of us go up with Bus. We meet at his house, clean up a bit ready to go into town for dinner. Just now my two good friends, Frank O'Brien,[49] Salt Lake newspaper man and Bill Eldrige show up. Frank has handled and arranged the pigeon business. Wish these boys were along to get pictures. Am partly thru dinner when see it is time for the show, so dash over to the auditorium. Owing to a mistake in announcing, a bare handful of people are on hand so the show is a flop.[50] Deason and Cutler return to sleep at the boats. Larabee and Southworth go to the hotel, while Doris, Mildred, and I are guests at Bus's house. Before retiring I make tentative plans with Bus and Mandy Campbell to tow our boats down to Ouray, some sixty miles. Would be a great thing as this rowing business is painfully slow.

ARRIVED JENSEN at 5:27 P.M. 22 mile day.

JUNE 30TH.

We had food stored with Bus, and busied ourselves in the morning with getting food to Jensen, the power boat down and the other incidentals connected with taking off. Mandy's boat, the LOLA MAY had two 16 h.p. outboards, with a motor of Bus's, a three [h.p.] as an auxiliary. After much ado we get loaded. Frank and Bill will go at least part of the way with us. In the power boat are Bus, Mandy, Lola, a nurse, and Lola's fiance. Right from the start we have much trouble with shoals, and a high wind comes up. I believe our distance won't be great from Jensen by nightfall.

MILE 175. Right. Cars come overland to meet us here. Buzz just got in and comes over too. Getting late, and plans are revised, with Bus now leaving too, so the next meeting place is a spot known only to Bus. We are to meet at the Leota Ranch, some 39 miles downstream. This looks impossible to me, but here we go!

MILE 165. Going really tough. Hard to find channel. Its trying to rain and we're all cold. Going to stop pretty soon. This point is the entrance to HORSESHOE BEND, 8 ½ miles around, tho barely a half mile across.

MILE 163 CAMP #10. We stop gratefully as its quite cold. Stopping raining but even so the outlook is uncomfortable. We find the ground covered with reminders that this is a cattle range. Get a couple of fires going and the warmth soon makes things more cheerful. Doris soon gets dinner for us all and the food really helps. Mandy decides to push on down the river to his meeting point. He is gone some time when we hear him returning. He gets close to camp then cuts downstream again. Wrong channel! I go to sleep thinking that Mandy and his party are in for a night.

JULY 1

Last night Doris worked on Larabee's hand which has developed a slight infection. Larabee lanced it with his pocket knife and the hand is better this morning.

SHOVE OFF MILE 163 8:35 A.M.

MILE 158 Here we find on the right bank Mandy's motorboat! The going got bad after dark so they stopped. We called, expecting to raise them—but no answer! Went across the bar and thru the trees and came upon a big abandoned placer camp. After some time raise a couple of men who are planning to do some mining. They advise us that Mandy's party got in around midnight, borrowed their pickup, and went for town, expecting to be back around noon. We fooled around exploring the property, then finally decided to borrow the light motor belonging to Bus. Reed and I rigged up a motor mount on the WEN and finally took off without any sign of Mandy. We figure on calling Bus from OURAY and explain our "theft," and try to arrange to get the motor to take on to Lees Ferry.

MILE 156. Wind starting up again. Having pretty good luck picking the channel, and this beats rowing all to pieces.

MILE 148 ½. Bucking a heavy headwind now.

MILE 144 ½. CAMP #11. This is a poor looking spot to camp, but best we can find. About fifty feet above river is a mesa that has a good place for beds. Not far across it is the river again, this being a loop of some three miles. Have dinner, then I decide to try the outboard on the WEN without the other boats holding it back to see what it will do. I get motor started and barely swing the boat when the motor races. Cutting it off and looking for a sheared pin I find the whole bottom section has dropped off! After fishing around a while close to shore I find the parts, all but the bolts. Get it assembled, but need two bolts. Decide to run on to Leota in the morning and pick up some bolts. And here comes the roar of a motor! And from upstream comes Mandy Campbell and a friend! We get them dinner, all being amused at Mandy prowling around in his stocking feet. They decide to go on, and for several hours afterwards we hear their motor racing, then a dead silence as a bar catches them! They have two of our flashlights to help them—but it's tough. Later we find that they finally, after about three miles waited 'till daybreak and made it to Leota and were met by Bus who took them in. According to the map Leota Ranch is at MILE 141, so Dell and I will slip off early ahead of the rest of the party and get the bolts—we hope!

18 mile run.

JULY 2

Reed and I hurry thru our breakfast and take off in the WEN to go after the bolts. The other two boats and the rest of the party will follow in about an hour.

Shove off 6:45 AM

MILE 140 ½. We finally stop here to go out and look around. Leota is marked here on the map but there is no sign of life. See a boy horseback and go toward him to ask for information. The boy takes off, and we go about a mile before catching up with him. He seems to think we're bogies or something, but we finally elicit the information that the LEOTA ranch was moved some years back and that ranch headquarters is now some distance down the river. Oh me.

MILE 137. We reach the Leota ranch . We are fortunate in finding two bolts right away, and have them installed and ready to go as the rest of the party shows up. We fill our canteens, thank our kind benefactors, and take off again.

MILE 136. We decided there isn't enough gas so stop to send back to the ranch or wherever possible to get some. I cast a speculative eye over the party picking someone to send when I discover Southworth is missing. About then he arrives somewhat winded. He had gone exploring back at the ranch and we took off without him. Lucky we stopped for gas! I decide to go on anyway with what gas we have.

MILE 134. LUNCH. For some reason or other a water boiling goes on. Cutler is fussier than an old woman, and I'd hate to see him really get up against some hard going.

MILE 128. OURAY. We call it "Hooray." Ute Indian Reservation and a general store. I call Bus and thank him for use of the motor. He's grand about it, but will need it soon so we can't take it on with us. Debate getting one from Salt Lake, but the non-rowers put up quite a fuss. We return to the boats slightly out of humor. Cutler doesn't like to stay in position, and we're barely under way when he complains bitterly about using the substitute light oars. To teach him a lesson, I give him my oars and take his, and the pace I set with his "worthless" oars has him well fagged by camp time. The long pull to Green River looks discouraging, but guess we'll make it after a while.

MILE 123. WEST BRANCH. Been bucking a heavy wind with very little current to help us.

MILE 122. CAMP #12. A good spot to camp. Make our beds on a little used road just back from and paralleling the river. We put up barriers to stop possible traffic. Explore around a bit and all in all spirits are much revived. We debate on how to speed up progress, and decide to hit the oars hard in the morning when there isn't any wind and just row hard and see where the day gets us. After all, we're only 123 miles from Green River, and every day's run clips off a good substantial distance. I think I may replace Cutler at Green River.

July 3rd.
Shove off 7:30 AM.

MILE 96. CAMP #13. Made good time to-day thru steady hard rowing and feel we can knock off a bit early, wash clothes, bathe, etc. Flies are terribly bad here, and during dinner we are pestered nearly to death with them. We run, fan each other, and in general have a tough time of it. Have

Photo montage of upper Green River, 1940: (clockwise from upper left) boats at Green River, Wyoming; start of trip; Horseshoe Canyon; Hideout Camp; Red Canyon; (center) boat at Green River, Wyoming

some extras to celebrate the impending Fourth. Find an old camp just below where they've been pumping water once.

JULY 4TH.

At crack of dawn we are awakened by heavy blast that seems to come from downriver. We speculate but can't figure the source.

Shove off 7:20 AM.

MILE 95. SAND WASH.[51] Here the explosion is explained. We stop here to find five men from Price, Utah fishing, and they set off the blast of dynamite to usher in the FOURTH. Names: H. Pressett. J. Birch. R. Pierce. O. Rasmasen. L. Pierce. After a short visit we take off again.

MILE 86. LUNCH. Cutler has been so unruly about keeping place on the river, etc. that am going to let him row the JOAN. Cutler is a damned sissy, and tries to say the JOAN is easier to row than the MEXICAN HAT II and he (Cutler) can't keep up. When we leave after lunch it takes less than an hour for Cutler to show a yellow streak and lay down on the rowing. Baker, Southworth and I get ahead and as Cutler has Larabee go in the wrong channel. Wind comes up. Reed stays in his position and is of course held up. We dawdle along in the WEN, but even so get quite a ways ahead.

MILE 77. LEFT. Here the other boats come dragging in. The canyon on the left is filled with weird rock-capped pillars. Just below and high up on the left is a natural bridge.

MILE 73. CAMP #145. We land and Hugh and Larabee promptly go off to explore, ending up by going high up on the cliff walls and starting small landslides. We have a nice dinner, tho Cutler and Larabee make it hard for the girls by getting in late.

JULY 5TH.

Shove off 7:30 AM.

MILE 73. See natural bridge high up right wall.

MILE 70. RAPID #1 DESOLATION CANYON.

MILE 69. On right bank at foot of rapid I see oar painted orange. Recovery proves it to be fine oar in perfect condition. The sequel to this is that its later found to have been lost by Bus Hatch this spring way up in Split Mountain Canyon when he wrecked a boat.[52]

MILE 60. Right. LUNCH. Hotter than blazes and we have a scanty ledge for protection from the sun.

MILE 59. These last two rapids had a real wallop in them as the rocks are very thick and the navigable channel narrow.

MILE 56 RAPID #11 DESOLATION CANYON. The roughness of some of the last rapids inclines Larabee to try to get a good picture of a boat in a hole, but indifferent success is met.

MILE 54. ROCK CREEK. Stop here to visit SEAMONTON RANCH. We go over but find it empty. Tenant probably out for the FOURTH. Find some luscious apricots and stock up.[53]

MILE 53 CAMP #15. Good camp here.

JULY 6TH.

First thing this morning Doris releases one of the pigeons, and it flies directly across the river and sits on a rock. In the meantime the remaining pigeon dances up and down in the cage and gives every evidence of much distress. We conclude that these must be mates, so another note is attached to the penned bird and it too is released. It speeds directly across the river, swings by the other bird who joins it, and they head for Salt Lake City. Its quite a sight! The need for a hike is felt by some, so Cutler, Baker, and Larabee take off, arranging to meet us at noon about a mile and a half below. Baker likes to play up as a good sport, because I know she doesn't like climbing. Doris and Dell do washing, while Deason fishes. Southworth and I go for a hike up into Rock Creek to see where the road goes. We find it ends just a ways up, thus showing that everything is packed in overland by pack animals.

Shove off 11:30 AM

MILE 51. SNAP CANYON. Pick up the hikers and proceed on to find a lunch place.

MILE 39. CAMP #16 Left. Over to the left a ways of this excellent camp spot is a farm house supposed to be the McPherson Ranch.[54] No one is at home tho it appears that some one is occupying the place. More fruit trees. After dinner we go over again and this time a cowboy-watchman shows up. He gives us a lot of eggs, we fill our canteens, and the man promises to be down in the morning to see us off. The ranch is being sold to the government to be part of the Ute Indian Reservation.

JULY 7TH

Yesterday we found a number of rapids not indicated on the map. Probably at higher stages of water they wouldn't be noticeable. I have named them and spotted them [on the map].

The first rapid below here is the first in the Gray Canyon series. Therefore we have run all the rapids of DESOLATION CANYON, which proved to be 27 in number.

Shove off 7:45 AM.

MILE 26. COAL CREEK. Had trouble with WEN and tapped several holes. Slid off into wrong channel so signaled other boats to hold up. Landed and went back and brought Cutler's boat thru in good shape. Made me mad. Reed thru OK. And on we go, altho I don't like the low water thru this section with it spread out so wide and filled with rocks.

MILE 22. RATTLESNAKE CANYON [rapid]. Looking this one over on general principles as it has a heavy indicated drop. Not too hard to run and all passengers go thru. This is the last chance for a real rapid from here to Green River, so we have a nice record. So far we've looked at but 6 rapids including this before running. Passengers have ridden all but 3. Those looked over and whether passengers rode or not:

ASHLEY FALLS—PASSENGERS
LOWER DISASTER FALLS—BOATMEN
TRIPLET FALLS—BOATMEN
HELLS HALF MILE—BOATMEN
7 SPLIT MOUNTAIN—PASSENGERS
RATTLESNAKE CREEK RAPIDS—PASSENGERS

MILE 20. We'll see the Price River soon.
MILE 18. RIGHT. CAMP #17. Grand camp, even found a plank to fit up kitchen with. We found several more unmapped rapids to-day.

July 8th

Shove off. 7:00 AM
MILE 12. This is the #15 GRAY CANYON and the last rapid of Gray Canyon. I hit three rocks in this baby, MEXICAN HAT II got hung up and broke an oar, JOAN hit one rock, or so Reed says, tho what the other two things he hit were I don't know. At any rate we have clear sailing to Green River, tho its going to be a hard row.
MILE 11. GUNNISON BUTTE.[55]
MILE 8. DAM AND HASTINGS RANCH. We pull in here to wash up boats, and Doris gets the use of washing machine to do a lot of laundry. Cutler, Reed and I ride the big power wheel. A car load of people show up other side of river to see boats. We were going to stay here overnight, but decide to run on in to Green River for dinner. We hope!
MILE 5. We bumped plenty going over the dam, but this last going has been discouraging hard work.[56] It looks like a long ways from here to Green River!
MILE 0. GREEN RIVER, UTAH. ELEV. 4046.
We go up to the hotel leaving Don Harris watching the boats. Reed is to go right back. We have dinner, I check to find that oars are on hand—and to bed!

July 9th

Up early and go to sorting food at Beebees. After girls are well started I get the oars and give them an oil coat. Then send them down to Reed to put leathers on. I talk to Cutler and against my better judgement decide to take him on thru. He and Reed hate each other and it's a bad set-up. Food is finally ready. At three o'clock Doris' mother comes with the baby.[57] Fox driving our car, to the hotel. I take the baby to the river but she doesn't want to ride in my WEN as it "plashes," and insists on my rowing her around in the JOAN.
We're having dinner when in walks Mother, Barry Goldwater,[58] Bill Saufley, and his fiancee. Its good to see Mother, and she joins us at dinner. After dinner we go to the hotel and find Ann Rosner[59] has gotten in.
A bit later we go to basement of hotel and see the movies of Harris' '39 trip. They are good and show plenty of action in the low water.[60]

Last night before leaving Deason[61] promised to see Emil Johnson in Salt Lake City and see if he could get us a motor. A wire arrives saying the motor will be in this afternoon. I find it at the Midland garage.

July 10th.

I get two cans for gasoline, and by good luck run into Arth Chaffin[62] who advises me he'll have plenty of gasoline for us at his place. He got our food all right.

We get the food all down to the boats, hook up the outboard motor and get everything ready to go. Harris is going as far as the Geyser with us. I get word that Wayne McConkie[63] and his father the Bishop of Moab will be over this afternoon and go down in their canoe to the Junction to see us run the first few rapids of Cataract Canyon.

After much last minute preparations we are ready and:

Shove off 4:00 PM.

MILE 6. THE GEYSER. The motor is a big help, tho am slow to get the feel of picking the right channel. Sheared several pins from the word commence. Make camp and are just about to eat when the McConkies show up. They have dinner with us then push on downstream. Doris and I sleep miserably as we're too close to the geyser and its intermittent bursts all night are disturbing.

July 11th.

Harris and I fixed my motor bracket better last night and we're all set to go this morning.

Shove off 7:30 AM. Harris goes a ways then turns back. The motor performs faithfully and we go right along. Don't make much better time than rowing, but at least we can keep up a steady hour after hour pace without wearing ourselves out rowing.

Grand Canyon,
July 11 to August 3, 1940

[Editor's Note:]

The section of Nevills's journal that covers the voyage from the Crystal Geyser through Labyrinth, Stillwater, Cataract, and Glen Canyons to their arrival at Lees Ferry, Arizona—July 11 to August 3, 1940—was not found in the Nevills papers when they came to the University of Utah in 1988; subsequent inquiries have turned up nothing. This section of the journey is described in great detail by Doris in her published account, "Woman Conqueror of the Colorado," which appeared in serial form in the Grand Junction Daily Sentinel *in the summer of 1941. The following account is summarized from that source.*

Nevills adding his name to "river register" just above Bowknot Bend, Labyrinth Canyon

JULY 11–AUGUST 3

The party left Green River, Utah, accompanied for the first few miles by Don Harris and some other friends. They camped together at the Crystal Geyser, and the next day all the visitors said goodbye and the party continued on downriver. They stopped at the river register above Bowknot Bend and added another inscription to the one they had left two years before; this one can still be seen and reads simply: "Nevills Expedition 7-12-40." Part of the group walked over the neck of Bowknot Bend, something often done today. They proceeded through the beautiful curves of Labyrinth and Stillwater canyons in good spirits. Rosner and Goldwater mixed well with the other passengers, and the days and nights were spent singing, joking, thinking up pranks, and exploring old cabins and Indian ruins. There were hints of tension, and other accounts of the trip describe a rising tide of dissension among the passengers, but Doris wasn't about to describe any squabbles in print when she knew how much was riding on the trip. She was often the foil to Norman's pointed personality, and she had a good sense of humor as well. On July 14 she wrote, "Today we will see the Colorado River, and Cataract Canyon. . . . Norm has long been promising us water when we would finally get to the Colorado so as we came into the mighty Colorado Norm said 'Well, our troubles are over, we at last have plenty of water under us,' and just then we ran onto a sandbar."

They had already arranged to meet Bishop McConkie of Moab and his son, Wayne, at Spanish Bottom, just below the confluence of the Green and the Colorado, and when they invited Doris to run Rapid #1 (later named Brown Betty) with them in their canoe, she jumped at the chance, being "consumed with curiosity to see how a canoe of this type 'rides." Their high spirits continued through the first part of Cataract, with Norman going through rapids #9–10 standing on deck of Wen as Goldwater rowed, a trick he'd first learned from Emery Kolb in 1938. But Cataract Canyon always has a way of extracting payments from those who run it, and in Rapid #24 (Big Drop 3), Reed missed Norman's signal and pinned the Joan between two boulders on the left side of the river. Norman, Goldwater, and Southworth clambered out to the boat and after several hours work, freed it. They wrestled the damaged boat to shore, but not before it capsized when it came loose, soaking all the food and gear in the hatches. While this was going on— presumably Doris and the others who weren't involved in the rescue—carved an inscription in a boulder at the head of Big Drop 3 that is still visible today: "Capsized #3. 7-15-40. Nevills."

That night, as the men worked to repair the damage, Doris waxed sentimental about the boats: "I feel almost a physical pain when anything happens to our boats. They are such gallant and courageous crafts. It's all right to tell oneself they are mere wood, but when they turn in such [a] magnificent performance time and time again one soon regards them with affectionate concern." Chastened, they went on more carefully. Camping at Dark Canyon, most of the party hiked up the canyon, while Norman, Doris, and Reed scouted the rapid. Since the water was rising, Nevills decided to run the Wen and the Mexican Hat II through, which he did successfully; Reed then brought the Joan through.

The rest of Cataract Canyon passed uneventfully, save for a stop to add their names to another river register at the end of Cataract. On July 20, they reached Hite, and everyone took a break to rest, read mail brought in from Hanksville, stow new supplies, and visit with the amiable Arth Chaffin, the operator of the ferry. They left on July 22, dropping off a prospector and his son at their mining camp, where they found the prospector's wife operating the mining machinery. From there, they drifted through the beautiful and peaceful reaches of Glen Canyon, admired the scenery, explored old cabins such as Cass Hite's (where Doris ate too much watermelon), and stopped at Hidden Passage and Music Temple. The whole group hiked to Rainbow Bridge, where they planned to stay overnight at the Wilson camp, but a hard rainstorm almost caught them in a flash flood and made Nevills worry about the boats, tied up back at the river. He, Reed, and Doris waited for the flood to subside and then dashed back to the river at dusk, making the six miles in two-and-a-half hours through driftwood and deep pools of flood water, where they found the boats just fine. The next day, while the others were coming back from their overnight stay at the Rainbow Bridge camp, Norman and Doris motored upriver and shared some private moments, always difficult to find on a river trip.

Doris stayed in camp while Norman and the others went in search of the Herbert E. Gregory Natural Bridge, rumored to be found in the Escalante River canyon. Measuring the bridge had been one of Norman's goals for the trip.[64] On August 1, they stopped at the Utah-Arizona line for Barry to paint the inscription: UTAH-ARIZONA WELCOMES YOU. But then Doris had a premonition that something was wrong at home, and from then on, she was "frightfully impatient" to reach Lees Ferry. When they got there the next day, she found that their daughter, Joan, was fine, but Doris's mother had broken her ankle. She and Norman borrowed a car and drove home to Mexican Hat over dirt roads, stayed overnight, got everyone settled, and turned around and came back the next day. Nevills's journal resumes on August 4, 1940. When they started on the river that day, the water level was at only 3,000 cfs, a very low level to be running the rapids of the Grand Canyon.

Aug. 4

Doris and I got in at 1:30 AM from Mexican Hat, so we're a bit sleepy and tired this morning. however, after breakfast Bill Brown and his wife help ferry us to Lees Ferry where we start getting stuff together. It's a big job, but finally all is ready and bid Ace Bush and his friend goodbye, the Cornelius' goodbye, and we're off at: 1:00:PM.

Its clouding up and starting to blow.

MILE 4. NAVAJO BRIDGE. Few people up on the bridge braving the rain that has now come up. Its miserable on the river and seems like a poor day to start a trip. But at that its good to get started.

MILE 7. BADGER CREEK RAPID. CAMP #33. This looks like a pretty tough situation at Badger Creek. There simply isn't a channel anywheres. Even row over to the other side to look for a way thru, but not a chance there. It looks like a lining job, and we decide to carry a lot of our stuff to foot of rapid to be ready for come what may in the morning. I hate to have this rapid beat me in more ways than one. It beat me in '38, and it will be the first this trip to be lined. Oh well, look it over some more in the morning.

Aug. 5th.

Looks bad. Am going on down to pick out our lining channel. On way back up can see possible chance to get thru. I decide to run! Announce that I will take all three boats thru. Both Cutler and Del seem relieved to miss this one. Don't blame them as it is mean.

Hung the JOAN up for a minute in mid-channel but slid right loose. Shove off 8:50 AM.

MILE 11. Soap Creek Rapid. Not too tough, tho a different looking rapid than in high water. All boats thru in good shape.

MILE 14. SHEER WALL RAPID. Look over but passengers and all go thru. These rapids require more looking over in this low water as the rocks are awfully thick.

MILE 17. HOUSE ROCK RAPIDS. No riders.

MILE 18. BOULDER NARROWS. Here is the famous huge rock perched in midstream with scant clearance for the river around it. The bunch landed against the rock and Charlie finally got to the top and started the driftwood on top afire. Its around fifty feet above the river at the prevailing low stage of water. As we leave it is quite a sight back upstream at the large blaze.

MILE 20. NORTH CANYON. CAMP #34. This is a fine camp on the right side and there's plenty of wood.

AUG. 6TH.

Last night around 8:00 PM we were startled to see a burning raft-like business coming down the river—a piece of burning drift from the fire atop the rock in Boulder Narrows! It was a spooky and beautiful sight. Twice more during the night I awoke by some instinct or the other to see burning embers floating past. The river is smooth here approaching the rapid, the firelit logs would approach the drop-off, seem to pause—then plunge quickly into the foaming waves to have the fire quickly extinguished.

I decide to let Barry bring the MEXICAN HAT II thru, and Charlie the JOAN. I shove off at 7:25 AM, closely followed by the other two, and we're all at the bottom and off again at 8:05 AM.

MIKE 21. TWENTY-ONE MILE RAPIDS. Give this a glance then run thru with no passengers. Mighty rough.

MILE 24. TWENTY-FOUR MILE RAPIDS. This one is bad in high water tho ran it in '38. Del wouldn't run this one in '38. Looks almost hopeless to run. Main water on right, but is so badly jammed with rocks and holes as to be impossible. I finally decide to try the left side. I take off in the WEN, get halfway thru, and some from twenty-five feet from left bank have to go between two rocks that are about same distance apart as boat is wide. Almost get thru, but not quite. Rescue crew comes out and we work WEN up on rock to left, then tilt it over edge and I shoot free again making it to bottom of rapid OK. While getting up on the rock the stern was under some little while and so there was water in the stern compartment. Next I try my luck in the MEXICAN HAT II. The boys are waiting to give me a push at the crucial moment, thus I get thru without completely hanging up. With the JOAN I start out bow first thinking to row in fast between the rocks and bulldoze thru. But find I can't steer well enough and at last minute whirl around, but it sends me into the rocks at a slight angle and we all but get hung up in a bad ways, but the boys get me loose and send me on with shove. I put this down as a bad rapid.

MILE 25. CAVE SPRINGS RAPID. Again no passengers. These rocks are thick.

MILE 27. Right. CAMP #35. 7 miles to-day!

AUG. 7TH.

Not a bad camp. At least we were tired enough to appreciate getting dinner and a good nights sleep. Baker keeps declaring she doesn't sleep, but I suspect she's kidding herself a bit—not us!

Shove off 7:25 AM.

MILE 29. TWENTY-NINE MILE RAPIDS. Nice riding for passengers and all. Hold against right wall.

MILE 31. PARADISE CANYON.[65] Here we try to climb up to find a skeleton that Buzz H. told me about.[66] Doris and I get up first, and I'd given up finding it when Doris announced her discovery of it. Its some 100–150 yards upstream from Paradise Canyon, top of second talus slope against base of cliff. A bit hard to climb to. Charley made it up fine, but Cutler seemed to be booed [afraid] of the climb. The skeleton is minus a head, has a broken arm and leg. We climb back down to the boats and shove off to Vasey's Paradise which we see downstream a ways.

MILE 32. VASEY'S PARADISE. A wonderful spot. Take baths here, do washing, and enjoy the luxury of plenty of fresh clear water. After lunch we get under the somewhat cramped shelter of a big rock—our siesta is soon interrupted by a drift fire touched off directly overhead. On we go!

MILE 35. Right. Natural bridge (called by Kolb "Bridge of Sighs.") This section is filled with caverns and cave entrances. I think it would pay on another trip to stop along here and investigate some of these caves. There are many springs along the right wall.

MILE 43. PRESIDENT HARDING RAPID. Have been warning the bunch about this rapid as in '38 it was plenty tricky. Frank Dodge wrecked a boat here in '21.[67] Barry was rowing the WEN on approach and kept right on rowing thru where the rapid was supposed to be. In low water it is not even a riffle!

MILE 44. LEFT. CAMP #36. A good camp with lots of wood. Reed amuses all by claiming that the first boat thru a rapid goes faster than the following boats. He can't get it thru his head how ridiculous this is! Cutler and Charlie find some carbide which is played with and is touched off by putting a few crystals of the carbide in a tin can with a lid, then spitting on the carbide and touching off the gas by means of a small aperture. The can is held by a foot lightly on it.

AUG. 8TH.

Shove off 7:20 AM.

MILE 47. SADDLE CANYON. Here the D.W.B.'s get to work (Damned Wood Burners)[68] and a large pile of drift is touched off. In fact stops to touch off drift piles have been numerous, tho the firebugs do it without causing the lead boat to hold up, but generally get the pyrotechnics done while a rapid is being looked over.

MILE 52. NANKOWEAP CREEK. Were going to spend some time here but after prowling around a bit decide to go on. There are interesting ruins here but a day or so is needed here to do any real exploring. In '38 I found a white arrowhead that I took home to Joan.

MILE 57. MALGOSA CANYON. LUNCH. Last forty-five minutes have been hunting and hunting for a place to stop for lunch. This is best shade possible. Co-incidentally in 1938 I stopped here for lunch too, finding this the best place around.

MILE 61. LITTLE COLORADO RIVER. Stop just briefly to walk over to look at discharge from Little Colo. A dirty red muddy flow of some hundred or so second feet. A very uninviting spot so on we go, eager to be in the Grand Canyon. Well, the rapids of Marble Canyon, 28 of them, are behind us. But passengers are walking around more now. There are too many rocks, and the added weight of passengers makes too much of a hazard for the boats.

MILE 62. FIRST VIEW OF HOPI TOWER!

MILE 65. Left, across from LAVA CANYON. Here in the early days copper leads were followed under the dikes on the left. Been quite a camp at one time. Still quite a bit of equipment around, all of it brought in by way of the TANNER TRAIL. Doris finds an old coal oil lamp that has turned to violet. A wonderful find! Most of us up to the tunnels, two in number, and John and I go way back in one that is the biggest. Beautiful copper compounds all over. Find dynamite, fuse, and caps in one drift. Return to the boats, then go down to look over the rapid. It's a hard job as we have to get on a sort of island first thru pretty fast water. We all get dunked well and proper. There's one big wave, biggest we've seen so far. Its only about six feet high, but sharp on the sides. I decide to go right over it and thus instruct the other boats. But when we take off John thinks there's rock there and I start to slide off to one side, see its OK and manage to get almost on top. Its fun! The other two boats come slap bang thru the middle.

MILE 68. Left, just above '38 camp. CAMP #37. Camp on a ledge here. Would be a fine camp but there's millions of deer flies to make things most uncomfortable. And its hot! After dinner Barry and Charlie row across the river to sleep on a bar in hopes that it will be cooler and freer from flies. We get along alright on our side as after dark the flies let up a lot. In the morning Baker claims she got no sleep again!

AUGUST 9TH.

Everyone wants to put in a full day and try to run thru to Bright Angel. I don't think we can do it as it is 19 miles of many of the biggest rapids in the river. We shall see! I'm awfully tired, and need a rest. Am too tired to handle the boat fast enough.

Shove off 7:15 AM.

MILE 72. UNKAR CREEK RAPIDS. These prove to be a surprise. In high water slid thru these without looking over or even making a *time notation!* But in this extreme low water they are tough because of a quick switching channel with lots of rocks. I give the WEN a bad blow near the foot of rapid. Worst I've had on the trip. Nearly threw Barry from the boat. Other boats come thru alright.

MILE 73. This little riffle here had some of the fastest water we've had on the trip. Open channel and easy. Run right.

MILE 75. SEVENTY-FIVE MILE RAPIDS. Not bad, and take passengers too.

MILE 76. HANCE RAPID. This is a real tough one. In high water I played the left side, and it seems that we have to do same now. Finally pick out a complicated course and set off in the WEN. But can't see over brink far enough to get spotted, and its acutely necessary to go in correct place here. So I pull in across the river to right bank and look again. Spot a big rock to go by and take off. Towards the bottom have to pull out of the main drag to get in below a big rock to cross over to a place I can go thru between two other rocks. I pull harder than necessary and the WEN shoots into this below rock eddy, then takes off bow first between the rocks. It hangs up so fast that I go clear off the seat into the bow. Get up, and by standing on a rock 'longside of the boat push off and go on. Cutler comes down but gets balled up in middle of rapid and takes wrong course, and nearly gets wrecked. Del comes thru in good shape.

MILE 78. SOCKDOLOGER RAPID. LUNCH left. Well, the snap is gone from Sockdologer in this real low water. There are lots of rocks, a more or less erratic course, but no speed to the water. While lunch is being gotten ready back in a little dead end canyon on the left I investigate the WEN and find it is taking water in the stern hatch on the left side facing stern. I work at it and cram in some rags to stop the leak a bit until we get to Bright Angel. Put out all the stuff to dry. Fortunately nothing that matters is wet.

It looks quite possible to get along the rapid afoot on the right hand side in this low stage of water.

MILE 81. GRAPEVINE RAPID. Let Barry run this one after we've walked way down alongside on the right to look it over. Would be hard if not impossible to walk clear down. We go thru fine except in one spot Barry goes right instead of left and we have a thrill for a minute or so.

MILE 83. 83 MILE RAPIDS. Land on left and see it's a matter of sliding left of rock in midchannel. I take off in WEN and catch my right oar on rock, snapping it in two and jimming up my fingers. Makes me plenty mad. Other boats thru OK. Plain carelessness on my part, tho I'm terribly tired.

MILE 84. ZOROASTER CANYON RAPID. Barry was rowing and took off wrong side of channel and gave us a wild ride. This was no rapid at all at high water but now is mean.

MILE 87. Bright Angel! 19 mile day. Did it!

We go right up to Bright Angel Lodge[69] to clean up and have dinner. Barry has asked Doris and me to be his guests—which we do to the extent of the room—but we pay our own meals, which are later refunded by the Harvey people.

AUGUST 10TH.

Round up some tar from Lehman, the Phantom Ranch manager, and along with some tin from the U.S.G.S. we are able to do a real respectable job of repairing the boats. Reed and I finish around noon and are glad to get back up to the ranch to loaf.

AUGUST 11TH

This morning Reed and I go down to the stables and get the garbage truck, a two wheeled cart. This we take up to the ranch and load with our supplies. Cutler cleverly evades helping us as usual and takes off. Never again do I get involved with Cutler on anything! With Doris and Mildred pushing, and Del and I pulling we get down to the government cabin where the food sorting goes on in the shade. As we finish Charlie and Barry show up and while the girls return to the ranch, we all pull the truck down fairly close to the boats and pack over the sacks to the boats from there. Barry and Charlie go back, while Dell and I sort the food sacks in piles for their respective boats. We start back up finally with the truck, but go just a ways when the trail guide saves us terrific labor by hitching his horse to the truck and pulling it back up to the stables. Rest of the day is spent resting!

AUGUST 12TH
Shove off 9:50 AM.

MILE 89 PIPE CREEK. We stop here to fill our canteens. We have brought two girls from Phantom this far also a couple of young fellows who are going up the trail from here. Last night John escorted Anne up the trail to the South Rim, and this morning John looks tired. Deason is back with us and I am grateful for his company. Between Charlie kicking about there not being bread, and Barry morose because we couldn't take Anne along it's a different spirited group than the upper river party. Baker had declared she would leave at Bright Angel if Rosner didn't, but I still feel an implied criticism in her because of Anne not going on. Talk about hypocrisy!

MILE 90. HORN CREEK RAPID. This rapid is mean at any stage. We run on right, but all three boats bang the right hand ledge before cutting back out to midstream to avoid the dike that sticks out half way down from right shore.

MILE 93. GRANITE FALLS. This is still quite a rapid to be reckoned with in even low water. Have to ride right wall. I tap the right wall in going thru.

MILE 94. HERMIT FALLS. CAMP #38. Left. This is a wonderful camp and good water. Only thing tho wind is blowing. The rapid itself is nothing. In high water in '38 I lined this one, but tomorrow will run, and probably let Barry and Charlie run it too.

AUGUST 13TH
Shove off 7:15 AM. Let Barry and Charlie follow me on this one.

MILE 96. BOUCHER RAPIDS. Be careful, high or low.

MILE 98 CRYSTAL RAPIDS.[70] High water easy, but in real low water lots of rocks and crooked channel.

MILE 99. TUNA CREEK RAPIDS. Here on the right at head of rapid is the wrecked, green canvas boat that Barry and Emery Kolb used in the Ripley broadcast this spring.

MILE 104 RUBY CANYON. Cutler hits a hard blow on a rock here and punches a hole clear thru bottom of MEXICAN HAT II. This is first hole to ever be punched right thru the plywood.

We have to stop here as Cutler's boat is filling fast. After lunch Reed and I put a patch in the bottom and stop leak. Nasty hole. And Cutler slips on a rock and claims to have hurt his back badly. I don't think there's a damn thing wrong with him except nervousness. He's a mess.

MILE 105. The WEN hangs a minute mid-stream, and Barry gets washed off when he starts to push us free. Get thru OK. Cutler comes along and hangs completely, all efforts to get loose no good. Looks tough, and after much rocking, etc., a line is thrown to shore to Barry, Charlie, and Reed. Over the taut line comes John with Baker. Then Cutler, after affixing the line so as to pull boat free from shore comes in too. Doesn't work, so back goes Cutler. This time when he gets back boat is free and comes down rapid to be picked up by Doris and me who are waiting in the WEN for just this happening. We get to shore with trouble as there is a shore lash. The boys come down and help bail the MEXICAN HAT II out. Then signal Reed thru without passengers and his empty boat makes it alright, barely touching the rock.

MILE 106. SERPENTINE CANYON RAPID. This is a bad one at most stages of water but its not tough to-day. Barry runs the MEXICAN HAT II thru as Cutler is played out.

MILE 108. SHINUMO CREEK. CAMP #39. We pull into this camp really tired and worn out. Oh me! Boys go fishing by running fish into shallows. After catching them they let the fish lie on the ground, evidently on the assumption the fish will clean themselves. Makes Deason mad. Wind blows during dinner and we get plenty of sand in our food. But this creek has wonderful water and is a real luxury to drink and bathe in. Am tipped off that Cutler, Charlie and Barry plan to take off in the morning and explore, deliberately holding the party up. I'll get the jump on them in the morning and ask them why they don't go upstream a ways and look around and get some pictures. That should shame them into being ready quicker! This low water is tough and too low to be running. Am sorry now that I didn't cancel trip until there was more water.

AUGUST 14TH

The ruse worked, and the boys showed up in fairly good time. Its like having children out on a picnic or boy scout trip handling this bunch.

MILE 112. WALTHENBERG RAPIDS. Right. This is clear sailing in high water, but this low water makes a mean channel to run. Its quite tricky.

MILE 116. ELVES CHASM. Lunch. Get water here. Take nap in cave. Number of names on wall here. Beautiful spot.

MILE 120. HUNDRED AND TWENTY MILE CREEK. These little rapids that ordinarily wouldn't look at need checking as rocks have a tendency to stick up right in the least expected place and invisible from above.

MILE 128. HUNDRED AND TWENTY-EIGHT MILE CREEK. CAMP #40. We've been trying to get to a camp with water, but this seems our best and last chance. There's a trace of water up the canyon a ways but not enough to do any good. Plenty of wood and a good campsite. Some are determined to sleep in the middle of wash and can't seem to realize the danger of this practice.

AUGUST 15TH

SHOVE OFF 7:25 AM. Foot of rapid and on again. This is a zippy plenty fast little fellow in this low water.

MILE 130. BEDROCK RAPID. Land mouth 130 MILE CREEK. Only we don't land to look it over! In high water this rapid presented a really tough problem. Didn't dare go to left, and to keep right was awfully hard as current drove against huge rock midchannel. But in this extreme low water we go *LEFT* and weave around the rocks in the very slow current. A duplicate of the President Harding surprise.

MILE 131. DUBENDORFF RAPID. Land right, Galloway Canyon. This is tougher channel than high water running. I finally pick the channel which is a long complicated one to follow. Some of the party stupidly think we're spending too much time looking them over, but just why is it that I have one of the best records running rapids ever made? I come thru per schedule, Cutler gets balled up a bit and hits two rocks, Reed goes clear out of control and gets into a hole at foot which nearly swamps him. Reed blames his arm, but that alibi is getting worn thin.

MILE 133. TAPEATS CREEK. We land here and fill canteens with this wonderful water. Charlie, Barry and Cutler wander off to see canyon. Finally I get tired waiting for them so Reed in his boat, Deason, John, Baker, Doris and I take off. The rest of the party overtakes our slowly drifting boat in the GRANITE NARROWS. It shows how irresponsible the rest are. They ran blind into Tapeats Creek rapid and almost wrecked and capsized the boat. While drifting along waiting for the errant MEXICAN HAT II I try out my life preserver. It like the most of them has been packed so hard, taken so much mud that it is practically useless.

MILE 136. DEER CREEK FALLS. Lunch. A beautiful spot and we eat lunch under a rock with the cold spray from the falls keeping us almost cold. The water here is icy-like.

MILE 138. This unnamed little riffle at this real low stage of water is nasty.[71] Current and rocks crowds to the right and drops into a hole. Its just possible by dragging left oar in shoals to hold far enough left to ride hole and get thru. On approach I asked John what he could see. Nothing much was his reply, tho he thought a small hole was at the bottom. I got up to look but didn't see much wrong. We took off, and at the bottom hit a hole! WEN went clear under, threw Doris and John off—no life jackets on—then came up standing on its side. I climbed side to right it then reached down and pulled Doris into the boat. John by then got ahold. Boat clear full of water and was difficult to land below. Most water I've ever had in a boat. We bail out fast so as to keep compartments dry, then I go back and after much study decide to run. Reed isn't anxious to run it, in fact is leery of it, so I bring his boat thru, followed by Cutler.

MILE 143. KANAB CREEK. Right. CAMP #41. Good camp and lots of good water. Our kitchen is set up just upstream from Kanab Creek, on the talus. Some of us sleep close by while the rest sleep down in close to the creek. Charlie blows off again about not having bread.

AUGUST 16TH

Shove off at 8:00 AM. [Kanab Creek Rapid] is a long baby and plenty full of rocks. We ran fairly close together.

MILE 149. UPSET RAPIDS. Nasty channel tho easy enough to run.

MILE 156 HAVASU CREEK. CAMP #42. The water doesn't seem as blue as in '38. Maybe because its lower. After lunch Barry, Cutler and Baker took off to walk to the Indian Agency some ten miles up the canyon. I have my private opinion of how far they will get. This is later born out when they come in around dark with a gruesome tale of many hardships![72] In the meantime, while Reed slept, Doris, John, Charlie, Deason and I went up to the first waterfalls and played around. Then took a nap. Had trouble getting wood for fire as there is no drift near here. Had to get wood from mesquite trees.

AUGUST 17TH

Shove off 7:15 AM.

MILE 164. HUNDRED AND SIXTY FOUR MILE CANYON. This was one of our '38 trip camps. Here we found a cache of supplies and equipment left by prospectors. We go up to cache and look around. The rapid here now is just a riffle, tho in high water it's a boomer.

MILE 171. GATEWAY RAPIDS. John goes thru this one without touching a rock, while both the MEXICAN HAT II and the JOAN hit hard. I really think John has more on the ball in every respect than the rest put together.

MILE 173. Lunch. Get into shade of little canyon on the left, at head of little rapid. Making good time to-day. We're riding the crest of a little flood and here we've made 16 miles already this morning.

MILE 179. LAVA FALLS. This looks like a sure lining job, but would like to run it. I study and study the set up, while the others have started portaging the equipment. Finally I work out a complicated tho possible way to run. It all hinges on making the perfect moves at the exact correct time. I finally take off and make it! The MEXICAN HAT II gets fiddled a bit but makes it, and the JOAN comes thru with only slightly less ease than the WEN. This makes the fourth party to run it, or seven of us to do so. First time was by Jack Harbin of the Grand Canyon in 1927. Then Holmstrom in '38, then Harris and Loper in '39. Now us.[73] We have dinner at bottom left, then as it looks stormy, I decide to run a ways below to our '38 camp in cove on left where possible high water won't be hard to handle. Of course

Charlie, Barry and Cutler elect to remain. We go below to a fine camp and take baths and talk.

MILE 179 Left by warm springs. CAMP #43.

AUGUST 18TH

Shove off 7:45 AM.

Mile 185. Have another little flood to travel on to-day. We're really taking off.

MILE 204. SPRING CANYON. CAMP #44. Had a good day. Been riding this little flood and its made a world of difference in our speed. Hope it will stay up. Looks like rain and our camp is next to cliffs upstream side mouth of canyon. Going up the canyon a ways find a nice little flow of good water. Rain all around us but practically none falls here. Tired tonight. Staggered as I got out of the boat. Am nervous of a flood coming down Spring Canyon.

AUGUST 19TH

No flood in canyon, no rain here, and the river's gone down! We're going to try to make DIAMOND CREEK to-day. Food is getting low. I insisted on supplies being left behind at Bright Angel as we had too much load for this low water. And at that they wanted an extra passenger! This heavy rowing by hour shifts takes more energy so we need more food.

MILE 205. TWO HUNDRED FIVE MILE RAPID. This one is full of rocks and Barry brings Reed's boat thru as he is tired or something.

MILE 209. GRANITE PARK RAPID. John starts thru but gives me oars as its nippy.

MILE 215. THREE SPRINGS CANYON. To land at all in mouth of canyon is nearly impossible. Have to land upstream a ways. Then its hard to get to the water as the canyon is deep and narrow. A poor place to get water or camp.

MILE 217. TWO HUNDRED AND SEVENTEEN MILE RAPID. This is a long baby and in high water was a long fast swoop. Its rocky now but a bit of care and you go right thru a-zipping. Nice ride.

MILE 225. DIAMOND CREEK. CAMP #45. We get in and fool around making camp. Wander around a bit and wash. We will stay over here tomorrow so feel glad to rest. This is a marvelous camp and just back of us are the remains of the government camp when here diamond drilling the formation as test for a dam site.

AUGUST 20TH

Up early as usual and have breakfast. After breakfast John, Deason and I go up Diamond creek to Peach Springs Wash. We find evidences of mining, but very unlikely looking prospects. We return about 1:00, have lunch with the rest, then the afternoon is spent reading, writing, inscribing hats, etc. After dinner fire is set to all the old cabins back of us. It makes a mighty blaze. Looks like rain again. River is still falling off a bit. With all this rain one would expect a rise in the river.

AUGUST 21ST.
After breakfast John, Barry and Cutler get ready to ride their air mattresses thru DIAMOND CREEK RAPID. Cutler and Barry will ride together, John alone.

Shove off 7:15 AM. Cutler and Barry soon get thrown off and take to their pickup boats. John sails on thru, and clear on down and thru the next rapid!

MILE 226. John climbs aboard and we go on.

MILE 231. Snappy drop at bottom. This is called TWO HUNDRED THIRTYONE MILE RAPID.

MILE 232. We all get caught in a hole going thru this one and get a good dunking. Not dangerous.[74]

MILE 238 Left under ledge, Lunch. John refused to go further without eating! He's right, I'm hungry too.

MILE 239. See a stick on right bank with a bottle suspended from it. I go over and open jar to find a note. It advises that my friend Harry Aleson and his friend Lewis West came up to meet us. While walking up Separation Canyon a few days ago a flood came along and took their boat and motor! They say meet them at mouth of Separation! I look downstream and see two figures on bank at mouth of canyon!

MILE 239. SEPARATION CANYON. Good to see the boys, and we decide to push on down with them to find the outboard and boat which they're sure wasn't sunk. We have our pictures taken by plaque to Powell party separation that occurred here, then load in them and their ample supplies and take off. Wind comes up, and what with nervous reaction etc. our nerves are somewhat jumpy. Its hard rowing and little progress. Separation Rapid is covered. I'm sorry. Well, at any rate we're on LAKE MEAD.

MILE 249. LOST CREEK. CAMP #46. This is a poor camp, but tonight we go to sleep with the 151 rapids of GRAND CANYON behind us. All rapids run from Green River, Wyoming by myself, some three times! Our camp is on a sort of damp mud flat. Have a good dinner by mixing in supplies of Aleson and West. After dinner I row across the lake and find an average depth of only 6 feet. Barry and Charlie are agitating along with Cutler and Baker that I won't be met by the government boat, but that I had planned all along for Aleson to meet us. I'll be glad to get away from this ungrateful bunch. A lot of work went into this trip and its disgusting to never have a word of thanks or appreciation. Harry Aleson and I pore over maps trying to figure out where the boat will be. I'm pessimistic over our finding it as there is no driftwood anywhere so eddies aren't holding things up. I had told the Park Service we would be at Spencer Canyon the night of August 21st, so we're exactly on time. I suspect that the low water level in lake is holding up the boat.

AUGUST 22ND.

Shove off 7:38 AM. Tried to rain last night.

MILE 252. We've made 3 ½ miles rowing and I bet Harry I see his boat. I win the dollar! Sure enough, over against a sandbar on the right is the boat. It's a sixteen foot metal boat and is half submerged. Puzzled why its still there I feel the anchor rope and on the end of it a 150 lb. rock. Lucky for us. The rock evidently caught on the bar and held alright. Bail the boat out and find everything intact. Finally get motor started and it heats. After a long complicated series of tests I find the water pump stuck. Soon get it fixed and away we go. Go a mile or two and a hue and cry made to stop and stretch legs. We do so, also fix up lunch to eat in the boats. Almost thru eating and there's the government boat. Its waiting for us so down we go. Mother is on front deck and it's a thrill to see her. Charlie's wife, Barry's wife and daughter are there. Soon make the boats fast and we're off. Pull in at Pierces Ferry to have dinner about five o'clock. Reach the dam at midnight. Meet Ethel Farrel and Marie Crane[75] again. Take Mother to her lodgings, then we get together in Ethel's cabin to see some of Hugh's pictures. They seemed quite good. Tired! Hugh leaves, Mildred, Doris and I flop on the floor and go to sleep.

Grand Canyon,
July 14 to August 5, 1941

By 1941, even though his San Juan River trips were doing well—and he conducted quite a few parties down that stretch of river in the fall of 1940 and spring of 1941— Nevills realized that the Grand Canyon was the real attraction in terms of whitewater, scenery, and what advertisers today call "name recognition." His tourist lodge at Mexican Hat was getting to be known, too, and enough adventurous travelers found their way along the atrocious dirt roads to stay with the Nevillses. Another visitor was the stork: Sandra Jane Nevills was born on March 28, 1941, so Nevills now had even more responsibilities.

But the big water in the Grand Canyon had gotten into his blood, and 1941 promised to be a high-water year. Unlike most early river runners, Nevills preferred to run on high water rather than low, as the rapids were more thrilling and the rocks were covered. His experiences on low water in 1940 had only confirmed this view, and he was anxious to go through the canyon on the peak of the runoff. He was lucky with the runoff this year, for the river stood at 27,000 cfs on the day they launched.

Despite all the publicity engendered by the previous two expeditions, Nevills felt that he didn't have enough photographs and films to adequately sell his trips to the public, so he decided that 1941 would be a filming trip and priced it accordingly. Passengers were only charged $350 for the trip if they brought color film or still cameras. Even with this bargain price, he had only four paying passengers: Agnes Albert, a thirty-three-year-old housewife from San Mateo, California; Bill Schukraft, a thirty-three-year-old manufacturer from Chicago; Weldon Heald, a forty-year-old architect from Altadena, California; and Alexander "Zee" Grant from New York. The latter was an interesting addition to the group in that he brought along his own boat, a 16 ½-foot folding kayak called the Escalante. Despite Nevills's misgivings, Grant's whitewater skills (he had won every major foldboating race in the country by this point), the boat's durability after two capsizes in the first two days, and Grant's personality won him over; by the end of the trip Nevills was an enthusiastic proponent of kayaking.

There would be only two cataract boats, the Wen *and the* Mexican Hat II, *with Nevills, as usual, rowing the* Wen, *and Del Reed returning to row the* MH II. *Reed's presence on the trip is surprising, given that he had not shown much talent for rowing a boat in 1940—and would not give any evidence that that had changed on this trip—but it's likely that there simply was no one else who had any kind of boating experience that Nevills could call on. It was Reed's last trip with Nevills.*

Agnes Albert and Norman Nevills at start of 1941 trip

Unlike the previous two trips, this one was not marred by any kind of tensions, "whispering," or "griping," and Nevills comments several times on what a good group this was and what a grand time he was having. Part of this relates to the size of the group; with only six people, it was an ideal size for a Grand Canyon river run, as modern river guides will attest. The other aspect has to be Nevills's growing confidence in his ability and place as the premier riverman of his day. He didn't feel the need to either assert his authority or bark orders, and it shows in the relaxed tone of his journal. By the time the party reached Lake Mead on August 1, all agreed it had been a marvelous trip. Only one thing marred an otherwise perfect journey: Norman's father, William Eugene Nevills, died at the age of seventy-five on July 30, a fact that was left to Doris to break to Norman on August 3. The elder Nevills had been ill for quite some time, and his passing was not unexpected. Perhaps that was why when Dr. Harold Bryant, the superintendent of Grand Canyon National Park, asked Norman to donate the Wen to the museum at the south rim, he agreed so readily.

Thousands of feet of film were shot on the trip, and for the next few months all were busy giving talks and lectures, and showing the films. For Nevills, the 1941 expedition had turned out to be a triumph—a success both in personal terms and for his growing business. As is shown by his correspondence of the period, he was starting to set his sights even higher, talking of running rivers in India and Canada. Soon, however, world events were to intrude on the little world of Colorado River runners. Within three months of the end of the trip, Grant, Schukraft, and Heald had all been called up for military service, and Nevills himself was beginning to wonder about his draft status if the nation was plunged into war. There would be time for one more Nevills Expedition trip down the Grand Canyon, but after that, events would conspire to keep Nevills away from the Grand Canyon for over five years.

JULY 14

We load the MEXICAN HAT II on the trailer, with the WEN on top. Zee[1] by this time has the foldboat, ESCALANTE,[2] enough assembled to be placed upside down on top of the WEN. As my car is broken down we have hired a Chev[rolet]. pick-up truck to haul the outfit. I drive the pick-up, with Doris and the truck owners' wife in front, Red (truckowner), Zee, (Alexander G. Grant Jr.), Bill (W.J. Schukraft)[3] and Del[4] in back on top of our supplies. We leave at 9:00 AM.

Lunch with Wetherills.

At Cameron. Have a light lunch. Here we meet Agnes[5] (Mrs. Agnes Albert), who has been hopefully waiting since noon. We go on, Rex now driving, with Agnes and Rex's wife in front.

Gap [Trading] Post for dinner. The meal is much the worse for Mrs. Johnson being away, but we make out.

Arrive Marble Canyon where we are greeted by Weldon,[6] his wife Phyllis, and Weldon's mother. We leave Doris and Agnes at Marble, while the rest of us take off for Lees Ferry to leave the boats. It becomes obvious, after much jockeying around that the road is impassable to Lees Ferry across the Paria.[7] We decide to wait 'till morning, so unhitch from the trailer, and Bill, Weldon, and I return to Marble Canyon. We are much amused as Bill is given the honeymoon cottage. Our amusement is heightened by the fact that Bill is conducted to his quarters by a very young girl barely reaching to Bill's waist! And so to bed at MIDNIGHT.

JULY 15.

We waste few ceremonies in getting away after breakfast, and go to the Paria to get the boats. We all drive back to MILE 1 to where we will launch and embark. There we find Del, and Hull Cook and his father who have come over to ride as far as Badger Creek Rapid with us. Also in our party is young Jimmy Fisher who will also ride to Badger Creek. Our big boats are quickly readied for the start, but the foldboat needs lots of tinkering with. I design and build a splashboard for Zee. It later proves to be of much use. As I look at the frail foldboat, I, like the others have serious misgivings as to any possibility of its surviving the heavy water of Marble and Grand Canyon. But my judgement tells me that its safer with plenty of water to cover the rocks, so I am hoping for the best. At any rate we will be able to pull Zee out even if we can't save the Foldboat. These embarkations are awfully nerve wracking, and it is with a great feeling of relief that I finally give the signal to shove off at 12:15 PM.

Just before we get to the Navajo Bridge I turn over the WEN to the elder Cook and climb out on the rear deck of the foldboat.[8] I ride thus under the bridge. Can see Doris up on the bridge waving! As we approach Badger Creek Rapid I transfer back to the WEN.

We pull in on left and under the very slim shade of a great boulder have lunch. As soon as possible I walk over and glance over the rapid. My

Norman Nevills paddling the *Escalante* with Zee Grant on back deck

first hunch is confirmed, it can be run! This is a great satisfaction, as in
'38 I lined, and last year I had to run all three boats myself, and it was a
mighty tough and rocky channel. But this year it is a straight shot thru,
guarded by two holes, but with a well defined tongue. As it is obviously
hard to see the tongue I have Del signal me for position so I won't miss the
tongue. All is set, and at 3:50 PM I slide thru with the WEN, soon followed
by the MEXICAN HAT II. I leave Del to bail and be ready in case of an
accident to the foldboat, and go up to signal Zee. He starts. Too far left.
Signal him over. Now he's too far right. I signal him over. Still too far to
the right. I signal him again, and this time he whirls his boat about and a
few heavy paddles and he's way too far left (looking upstream). I yell and
signal frantically, Zee raises up in the boat and sees his predicament, turns
the foldboat around, paddles frantically—but is swept on into the worst
hole in Badger! As I start to run for the WEN, some two hundred yards
downstream I watch the river. The foldboat almost immediately sticks its
nose thru the big wave at the lower edge of the hole—but no Zee. The
boat comes on thru, goes maybe a hundred feet when I spot Zee about
30' in ahead of the ESCALANTE! He holds himself back and gets ahold of
the boat. Del has by now made it out into the river. Hull and I start to take
off, but as I see Zee is OK and that Del is out anyhow I pull back to shore.
Later Zee explains that his air inflated life preserver went to pieces, and
all that saved him was an emergency gas bottle preserver![9] From the time
I shoved off in the WEN, until Zee got to shore downstream a ways, only
25 minutes elapsed, but it seems hours. I feel a great relief at knowing that
the ESCALANTE can get into such tough water and come thru in such
good shape. Zee never let loose of his paddle during all the underwater
maneuvers!

Here at MILE 8 ½ is where Zee landed on left side. We all assemble here for final farewells, and then the two Cooks and Jimmy wave as we once more shove off—with Soap Creek ahead.

SOAP CREEK RAPID. We land on right and a glance suffices to show that its easily run. Altho it is getting late we all want to take a crack at it. I think its good psychology for Zee to take it on.[10] I slip thru riding the big waves. They *are* big fellows. Good twenty feet high. I say to myself in the middle of them "Why they're just like mountains." Grand ride. Del slips off to the right and misses the big fellows. Zee comes thru riding the big ones high, wide, and handsome! The boy can really take it! My respect for the foldboat is rapidly mounting, tho I do know that fast hitting side waves or breaking waves will flip him. No good spot to camp below so on we go.

CAMP. Nice camp. Left hand side just below canyon at mile 12 ½. 11 ½ mile run today. This is the most we've made the first day out. We're all dog tired, but spirits are high.

JULY 16

EMBARK at 8:25 AM. River is about the same. We are all eager to be on our way. I cook breakfast, the dishes are done by Del.

SHEER WALL RAPID. Lots of fun. Agnes gets splashed!

HOUSE ROCK RAPID. Mile 17. I have had an idea that this may be a tough baby, but upon drifting down upon it I see that one can easily slip off on the right side of the tongue to miss a few of the rather heavy waves in the main channel. I give the go ahead signal and Agnes and I run on thru, followed by the ESCALANTE. Zee doesn't back paddle enough and goes right on into the heavy water. About the third wave proves his nemesis, and over he goes! He climbs right back on the upside-down boat and paddles to shore. He made shore without any assistance. The MEXICAN HAT II comes thru OK and Zee's boat is soon ready to take off again. An upset a day! Oh me, what is this going to mean before we get to Lake Mead?

NORTH CANYON RAPID. Land passengers on the right and I run thru with WEN taking most of the big water. Zee takes the big water all the way and makes a very beautiful run. Del slides off and misses the fun.

TWENTY ONE MILE RAPID. We go on thru with passengers and get a real ride tho its not hard to run.

MILE 24 ½. WEN, MEXICAN HAT II, ESCALANTE. All thru in fine shape. This is a bearcat in real low water.

Lunch left. Good shade just above CAVE SPRING RAPID. In the cover here, stuck in a crevice is an old rusty, handle-less pick.

MILE 30. This little rapid has a lot of whirlpools at the bottom and we are much amused to see the ESCALANTE spun around three times in short order!

CAMP. Vasey's Paradise. Hard to land here at this stage of water and very poor anchorage. We finally contrive to moor the boats, then all indulge in the luxury of the fresh cold water from the spring, which is running more water than I've seen on the other two trips.

July 17

Embark at 8:50 AM. This morning I am taking over the foldboat for a try at it, and Bill and Zee are going to manage the WEN. At MILE 34 I run a little rapid in the ESCALANTE, and get thru fine, tho I find turning the foldboat much harder than one of the big boats. The trick seems to be to quarter the boat away from what you want to miss then back paddle like the dickens. I take Agnes aboard with me! We cause some consternation when I announce that Agnes and I are going to run the next rapid together on the foldboat. We do so and come thru with no more than a ducking. Then I turn over the foldboat to Agnes and get back aboard the WEN.

MILE 36. I pull in on left, followed by MEXICAN HAT II. Agnes comes along drifting well out to midstream. I yell at her to make for shore as there is a heavy current into this rapid. Her efforts are not enough and just by a miracle she gets the ESCALANTE close enough to shore at the very brink of the rapid to get hung up on a rock. Del goes by her boat and I dive over to her and get a firm grip on the foldboat. A line from shore is thrown us and we soon get landed.

At 10:25 I shove off in the ESCALANTE and run my first snorter in it. Make it fine and ride the big eddy right back to near the top. Then run it agin! All in all I run this one three times. Del brings Zee thru in the WEN, but the WEN seems to feel a stranger at the oars as it nearly capsizes with Del and he get half full of water. Zee looks much perturbed.

We pull in on right into the shelf of the upper of the ROYAL ARCHES. Good spot to eat lunch. It's windy out on the river.

PRESIDENT HARDING RAPID. We arrive in high disagreeable wind. The rapid, as usual in high water has quite a zip to it. We run on the left without stopping, tho Zee lands for a second to get a better view.

Saddle Canyon. Oh me! Wind and rain!

Little Nancoweep. We decide this is a poor camp and that we should drop to next landing below.

CAMP. After dinner tonight we light a great pile of driftwood that lights the whole canyon up. It sends light to the 3000' rim above and a great ways up and down canyon. Pictures are taken, All in all it's a great camp. Wind has died down and the weather looks pretty good.

July 18

We stay in camp today as we are ahead of schedule. The morning is devoted to a climb up to some ruins some 500' above the river and at the mouth of Nancoweep Creek. Get back at 1:00 PM and the rest of the day is spent just lazying around and talking about the big ones that got away, etc. Yesterday Bill got quite a thrill out of a little rapid above MILE 36. He was much perturbed but came thru grinning from ear to ear.

When Del brought the WEN thru yesterday he overlooked Agnes's camera equipment that was uncovered and it got quite a soaking. Just for fun I have put two x's with mileage point above them to indicate the two upsets for the foldboat so far. Zee joins in with the idea gleefully.

Norman Nevills paddling the *Escalante*

Funny, after breakfast today we all took two salt tablets and Bill and I were positively sick and almost lost our breakfast.

Tonight we have another big fire that is terribly spectacular and sit around and talk until midnight. How time flies! We have lots of fun working ourselves into a lather over Hance, Sockologer and Grapevine. I really believe that my psychology will work as usual in painting such an awful picture that the reality will seem much lesser.[11]

JULY 19

We get up at 6:45 AM after a night of wind and sand blowing. Everyone seem happy and rarin' to go. Ski is overcast and maybe holds a storm for this afternoon.

SHOVE OFF 8:30 AM. The Nancoweep Rapids are just fun.

Foot of KWAGUNT RAPID. Splashy and fun. No need to look over. WEN and ESCALANTE come thru without shipping, but MEXICAN HAT II gets a ducking. We stop to let Bill dry his camera.

SIXTY MILE RAPID. Lots of fun and nice going.

LITTLE COLORADO RIVER. Small flow in L.C. and I win one milkshake. We go right on as it is an uninviting spot.

Lava Canyon Rapid. Nice and Splashy. Have trouble through here in keeping bearings as at different stages of water the rapids come and go and the topography is confusing.

LUNCH. We go a few hundred feet over to Tanners old camp for lunch. This in on left side at foot of rapid, MILE 65 ½. After lunch we elect to explore the old workings. At the mine entrance the exploring party

Agnes Albert

dwindles down to Agnes and I. We go way back in every tunnel end and have much fun in making spooky noises in the dark, There are several hundred feet of workings, at spots caving quite badly. In one place I go across an old plank that spans a water filled shaft. It's quite a thrill. Upon returning to the mouth of the mine we sit around awhile and talk. Return to Tanners Camp, pack up the lunch equipment and take off.[12]

MILE 68 ½. CAMP. Left. 16 ½ mile run. We have the same camp as in '38. Even using the same fireplace. We got over to build a big woodpile for a signal fire and get in for some heavy work! At just near its completion I discover the pile we built in '38 to burn. We decide to burn the '38 pile and leave this new one for the '42 trip. In '38 after building this pile we found a natural drift stacked up near camp which we burned. After dinner we go over to burn the pile. It makes a beautiful blaze and we watch anxiously for answering lights but see none. Next year will arrange to have a rocket set off as signal that we are observed. I later found that we were observed coming into camp this afternoon. We entertain ourselves with gruesome stories of the horrors awaiting us tomorrow at Hance, Sock., and Grapevine.

JULY 20

Up at 6:00 AM. Everyone in fine fettle and anxious for the thrill promised in todays run to Bright Angel.

SHOVE OFF 7:50 AM. Tanner Rapid lots of fun.

Land Right at UNKAR CREEK RAPID. We look it over and find it will be a lot of fun tho must use a bit of care. Away we go and have a marvelous ride.

Zee Grant in Unkar Rapid

A glance and away we go. Only trick to it that you have to pull hard
right at the bottom and I don't get over far enough. We land in a hole and
what a ducking. I have taken Weldon over in my boat with Agnes ready
for the big fellows ahead. This will leave Del with only Bill. This rapid was
SEVENTY-FIVE MILE RAPID.

To enliven things further I have a new poem:

Grapenuts in the morning.
Grapevine for lunch
But I have a feeling, in fact it's a hunch;
When old man HANCE sees us, walking on the beach,
He is a mighty lesson, to us agoin' to teach!

HANCE RAPID. This is a whizzer. We look it over until 10:15 at which
time I shove off in the WEN, running towards the left from the middle. I
go thru three holes in succession and fill up to the seat. What a ride! Pull
in some ways below, bail, then signal Del thru. Del comes thru fine, then
ESCALANTE runs thru by playing the left bank. This rapid is a number one
toughy at any stage of water.

SOCKDOLOGER.[13] 11:27–11:40 at top looking over. 12:05 PM. All safe
at bottom. Well, this was a honey. After my big build-up on it I was even
surprised myself. In '38 this looked like a pretty formidable piece of water—
but this year—oh me! In '38 we dropped down the tongue, slipped off the
tongue to the left—and that was that. But this year the tongue drives hard

to the right wall, bad holes on both sides and it's a tricky problem to get thru. We had a real thrill taking off, made it fine, tho the water below was a disappointment. ESCALANTE and MEXICAN HAT II make it beautifully.

GRAPEVINE RAPIDS. After Sockdologer and the sight and ride it presented I didn't seem to feel quite so impressed by this fellow, altho it had a mean channel. I took off with Agnes and Weldon, drifted down on the tongue, saw I was going too far right, so pulled hard left, and almost pulled us into some really tough holes. I pulled back hard to the right—and we had it made. For a minute tho I thought church was really going to let out! We had promised ourselves to not eat lunch until Grapevine was under our belt so we now are looking for a lunch spot.

LUNCH. Mouth of Boulder Canyon. Here we sample Bill's Scotch as a celebration of having the toughies behind us. The Scotch goes to all our heads and first thing I knew the whole caboodle of us were talking at the top of our voices at once![14]

EIGHTY-THREE MILE RAPID. At this stage passengers practically have to ride. Its nice running though waves are high and sharp. This is grand going from here on in and we're riding 'em high, wide, and handsome. We go out of our way in the WEN to get a ducking—and get it! I get off my bearings a bit and keep thinking each rapid we come to is MILE 83. This logging here is correct.

Just above Bright Angel we are horseplaying. Agnes fell off the stern deck on top of me, I lost my balance and collapsed onto Weldon in the bow! What a day and what a grand bunch. This is truly the merriest and happiest outfit that ever tackled the Colorado. This crowd bears out my theory that one or two gripers and whisperers can spoil a whole party.[15]

We have fortified ourselves for a gala reception at Bright Angel trail. Zee in particular feels sure there will be a clamoring multitude on hand to welcome us.

Bright Angel CREEK. Woe is me! I really thought we would have at least some kind of a reception committee. But no a soul! Not a solitary person was in sight as we came majestically in, holding perfect formation for the photographer! Serves my ego right!

We tie up the boats on the beach just below the bridge and go over to the trail house to telephone. I call Phoenix A.P.[16] and also Harry Franse on the South Rim. We then go on up and get ourselves installed at Phantom Ranch. After dinner Zee gets ahold of Bolati on the North Rim and arrangements are made for Zee to go up to the Rim early next morning. A short while later I am delighted to have Doris call from the South Rim advising me that she will be down in the morning afoot with her friend Jimmie Redd. So a grand day ends. So tired, and bed feels good.

July 21

Up bright and early and I go for the Bright Angel trail to meet Doris. Sure enough! Half mile from the bridge I meet Doris and Jimmy tramping their

Del Reed

weary way in. Boy its good to see her and we start jabbering at high rate of speed.

We meet Bill and Agnes at the trail house. We talk for a while, then Agnes and Bill take off for the South Rim where they will stay overnight.

When we get up to the Ranch we find Weldon had left for Roaring Springs,[17] and Zee for the North Rim.

Late afternoon, Doris and I go down to the river and sort and stow the food for our next, the last lap of the trip. Get back to the Ranch and have a swim.[18] Weldon has just gotten in and is cooling off in the cabin. We write letters, etc. Zee [reports] in from the North Rim reporting good progress there.

JULY 22

We get up usual hour and have breakfast at 7:30. The day is spent in complete relaxation and rest. Write a few letters.

Agnes and Bill get in from the South Rim awhile before dinner after a very hot ride down. They bring the movie film from Super Harboard.

Zee puts in an almost belated appearance but makes the dinner. Zee had quite a trip up and back. Not liking the horses on the narrow trail, Zee elected to walk.

July 23

As we are eating breakfast at Phantom Ranch Barry Goldwater and six YMCA leaders roll in for breakfast and to see the gang.

Doris and Jimmy take off on the mules a bit ahead of us. I sure hate to see her go and miss the rest of this trip.[19]

9:05 AM Shove off. Loaded to the gunnels. In the WEN: Barry at the oars. Agnes and myself. Three YMCA's.

MEXICAN HAT II: Dell, Weldon, Bill, three YMCA's.

We have a somewhat precarious ride to Pipe Creek as the water is high and we have a tremendous load.

PIPE CREEK. Here we land on the left to discharge our excess passenger load and bid final farewells. I get to see Doris again. Here too is quite a large group of pack trailers[20] to see us run this little rapid which we do in grand style.

HORN CREEK RAPID. This is a toughy at any time and its particularly mean in the high water. In '38 we ran the right side, cut to the center and slid across the big middle hole and on down to easy water. This year its obviously better to take the left side, play in close to the big center hole. It's a tricky job as there's a hard pull towards holes each way from the channel to be run. I go thru with the WEN and don't ship a drop of water. Dell gets caught in the edge of the big center hole and takes on quite a load of water. The speed above the rapid fooled him and he didn't get over quick enough. Zee comes thru right in my track in grand style.

Carrying the *Escalante* around Hermit Rapid

GRANITE FALLS. This one has the big water of '38 and I am anxious to see if I can contrive to run the main channel and not have an oar send me into the cove as before. This is the biggest water we have seen so far. I run right down the main drag and what a thrill. The waves are huge, and two of them are big enough to cause me to throw my weight forward to prevent backflipping. Get plenty of water and work hard to pull in on left some ways below. Dell gives me a bad moment when he gets slid off to the right near bottom and doesn't show up for what seems like ages. He too gets a boatload of water. He and I land with water to top of seat level. Zee takes the left hand side and dodges the big water in good shape and comes thru nicely. This high state of water doesn't take much looking over.

HERMIT FALLS. This presents the same problem as in '38. Impossible to slide away from the second and third big waves, and the chances of pulling off on left are remote as main current is powerful. The lining is not too easy but we get it done with considerable dispatch. High winds and sand blowing make it a disagreeable spot and we decide upon dropping downstream a ways on the theory that any camp could beat this. Besides there is a heavy shore lash at the foot of the Hermit which is giving the boats a hard pounding. In lower water this rapid is a joke. Line WEN first, then MEXICAN HAT II in one third the time. ESCALANTE is carried around.

CAMP BOUCHER CREEK. Left. We pull in just upstream from Boucher Creek so as to allow plenty of room for possible floods. The wind is blowing, but rain doesn't look too likely. Getting dinner eaten in the blowing sand is somewhat difficult but it is accomplished with much good nature evinced all the way around.

Escalante in big waves

JULY 24

What a night! Blew sand in our faces all night long and we literally had to dig our ways out this morning.

8:10 AM Shove off. Run Boucher Rapid right off the reel and its wonderful fast going. Surprisingly enough its about the fastest water we've had so far on the trip. We made a good twenty miles an hour.

CRYSTAL RAPIDS. Just land her a moment to check the channel but is as remembered, nice going in high water. In extreme low water it is very rocky.

This stretch thru here is real sport and goes like the dickens over these small rapids. Hardly a place in the canyon more fun to run than these.

RUBY CANYON RAPIDS.[21] Run all these just looking over from boat. River a bit red this morning but doesn't seem to be any higher. In '40 we had quite a bit of grief thru here with rocks, but this high water is a cinch and is perfect going. We get a few drops of rain.

SERPENTINE CANYON RAPIDS. Well! This rapid has definitely changed! In '38 the channel *was* a sort of serpentine affair, staying mostly to the right, but this time the takeoff is near the left and switches over to the right a bit then drops right on thru. Dell is complaining about being overloaded so I am taking Bill into my boat. Actually there is little difference in our loads, but I think it will be fun anyhow.

It's beginning to rain.

SHINUMO CREEK. Lunch. We are glad to pull in here tho it's just stopped raining. We are cold and the boys build a fire. Funny weather. We stop here quite a while and take naps. We are finally disturbed by the sun driving down hard on us.

Zee Grant, Norman Nevills, Agnes Albert, Bill Schukraft, Del Reed, Weldon Heald

[Just downstream] We pull in here driven to shelter by a terrific upstream driving rain! We are thrilled to the sight of many waterfalls forming from the literal cloudburst. Across the canyon rocks are falling from the cliff. It's fun and we are all enjoying it.

WALTHENBERG RAPIDS. Another surprise! In low water this is rocky. But in the high water of '38 the channel was easy and we ran without a second thought. But a flood has overtaken us and now this rapid has strong lashing waves in the center of the main drag. We look over the right side where one can slip along thru the rocks near the cliff, but I decide to run the main channel. I land on left, but around shoulder of rock that is almost impossible for people to reach. Dell lands just upstream so in shape to get passengers. This *was* tough water. The waves had an awfully hard lash to them. The ESCALANTE sneaks on the right and plays the filth, hits two rocks, and in crossing the channel to left at bottom gets some hard going over by heavy water.[22]

CAMP—ELVES CHASM. Difficult landing but we anchor on left. The creek is running a red colored water. Creek is on left, then a hundred and fifty feet of sand bank offers a good camping place. The boats are tied up and I have just put out the camping equipment when I see figures dashing madly around. I join the rush and find that another fork of the creek has discharged and a flood is coming down clear across the sand bank. We gather up all equipment and lose nothing. It's quite a thrill and novel experience. This second water is dirty brown. Altho the flood passes over the boat anchorage it holds fast. The flood hit at 6:15 PM. A grand nights sleep nevertheless.

At top of a big rapid, Nevills standing in boat for a last look

July 25

Shove off 8:50 AM. Well well well! In taking off I bang into a rock, bounce off and hit another!

Yesterday the river raised 3' in this 300' section. I almost forgot, yesterday, in climbing from his foldboat at Walthenberg Rapid, Zee went up the cliff some fifteen feet, lost his grip and came tumbling down into the river. What luck that no rocks were lurking under the surface! This creek at Elves Chasm is known as Royal Arch Creek. We leave a register up in the cave for future parties to sign. I am going to get the names of past parties gradually filled into it.

Its clouded up again this morning and it looks like rain is going to overtake us again today.

MILE 121 [rapid] The bow heavy WEN really got us slugged in this one! Going to have to shift my load. The foul red water is unpleasant stuff to get socked with.

FOSSIL RAPIDS. Fun to run. Starting to rain and it's getting cold!

LUNCH. Build a fire here where we've pulled in on the right. See a snake thought to be coral [snake], its black and white banded, 18" long.[23] Finally stops raining.

BEDROCK RAPID. In low water this is no rapid at all, but like President Harding, in the high water it has a real kick and is a dangerous piece of water. We have a bit of a time getting Zee to a vantage point to look it over. Weldon goes overland to lighten Dell's boat and meets us at the bottom. It's a hard one to get around. Agnes and I shove off in the

Waiting their turn to run a big rapid, Agnes Albert (left), Nevills (standing), and man on stern deck in common position for passengers to run rapids

WEN. Near bottom get a good ducking. Dell and Zee come thru fine. Bill rides with Dell.

DUBENDORFF RAPID. This is a honey. The main drag is on the right and the obvious course is to try to slip off the tongue to the right and play on thru. There is a terrific thrust to the left and I calculate that I will be shoved over just right to hit a big hole in the main drag. On the other hand we could slip down the right hand side, but lord oh lord I want take on Dubie the way it should be done, high, wide, and handsome! I go thru as planned, get socked by the hole, blinded by muddy water. Dell right in my tracks. Zee plays the right hand bank and keeps out of the big water. Good thing as the power in these waves would have thrown him over like lightning.

TAPEATS CREEK. Land on right looking for a camp spot but this is definitely no good for several reasons. No anchorage, a flood down Tapeats would catch us, and there's quicksand here! Therefore we decide to drop down a ways.

CAMP. We are now camped on the big bar just below Tapeats Creek. Plenty of wood and a short walk to Tapeats Creek. Tapeats is like ice water but most of the gang take baths. I never saw a person like Agnes for taking cold water. Looks stormy a bit but don't think it will rain. Nice camp. The sunset lights back on the Powell Plateau were gorgeous.

JULY 26

Up this morning with just a few clouds. River up 6" to a foot.

8:55 AM Shove off. Fine going this morning.

DEER CREEK FALLS. Water over falls half again as big as in '40. Brrr! The air and water are cold! Get some pictures then take off again.

50' above prevailing stage [are] cliff ruins. Stopped at the lower ones in '38. See some new ones this trip just upstream. Don't stop tho.

MILE 138. This is the famous rapid where I dumped Doris and John out into the river in '40. At this stage of water its hardly a riffle. Bill takes a picture.

MILE 139. Small rapid here. We've been cutting up a bit in this boat and to clap the climax I stand on my head going thru this little rapid with Bill at the oars. I suggest no pictures are taken! We get a real laugh out of the MEXICAN HAT II. Dell has no sense of humor whatsoever, and he conveys to Weldon his disapproval of such antics. After a trick like this both Weldon and Dell are seen to sit up real straight in the boat and not crack a smile.

KANAB RAPIDS. Glance over from right. Marvelous riding and we hate to see 'em end.

MATKATAMIBA RAPIDS. Water here but no landing.

LUNCH, MILE 148. We are just eating lunch when a heavy rain comes up. We are really pleased as it has caught us in a grand sheltered spot. After a bit of rain some beautiful waterfalls begin to come over the cliff walls and we are treated to a rare sight. The high ribbon-like falls come down from around 1600'. Sky clears and we have blue skies for the take-off.

Just before UPSET RAPID I shove the WEN under a big waterfall and try to get Agnes and Bill wet. This is at Mile 149. Waterfalls everywhere.

UPSET RAPID. This would be a tough nut to walk around in this high water, and anyway, we're all spoiling for a good ride. Off we go! Boy oh boy! One big wave passed us up going like a big freight engine. I swear if it had hit us we'd have stayed hit![24]

HAVASU CANYON. This *is* a disappointment! Here I've extolled the beauties of the sky blue water and we find the rains have made a red stream instead! We row, because of the high water, right up thru the sides of the canyon in the boats! We try climbing out for a camping spot much to Zee's chagrin. Zee does hate the climbing and pleads with us to go on. Dell shows the first, last and only display of temper on the trip when he pulls in to tie up. He seems to be displeased with Zee. I remark this as no one else at any time on the trip let his good disposition get out of hand. Old oar here, one we've seen on both previous trips. Well, although it's late we decide to look for a more favorable camp. Remembering the high walls thru this section I have qualms about picking up a camp spot this side of 164 Canyon.

CAMP. Right 164 MILE CANYON.[25] We came rolling in anxious to make camp. Last year this was barely a ripple, while in '38 it had plenty on the ball. At any rate into it we went. It was rough. Current drives hard to the left wall and there's some ugly waves. We were barely thru when Dell ploughed in. Dell later reported he came very close to upsetting when

Agnes Albert watching boat run rapids

a hard lashing wave struck him. But Zee, over he went! The one wave flipped him over, then the next righted him again! Zee climbed in, found he was facing wrong end and turned around! We all landed laughing and completely exhilarated by our experience. Zee made it right on in under his own power. Nice camp here and we like it. As we are ahead of schedule we plan to fiddle around in the morning and take our time. This is a marvelous camp and we're all glad we came on.

JULY 27

Day dawns bright and clear tho we have grand shade. It is now 9:00 AM and we're just fooling around. We are ahead of schedule and there's no need to hurry. My oh my this has been a marvelous trip!

LUNCH. Looking for shade. We go into mouth of canyon a ways and find shade under a tree. Partly thru lunch I glance up and see a bull snake resting above Dell's head. This evokes a mad scramble. We shortly move on and take off again.

LAVA FALLS. This is a tough set-up as in '38 and we obviously have to line. We landed on left and line this side. Not too hard a job. Soon as the WEN is down I run it on below to the cove then walk back up. We carry all the equipment around to the foot of the rapid then run the MEXICAN HAT II thru in short time. Load it, then all pile on to drift down to where Zee and Agnes [are waiting].

CAMP. Left. Good camp and we all enjoy the stop. Ahead of us lies very little hard water. This is our last major obstacle.

JULY 28

Good nights sleep. We talked over ways and means for editing the movies, and the consensus of opinion is that Bill should use his own judgement. The springs here forming the travertine are called "warm springs" but actually their temperature is very mild. I imagine most parties have seen them in cold water and their temperature remains constant thru the year and by contrast seem warm.

8:20 AM. Shove off. We tear thru the rapid just below in good style tho it's a mean looking customer the way it drives into the left hand wall.

MILE 185 [rapid]. Agnes takes us thru this rapid in fine style. We are going to kill time today as we're quite ahead of schedule and don't want to have to spend all our extra time at Diamond Creek. Its fun to have to place to go and lots of time to get there. Clear nice day. Few high fleecy clouds.

CAMP. Right. Nice willow tree and a dandy place to lay over. Agnes and I are going to do a bit of climbing after lunch. After lunch and a siesta Agnes and I take on a 60' basalt cliff back of camp. I take one ten foot spill and never do get anywhere. We all join in a good laugh at my expense as I'm supposed to be giving climbing lessons and can't even climb it myself. Nothing daunted, Agnes and I set out to climb a peak back of camp that raises some 800–1000'. We take no water and reach the summit dry. Grand view. Take movies. See signs of mountain sheep. Going down Agnes gets some cactus thorns! We land in camp *dry*! Some grapefruit juice really hits the spot. After dinner keep awake for some time swapping yarns, singing, etc. At 3:00 PM a big plane passed overhead, and another passed north of us around 3:30 PM. Agnes and I got into camp at 4:30 PM. The river is falling off a bit. We are anxious to get some clear water as this river water is a bit flat. First quarter of moon is overhead.

JULY 29

Shove off at 8:45 AM. Yesterday was a bit cloudy and relatively cool, but today looks like a scorcher.

PARASHONT WASH. As we were going by I looked toward ledge at right of canyon mouth and saw something suspended by a wire and possibly a camp. We landed and immediately investigated. It proved to be a cowman's or trappers camp. A coyote trap was sprung close by. A stack of dishes under an oil can. Around the corner more evidence of camping. Been children here. I take along a child's book of stories.[26] Leave note for whoever would find it to please get in touch with me.

Here is contents of letter just received from St. George, Utah, and postmarked Sept. 17, 1941.

> Dear Sir—I found your note at my camp and as you ask me to write you, I now take pleasure to do so. I am going to ask a few questions. What I am interested in, is what type of boat did you have? That you got down over those rapids with out having a reck.*[sic]* Did you get thru to the Lake and

how much trouble did your have? I have heard there was a boat that would carry eight or nine hundred lbs. that can be carried [around?]. If you should know of anywhere I could get that kind of boat or pattern of same I would greatly appreciate it very much. Hoping to hear from you soon,

Roy Wood
St. George Utah

Bill runs the WEN on thru Parashont rapid. Last night the river dropped nearly a foot in a 400–600' section and I think we lost about 5000 sec. feet.

CAMP. Same as '38. We go a ways up on left side of canyon (SPRING CANYON) and have lunch in welcome shade and with a nice clear stream of water running by. After lunch all but Dell and I go on up the canyon to bathe. Dell and I lie in shade and talk. After dinner at same place we go down to bar to sleep. About nine o'clock the air cools of nicely but talk goes on 'til 11:00 PM. The talk is on intricate phases of astronomy, and I for one am left way behind. The river canyon thru here is not as spectacular as up above, but its still classy scenery.

JULY 30.

Up at 5:30 AM as want to travel while it's cool. It's 21 miles to Diamond Creek from here and we plan to get in fairly early. Weldon talks of walking out to Peach Springs for some steaks, but the distance being uncertain and that fact the shade will look pretty good inclines me to believe we will all be together at Diamond Creek.

Looking forward to a few rapids with a bit more zip in 'em today.

7:10 AM. We're off!

TWO HUNDRED AND FIVE MILE RAPIDS! I look this baby over from the deck and take off. What a ride! All possible channels are full of holes and there's some big time water in it. It was a grand ride and just what we were looking for—tho still a real surprise. This, in low water my notes show was a meany—full of rocks. Last year Dell's arm hurt and Barry took his boat thru here. I am listing this one along with 164 [Mile Rapid] as a major rapid. 164 is not a major rapid in low water really, but its mean in high.

Mile 210. A burro is seen on the bar.[27] He runs a few steps then ee-awws. Runs a few more. Eee-aws again. Its ludicrous but too dark to get pictures.

FALL CANYON. River dropped again during the night. About 6". I figure we now have 15–17000 sec. feet.

THREE SPRINGS CANYON. Water here but too hard to land and no camp. If ever necessary to get water here land upstream.

TWO HUNDRED AND SEVENTEEN MILE RAPIDS. Look this baby over from boat and take off. It's a real ride and is no slouch. Fast and big waves. Plays right wall at bottom.

Zee Grant and the *Escalante*

12:00 Noon arrive Diamond Creek. We eat lunch under the old willow tree. Then a siesta, tho Zee goes around corner in Diamond to build a dam. Much later in the day I contribute an hours work. By dinner time Zee has a rather large pool backed up. Agnes and I wash the WEN. Weldon and Dell scrub the MEXICAN HAT II. Hotter than the old Hub here. Shade feels good. Eat dinner and to bed. I spend a restless night and am bothered by a feeling of apprehension towards folks at home.[28] (2:45 PM today Dad passed away.)

July 31

Up about 8:00 AM. After breakfast Bill gets pictures of the boats, and some of me explaining the features, etc., of the WEN. Oh yes, be sure to keep an eye on 224 MILE RAPIDS. They're vicious at this stage of water and have a big whirlpool at bottom right side. Trip to Peach Springs definitely abandoned. Agnes declares she and I must go exploring, but this heat will probably find us all hovering around camp. Zee goes after his dam again. Eventually everyone pitches in and the dam gets to a good three feet high. This morning I wash all my dirty clothes including my sheet. I am not much of a launderer, but at least they're some better. The eggs have held out right to the last gasp!

This afternoon take a bath and wash my hair. We have the air mattresses in the pool and much fun ensues. My parading around in my shorts creates a near convulsion on parts of all and I submit to photographs. Last couple of days my left ear has hurt way deep inside. Water.

At Separation Rapid plaque: Norman Nevills, Weldon Heald, Agnes Albert, Bill Schukraft, Zee Grant (standing), Del Reed.

AUGUST 1

7:45 AM. We're off! It feels good to be traveling again and we eagerly anticipate some fun riding on down to the Lake. We bet on where we will meet Harry Aleson and I gamble he will be right at Bridge Canyon.

BRIDGE CANYON MILE 235. Harry Aleson and Jim Savage meet us here. Harry's boat tied in eddy middle of rapid. Harry serves us grape juice and boy its good! Harry and I go down to try his boat on an attempt to make up rapid.[29] No dice. Motor not enough soup. We tinker with motor and still no dice. Idling valve evidently plugged. We have lunch.

On we go with Harry's boat towing the three boats.

We stop at SEPARATION CANYON to get pictures.

Pull into SPENCER CANYON around 4:00 PM and find a delightful camp spot. Just getting squared around when in comes the [Grand Canyon] Tours boat the "APACHE." Jack Hudson, Harry Fitch, Willis Evans.

They offer a tow to Pierces Ferry. We debate awhile then all decide to go except Zee, Harry, and Dell. They will follow on in the morning. I get dinner for whole crowd of 11.

We get to Pierce's at around nine o'clock. Have a sandwich. To bed!

AUGUST 2

Up fairly early and send messages from the radio station. I send one for Zee. Am told that Doris is "unavoidably detained" but will be in afternoon of tomorrow.

The morning drags. We go out to meet the Tours boat and look for Harry and party. About one or two the Tours boat hoves into sight towing our boats. The APACHE tows the whole shebang into Pierce's landing. After much discussion, exchange of radio messages etc., it is decided that we will have dinner, then have Jack Hudson in the APACHE tow us to BOULDER DAM.

Harry leaves his boat at the dock. Then with the ESCALANTE tied on top of the WEN we take off. Around midnight we pull into a canyon above main basin and finally get anchored. Zee and I bed down on a ridge. So does Harry. The rest sleep on the boat. No food. It's all buried under the ESCALANTE. Just at sundown in BOULDER CANYON we came across a coyote swimming for the south shore. It was quite a sight. Looked like a mountain lion at first.

AUGUST 3.

Around nine AM we approached the BOULDER LANDING. Met by big boats. On one, and transferring to APACHE is John Southworth of '40 trip! Friends of Agnes also are on boat but go on. Pictures are taken and Zee is the sensation of the hour—and justifiably so as he turned in a swell job of bringing his boat thru. We go right up to the GREEN HUT for breakfast— and in walks Doris and Joan!

After breakfast Agnes and Major Robertson take off, Bill leaves—so do the Healds. Harry, Dell, Zee, Doris, Joan and I hold down Boulder City Hotel. Zee runs his pictures to a very appreciative audience at the theater and I make a sort of hit and miss running narrative. This afternoon Doris tells me of Dad's passing.

Go to bed early tonight.

AUGUST 4

Get the boats loaded and make a late start for Mexican Hat. Bid Zee and Harry good-bye. Harry is taking the ESCALANTE over to Las Vegas where it will be entrained for the North Rim.

Midnight. Bed down in Williams.

AUGUST 5.

Visit at Grand Canyon and have lunch. Visit with Dr. Bryant. Am asked to have WEN put with remainder of Powell's boat and one of Stanton's in museum.[30]

MEXICAN HAT 10:30 PM.

GOOD-BYE.

Grand Canyon,
July 12 to August 7, 1942

1942 was a watershed year for Nevills, in ways good and not so good. During the winter, Nevills threw himself, with his usual enthusiasm, into drilling a well for his home and the Nevills Lodge. After months of work, the well came in with a small flow of oil, not water, and he was forced to continue hauling water by truck.

Nevills was also concerned by his draft status; at thirty-three years old, he was on the upper end of draft age, and since 1940 had been considered III-A (not likely to be drafted save for national emergency). But when the U.S. entered the war, he was reclassified as I-A, or eligible for the draft. The uncertainty about his status with the Selective Service was to continue throughout the war; he was the head of the family, had dependent children, and a dependent mother, and so was not really likely to be drafted. But as the war dragged on, he couldn't be certain. So he contacted his local draft board and also thought about moving to Provo, Utah, to work in the Geneva steel mill. By then his San Juan River trips were fully booked, just as it became difficult for Americans to travel because of wartime rationing of gas, oil, and tires. Yet Nevills was determined to make another Grand Canyon run, despite the difficulties of getting supplies. His San Juan trip in May 1942 paid off by introducing him to two men who would gladly overcome any problems to go on the Grand Canyon: Neill C. Wilson and Ed Hudson. Wilson signed up for the Grand Canyon run, along with his young son, Bruce, and persuaded a friend of his, Otis Reed Marston, of San Francisco, to come along and bring his son, Garth. This made Nevills a pioneer yet again, by allowing children to go on his river trips. The thought of children on a river expedition would have been absolutely unheard of at any time previous to this, yet Nevills felt he could take them with no danger, and he was right.

For the 1942 Grand Canyon trip, Nevills raised his prices to $1,500 per person, a princely sum in 1942. He had mentioned in earlier correspondence that he was thinking of raising the price; perhaps he was inspired to do so by a letter from Wilson, in which he advised, rather crudely, "Make yourself some money. Don't give your stuff away. . . . But for crise [sic] sake make 'em pay—don't be like the beautiful lady who gave away one million dollars' worth before she discovered it was worth $3 a crack."[1] At any rate, with this price structure, Nevills had suddenly reached into the higher levels of the adventure travel market. As it turned out, all involved felt the trip was well worth the money, for in this trip Nevills's boyish personality came to the fore, and everyone had a great time. The water was at an ideal level—21,700 *cfs—making for wonderful rides through the rapids. They rode on logs; they took silly photos with "Irene," the cardboard stewardess cutout; they started huge fires; and they played pranks on each other. In Wilson, Nevills made a lasting friend whose advice would serve him well in the future. In Olsen, Nevills had lucked into a mother lode of advertising, especially after World War II, when Olsen's film* Facing Your Danger—*starring Norman Nevills as himself—won an Academy Award for short subjects. Garth Marston later became a boatman for Nevills Expedition, as did his father, Otis.*

Of course, all those events were far in the future when the happy crew got off the river in August 1942, wearing the tan and glow that comes from a wonderful river trip. Nevills felt on top of his own particular world, the most famous and well-known riverman of his day, and the future indeed looked bright for Nevills Expedition. But by the end of that summer, world events finally caught up with the isolated little world of Mexican Hat, and Nevills was reluctantly forced to conclude that river trips would have to wait until the great conflict raging overseas was finished before he could once again set sail on his beloved Colorado River.

JULY 12

We leave this morning in order to have a good start in getting the two boats, MEXICAN HAT II and JOAN to Lees Ferry. The WEN was taken over on last San Juan trip, along with some of our food supplies. Leading the procession was Ed Olsen[2] in his car, followed by Doris and me with the JOAN. Pres and Wayne were in Pres's car with the MEXICAN HAT II in tow. Had lunch at Kayenta. At Tuba City found that the big trailer that Pres is towing had an inner wheel bearing shot, so had to do some tall hustling around to get it fixed and get another axle bolt nut. Mr. Miller of the government garage supplied the nut. Then Pres and Wayne took off for Lees Ferry, where they would unload the MEXICAN HAT II, and then rejoin us next day at South Rim, where Pres's car would be left along with Ed Olsen's. Doris, Ed Olsen and I had dinner at Cameron, where we also learned that Harry Aleson was waiting for us at Marble Canyon. Arrive at South Rim in good time, and at South Entrance met the ranger, Don McLean, who wants to go on next Grand Canyon trip. Beautiful sunset over Canyon. Looked down on Canyon from Desert Watchtower. On to El Tovar and bed.

JULY 13

Up early and arrange to have our food supplies packed down to Phantom Ranch. Arrange to have Dr. and Mrs. Bryant[3] meet us at Phantom Ranch and ride down to Pipe Springs on our take-off from Phantom July 23rd. Harry Franse[4] arranges to burn a signal fire in answer to ours that will be made foot of Tanner Trail July 19. We attend the morning show at Emery Kolb's. Arrange to have Edith Kolb Lehnert[5] drive Ed Olsen's car to Boulder City. Pres[6] and Wayne[7] show up about noon. We visit around a bit more then take off for Marble Canyon in my car. Dinner at Cameron. Arrive Marble Canyon ready for bed.

JULY 14

6:00 AM state finds Ed Hudson[8] among us. To my consternation I find Ed has misinterpreted my letters and has arrived with 4000' feet of 16mm film but no camera other than an 8mm![9] We decide to get our equipment ready, then in afternoon drive to The Gap and make some kind of arrangement to get a camera. After breakfast we go to the boats, and there, assisted by Frank Dodge[10] get the three boats down into the river. The food in then sorted and equipment sorted. All the boats have small seep of water which will stop in a few hours. As we leave to return to Marble Canyon Lodge Harry Aleson comes up the river in his boat with 22 H.P. Evinrude. We visit a while, then arrange to view his pictures at Marble [Canyon] Lodge; together with one or two reels of my '41 trip. Leave Wayne McConkie to stay with Frank Dodge in order for Wayne to familiarize himself with the JOAN, and our turning technique. Wayne is a canoe man, and naturally his method of missing a rock or maneuvering is diametrically opposed to ours. After lunch Doris and Pres stay at Lodge while Ed Olsen, Ed Hudson, and myself drive the 40 miles to The Gap to do some phoning. About the time the calls are placed it is decided for Ed Olsen to take over a goodly portion of Ed Hudson's film, aside from the 4000' he had ordered, and that Ed H. would do his work with the 8mm. Thus we decide the issue. About half way home I am floored by having a bad blowout in one of what I thought to be my best tires![11] Arrive in time for dinner, then until the wee small hours quite a crowd of us view 16mm movies. Bed looks very good when we finally get to it!

JULY 15

Up at 6:30 AM to find the stage had disgorged four more of our expedition members. Neill and Bruce Wilson,[12] Otis and Garth Marston.[13] Am pleased to find that Otis has a 16mm cartridge loading Bell and Howell, with *6000'* of film! Thus there is between eleven and 12,000 feet of film in the party to record our descent. Breakfast over we repair to my car and a pick-up to get to the river. Final checking of equipment, particularly personal, is made, and I soon have the loads allotted to the respective boats. It is easier each trip as one always learns. Harry Aleson will meet us at head of lake, so I am saved further persuasion in the matter of his not accompanying us in his power driven boat![14] Instead, he will go as far as Badger Creek, taking with him Frank Dodge, Riley Baker, Snooks Jackson and his brother. Doris says good-bye, and that will not be on bridge to wave as has such a long trek home. The fact of our imminent departure is thus brought to home. This is my fourth trip. One man, Frank Dodge, has made three trips, but two of them clear thru. This is the first time I haven't had at least one woman in the party. Again, have two boys, and predictors have it they will raise the hazard. This trip I have two green men. Pres I have trained and drilled for seven months so I feel sure of his ability. Wayne is completely new to the job, but I am relying on his complete dependability in following orders to fall right into the swing of things. Our crew looks like a good one. All have had plenty of outdoor experience, plus quite a bit of boating of one kind or another. Our starting line-up, and one we will follow with one or two exceptions thru the Canyon is:

WEN   Neill, 52 yrs; Bruce, 12 yrs; Garth, 16 yrs; myself, 34 yrs.
MEXICAN HAT II   Otis, 53 yrs; Ed Olsen, 43 yrs; boatman, Pres, 29 yrs
JOAN   Ed Hudson, 35 yrs; boatman, Wayne, 32 yrs

Embark. Beautiful clear day. River at 23,000'.

NAVAJO BRIDGE. Dozen or so persons on bridge. And Doris! It is great to see her and now the trip begins to take on an even better complexion. Pres and Wayne are both hooked by an eddy, much to Doris's amusement, and she calls down joking remarks to them. We keep traveling with Harry Aleson occasionally weaving in and out with his motor boat.

BADGER CREEK RAPID. I land usual spot on left, while Harry Aleson and crew land across the river. Go right down to look over so we can eat lunch at foot. All members, particularly the boatmen are quite anxious to see this, their first big rapid. I point out the channel to Pres and Wayne, then have Wayne installed as signaler for Pres and me. I shove off in the WEN and have a fine ride thru. It feels good to have the big water under the boat again. Pres comes through next and turns in an excellent job of running. I go up to signal Wayne through—and here he comes! Too far left. (His left). Over. Too far right. Over. Still too far right. Over. Now he's too far to the left so I send him back. Too far right and he's coming down fast now on the narrow tongue, guarded by a huge hole on the right, and several holes and rocks on the left. I motion frantically for him to get over to the left, he turns, still with plenty of time, but instead of getting full right angles to the current he holds his boat in such a manner as to be pulling against the current. He is swept now right to the very rim of the hole, pulls tremendously with his left oar and just does get the JOAN headed stern on as he drops down into the hole! I have a bad moment and get set to dash for the WEN when here he comes through the big reverse wave below![15] All boats are now safely at the foot of Badger Creek Rapid! I start getting lunch, and in the meantime the crowd of five from across the river come over and we all have lunch together. The unexpected addition puts a strain on our larder but we make out fine. Everyone has a swim as it is quite hot. I write an account of our experiences thus far for Doris, to be taken out by Harry and mailed. Otis digs up an old envelope for the missive. Final adieus are made, and now we're off again. Cooled off a bit and is fine traveling.

SOAP CREEK RAPIDS! Land right. A hasty survey shows same channel as '38. Good going. Through Wayne had a bad shaking up in Badger Creek he is ready and rarin' to try out Soap Creek. Just before I take off Neill comes to me and asks that whenever possible to please give Otis a ride in a big one as Oty wants some real thrills. My desire of several years standing to take a passenger thru SOAP CREEK crystallizes on the spot and I offer Oty the chance. He accepts. Oty and I take off. Have a fine ride. Next signal Pres to come thru. Pres does fine, though gets a bit too far to the left and thus has to land below me on a very rocky shore. I get my boat swung around again and ready for a rescue if necessary, and signal for Wayne to come thru. Wayne tries to sneak off the tongue to the right but the angle of his boat gets him slapped back onto the tongue and into the first big waves out of control. He makes two complete revolutions going on through and his ride in wildness fully equals that of the BOTANY in 1938. Needless to say poor Wayne arrives at the bottom near Pres with his confidence quite shaken! As the anchorage is bad I send the other two boats on to await me in an eddy below, then I get off in the WEN. All boats were at bottom at 5:00 PM.

CAMP. Left. Same as '41. Everyone in fine spirits and have a swim. Get dinner. Water temperature 78 degrees and air 86. We plan to keep temperature readings all way through, but thermometer is tied to boat for night and next morning finds it gone. Wood scarce, but the two boys rustle around and dig up enough for dinner and breakfast.

JULY 16

Up at 6:00 AM. Everyone seemed to have a good night's sleep despite the fact that during the night the wind blew and drifted sand on us. I alone seem to feel the hardness of an air mattress-less bed! Neill and Oty brought along a life sized model in cardboard of a TWA airline hostess which they assemble. It then develops that Ed Olsen's brother is married to the model for the figure—Irene! During the day many amusing shots are taken of "Irene" in different places, including my taking her through #24 [24½ Mile Rapid]. Last night had a long talk with Wayne and think I've built up his confidence a bit. I know he will turn in a good job. I suggest to Wayne that he should take Ed Hudson with him in one of the bigger rapids to give him a thrill, and Wayne's reply was almost an epic for self depreciation and frankness: "Anyone that would ride through a big rapid with me is crazy"!

7:55 AM. Leave camp at Mile 12½.

SHEER WALL RAPID. Run right through. Good channel.

HOUSE ROCK RAPID. Land right. Quite rough. I take off with Ed Olsen and Bruce as passengers. Fine rough ride. Then Pres and Neill come through. I intend to return and ride through with Wayne, but it's such a long walk back that I decide not to. In the meantime an argument ensues between Ed. H. and Wayne as to Ed's riding as passenger. It ends up with Ed riding through with Wayne. Whereas I normally wouldn't like this I feel it was a good confidence builder and for the best.

At Mile 18½ just below huge boulder or rock at BOULDER NARROWS we stop on left and pry huge drift log into river. On the log then ride Neill, Ed Olsen, Garth, and Bruce.

"Irene" at camp

Mile 19½. Log grounds here on right so that its passengers transfer back to their respective boats.

NORTH CANYON RAPID. Quite rough. I shove off in WEN with Garth and Bruce as passengers. Comes next Pres with Ed Olsen. Wayne with Ed Hudson.

LUNCH. Right, Mile 21. Sort of a cave and a fine shelter.

#24 RAPID[16] [24½ Mile Rapid]. This is a toughy at all stages of water, though tenfold easier to run in high water. In '38 I ran Del Reed's boat too in it. In '40 I ran all three boats. Main thing is to slip off tongue to left. All boats make a good run. No passengers.

TWENTY-NINE MILE RAPID. Neill at oars on this one.

CAMP. VASEY'S PARADISE. Bad anchorage and we are compelled to drag the boats up out of the water. Everyone thrilled with the beauty of the water here and we plan to stay over at least part of tomorrow. Been an amazing number of small rapids today that had a real hard throw to them. Plenty of eddies and whirlpools at bottom. Neill ran the WEN quite a bit today, and Ed Olsen the MEXICAN HAT II. Been overcast almost all day and consequently marvelously cool. Wish Cherry could be here for this perfect stage of water and fine weather. Wayne's hands are blistered and sore from having to pull more on the oars than necessary, but his technique is getting better every hour that goes by. Water a bit slowish between rapids but at that it's a pretty good current. At dark Bruce and Garth are setting off a drift pile up by the cliff for a bonfire. Pres's boat is tied up right near spring. Wayne missed landing and had to have his boat beached, but my cove anchorage was poor so WEN is out too.

July 17

Started raining lightly at daybreak and keeps drizzling up until noon. Despite this fact we have a good breakfast and I even turn out some french toast. Harry Aleson gave us a can of syrup which goes well with it. I personally put in a restless night as the bare rock is a most hard bed. Will have air mattresses next trip. Would have brought them this trip but was afraid of the weight. The ideal combination is an air mattress, single army blanket, sheet and very light waterproof tarp. After breakfast all of us but Pres take off to explore a cave a quarter mile upstream, and to see the dead man we found in 1940.[17]

Upon reaching the cave a preliminary survey shows us that its extensiveness demands better lighting, and, as we have but one flash along, Wayne volunteers to go back to camp for at least two more. Neill, Bruce, and Ed Olsen, and Garth left with Wayne. At mouth of cave Neill had a very narrow escape when a large chunk of limestone fell from above and missed him by not more than a few feet. Rock weighed close to a thousand pounds. Upon Wayne's return back we all went on into cave some 200' more thru rather tortuous passages. All along we explored every possible passageway hoping to find more chambers. Another 100' of passageways and Wayne and Ed Hudson were left behind to await Oty and me. Oty and I made some thrilling stomach crawls thru passageways and vertical chutes, eventually reaching the limit of the unblocked routes. One room we went thru was a good 75' high. In last room, wedged in a crack of the rock and held in place by a rock chip was a note that purposes to have been left by the Stanton Party in 1890.[18] I somehow doubt its authenticity, but it's a fact that on the first Stanton trip that this was the point that the members all crawled out of the canyon. In this same cave they stored some of their remaining supplies. This, it's quite possible that the note may be authentic. Its text:

STANTON SURVEY PARTY
E.H. Brown
—— Pierce
W.H. Edwards
Jan. 14, 1890

I bring the note along and will take it home. Oty writes on the wall in chalk indicating the fact of our finding the note etc. Oty and I work our way back to Ed and Wayne. Everywhere is smoke evidence and some basketry showing prehistoric occupation.[19] Soon arrive at mouth of the cave and find it still trying to drizzle. We go on up main canyon past Paradise Canyon and climb up to see the dead man. Don't stay long, though go over to another shallow cave to see some cliff ruins remains. We found the main adit of the big Stanton Cave blocked in such a manner as to render almost impossible its opening by any but the most difficult and elaborate work. Go back to camp and have lunch. A bit of blue sky opening up in the south, and we decide to go at least as far as President Harding Rapid. River up a few inches this morning. It's a more reddish color.

SHOVE OFF FROM VASEY'S. In taking off, Ed Olsen, sitting high on the bow of the MEXICAN HAT II is thrown into river when the boat is whirled around fast in leaving the eddy and caught by the main current of the river. Fortunately Ed didn't have his camera in his hand so nothing more serious than a ducking and a lesson came to him.

REDWALL CAVERN. At a stage of water no higher than 20,000', this could make a fine camp though very little wood around.

THIRTY-SIX MILE RAPID. Neill at oars. I ride deck holding onto stern rope but come close to getting bucked off. Lots of fun though.

PRESIDENT HARDING RAPID. And a thrill! Neill at the oars. I suggest that this is a toughy, but Neill says he would like to have a try at it so away we go! I attempt to coach Neill, but my instructions seem to confuse rather than help him. As a result we go slithering up almost on the huge rock in midstream, swing around into the hole and only by a miracle and the wide beam of the WEN keep from tipping over. As it is I have to throw my weight all on one side, at same time sort of helping Bruce to stay on deck. The WEN gets water in her to seat level, which is a very rare occurrence. It was fun though, and Neill gains appellation of: "Big Water Wilson." Otis at oars of MEXICAN HAT II comes thru very smoothly, as does Wayne. This is no rapid at all in low water, but from 15,000 up it's a good one to watch out for. Best channel is to slip off on right side of rock.[20]

SADDLE CANYON. So early we decided to go on to our Nankoweap camp. We see the effects of our big '40 fire when we touched off an enormous driftwood pile here.

CAMP. NANKOWEAP. Fine camp here. Although it threatens rain it doesn't materialize and we have dinner in good style. As darkness comes on a sliver of moon rides the western cliffs. After dinner we had a D.W.B. initiation, with all but a few getting admittance by lighting with one match a fire to touch off a big driftwood pile just across from us on other side of Nankoweap Creek. Wonderful big fire and lit the whole canyon up from top to bottom all around. All had retired when something in the pile exploded with a great bang very similar to a dynamite blast. To sleep, starlight night. No wind.

July 18

All day camp at Nancoweep. After breakfast all but Pres, Wayne and me took off to climb up to the ruins at the head of the talus slope back some

Neill Wilson

half mile from camp. I fixed some of the oar locks that needed attention. Tried to build up my left lock to prevent the oar from turning in my hand. Pres found an old boat clear over past Little Nancoweep Creek, so the three of us lugged it over to camp. It looks to be the boat I found at Outlaw Cave a year ago, and later turned loose at Lees Ferry. River is bright red this morning. Apparently a flash flood from up country. Ed Olsen was sick for a while this morning after taking salt tablets.

The party returns from the ruins. In meantime Wayne has found an arrowhead in old surface sites just back of camp. After lunch we prepare to loaf around and rest. Pres finds an old Eastman camera much the worse for wear in a drift pile. He also finds a good 7' oar. He seems to have caught my driftwood pile fever! Few flies to date, but the red ants are awful pests. Ed Hudson and I build a small dam and spend an hour or so lying in Nancoweep Creek. In early mornings water is quite cool, but during the day it's just a nice temperature to lie in. Ed Olsen has a good sunburn on his legs this evening, and it looks like he'll have sore legs for a day or two. This evening the water is clearing up in color and should be back to normal in a day or two. This evening Otis gave me a set of the East and West quadrangle sheets of the Grand Canyon for which I am very glad. Lots of pictures being taken. Over a thousand feet [of movie film] a person, that is Oty and Ed Olsen, to date. Late dinner, and we decided to go to bed without another driftwood fire. Just before dinner I really gagged in the process of trying to hold down a couple of salt tablets.

Boatmen Pres Walker, Norman Nevills, Wayne McConkie

July 19

This is the day! Tonight we will sleep within the Grand Canyon and light the signal fire at Tanner Trail. My, time has flown to this point. This trip has seemed the fastest in passing of time of any of the trips.

7:45 AM. EMBARK. Shady this morning and the lighting of the canyon is really something. It's the most beautiful thru here that I've ever seen it by far. Nice setting of clouds which adds a lot.

KWAGUNT RAPID. Quite rough and get a bit of a ducking.

LITTLE COLORADO RIVER. Cape Solitude a grand sight! A small discharge coming in form the Little Colorado. Maybe 50'. We go on by as this is not an inviting place to stop and there's not much to see unless one were to walk the six miles up to the first cataracts in Little Colorado Canyon.[21]

We round a bend and get our first view of the HOPI tower. It's still a great thrill to see it and immediately we discuss if we are being observed.

OLD TANNER MINE—LAVA CANYON RAPID. As I drop down on this rapid I decide to dive off to the left and thus come into shore at a good spot to get to our lunch spot and take off for the mine. I do so, see a hole, pull left, miss it, and make shore. Pres does likewise though gets quite close onto the hole. In meantime I have beached, Bruce is going up to anchor the bow rope, I have my maps out, have just written as far as the colon in the time, when Neill says: "The boys are over." He says it without any particular feeling and I think he means they're through the rapid. Again he says the same thing, but with an urgency in his voice which causes me to look over my shoulder and see the JOAN, bottom side up, with Ed Hudson in sight, but no Wayne. I call Bruce in with rope, then Neill, Bruce and I shove off, all this in a matter of seconds. As I approach the boat I have a terribly anxious moment when I still can't locate Wayne. As I come up close to the bow of the JOAN I see Wayne around the side working up to the JOAN's bow. I have Neill grab hold of the bow rope and in a very short distance they are beached. All this was filmed, including actual upset by Ed Olsen.[22] We all grab the JOAN and flip her over. I take off after Neill's canteen, which was in the JOAN, and Garth swims off down-river after Ed Hudson's hat. He gets it at foot of rapid below! All that is lost is Ed Hudson's pencil. I could have rescued it but wanted to get boat ashore. Nothing in the JOAN was wet or injured. The boys didn't have on their preservers so had quite a time surfacing. This is not a bad rapid, but the channel I took in order to make a quick landing demanded quick handling to miss the hole. Ed Hudson maintained that they tipped over going over brink sideways, but what really happened was that they went into the hole sideways and bottom reverse wave rolled them over upstream. Just a minute or so before this all happened one of the boys, I think Neill, maybe Garth, asked me about the real danger of "holes." I told them that they were always dangerous and even the most innocent looking small hole could spell disaster. It surely did! In a way I'm glad this happened as it demonstrated only too well just how fast this river can catch up with the unwary. So on we go for lunch! This we do in regular manner. I gather up an aluminum plate, tin cup, knife fork and spoon to take home for a souvenir. By the way, Wayne got two large marble rocks at Vasey's, from them, he will cut us each a pair of bookends. One rock in each of our boats. We go on up to the mine[23] and explore its different passageways. Coming out we seek shade. All of us are restless and its hard to find a comfortable spot, so on we go. I gather the upset has Wayne perturbed about the big fellows that are coming tomorrow. He'll do fine, I know, in them.

TANNER TRAIL. Well, here we are! It's hot so we all lay around awhile to rest. Talk awhile, I am going to have Bruce wear his preserver more now, as well as rest of party in order to take no chances. In meantime Neill advances the idea himself much to my satisfaction, so all is well. We soon get restless, so all but Garth take off the half mile down the rocks and sandbar to the point on which I expect to see the '38 driftwood pile we made. But since last year the floods have taken it apart so we set to work to build a new pile. It's hot. We're tired, and every effort comes hard. The excitement of this morning is taking its toll! We get the pile big enough for our satisfaction and wearily pull back to camp. Everyone goes in swimming and my how refreshing the water is. I had been telling the gang how I was sure Harry Franse would have spotted the upset in the telescopes, and in this same vein joked about swimming around naked as the tourists on top might spot us. They did! After trip, on the Rim, was told that people were watching us swimming around at foot of Tanner Trail! Before, during, and after dinner we had lots of fun discussing the big run coming up in the morning. Hance! Sockdologer! Grapevine! Barely had time to get dishes washed when it was time to get down to light the fire. I had arranged to have it lit at 9:00 PM sharp so that watchers on the Hopi tower would spot it and could send answering light. We found the ashes of the '41 fire this afternoon. 9:00 PM. We touch off the fire, and almost immediately a red glare appeared on the Hopi Watchtower. A red railroad flare. Then two rockets were set off. In conclusion a blinker light (which we found later to be from a flashlight of Harry Aleson's) sent us a message. Neill interpreted it to say: "See you." We find later that it said: "Good night"! At any rate it was a great thrill to see the answering signal and we returned to camp in high good spirits. A cool wind is blowing, the moon is playing around in a cloudish sky.

JULY 20

Found the old '38 camp spot this morning with the plank still in place. Wayne found old pick about a hundred yards back of our camp here. Over near big mesquite tree. We take off into Tanner Rapid and have a fine ride.

UNKAR CREEK RAPID. A bit tricky, but not hard to run. Gives a fine ride. We play right tongue on right side. Second drop at bottom easy.

SEVENTY FIVE MILE RAPID. Was going to run this without stopping but in safety measure for other two fellows pulled in. Not hard to run and gives a fine ride.

HANCE RAPID. The same old Hance! It's a toughy, sure enough, but by playing down thru the holes on the left hand side there's an easy channel to take and stay out of trouble on. Wicked looking customer, sure enough! I take off in WEN and Pres gives a good run too. Wayne is unsure on this fellow so I bring the JOAN thru, making, strangely enough, the best run I've ever made on Hance. Barely got wet. The water down below is very rough but we all bang thru in fine style.

SOCKDOLOGER RAPID. Same channel as in '38. Much easier than in '41. However it's quite a rapid. Ed Hudson swears he shook all the way thru it. I think he did! Everyone seemed quite impressed. Big roar and some big water. I have the boys watch their watches so as to time their descent on five minute intervals. At 11:50 AM the WEN is off. Most passengers I've ever had in Sockdologer. Neill and Bruce on the deck. Garth in the cockpit. We make it fine shape and just at foot of first drop I pull into cove on right in order to watch the fun of the next boats coming down. We are bailed and just squared around when here comes the MEXICAN HAT II. They do fine and come into this landing too. Soon Ed and Wayne come down the line and they both wear very relieved expressions when they see us. We shove right on, determined to get Grapevine behind us before eating lunch.

GRAPEVINE RAPID. Well, this really was something! Whereas I thought Sockdologer was a very good channel, this baby presented at first glance the most channel-less looking job I've seen next to Lava Falls. So I went on along the cliff further downstream so as to get a better view, and then the set-up becomes clearer. But what a confusion of holes! However, by going right down the tongue, and bearing slightly left in the big water it could be made very nicely. Frankly though, it was tough and I was only too glad to get it behind us. We shove off in the WEN 1:00 PM. Again we lay low in an advantageous position in order to watch the other boats come thru. Five minute intervals. Both boys make a good run, and I have never seen a more relieved looking person than Wayne. After he's been dreading these two babies, and he certainly turned in a fine run in both. From now on Wayne will really be ready to take them on!

LUNCH. BOULDER CREEK. Same spot as last year. Plan to lay low here until time to get into Bright Angel trail. Want to get in around 4:30 to 5:00. Bruce is 13 years old today, and there will be a birthday cake and all for him at Phantom Ranch. We came booming thru Sockdologer and Grapevine singing lustily: "Happy Birthday to you," supplemented with one or two other songs. The front boat seems to be a noisy and carefree one. I work on my left eye which has been sore since Nancoweep. A sty. Ed Hudson is very disgusted at my lackadaisical treatment.

EIGHTY-THREE MILE RAPID. And is this a round customer! By George there are some real whirlpools here. Water is fast and tosses us about. In fact this five miles into Bright Angel is marked by a number of really rough and ready pieces of water. In high water no need to look over, but they must all be handled carefully.

BRIGHT ANGEL TRAIL. Several people on hand to see us come in. About half a mile upstream stood Harry Aleson and one Dot McLaughlin! I kept going but was obligated to have Wayne pick them up and bring them on down. Also were met on shore by U.S.G.S. couple, Mr. and Mrs. Talvity. We pull the boats high up on shore after taking out personal luggage, pose for a group picture. We stop in at Talvitys and have ice water. My it's good. On to Phantom where we are greeted by Emma and Phil, Virginia Opie.[24] I wash up, then get my log ready to mail to Doris. Dr. Bryant and Mrs. Bryant will be down tomorrow instead of tonight for the birthday dinner. Am sorry I mixed up the original plans which called for their being here tonight, but I did think they would like to ride downstream a ways with us. A very grand dinner as guests of Neill and Bruce. I make several calls, one to Harry Franse to get our news story out. We find that Harry F. saw the upset but didn't positively identify it as an upset. So we decide to not disclose details of the upset in order to not unnecessarily worry folks at home, particularly Wayne's folks. Go down and check the boats. Tired. Bed feels good. Had some mail, which ended a swell day perfectly.

JULY 21

AT PHANTOM RANCH. Have 140 cards to address and write messages on, so directly after breakfast I sit down to have at them. By noon I'm really

Sorting supplies at Phantom Ranch

tired of the job. However, after lunch I take to them again, and by dinner time am thru—but tired! In meantime Oty, Garth and Ed Olsen have gone to South Rim. Ed has an infected ear and wants to see a doctor. Others left here mostly lie around and sleep. About five o'clock Dr. and Mrs. Bryant walk in, accompanied by a Mr. and Mrs. Bauer from N.Y. The Bauers have been by Mexican Hat and bring messages etc. We have a fine visit, then go into dinner. After dinner we all go down and sit around the swimming pool. About 9:00 PM Garth comes in from the Rim, followed shortly thereafter by Oty and Ed. Singing and talking continues, then to bed!

July 22

AT PHANTOM RANCH. After breakfast we go out and sort the food and get it into the proper sacks. It's quite a load, particularly with so many fruit juices. The Bryants, Marstons, and Mr. Bauer take off up Bright Angel Creek to go fishing. Take a lunch. Upon sacking the food we hitch up "Old Supai" to the garbage wagon and haul our supplies down to the river. Load the boats. Then Wayne, appearing as a Roman chariot driver takes off with Mrs. Bauer in the cart. We follow along and round the first corner to find that the cart had almost fallen apart and Wayne making emergency repairs. We get a drink of cold water at government cabin, then get back to Phantom about right for lunch. After lunch Neill and I go over details and information which he plans to use in working up a story or so for different magazines. In the course of talk get on chinning, which results in our going

"Old Supai" hauling supplies at Phantom Ranch, Wayne McConkie at the reins

out and trying our luck. Neill is one of the few persons I've see who could chin 14 or 15 times right off-hand.

Write letters, loaf; after a very fine dinner (we had dinner for lunch too!) we sit out in front of the lodge and talk. The Bryants are going to ride as far as Pipe Springs tomorrow, also the Bauers. They are very much thrilled at the prospect. Harry Aleson will go as far as Hermit Falls with us and then walk up the old Hermit Trail. In the course of the evening I attempt to speed things up by assisting in computing the various bills owed by our party. My perfectly remarkable series of miscalculations earn me the title of: "Counter!" And so to bed!

JULY 23

Breakfast at Phantom Ranch. I call Harry Franse reporting our leaving and giving him the probably time of our arrival at Granite Falls so he and others can watch us shoot the rapids.

9:00 AM. EMBARK. Going overland are most of the party. On deck of the WEN is Dr. Bryant. In bow, Mrs. Bryant. Deck of MEXICAN HAT

II, Mr. Bauer. Deck of JOAN, Mrs. Bauer. We hit the first riffle, pass quite a crowd assembled on right bank to see us shoot next "rapid," and are quickly underway. Water is around 17,000 feet and choppy. Give Doc a good ducking. Despite the fact, though, Dr. Bryant keeps his camera clicking. Only too soon we pull in at mouth of Pipe Springs. Our passengers on this stretch are extremely grateful for the ride and can't express their gratitude enough. Mrs. Bryant arranges to have our party, that is those who will be on South Rim after trip come to dinner on August 5, followed by a showing of the '41 pictures at the campfire afterwards.

PIPE SPRINGS. We send mail up with the Bryants. They are mailing 75 of my cards. We're off!

HORN CREEK RAPID. Arrive in good time. Harry Aleson riding bow of JOAN. We're back again at the serious business of rapid running, and here we have a real one. A short survey convinces me that the channel used last year over on the left side is best. No passengers in this one. I take off in WEN. Easy run; MEXICAN HAT II good shape too. Anxious moment as Wayne almost doesn't get over far enough to miss big middle hole. But he makes a good recovery and comes through in fine shape. This is a dangerous rapid if a miscalculation occurs. Feels good to have big water under boats again. The take-offs from a lay-over point are always tiresome and a strain.

GRANITE FALLS RAPID. We really have something here! A wild confusion of big water and a terrific current. Plays the right wall, big hole near bottom. Leaving the big hole the current heads into an island, the only good channel being to the left. In '40 Dell started down the right channel and had to line his boat back up. This is a toughy and promises a very real thrill. I take off in WEN at 12:00 noon. This rapid is at mouth of Monument Creek and is sometimes called Monument Creek Rapid. What a ride! I slide a bit to the right to miss a big hole, come up on a wave and get tossed off to the right, into and out of a cove! I swing around a bit then head the bow into the big water, working toward the wall and thus missing the big hole at foot. Pass the hole I swing the stern around and start pulling so as to get left of island. Miss it, drop down a riffle and beach in cove on left. Least water I have ever taken on in GRANITE FALLS! Tie up and bail. I waved as I rounded island and wonder if that was taken as "come ahead" signal by Pres. Finish bailing and clamber up on rock point above the boat and look upstream to see Pres standing up in boat, approaching island, and straightening his left oarlock. As he gets it straight and starts to pull he is swept onto rock at head of island! Struck hard. Commences to bail. Then wiggles boat. Then for some reason or other just sits. I bellow at him to bail, but of course he can't hear me. After considerable bailing the boat swings free, taps another rock or two, and finally is brought into berth close to the WEN. It seems that at the hole, Pres was thrown from seat, fell half out of the boat, but made it back in somehow. Took on a real pile of water. I look for Wayne to come down to discuss the situation with me as this rapid is

Neill Wilson and Bruce Wilson

obviously having a field holiday with us. Later I learn that he didn't see Pres make his wild run so that helped! At any rate, in a very few minutes Wayne came down riding them high, wide, and handsome! He took a trouncing in the big hole but came through perfectly, missed the island and was soon beached. Anchorage bad here, so we decide to drop down to Hermit Falls for lunch.

HERMIT FALLS. CAMP. Same proposition as I've seen it from first trip. Easy to run as we had it low water of '40, but above 15,000 feet no way to miss the series of almost explosion waves in main channel. One of these big waves along could probably be run, but not in conjunction with two others. We will line. LUNCH. Harry has a few things with him also makes tea to carry up on his hike to the Rim. I write a letter to Mother and Doris on the back of a fruit can label, and gave them to Harry to take up, put in an envelope and mail. Incidentally, with a twenty pound pack, Harry made it up to Rim in 5½ hours! Some hiking! After lunch we decide to stay here overnight as we have water and a good camp. Ate lunch on South bank of Hermit, but will have main meals same spot as '40 on north bank.

2:30-3:45 we tote equipment to foot of rapid where it can be reloaded in the morning.

This crew worked well together on the lining and we really did a fast and efficient job of going thru. Bruce slept thru the lining operations so he is delegated to get wood for fires. Clouding up a bit and a mild wind is blowing, but no sand drifting. Bad surge at foot of rapid so we had to take

Ed Hudson

the boats clear out of the water, and build sort of piers under them. Wayne has gotten a lot of confidence from this day's run. He should! He's run some real toughies today. He'll do beautifully from here on. Everyone really tired tonight and bed is most welcome. Harry gave me a blanket sheet that was left behind at Bright Angel by a camper and it felt good under my hips. I just can't seem to get used to the hard bed. Trouble sleeping, despite the fact that this trip to me has been the easiest from standpoint of navigation that I've ever made.

JULY 24

Up early and most of us feel a stiffness from yesterday's exertions. I slept without anything until about 3:00 AM, then a sheet. After breakfast toted the kitchen equipment and a few odds and ends to the boats. Pres had his stuff loaded in so we contrived to launch the MEXICAN HAT II load and all. Then Pres dropped downstream a ways as terrific shore lash here. Ed O. and Bruce went with Pres. Two of us held WEN while rest tossed in load. With great difficulty I store the equipment under hatches, as the WEN tossed and pitched. JOAN was a bit less of a problem, and we soon all were off and ready for the day's adventures.

BOUCHER RAPID. Land here on left to check tongue. O.K. We take off and have a fine big water ride to start the day with.

CRYSTAL RAPID. Land here for just a couple of minutes to check the tongue. Could easily run these by just looking over from the boat but there's a much higher safety margin in checking the tongue first and making sure it doesn't dive into a hole.

Stop to check this one as at first I thought it was SERPENTINE. This is wonderful riding thru this section to Bass Trail. Although I get much kidding as every little bit I seem to come to Serpentine Rapid!

SERPENTINE RAPID. Quite a rapid and gives a plenty zippy ride. Not hard to handle though must take proper channel.

SHINUMO CREEK. CAMP. First landed upstream in a cove but soon found we could get safe and handy anchorage at mouth of creek. Have lunch on south side of Shinumo in cave. Wet the sand down and makes nice spot. At this creek Dr. Bryant wants to learn if there are trout, so after lunch Oty and Wayne leave to make a check. Oty is soon fishing for catfish, and lands 9 or 10, also a big carp. No trout. Upstream, Wayne, Neill and Bruce go over a mile but see no trout. Do find a small dead burro [and] kill a Grand Canyon rattler about 20–24" long. Afternoon spent mainly in loafing, though I checked over the topog maps. Wood very scarce here and cooking was difficult. As a result the fish weren't ready until after dessert was served! Beautiful moonlight night and everyone seemed to have a good night's sleep. No bailing can in the WEN today so we had quite a time bailing with only buckets.

JULY 25
A good start this morning.

WALTHENBERG RAPID. This doesn't look like a passenger rapid, but we're going to take them as there's just all water under us. It's a wild and rough ride and plenty of fun. All come thru in fine shape.

ELVES CHASM. Swell ride from Walthenberg to here. Even the little rapids packed a real punch, and most of the rapids were characterized by sinks and whirlpools at the bottom. Strangely and luckily enough the WEN hasn't taken on any water in any of the rapids today up to here! We walk up to our register placed here last year and find the can several feet from where we left it, the plank that was on top of the can tossed to one side, but the leather notebook unhurt though lying open nearby. We all sign the register then pile rocks, etc. on the can so that it would take quite some strong sheep or burro to disturb it. Neill is going to send me a Sierra Club copper can for the register can and I will then hang it from a drilled hole in the wall here. This place makes a good spot for a Grand Canyon boat trip registering point.[25]

LUNCH. Right. Head of FOSSIL RAPID. Climb up to top of talus slope and get some good shade. I break a jar of peanut butter on way up. I no longer eat peanut butter as I found it caused me to get sickish after taking salt tablets.

128 MILE CREEK [rapid]. Goes to left wall. We're back in the Granite again.

BEDROCK RAPID. Rapids above here really rough and tossed us around plenty. Makes for really fine boating, though. Bedrock is still a toughy and is one to handle very carefully. I decide no passengers are to run with the exception of Garth who I will take in my boat. Am trying to divide up the thrills amongst the bunch as well as possible. We will run 1,2,3, on this one and I take off. Pres and I both slip off tongue to right in good shape, but Wayne falls off seat, and only a very speedy recovery keeps him from getting unpleasantly close to the big rock in the middle of the river. Rest of crowd get around overland in good shape and soon join us.

DUBENDORFF RAPID. Here it is! The almost most famous of them all. And what a ride in sight! Big water and an awfully fast current. I have long wanted to take a passenger thru this one and as it's Neill's turn to ride I suggest that I may, after looking over, be willing to take him. He declines in favor of Otis, who, he says, is more out for the thrill than he, and as he got him to take trip feels he should give him first chance. Therefor I decide to let Pres bring Neill thru, if, after Oty and I run thru I feel it is safe for Pres to bring a passenger. I arrange to signal with one hand if Pres is to come alone, two if he is to bring Neill. Oty and I off in WEN at 3:55 PM. Have a grand ride in the big water. Pres comes thru with Neill in good shape too. Wayne, alone, makes the best ride of all, but just at the bottom a hole opens up and he really goes out of sight. Seems like forever before he comes on thru. He really got a boat load of water! Pres and I went over same spot, but had smoothish channel. Wayne says that he was on a wave, and suddenly before his eyes the water opened up and formed a great enormous hole! Wayne's descriptions are really something. Back at Lava Canyon Wayne declared that he really could see gravel at bottom of hole that upset them.

Getting stormy. Small rapid here, but quite good sized hole just to right of tongue. I slip thru to left, as does Wayne, but Pres and his passengers drop right into the hole and come close to getting into real trouble. Take on lots of water, and I never before have seen such quantities of water coming out via buckets at such a high rate of speed. Several reasons for the mishap were given. At any rate it was a bad piece of navigation and could well have caused a serious accident.

TAPEATS CREEK. CAMP. We first land at head of rapid and discharge passengers, then Wayne and I drop onto bottom at camp tie-up spot. Pres comes thru but hits another good sized hole, getting lots of water aboard. The other hole was supposed to have been to scare his passengers, but this one coming on top of that makes me wonder. At any rate it's a swell camp here and though a storm drives us to shelter after first landing it soon clears off and dinner is under way. After dinner Wayne and Otis, later joined by Garth go fishing in Tapeats Creek. I write in my journal, Pres boils out dish towels. Last night couldn't find the "butter," thought it was left at Hermit, but tonight I got the sand out of my eyes and discover it tucked away in my stern hatch. Spectacular lighting effect. Dark sky. Canyon almost somber. Brilliant lighting on two big towers up near Powell Plateau. Wayne and Otis come in with 10 RAINBOW TROUT. Five apiece. Garth one, the second

Ed Olson

largest at 13". They ranged from 10" to Wayne's champ at 14." And so to bed after a very full and enjoyable day. A grand cool night to sleep.

JULY 26

Up this morning to a grand breakfast of Rainbow trout. They are delicious, even tho we are almost out of salt. Will try to get some at miner's cache at 164 [Mile] canyon, or else at cowboy camp at Parashont Wash. We have all discussed making this camp a longer stop on future trips and undoubtedly that is the thing to do. Now that I know the Canyon so well can travel with less margin from here on down as there really is no water to bother us. After breakfast Oty offers to coach me a bit on the art of catching trout. We go over to Tapeats and from the word go I see that I have more than a lot to learn. Soon do get a strike, but naturally I get no more than the experience. But from it all I do get an idea of how to go about it, and with quite a bit of practice might catch one. Salmon eggs seem to be a sure bet, along with grasshoppers. Tho flies too will work. Oty also outlines a drying-carrying plan so that a good catch could be taken along for a meal or two below. Oty catches one more trout this morning.

GRANITE NARROWS CAVE.[26] Pull in here and climb up into the rather large cave on the right. Big and dry, with floor covered with rat dung.

DEER CREEK FALLS. Decide to have lunch here, and big helpings of Kool-Aid. But first pictures are taken, then I try to inveigle everyone

Otis Marston and Garth Marston

into going thru the water to the wall behind. This water is really chilly and pounds the top of your head in its 125' descent. No takers. So, in order to carry the story back to Doris, who, in 1940 kidded me because I wouldn't go under, I go on thru the falls! Coming out am inspired with the idea of everyone going under and standing, the first one out being stuck with milkshakes for the crowd at Boulder City. Away we go. Pres is first out. This is a really beautiful spot and such grand water.

We pass the old cliff ruins on the left just below here at Mile 137¼.

Mile 138. This is the rapid I spilled Doris in in 1940. It has no name, and so this trip I am applying the name: "DORIS RAPID." In low water this is a meany, but in high water very simple to run.

KANAB CREEK. Water in creek low and a bit cloudy from rains. This is the canyon that marked the end of the 2nd Powell Expedition.[27] Funny, whenever I come down on this canyon I have a very peculiar hallucination. It seems that the Powell party is just actually leaving here, and I see the men just disappearing into the Canyon, casting final looks at the river over their shoulders. We waste little time looking over the rapid. It has the usual high water channel, lots of holes and big waves but very easy to run. I take the WEN thru standing up to handle it all the way.

Beautiful day. A bit cloudy, pleasantly cool, and the lighting effects great. At Deer Creek Falls Garth trades places with Ed Hudson in order for Ed to get certain types of pictures by riding the bow. His weight in the bow is more than noticeable in handling the WEN.

Deer Creek Falls

UPSET RAPID. And now *here* is a whizzer! The tongue drives right into a very good sized hole, and the only chance to miss it lies in slipping to the right. But this seems more than a poor chance as the lateral drive towards the hole is terrific. I decide to try to slip to the right, but actually plan that I will be swept inevitably into the hole. On this type hole I see no danger if it's hit head on so decide to take passengers. I keep Ed Hudson in the WEN with some misgivings as his weight will not give me a chance to pull over. And do we run smack dab into the hole! Go right thru with a complete drenching. I pull in easily to shore near the reverse wave, but on they come. Can't make the landing, so pull in on rocks downstream a ways.

Comes Wayne! Wayne is loaded very light, and tho he pulls hard to miss hole goes right on in slicker than a whistle. The big waves stops the JOAN dead in her tracks. Garth is swept over the side, retaining a precarious grip on the lifeline. Finally the JOAN comes on thru the wave, Wayne grabs Garth's leg and hoist him back on deck and they're off. I push on out to mid-stream to save Wayne pulling in and away we go! Some ride!

Day is darkish now, rain threatening. I am apprehensive that the Havasu Creek will have become clouded with storm waters. It's nice boating in the cool, tho. This is one of the most beautiful sections of the Canyon.

SINYALA RAPID. Left oar turning in my hand and my hand is plenty sore. Wayne is running in #2 position today in order to get the experience and to get a chance to have the fun of watching the boat behind coming thru. We always in the front boat lay in wait at the foot of a rapid like a flock of vultures ready to pounce on any morsel of humor contributed by a boat in an eddy. No sign of the MEXICAN HAT II. They are dropping behind much to my annoyance. Tomorrow will have Wayne back in #3 to kind of ride herd a bit.

As Wayne and I run around a rock in midstream the MEXICAN HAT II finally shows up with Oty at the oars. Was really getting worried as the landing at Havasu is tricky and they would surely have swept on by. To cap the climax the MEXICAN HAT II goes around wrong side of the rock. In no uncertain terms I instruct Pres to take over the oars and keep in line. Perhaps if I hadn't been so dead tired I wouldn't have been quite so obviously touchy—but on the other hand it's the small things like this that can bring on real disaster in a hurry.

HAVASU. Pull into the cove at mouth of canyon and row on up thru the narrows to the foot of the first falls. What a sight! Water is its regular turquoise blue. Fish jumping and swimming all around. Catfish, tho at first some thought they were trout. We pull on out of Canyon and, just as it starts to rain tie up the boats.[28] This is hard to do as the anchorage here is really tough. By securing the WEN, then hitching the other boats to the WEN we make a satisfactory tying. And then it rains! It's soon over and the boys have gotten wood for dinner and we soon are eating. Food tastes good. Thunder and lightening very spectacular. Expected to see high cliff waterfalls, but the exceptionally dry top country conditions squelched that. Oty has one trout left which he shares with me—it's good! While hunting for wood the boys found a high ledge with sand on it, so all of us but Ed Olsen repair to it for the night. Middle of the night have a very light sprinkle, but it stops immediately, the skies clear, and we have a beautiful moon. I go down once to check the boats. Have had a better bed, but sleep pretty well despite it.

July 27

Up early and glad to quit the bed. Believe me, next year we'll all have air mattresses. Take our time having breakfast as want to stay here until at least noon in order to get pictures of Havasu Canyon. Tell Ed Olsen and Oty that they can run 164 [Mile] Rapid below here and they are both anxious to get there and have at it. This is surely a fine balanced group. For me this has been the smoothest and best trip of them all. What apprehensions I may have had before we started were quickly dissolved. And now, if only we can make good connections for the trip across Lake Mead. Most of the fellows go ahead up canyon via overland route. Upon finishing my diary I join Garth and Bruce, Pres joins us, and we swim up thru the narrow and work our way up over the lower falls. There the boys slide down the water chutes and we all have lots of fun splashing back and forth. Rest of crowd show up, and Wayne takes all cameras overland while rest of us all swim down the canyon and to the boats.

We eat lunch, then wait around so as to get a sun shot in order to get the correct time. All watches have stopped. A great long discussion of proper technique to use in getting time from solar shadow ensues, but it finally boils down to simple terms and we are convinced of our accuracy finally.

Shove off from HAVASU at 1:05 PM. And is it hot! Heat most depressing. I notice it more than usual and finally take to going overboard to cool off.

HUNDRED AND SIXTY FOUR MILE RAPID. First we go up to the miner's cache on ledge up from mouth of canyon in the hopes of finding some salt. No luck. Few matches, tea, etc. It's hot. We return to the boats and after coaching the rapid runners a bit I shove off in the WEN. Oty comes thru in the MEXICAN HAT II next, gets swung around once, but comes on in fine shape. Ed Olsen comes next and makes a fine run. On we go.

Just below Cataract Canyon. Right bank. SEVEN MOUNTAIN SHEEP.[29] They are quite a sight.

FERN GLEN CANYON. CAMP. Land here as it looks to be a good possibility for water and shade. Pres, Oty and Garth stay to tie up the boats, and we leave expecting them to follow along. At mouth of canyon I spot a note in a jar in a rock cairn. I later make a copy of it and take original along. Will write the party leaving it.

> Jan. 4, 1932. We have explored the North side of the Colorado River from the Hell's Trail [I believe they mean Red Slide Canyon—NDN] to this point. All of its side canyons. We have found one vein of white gold quartz. But the things we find in the driftwood and scenery are by far the most interesting up to date. We are out of supplies now. We will have to climb out and find some meat as there is no life along the river.
> Signed: M. Johnson, J.L. Bybee, Glendale, Utah, U.S.A.[30]

Up canyon a little ways we find a small seep. This encourages us to go further and we soon come to a nice little trickle of quite cool water. It's very brackish tho with alkali. Altogether we go up some half mile until a waterfall impedes our progress. Take a dip in a cool pool of water then return to the boats. And find our friends still on the hot sandbar awaiting our return! They then go up the canyon while rest of us wait in shade for sun to go down and allow us to set up camp. There's a big window in limestone wall, up right hand side of canyon ¼ mile. Very interesting discussion during dinner of brokerage methods, etc. River here is about 350' in width. Red flood marks on bar shows a drop of 2' since the flood that hit us at Nankweap. Clouds have rolled in again and a bit of a breeze is blowing, assuring us of a cool night to sleep. Just before going to bed lit a biggish driftwood pile which illuminated the canyon walls beautifully. However, we didn't bask long in its glow as everyone was sleepy and ready

Nevills at the oars

for sleep. Last awake was Wayne and me. We talked—rapids!

JULY 28

Wind blew constantly during the night and we awoke this morning to find ourselves about sanded in. High light clouds in the sky this morning, suggesting possible shower for this afternoon. A big day lies before us as today we have to get past Lava Falls.

RED SLIDE CANYON. On right side up some twenty feet above river spot old boat. Galvanized bottom. Dory type. 14' long, 30" bottom, 42" beam. Oarlocks beginners type bolted to sides. Iron stays to hold sides in place. Nearby a piece of ¾" X 30" drill steel. I get the impression that this boat has been brought down the trail here and assembled here for prospecting purposes. One side is a bit rotted, but with a bit of work the boat could be used in an emergency.

LAVA FALLS. This is definitely a lining job, tho how I would like to take this baby on in the high water. A twenty-two foot boat could do it with more than a reasonable chance to land right side up, though the bad water below would make the attempt very dangerous. At any rate we immediately set to work to carry the equipment and pile it in separate piles at foot of drop to which we will line. By 10:30 AM this is done and we start lining the JOAN. This is the toughest channel to line thru that I've struck on my two other lining jobs here. Too little water thru the passageways and it means hard tugging and pulling. Hard on men and boats. Only injury sustained in the operations was a banged-up knee for Wayne.

JOAN 10:30 AM–11:50 AM. Loaded up JOAN and ran her below in cove for anchorage. Walked back. Tough lining. Decide to experiment in trying to carry the other two boats around but this is quickly shown to be a highly impractical idea.

WEN 11:50 AM–1:15 PM. Taking too long.

MEXICAN HAT II 1:15 PM–2:40 PM. It's over! We all gather in cove plenty tired, hot and hungry. Bread has turned moldy so we are switching to Rye Crisp. Make little ceremony of eating so as to be on our way. At least the clouds have now come up and there's a cool breeze. By checking the direction of the Canyon we have determined that at Whitmore Wash we should have a North-South canyon trend thus gaining shade on right bank.

WHITMORE WASH. CAMP. As we pull in here see 3 adult and 2 young mountain sheep. They follow on downstream a ways and keep in view a good half hour. I believe some good pictures of them were taken. Wind is blowing here and the sand drifting quite badly. I spot a cove and soon get a good camp rigged up. Wood plentiful and we have a very good dinner. Tired. Marstons and Wilsons erect a drift fence for their beds. It worked all right until during the night the wind shifted. Ed Olsen had the same experience. Wayne, Pres, and I slept back in the catclaws and kept completely free from the sand. To bed at 10:30. Pres and I sat in the WEN and were too lazy to get up to go to bed. Our thoughts are beginning to turn to Lake Mead and our arrival. Am determined to bring Doris next year so she too can have the sport of running this high water thru the Canyon.

JULY 29

Had a good nights's sleep last night. Believe I am beginning to get broken in to the hard sand! Today Oty will ride with me in order to get pictures of the two boys. Neill rides with Wayne. Ed Hudson with Pres. Late start today but only 16 miles to go. Plenty warm.

WILLOW CAMP. Fine camping spot. Along here we are getting trick pictures of the two boys, including shots of buckets of water being thrown at them. Garth at oars.

PARASHONT WASH. Go up to camp of Roy Wood of Cedar City that we found last year and are lucky to find some salt in a Postum can. I take all but a little and leave a note thanking him. Will return some next year. Also here is dynamite, fuse and caps which I suspect he uses to dynamite fish.

Mile 199. See can perched on stick high on right bank. We land to investigate and find old cowboy camp. The can is wired to the stick, is full of holes and obviously has been used as a dipper to catch fish.

At Mile 202 I pull in on right thinking it's SPRING CANYON, as it certainly resembles it. Find it isn't and ready to go right on. In meantime Wayne comes in close to rocks and as Neill stands up to fend off or make landing he falls overboard, camera and all. Nothing hurt, tho later on camera is gummed up a bit by case sweating.

SPRING CANYON. CAMP. Tie up and go up canyon to our last year's camp and find table as we left it and shade. Eat lunch. Then all disappear to relax. I see that camp has been visited at least once since last year. In fact I write note and leave in jar for next visitors. Wayne goes in cave just below and stirs up a domestic buck sheep! Drum (oil) that was across wash last year is now in cave. Water in canyon is fairly cool and of quite good quality. Afternoon is spent laying around. I work on my notes and maps, then too lie down. It's a constant battle with the red ants, tho. All in all I find this a long afternoon, as do the others. It brings home to mind even more the attractiveness of a longer layover at Tapeats Creek. Ed Olsen's ear is paining him badly again and he's really suffering. After dinner and before going to bed we all swim around down by the boats. A

beautiful night but bugs and red ants a nuisance. For some reason or other wasn't at all sleepy and spent quite a few wakeful hours.

JULY 30

On to Diamond Creek today! Ed Olsen's ear much better and he's 100% improved.

205 MILE RAPID. This rapid always comes as a surprise as it has no reputation yet is a tough little number. Holes, big water, and quite a turn at the bottom. I pick out the channel, then at 8:00 drop thru with the WEN, landing in big eddy on left. Neill then brings the MEXICAN HAT II thru in fine style making a good landing here too. Comes then Ed Hudson in the JOAN. He does fine until the lower end of the rapid where he lets his bow get swung around towards the wall and loses control. He is swept in sideways against the wall with an almost directly impinging current holding him there. I'm afraid of his being rolled over and motion him to sit tight as I go over to land below him and get to him over the top of the rocks. I land and am just about to him with a big surge wave cuts him loose and away he goes. I tell him to land foot next rapid or riffle below. I have to do some tremendous rowing in order to get across river and back upstream, in order

to pick up the gang. I like to give everyone a crack at running rapids but it gives me the willies to see these fine boats getting banged around. Wayne wishes to exercise his own judgement in matter of which boat he will ride in as we are quite overloaded now that the JOAN is below. I end the debate by ordering him into the WEN. We quickly are with the JOAN, passengers redistributed, and on our way.

GRANITE PARK. We land here in order to get a picture of the two boys running some fairly big water. It is arranged that I will ride the cockpit, concealing myself with a preserver held up on the left side that will be exposed to the cameras. The other two boats go over to the island in order to get a good shooting position. First we are all very amused by Bruce's concern over thinking he will have to run the boat. Everything set, and off we go. Garth makes a nice run and we are quickly joined by the other boats and on our way.

TWO HUNDRED SEVENTEEN MILE RAPID. At it again! Going to let the fellows try this one out too. It's the last major rapid in the Canyon. I take Pres thru with me, as passenger in the WEN. I give him a boat ride as I shove right into the big water. Land bottom good shape and next comes Otis in MEXICAN HAT II. Makes fine run and landing. Ed Olsen then comes in JOAN but doesn't make landing and gets caught head of next riffles in the rocks. He lines back a ways, gets off, then joins us below.

LUNCH. Passengers walked from 217 to [Mile 218] where we are eating lunch. Everyone cools off with a swim. After lunch Bruce gets sick on salt tablets. After lunch Garth and Ed Olsen exchange places so Ed can get pictures. He soon takes over the oars from Neill and what a pace he sets. We really take off, despite the fact that there are a lot of mean eddies and whirlpools thru this section.

DIAMOND CREEK. At 220 Mile Canyon on right we spotted cairn and flag left by Harry Aleson in May when he got to that point by motor. Too hot to stop, so went right on by. It's hot here at Diamond Creek and the afternoon is spent in building a small dam and lying in the pool thereby created. Flies are miserable here and a real nuisance at mealtimes. After dinner I perform the rites of initiation on Pres and Wayne, thus having them ready to assist in the general initiation scheduled for the morning.

JULY 31

At DIAMOND CREEK. Up fairly early and flies are hard at it again, tho during the night they retired. Stock has been around here and that explains it. It's cooler this morning as a few clouds are around overhead. After breakfast we get out supplies to check over. Want to hold initiation until good light for pictures. Get all the food sorted, meals planned for Lake Mead, etc. We then get the scene laid for the ceremony of induction and members are called, one by one in the following order: #1 Otis, #2 Neill, #3 Ed Hudson, #4 Ed Olsen, #5 Bruce, #6 Garth. On all but Ed Olsen, Wayne wielded a thorough and powerful paddle. Ed Hudson needed more pictures of his initiation

"River Rat" initiation ceremony, Diamond Creek: (standing, left to right) Pres Walker, Wayne McConkie, Norman Nevills

and blessed if Wayne didn't give him *another* good whack! Pres tapped Ed Olsen. His delivery was terrific and the paddle broke! A one inch board! Pres and assistants are now scouring pots and pans, while Wayne and I scrub and clean our boats. Then Pres comes over and cleans his. Just before lunch we congratulated Pres on his 30th birthday and I gave him some bathing trunks which I had brought for the occasion. Lunch to accompaniment of swattings at flies! Glad when lunch was thru! Afternoon spent in loafing— tho the flies, bugs and red ants made rest almost impossible. Ed Olsen and Wayne took off up Canyon. Garth and I climbed peak north side of Diamond Creek. At 1:10 PM seven P-38s[31] came over flying low and fast. It's cloudy and I'm afraid of Doris running into storms on her way over to meet us at Boulder Dam. This morning I trimmed Otis' beard and it proved quite a workout for both of us. However I think it's quite a creditable job and that he looks fine. Ed Hudson borrowed my razor and gave himself a sort of country doctor trim and shave. All in all it shows we are conscious of our impending arrival at Lake Mead. All in all the day dragged very slowly. After dinner I made fudge which wasn't too bad considering the manner in which it was made. Did a bit of clothes washing today, and now, tonight it would seem that we're all ready for bed and rarin' to go in the morning.

August 1

Embark from Diamond Creek at 7:10 AM. Had a grand night's sleep and everyone up bright and early. Very stormy looking this morning. We're glad

to be under way again this morning tho hate to see the trip end. This has been a fine party and undoubtedly the best group to ever run the Colorado. Away we go and I drop into edge of hole near foot of rapid to start the day out right. We are much disgusted to see the other two boats "nigger"[32] on us!

TRAVERTINE FALLS. Zippy going to here and we're having a boat ride. Much singing going on in the WEN, and we're running rapids in every conceivable manner to have fun, this our last day on the river. Pictures of falls taken, also, Oty gets shot of two boys taking off and landing the WEN. On our final takeoff Bruce falls in the river!

232 MILE RAPID. Pres hits a rock in bottom of this one. This makes the second rock for Pres. Wayne hits one in coming in to land at Boulder Creek. Ed Hudson hits wall at 217. The WEN has a clean bill of health. These rapids have a wicked zip to them thru here and plenty of big water.

234 MILE RAPID. As we drop down on this one I spot Harry Aleson's boat, *UP COLORADO* anchored below first drop on left. I attempt to drop over to him but big lateral wave sets me back in channel. I slip out near foot, but wave other two boats on. We get anchored, then I go overland, meeting Harry a hundred yards or so upstream. Exchange greetings, then agree to meet on down at Bridge Canyon.

BRIDGE CANYON—HEAD LAKE MEAD. Arrive here to the minute, day, and hour as last year! Harry soon shows up, and we clamber aboard his boat to go back up and see him try to get up 234 RAPID. Finally get up there, then Harry tries it out. Can't get up over last drop tho makes a quite thrilling attempt. He pulls into eddy, I get on bow—and do I get a ride! I find it very thrilling and quite an experience. Otis, Garth, then Bruce tries it out. Bruce gets the wildest ride! In meantime Wayne has caught a big carp weighing around six pounds with his bare hands! Finally finish here, drop

Harry Aleson in his powerboat *Up Colorado*

below, pick up rest of gang, then return to Bridge Canyon. We drift thru Bridge Canyon Rapid, Harry ties onto us and we're off to the engineer's camp, left side, Mile 238½. It seems that Pierce's Ferry is closed, but Harry has arranged for us to have dinner at the engineers camp at 1:00 PM.

Pass a drilling crew getting here and call greetings.[33] Are greeted here by a Mr. Whipple, surveyor. Air cooled tents, ice water—showers! The meal we have later on is really something. Not just because we were hungry, but it really was an excellent meal. We then arrange to have dinner too! So we repair to the tents to while away the time. After so long Mr. Whipple very kindly takes us for a spin in a peculiar powered scow called the *SURE SINK*. There's an old Mississippi River bayou boat here, and a couple of Alaska-type poling boats. All in all it's as weird a collection of river boats as to ever be seen in one spot. I can't help but feel that our three boats stand the comparison more than well. Henry Hart, old timer on the lower river admires our boats, tho frankly confesses that that upper canyon water is not for him. It's funny, I've run into so often these old timers who have spent their lives along the Colorado, and they nearly all have an almost superstitious fear of trying out the rapids.

SEPARATION CANYON. Our plans for a group picture don't quite jell, tho there's enough light for Ed Husdon to try a still. I hope it turns out as this is *the* place for a group picture.

At Spencer Canyon we change to Pacific time.

Harry Aleson towing boats out on Lake Mead

LOST CREEK. CAMP. Here we make camp, as we did in 1940. Funny thing tho, the canyon of Lost Creek in 1940 entered the river on downstream side, whereas now it's on the upriver side. Fine big bar, tho several of us are suffering from overeating at the engineer's camp at Bridge Canyon City. Ed Hudson is particularly affected by the meals and gets up several times during the night with a dysentery.

AUGUST 2

We decide to drop on down to Quartermaster Canyon for breakfast. Arriving there I recognize this to be the camp we made in 1938. On the navigation maps it's called WATERFALLS CANYON. In '38 it took us a day to make here from Mile 241 or thereabouts. Fine breakfast, considerably aided by flapjacks a la Aleson. Again we take off. Around noon we meet Jack Hudson in a marine landing boat, heading up to the engineer's camp with supplies. We have a swell visit, plus some ice water. It's good to see Jack again, and he told me he had hoped to tow us from the engineer's camp to Pierce's Ferry!

On we go, eating Rye Crisp, cheese and grapefruit juice for lunch. Just past Emery Falls we meet the Tours boat piloted by Fred Hilty, but it doesn't stop, Fred thinking Harry was going right on. We pull into a cove on right to look for turtles. Ed Olsen gets final shot of me with cowboy hat on, the final shot for his cowboy Pete series. The turtle hunt proves fruitless and we again take off. It's really hot! Pres and I ride on top of two luggage

(Left to right) Norman Nevills, Ed Olson, Bruce Wilson, Otis Marston, Neill Wilson, Garth Marston, Pres Walker, Ed Hudson, Wayne McConkie

compartments at stern, Oty, Neill, and Wayne on seat. Garth on seat. Ed Hudson in front compartment, Ed Olsen on the bow. Thus we ride clear across and on far side of Gregg Basin. Here we have dinner and determine to run all night. Taking off, I ride the WEN, Pres the MEXICAN HAT II, Wayne the JOAN. We've been averaging five or six miles an hour. Fumes from motor are bad. Only get lost once during night and then but for a few miles. Harry certainly turned in a remarkable piece of night navigation.

AUGUST 3

DAYLIGHT. I awaken to find us just pulling in to Sheep Island, 45 minutes from Boulder City! Awoke once in night while in Virgin Basin in roughish water to see the moonlit waters of Lake Mead. Other than that had a fine night's sleep.

We drink our fruit juices, bathe, shave and impatiently watch the clock. Arguments prevail as to the right time. We finally take off tho I protest that we're ahead of time.

Boulder Dam Landing! DORIS—Mrs. Walker—Marion and Edward Hudson. THE TRIP IS OVER.

My fourth trip is successfully completed. It's a thrill. I have a real gratitude to Neill Wilson who first made this trip possible, and to all of the gang who made this a success by their ever cheerful cooperation at all times.

'Nuff scurrying around getting breakfast, checking air transportation. All together for lunch. Ed Hudson has some stills we see. I am presented with a dish of mashed potatoes—with pepper for sand!

After seeing the Wilsons and Marstons off on the plane, get a haircut, then go down and load the boats. WEN on small trailer. MEXICAN HAT II on top of JOAN on big trailer.

Go to a show in the evening.

AUGUST 4

We leave early, taking Edith Lehnert with us. Since noon yesterday haven't seen Ed Olsen, and all are concerned.[34]

Lunch at Kingman. Dinner at Ashfork where we see papers telling of our arrival.

To bed at Williams.

AUGUST 5

Arrive South Rim 3:00 PM. Dinner with Bryants in evening. Rain descends on us at campfire so we all go over to Kolb Studio for the show. My '41 pictures are shown to a very responsive and appreciative audience.

AUGUST 6

Up early and away. Trouble with big trailer several times as bolts shear. But we get along well, roads aren't too bad, weather is on cool side—and we arrive Mexican Hat at 11:00 PM!

AUGUST 7

First thing we unload the equipment and put it away from the boats. Then off come the boats, they are turned over, await painting etc. for the next trip.

Pres and Wayne take off for home!

In afternoon a letter comes from Neill indicating his wish for material for his projected stories. Thus all day yesterday and today I've worked on these notes! 8:00 PM—and the END!

Salmon River,
July 11 to August 3, 1946
Snake River,
August 4 to August 17, 1946

The period 1942 through 1946 was one marked by world-shaking events, but besides shortages, newspaper accounts from the battlefields, and an occasional warplane passing overhead, life went on unchanged around Mexican Hat. Nevills's draft status was finally settled when he became the resident engineer for the US Geological Survey in Mexican Hat, responsible for taking samples of the San Juan River and measuring its flow several times a day, and sending in periodic reports. With his dependent family and age, he was at little risk of being drafted, although just in case he explored the possibilities of a commission in the military or defense work at one of the plants in Utah. The engineer post was an ideal job for him; his time was mostly his own to drill for water, perform upkeep on the lodge and houses, guide the rare tourist around Mexican Hat and Monument Valley, write long, detailed letters to a wide variety of correspondents all over the country, and type his journals. Doris home-schooled Joan and Sandra using the Calvert System, while Mae Nevills helped in the lodge.

Despite the wartime shortages, Nevills managed to run an occasional group of passengers down the San Juan, and kept his hand in with day trips from Bluff, Utah, to Mexican Hat. In May 1945 he took a trip on the Colorado from Moab through Cataract Canyon to Hite, Utah, with Dock Marston and found that he still had his big water skills. Bookings for river trips started coming in immediately after the war, helped along by articles in national magazines like Life, *which featured a story about Nevills and Badger Rapid in the October 23, 1944 issue;* Desert Magazine, *to become a frequent source of articles about Nevills Expedition after the war; and former passenger Neill Clark's, "Fast Water Man" in a May 1946 issue of the* Saturday Evening Post. *But publicity wasn't always positive, as an incident that occurred during the war proved.*

In 1944, 20th Century-Fox contracted with Nevills to take a newsreel camera and film of one of his trips. Nevills quickly agreed and the trip cast off on September 18, on low water. Not even ten miles into the trip, the boat carrying the camera and crew hung on a rock and capsized, throwing the whole outfit into the river. Lost was a $6,000 Bell and Howell Eymo camera, most of the exposed film, and other gear; the only thing saved was the tripod. Fortunately for Nevills, the camera was insured, and the crew came back the next year to complete the filming.

Oddly enough, for his first big trip after the war he chose not the Colorado or Green, but the Salmon River, the famed "River of No Return"—today known as the Main Salmon to distinguish it from the Middle Fork of the Salmon—and the equally famed Hells Canyon of the Snake River. It's unclear why he decided on trying out these new waters, but in the small world of river runners at the time, quite a number of people that he knew well, such as Bus Hatch, Buzz Holmstrom, and Zee Grant, had already run Idaho rivers. Marston, who was now completely given over to the river running bug and was acting as an informal booking agent for Nevills Expedition, had wide connections in the world of moneyed sportsman and had no doubt heard of the salmon and steelhead fishing along the Salmon. All of them must have urged him to give it a try. In making the decision, though, unlike the Colorado, Nevills was not going into a river-running vacuum; there was a long and rich heritage of boats and boaters in Idaho, dating back to the days of the mining booms that first brought whites into the area. Boating legends like Harry "Cap" Guleke and the Smith family had been on the Salmon and Snake long before Nevills ever set oar to water. So for a change, he was the inexperienced one, in the eyes of the old men and young who stood on the dance floors of their big scows and handled the long sweeps.

These rivers were very different in other ways, too; although they floated through over a hundred miles of wilderness, it seemed crowded to Nevills. There were two towns along the Salmon River—Salmon and Riggins—a bridge at Shoup, and a few roads and trails that led to isolated mining camps. After the emptiness of the Grand Canyon, the banks of the river appeared to be populated with miners and prospectors, homesteaders and their cabins, and the occasional hermit. During the trips, many people came and went, including newspapermen, local fishermen and ranchers, Doris and the children, and others. Nevills scoffed at the rapids on the Main Salmon as not being of the same caliber as those in Cataract and the Grand Canyon, but was surprised by the rapids on the Snake such as Buck Creek and Rush Creek; they gave nothing in difficult and fierceness away to the Big Drops or Hance, and Nevills had to use all his big water skills to successfully navigate them. Still, he was so impressed with the potential for commercial river running on the Snake and Salmon that he immediately made plans to return. Alas, as it turned out, he was never able to go back and establish himself there.

The trips generated great notice in Idaho and the region, and the stories were picked up by the wire services around the country. As usual, Nevills gave radio interviews from towns along the way. After the trip, however, he was to learn once again that all publicity was not necessarily good. In the July 24 issue of the Deseret News from Salt Lake City, a reporter named Hack Miller wrote a brief article responding to all the attention that Nevills had gotten that summer. Headlined "Not Much left for Nevill's [sic] River Expedition to Prove: Doc Frazier, Burg and Holmstrom ran 'The Snake' in tiny craft," the article was a mild rebuke of Nevills' claims of being a pioneer of small boats on the Snake and Salmon. Miller cited trips on those same rivers in the 1930s by Amos Burg, Buzz Holmstrom, and Russell Frazier,

to demonstrate that Nevills was not a pioneer. To add salt to the wound, a photo of Dr. Frazier was captioned "Dr. Russell G. Frazier . . . He Beat Mr. Neville [sic] To It, In River 'Test.'" Miller innocently sent Nevills a copy of the article, but the response was nothing like he must have imagined. Nevills was livid, and as soon as he saw the article, he responded in a long, scathing (and no doubt expensive) telegram that began, "Your letter and clipping of Aug. 24 received. Am disgusted with both," and went on from there to blast Miller in the roughest terms. After the trip, Nevills went to Salt Lake City and confronted Miller in his office in the Deseret News building. No doubt overwhelmed by the wrath his little piece had engendered, Miller stammered an apology in person and published a retraction in print.

The editor is, unfortunately, not well acquainted with the rivers of Idaho, so for the footnotes in this journal, he relied heavily on two of the standard works on Idaho river history: River of No Return by John Carrey and Cort Conley, and Snake River of Hells Canyon by John Carrey, Cort Conley, and Ace Barton. Together with other books by this same team, these volumes comprise a delightfully comprehensive and readable depiction of life along these mighty rivers. The editor is greatly indebted to these authors, and any errors of fact or interpretation in the notes are no fault but the editor's.

SALMON RIVER,
JULY 11 TO AUGUST 3, 1946

JULY 11
MEXICAN HAT. A late start. But finally, with the WEN atop the SAN JUAN boat MYSTERY CANYON,[1] on the trailer hooked to the station wagon, and the MEXICAN HAT II atop the JOAN, on the trailer attached to the army recon car,[2] we start. Doris with me, followed by Kent[3] in the recon car. We get a tire and tube in Monticello. Pres Walker drove the car with Kent's wife in it to Moab. We arrive in Moab around 7:00 PM, finding Pres's mother, and our old friends Lu and Marg Moore[4] there to meet us. Talk a bit late—to bed.

JULY 12
Arrive Salt Lake late afternoon and stay at Covey's.[5] [Salt Lake] Tribune photographer and two reporters come in to get story. Kent and Pres go to a show, while Doris and I join with friends at Hotel Utah for a party.

JULY 13
Equipment all working fine. We stop in Pocatello for a few odds and ends. There we hear more talk of rain, and I promptly buy a rain jacket! On to Blackfoot, Joan and Sandra still riding in the station wagon. At Blackfoot the chief of police gives us much help in getting parking space and supplies police [to] watch for the night. Doris's grandmother, cousin, and later uncle meet us for a visit.[6] They came in from Idaho Falls. Pres a bit liquored up.[7]

JULY 14
This is the big day. Will get my first view of the Salmon. Leaving Blackfoot we cross a very smooth and tame looking Snake River. At ARCO, rather just beyond, we don't see the recon car behind after quite a wait. Deciding they somehow took the wrong turn, we drive on to a phone at MOORE, and call the county sheriff at MARTIN, and have him flag the boys down and turn them back. We go on under rather threatening skies, and have lunch at CHALLIS. The Salmon on its first view looks like a little tiny tumbling mountain stream. Pretty, tho! Around three o'clock we get to Salmon City, soon followed by Pres and Kent. We get rooms at an auto court, and are soon running into more members of the party—June[8] and Pauline,[9] then the Marstons.[10]

JULY 15
A full day. Boats in the river tomorrow we decide. Conferences. I hear about foaming terrible rapids that are sure to spell doom. We are given an extremely friendly and helpful reception everywhere—but as could be

expected, and is natural we are looked upon a bit as smart alecs from the south who are going to be somewhat flabbergasted by the river. But in such a good spirit. The Clydes, Mother and Daughter-in-law pay their respects. Nice of them. Mrs. Clyde Sr. looks too young to be mother of Don [Smith]. Everyone is finally arrived. We're all thrilled and eager for the trip. Doris and I drive along the banks a ways to check appearance of river against a given drop. It's mild.

Doris gets the food ready and assembled. I meet an A.A. Bennett who has a ranch on the Middle Fork. He's a real flyer. Helped organize Alaskan Airways.[11] Arrange for him to pick up supplies and fly them in to us at Mackay Field at the SOUTH FORK. A conference with Dept. of Interior officials who participated in an earlier trip with Don Smith.[12] Am given grim promises of a *very* rough trip. Their pictures don't confirm this. A bunch will be down to see us run PINE CREEK RAPID, which they say will really whizzer us.

In the evening I show my Colorado pictures, and most of them are quite surprised at the real big time action. A good many comments are now made that these rapids may not look so tough to us! To bed!

July 16

5:30 AM. Up, and Kent, Pres, and I take the boats down to just above the bridge at MILE O, and put them in. Pres terribly drunk, almost falls in the river. Back and have breakfast, then back and load in supplies. We're using CO_2 belts for passengers this trip. But are inflating by mouth, not using the gas. We're a bit late in finally getting started as the Dock doesn't show up! Take-offs are always nerve-wracking—and this is worse than usual. With a big crowd assembled, Pres falls in the river trying to get into his boat, the MYSTERY CANYON. He was originally supposed to run the MEXICAN HAT II, but under the circumstances he is transferred.

11:00 AM. We're off!

#1   WEN: NEVILLS—JUNE CHAMBERLAIN, JOAN NEVILLS, NEILL WILSON,[13] FRANK STAHL (from Salmon—wants to ride a ways and fish)

#2   MEXICAN HAT II: KENT FROST, PAULINE SAYLOR, LOEL MARSTON, BRUCE WILSON

#3   JOAN: DOCK MARSTON, MARADEL MARSTON, HOWARD WELTY[14]

#4   MYSTERY CANYON: (San Juan semi-cataract) PRES WALKER

Passing under bridge a Salmon Sport calls to Kent: "Four bits you never make it!" Kent calls: "$50 we do!"

LUNCH. Mile 8. Right. Few mosquitoes. Bit of a dreary day, but we're having fun. Water a bit shallow over some of the bars, but not bad.

Norman Nevills, Kent Frost, Preston Walker

CAMP. Right. Well, not a bad day. Averaged 4 MPH. Just below us the NORTH FORK comes in. Damn creek! Kind of a dirty yellow mud color from mining operations further up. The highway is less than a hundred yards to our right. A sort of store or so is on the highway. Mosquitoes very mild, and they all disappear at sundown. Thing I notice most is that these bars don't have sand on them. Gravel. Mean to make landings, and a bit hard to get good places to sleep. Scenery not startling today, but it holds promise of getting pretty. So far have seen plenty of tame and wild ducks. Numerous magpies and crows. Doris meets us here, also friend of the Docks. Have dinner together, then we're left to our own. Find rather waterlogged driftwood for fire. Have a few stray visitors so get the equipment sorted etc. A truck rolls in during night and camps close by. This is a novel experience to see so much civilization on a river trip! North Fork is about 20' wide and flows maybe 200 second feet. The Salmon was flowing 2,340 second feet today.

July 17
2,250 second feet.

Up and have breakfast. Get our equipment all sorted and stowed. The MYSTERY CANYON will carry no food, just bedrolls. Wind is blowing mildly. Temperature: 54.

8:00 AM. Shove off from camp #1.

We see buildings and land to investigate. Find it's a ranger station. Agree to take two passengers on to SHOUP. MARIAN MAHONEY in WEN. BERNICE GUBERSBULER in JOAN. This is at INDIAN CREEK.

SHOUP. CAMP #2. *19 miles today.* We camp ¼ mile below bridge on left at site of old camp. It first appears a bit dirty, but looks like it'll have to do. We have lunch, then go over to post office and write and mail cards. Thence down the road to PINE CREEK RAPID. It *is* a mean looker, tho obviously it can be run. Study it awhile, then back to camp. This is quite a village. Old mining camp, populated with rather picturesque characters. Meet the "town bootlegger," an odorous mustached character who supplies Pres with tequila—we find later! Charles Sturmer, 10 year old boy and father come to camp to visit. Boy fascinated by boats so take him for ride. He will come in morning to ride down to PINE CREEK. Pauline, Bruce and I work our way up mountainside to an old mine. All of had visited the mill adjacent to camp. A terribly steep, long climb. We see many grouse. Find the mine tunnels and go exploring. Fascinating old stopes, chutes, tunnels, coyote holes etc. It's a thriller. In another tunnel we shove car way back in drift. With Pauline and Bruce in the car, myself hanging on the back we take off. Lots of speed. Rounding left turn we derail and have a hell of a wreck. THE GREAT SHOUP WRECK! Haven't had so much fun in years.[15] Getting late, so we repair to camp, trying out coasting on boards down the mountainsides. Watch for ticks. They seem to be past season tho. Threatening rain. We find dinner over with at camp but we make pretty good shift. A rat trap cabin adjacent to camp provides indoor shelter for Pres, Kent and I. We sleep on the tables!

JULY 18

This is the day! I am a bit on edge to get our first major Idaho rapid, PINE CREEK, over with. I expect this to be a criterion for the rest of the Salmon river. And in a way, I would still say that it provides the complications typical of the lower rapids. After breakfast we are soon packed up. Young Sturmer will ride as far as Pine Creek Rapids.

8:00 AM. Shove off.

Arrive PINE CREEK RAPIDS. MILE 42. River running 2,130. People line the bridge to watch us run this one. Spectators have come down from Salmon City. I anchor and go up on the bridge to study the channel. It's a bit tricky, but unless the water packs more punch than I think, can do!

With Maradel as passenger I take off and make a nice ride thru the rapid. It's a thrill to feel that the enemy has been met and conquered, so to speak!

MEXICAN HAT II with Kent, Loel as passenger. Nice ride.

Pres in bad shape. I elect to run the MYSTERY CANYON. In this open type San Juan boat I load in Bruce Wilson, and the game warden, Glen Richardson. I touch rock as we're loaded a bit, but run OK.

Dock Marston solo in JOAN. Nice ride.

Final farewells and on again. The trip's really started.

DUTCH OVEN CREEK. River to here from Pine Creek has been snappy and vicious. Look this over with Glen Richardson, run it—and on. Find another bottle in Pres' boat and threw in river. Tequila.

LUNCH. Mile 49. GARDEN CREEK. Pull in on left. Car or so belonging to fishermen here. Pres in bad shape. Passed clear out. Serious situation. Hold a conference, and it is decided that Neill will take over the MYSTERY CANYON until Pres OK.

CAMP. MILE 59. LONG TOM FOREST CAMP. Clear skies all day, but not too warm. Nice riding water all day. Neill had one or two real thrills, but did very well. Find another bottle of Pres'. He had it hidden in bow hatch of *my* boat! Nice evening, beautiful camp, but we're tired. Not a good bar to sleep on here, so we sleep up in the camp about fifty feet above the river. The road from Salmon runs right by here! We walk down to look at the Middle Fork. It's a beautiful stream. The Cowboy sleeps on one of the camp tables. We're all having fun, anyhow.

We are fascinated by a sign indicating this as IDAHO'S PRIMITIVE AREA. Road right alongside!

JULY 19

A good breakfast, and then prepare to get pictures of the famous LONG TOM RAPID. The light isn't too good as sun doesn't get to it until later in the day. Frankly it's a kind of weak rapid, anyhow.

8:35 AM. Break camp and off! River about 2000' today. Nice splashy ride.

Bottom of second drop in LONG TOM and on. Nice riding. The Salmon rapids mostly seem to comprise two drops, rather than one violent plunge.

All but the WEN stop upstream on the MIDDLE FORK to fish. Twins, Bruce and I land on right, and cross on old cable car to abandoned house. Spooky old place which we find later was the abode of an old prospector who had died a month or so before. Rest of party finally show up and we eat lunch near old cabin.

EEL RAPID. Vicious rock in center. Can run either right *or* left. I go back and bring the MYSTERY CANYON thru too, with the twins and Neill as passengers. Kent MEXICAN HAT II, Doctor[16] JOAN OK.

CAMP. MILE 69. BUTTS CREEK. Camp right. This river, running almost due west, is as Don Smith said in a letter, mean after middle of afternoon as sun is right in your eyes. Beautiful place to camp. A house and orchard are across the river. After dinner I row the MYSTERY CANYON across the river with *SEVEN* passengers to visit a Mr. Stevens who has the ranch and placer claim here. We gorged on his cherries and black raspberries. The hospitality of these folks along the Salmon is really impressive. All had a swim before dinner, and the water was more than frigid! This is exceptionally nice camp.

JULY 20

Had 6 of rainbow trout that the Doctor caught on the Middle Fork to supplement the regular breakfast rations. River a bit lower today. About 1950.

9:25 AM. Shove off.

LUNCH. LITTLE SQUAW CREEK RAPIDS, including the famous "RAINIER" just a lot of fun. Nothing tough so far today.

DISAPPOINTMENT CREEK. Left. We were drifting along when we spotted a house being built on the bank above. Landing, we found a Mrs. Rowe, working around the house. Her husband was off hunting. At great expense of labor they had dragged in logs to build the house. Don Smith had brought in quite a few supplies. A garden was going in, and placer mining is supposed to fill in the money gap. Never saw so damn many people in a river canyon before!

DEVIL TEETH RAPIDS. We stop to look this baby over as it has a bad name—and a sinister one. Actually as a rapid it's a real joke and very easy to run. Even the Frazier-Swain outfit could get thru here without an upset.

This whole section thru here is difficult to follow on the map. So many of the creeks are alike, and the bends in the river are hard to follow. We're set and tensed for the famous SALMON FALLS. Even tho it's getting late and camping is indicated, we're determined to get the famous "FALLS" behind us. The sun glare is tough! We're tired. The canyon walls assume some of the aspects of a gorge, and to my way of thinking, this marks the most awesome part of the whole Salmon River Canyon.

SALMON FALLS. MILE 90. This is also known as "Black Falls," and is at the mouth of Black Creek, which comes in on the right. It has a real first class boom to it, and at first glance it's a whing ding! Hard to get boats anchored. Best at head on right. Smith party tried to dynamite a big rock on the right channel to clear it, but only succeed in making it worse.[17] We were told that particular channel was impossible. However I elect to go thru on that route anyhow. I take off in WEN with Pauline and Bruce. Get over first drop, but don't allow for momentum just right, and take a VERY HARD blow directly amidships on the side. Left side. But we wallow on alright and land below on right as planned.

Well! So I go back and get the MYSTERY CANYON and hit the same channel again. This time I'm set, and slide thru so easy it's awful. Pres is still in bad shape. Kent then comes thru in the MEXICAN HAT II and hits the same rock, but with a very light tap.

The Doctor comes thru in the JOAN by taking the middle channel. Makes it easy and in fine style. The falls is caused by a series of four great rocks that literally block the river off.

CAMP. MILE 91. SABE CREEK. Right. We're tired, and the one of the few fine beaches we've found is most welcome. We ran the famous Salmon Falls with about 1900 second feet. Might have been a bit more. Not over 2100 though.

JULY 21

8:00 AM. River still dropping. We're off again!

BARTH HOT SPRINGS. They are easily seen running obviously warm water in from seeps on the left bank. Am, from here on tho, a bit confused as to our whereabouts. So we keep sharp eyes peeled for possible landmarks or people.

HILDA CREEK. Almost by, when I spot a boat pulled up and tied to the left bank. We land, and commence following a well, and recently used trail up the steep hillside. A couple of hundred yards brings us to a more level section—and an amazing sight—a flower-covered cottage! We directly spy an old man in shorts and bare feet! The famous old German hermit—ANDY STRAUSS.[18] He gives us a warm welcome, and is childishly eager to have us stay awhile. We go into his immaculately neat cabin and visit with him. He has lived here for 14 years, and is now 79 years old! Been a sailor. He treats us to some delicious wine, and tries to press a gallon of strawberry wine on us, but that somehow disappears! We do take some canned elk meat. Andy goes to the river with us and shows how he mans his boat. He was a sailor in the German Navy in World War I. I gather he finally jumped ship and drifted into this region.

LUNCH. BAILEY RAPID. This is one of the highly touted ones and *is* rough. After lunch I take off in WEN, followed at intervals by other three boats. It's a rough and very difficult channel.

FIVE MILE CREEK RAPID. Because of the light *and* nature of this rapid it turns out to be a beautiful long clear chute—and one of the prettiest looking rapids we find on the whole Idaho trip.

RICHARDSON CREEK. 1 man and 7 kids in house on left!

BIG MALLARD RAPID. All at bottom of rapid and anchored at mouth of MALLARD CREEK by 3:45 PM. Fishing proves to be fair.

JULY 22

Shove off. River 1800 to 1900 feet. Steadily dropping.

GROWLER RAPID. After the three cataract boats are run thru, I ride with Pres at oars in MYSTERY CANYON, standing on deck. It's quite a thriller this way and the one big rock looks a mite vicious. Pres is definitely now on the beam again.

LUNCH. MILE 121. Mines on both sides of the river. We stop on left, and there are quite extensive and recent workings here. Much machinery. Find two dead rattlesnakes at mine mouth, obviously killed this same day!!

MILE 123. As we round the bend, on the right, diving from a big rock we see three girls! IDAHO'S PRIMITIVE AREA! We pull in and find that they are Joan (16), brunette, Alice (14 and blond) Myerl (12 and redhead)—the Wilson sisters. They ask us up to their ranch, and are going to swim horses across the river for us. We drop the boat down to Mile 124 at head of THREE MILE RAPIDS, known locally as MACABER RAPID or some

Camera man filming boat at big rapid

such name, after a man killed there some years before. I take the three girls thru for a wild ride much to their satisfaction, and anchor the WEN for the night down below. We go back up and start dinner, after which we visit the ranch. Correction: We first see the girls swim some horses across the river, meet Mrs. Wilson, Mr. H.A. Wilson,[19] and their feeble minded daughter, 19 year old Allene. We all take a whirl at a bit of fast horse riding—some spills. Then to camp. In the evening we enjoy hot fresh bread, honey etc., at the Wilsons.

Oh yes, and also this afternoon Mr. Wilson starts up his truck and takes us all several miles upriver on a road that at times hangs by a thread to the cliff wall, with precipitous sharp grades. It's a real thriller. Later on after the trip is over, we are to learn that that fall Mr. Wilson rolled off this same grade with his truck and is killed! Our road ends at an elaborate home occupied by the man and some of his workers that own the mine upriver, the Painter Mine. They are most hospitable, and we eat cherries such as I've never seen before! Finally to bed after a very full day. We've all had a lot of fun, and it's a thrill to know we will meet the airplane tomorrow at Mackay Bar. A road goes out from here to DIXIE, and it appears to be a whing ding series of switchbacks. I had once thought that Doris could bring in supplies here!

JULY 23
Final farewells to the Wilsons—and we're off again.

MACKAY BAR and AIRFIELD.[20] The field is a bit rough, yet astonishingly good for its location. We land at upstream end of field, walk to lower end and find two men and a woman there who are mining—they appear just a bit dumb. This is quite a placer workings, but we mill around anxiously scanning the skies. TWO airplanes finally show up and circle and circle. We later find that one is a fire observation plane. We wonder if our plane is going to land, but after nearly a half hour of circling, a roar from upstream heralds its approach, and A.A. Bennett in his TRAVELAIRE is landed. Quite a fancy piece of flying. He was a great Alaska bush pilot and helped organized ALASKAN AIRWAYS. We exchange greetings, then he and I taxi back up to the other end of the field close to the boats. Unload our supplies, pay Bennett, send out mail with him, and having arrived at 9:14 AM, he is on his way at 9:45 AM. It's really a sight to see him take off and climb out of this deep canyon or valley. We go thru the throes of packing the boats, sorting etc., and at 10:30 AM are on our way again. We see the Wilsons one last time upstream across the river on the road.

SOUTH FORK OF SALMON. A very small flow being discharged. Just below here I see a very large fish swim by. Four or five feet long.[21]

Lord the water is slow here. Barely moving, it seems. 3 MPH.

MILE 128. No name on this rapid, but since the leaving the South Fork river has felt different. More thrust. We run this one in good style, but it packs a good hard wallop and has plenty of power.

CROOKED CREEK. Meet a Mr. Fleming here. He's a sort of caretaker for the quite elaborate ranch. Former owners buried here on the ranch. Kind of a funny deal. Mr. Fleming shows us former high water marks of river, and for one I was terribly impressed. My records show that this particular day we are on about 1700 to 1800 second feet. Yet the greatest all time flows high past this point was JUNE 1894. *120,000 feet!!* That would have been a fearful and wonderful stream.

GOOPIES! MILE 138. BULL CREEK. Right. Vacated house up on bar with an umbrella tent on top. Lets get the hell out of here![22]

CAMP. LEFT. Just downstream from CALIFORNIA CREEK. It's a really wonderful fishing stream and just about everyone catches trout. I learn how to clean them and work out on some for dinner. First really swanky sandbar camp that we've had, tho the sand has a mushy, sticky characteristic unlike our Colorado etc. Was a hardish day, as we bucked quite a bit of wind and had very little current. River running around 1700. We made a total of 16½ miles at that. Incidentally, this is still all on Mountain Standard Time.

JULY 24

MILE 141. Left. I spot a deer, get Kent's notice, and though deer goes up a hillside, Kent draws a dead bead and fatally hits it. We all pull to shore and Kent and I go up hillside after deer. Very steep. We jump a rattler. Kent goes on to track down the deer and I wait to see what he finds. Another rattler shows up, and I whistle at it and away it goes! A hail at last from the boats advises me that Kent is back—deer and all! We take all meat we can possibly keep and use, and shove off. A bit out of season, but then one is expected to live a bit off the country way down here! Deer covered with ticks.

SHEEP CREEK RAPIDS. Very easy.

MILE 147. Canyon comes in on right, forces river to left hand wall. Mean turn to make near bottom. WEN off at 11:20 AM, passengers and all. Pres fine, but Doctor and Kent almost get clipped by wall, having been slipped off course by the exceptionally sharp fast current.

CAREY FALLS. This is a sharp, very steep drop. All boat and passengers run it, but it's a breath-taking drop, and could only be done in very stable boats. There's a close to a vertical 8' drop in this baby. There's several sharp drops through here that all bear watching.

CAREY CREEK. Stop a few minutes to interview a woman we see on right bank. Want to check my navigation. Upon asking her where we are— she says she doesn't know! Seems to know absolutely nothing! Her husband is across the river where he has ferried melons across by cable car to his waiting pickup truck. I decide this is a bit of a dummy outfit so we shove off. The road on the left will now continue clear to Riggins.

LUNCH MILE 155. Hotter than blue blazes, and we've drifted and drifted trying to find a likely place to eat. We spot a boat beached up high here, with a ranch and possible fruit trees in the background. We land and find a Mr. and Mrs. Sig Burman and son Frank Burman. We get goodies from the trees to fill out our lunch, and altogether have a real swell stopover.

CAMP. HOWARD RANCH. After a lot of jockeying around, we camp on the right, use an old suspension bridge to cross the river where we visit with Mrs. Howard, member of one of the very old Idaho pioneer settlers. They have a very large and elaborate ranch. We try to phone Riggins, but can't make the connection. From this point the call is relayed through a Park or Forest Service line, and we can't rouse the Forest station. We have a most enjoyable visit and learn much of interest. Our camp isn't bad—about average for the Salmon!

July 25

Shove off. We're a bit impatient to get into telephonic communication with Riggins.

RIGGINS HOT SPRINGS. Quite a sanatarium here. We try to phone Riggins, but again no go! Visit around a bit, and also meet a stunning redhead who proves to be a Harry Conover model from New York. Also meet a newspaperman, and his sidekick. Jack Rottier[23] of Boise, Idaho. We are to see much more of the genial and good companion Jack from here on out! Well, one thing leads to another, and I convince the redhead, Virginia Herrick, that she should ride through the highly touted RUBY RAPID with me. She partly agrees. Her mother is about to throw fits. Quite a crowd assembles. Last week Don Smith hung up here with his Salmon Scow and had to be pulled loose with a truck!

RUBY RAPID. It's not so tough looking, and has one big navigable hole right in the center. After much finagling around, I load Virginia into the WEN, we get set, and I take her smack dab through the hole! It's a whingding, and we really get ducked. From a nervous frankly scared

Ruby Rapid, Salmon River: Preston Walker at the oars, Virginia Herrick in the bow

passenger, Virginia gets the fever! Wants more. So I then let her come through with Pres in the MYSTERY CANYON, though they steer clear of the hole. MEXICAN HAT II and June through in good shape too. So we've skinned another big timer!

LUNCH. Left. Shady and nice. Pres rows over to bring back Jack Rottier and Fred Ulrich, who also in turn bring some bottles of pasteurized milk! We have a long talk, Jack gets dope for news releases—and is later proved to get some big time stories clicking. As we shove off, we touch opposite shore to let off Jack and Fred.

LAKE CREEK RAPID. This is supposed to be as bad or trickier than Ruby. We find it just another ride, with passengers and all.

Country is opening up a bit and is drab and gray.

CAMP. This is on right, and not attractive for camping, but we *have* to stop as RIGGINS is just below. However, we make out in pretty good style and have a lot of fun. A car or two goes by on the road across the river.

JULY 26

Shove off. Look out RIGGINS!

We round a sweeping right turn and see a big lumber mill. Our guess it's Riggins is confirmed by a welcoming blast of the lumber mill whistle. We land a minute to get bearings, and are told that the Smith parties beach just below the bridge on the left—at the garbage dump! Well, what's good enough for the Smiths is good enough for us!

MILE ZERO. RIGGINS. Garbage heap! We find a trail of sorts and set out to case the town. Doris shows up with supplies etc., I leave the boys to get the stuff to the boats more or less, and we check up on the hotel. Neill and his wife and daughter take Bruce and head for the Carey Nixons[24] at Payette Lake. We are invited to come up for the evening. We swing into food sorting and checking of equipment. I now meet a very fine fellow, the city editor of the Lewiston [Morning]Tribune, Irving Reynolds.[25] He will accompany us to Lewiston. Later afternoon Doris and I take off for the Nixons. Arrive in time to get a chilly dip, and ride or rather do aquaplaning for first time. I collar a small bet by riding the board standing on my head. It starts to storm, and after a swell dinner Doris and I drive back to Riggins for the night. Rains a good portion of the night. At this point we change to Pacific Standard Time.

JULY 27

Shove off. Met a George Fletcher and his folks up at Payette Lake. George towed me on the aquaplane. I invited him, together with the Nixons to see us run some of the rapids below here today. There's supposed to be some whingys. WEN—MYSTERY CANYON—MEXICAN HAT II—JOAN. Pres in not too bad a shape, though he tanked up a bit during the night.

Watching them closely as there's supposed to be some damn vicious water along here.

FIDDLE CREEK. This is a rough looker. A hearse even is up on the road! An ominous sign. I take Doris through on this one. Other boats come right on through in good style. This rapid requires a bit of sharp routing.

LUNCH. Right. CRAWFORD CREEK. An old boy comes down a bit querulously and wonders who told us we could stop here! Evincing a bit of interest in mineralology quick thaws him, and we're bored to death with rock specimens—full of gold! Yeah? Gladys Wilson, Doris, Carey and Arnold Nixon, and George Fletcher have lunch with us. I tentatively sign George up to run the Snake with us. We all like him. Doris will meet us this evening and have dinner and camp the one night with us.

RHETT CREEK. We stop to look this baby over as the sunlight glare and reflection is so bad that its impossible almost to see the channel. A big rock to miss, and then an impingement on the left. Finally get oriented, pick out landmarks and away we go.

CAMP. Mistaken, *this* is where we change from one time [zone] to the other. As of tomorrow, we will be on Pacific Time. Today, Joan Nevills,[26] Irving Reynolds, and Neill Wilson rode with me. Second boat was MYSTERY CANYON with the Marston twins and Bruce Wilson. Then the MEXICAN HAT II with Pauline Saylor and June Chamberlain. Margaret Marston and Howard Welty with Doctor Marston in the JOAN. Leaving off Joan Nevills here, we will continue in this order of passenger seats clear to Lewiston. Doris drives up to join us. Neill and I go out wood hunting. We get some from an old cabin that looked to have been inhabited by the early day

Chinese miners! Have a very nice evening. We speculate on the great and famous SNOWHOLE and CHINA RAPIDS that lie ahead. They're supposed to be the all time whingdinging wonders of this river.

JULY 28

Farewells are said, and we get off to an early start. This is rather somber uninteresting country, and is almost devoid of vegetation.

SLATE CREEK. Visible signs on the highway to our right prove handy in identifying these side streams!

Another DEER CREEK. We're still on a falling stage, but the water we've picked up here and there amounts now to a total of 6560 SECOND FEET.

WHITEBIRD CREEK. Here the highway takes to the right up the canyon, through Whitebird and across the mountain to Lewiston. We elect to walk what we think is a half mile up to Whitebird and get some malts. Its hot. No luck in hailing rides. We descend upon WHITEBIRD this fine Sunday with insatiable appetites. I consume 3 malts and a hamburger. Everyone does himself proud. This under difficulties as the Whitebird sports are hanging around the drink emporium trying to get sobered up after the night before. I engage a pickup for $1.50 to haul us back to the boats. A small crowd tags along and we finally get under way.

This added water we're running here has quite a bit more punch. These rapids have a very heavy surging effect to them.

MILE 38. About here a road on right quits. It had been worked on by CCCs before the war. Below a few miles at Pine Bar there will be another road coming in from the high country, and this road was to have hooked up with it.

LUNCH. That is, some eat. It's damn hot, and I relax in the shade of a cliff, and succumb to the sleepy effects the malts had on me. I snore through lunch, and don't waken until much later. We finally drag ourselves to the boats and cast off.

MILE 41½. A bit rough. Watch it.

PINE BAR RAPIDS. Quite a modern looking mining camp here, a good road. But all deserted. Apparently all out over the weekend. This is a toughy, particularly so with the sun glare on the water. After quite a bit of staring and studying I take off in WEN with Maradel as passenger. I misjudge the current and clip a rock near bottom of rapid. I go back and solo through in MEXICAN HAT II. Work hard and come through OK. Pres fine in the MYSTERY, and the Doc really struts through in the JOAN.

CAMP. Left. Huge sand bar. Road and old cabin across river. Eating dinner as cars show up, apparently returning to the camp upstream from us. We're glad to hit the hay. Early next morning we hear a motor, and two fellows in a motorboat come into camp. Durad Murray, and C.C. Robinson. They are mining. They show and demonstrate a doodlebug.[27]

It's a honey—can figure miles, feet, meters—anything you use! These boys were going upstream last month with a passenger and swamped, drowning the passenger. Boat lies below us and we'll stop to see it. Later on Robinson, through talking with Irv Reynolds gave quite a demonstration of doodlebugging in Lewiston. He also created quite a bit of interest by betting he could go UPSTREAM all the way to Salmon City from Lewiston! We shall see. I do see Robinson later on in Lewiston at the end of the Snake River run.

July 29

Shove off. Don Smith had definitely stated that we couldn't possibly reach Lewiston on schedule without motors. And now, to me, it looks like we'll have to kill time to keep from getting in *ahead* of schedule.

MILE 49. Left. Land here and photograph the wrecked boat that Robinson and party swamped in last month. It's a sort of death trap looking sort of boat typical of all the utterly impractical small boats we've seen in Idaho.

This is old RICE FERRY, but there's a bridge here now. Robinson and wife are on bridge, and in trying to get a picture Mrs. Robinson drops her box camera. We pick it up directly and land briefly to return it to her.

MILE 50. Another old mining camp.

LUNCH. ROUND SPRING CREEK. Nice spot for lunch. It's hot and rest is welcome.

MILE 61¼. SURPRISE! This turns out to be quite a toughy. Big rock in center that is hard to miss. I climb up on cliffside on right to get better look and drop my sunglasses! Thought I heard a rattler and I moved quick, though dislodging the specs. Had a few bad moments, but Pres came to the rescue by finding them. Rather thrilling ride, but all boats and passengers run it smoothly.

SNOWHOLE RAPID. As we pull in for landing on left, there's a really big roar, and to look over the brink and down shows this to be a real drop. A trick of vision amplifies the actual drop, and it looks like 30-40'. Well, this is it.

All climb up on ledge on left, and I survey the situation for a good half hour. Far side too turbulent, though a straighter drop. Left too rocky. Center is best, though it requires a bit of sharp handling getting around two big rocks. WEN off at 3:40 PM. Whoopee! Made it in good shape. Other boats through fine too, though all the boatmen get knocked off the seat. Begins then a fearful and wonderful excursion involving climbing etc. to get all the party from head of rapid to foot. It *is* a bit difficult, but all come through with equipment and selves OK. We ran this rapid with about 6440 feet of water.

CAMP. A bit small, but a very pretty spot to camp. We're all tired but much elated to have the great SNOWHOLE in the bag. Remains the equally famous CHINA RAPID, claimer of 15 lives in one shot when a scow carrying Chinese miners upset in it.

JULY 30

CHINA RAPIDS. Well I'll be go to hell! At the prevailing stage this rapid is an utter and complete joke. On close observation we find a big hole close to shore that will make swell picture. I arrive at foot seething as cross current kept me out of hole. Kent takes off with same results! I try again in MYSTERY CANYON, and miss! I bring the JOAN through, and this time plot smack dab into the center of the hole. Quite wet! And so goes the river.[28]

WAPSHILLA CREEK. A road comes in here, and there's a phone here too. Meet a man who is setting up a placer mine. Chester Wilson. He's not too communicative a duck. Working on a boat. It's a fearful and wonderful looking contrivance. Saw one like it once before. 3½–foot sides, narrowing down to barely a foot wide at the bottom. Supposed to use the high flaring sides to prevent overturning. Nuts. An overboard wave would sink it. This chap is a bit screwy looking to us so we shove off, and treat him to a sight of precision running in the moderate rapid taking off from his camp.

LUNCH. Right. Nothing better offers so we loaf it out here. Cloudy skies, country dull—sort of general uninviting prospect.

MILE 80. Am looking for the place on the cliff where the "ONE WAY CLUB" plaques are supposed to be.

MILE 82. Some nice rapids along here. Fun to shoot.

RIGHT WALL. ONE WAY CLUB.[29] We land in a threatening drizzle, dig up a bottle and insert all our names ala Colorado style.

From here to the SNAKE RIVER is a matter of *4 miles*. My navigation suffers at the expense of my impatience to see the Snake. Each rapid we run, and some of these are whing dings, I announce as the *last* rapid on the Salmon. I also keep spotting the Snake. Seems like I'll never learn!

SNAKE RIVER! We are now out *49 miles from Lewiston*. Mileages from here on will be those *out from Lewiston*. I do not have my Snake River maps as Doris forgot to bring them to Lewiston, so we will go on dead reckoning, and will pick up data on the next run thru this section as we come down from Hells Canyon.

Snake River is a bit of a surprise to me. Looks a bit bigger, and the water is a definite tawny color. A sort of rapid takes off as we enter, and I avoid the largish waves as they have very hard curlback to them, and I want to sneak up on this baby's punch before taking them straight. We are now on 16, 400 second feet of water. It's a big looking river.

Looks like rain. May need shelter. As we boom along on what I can't decide is a rapid or just fast current (at foot as we get into what seems like no current at all I know it for rapid!) we observe a great dearth of drift along here.

MILE 47. A swell cave here, but it's a damn hard pull up a steep sandy shore to reach it—and no wood. We decide upon trying our luck below.

CAMP. Left. Swell spot. Have to row across river to get driftwood, but this current offers little resistance! Does rain a trifle during night, but not too much. We're camped tonight in OREGON. No wonder it's raining!

JULY 31

CHINA GARDEN CREEK. M&M ranch. We spot this large ranch and house on right and pull in. Find a Mrs. Tippett and her children. Lois Tippett. Her husband is out at a sheep camp or getting supplies. She does not know the mileage from Lewiston! Came up with Kyle McGrady[30] about a month ago. Irv calls Porter Ward at the Lewiston Tribune and tells him name of ranch we're at, and gets our mileage from Lewiston. Mrs. Tippett has us as her guests to a really bountiful repast, featuring wonderful hot rolls and cherry pies. I go into a nearby shed for the obvious reason, and suddenly find I'm sharing the place with one of the characteristically green Idaho rattlesnakes. We kill him. What a playmate for the children!

GRANDE RONDE RIVER. It's running very little water, comes in on left. Another road starts here on left side, and we directly are informed it's a good road right into Lewiston! A house is located on upriver bank at mouth of Grande Ronde with telephone and all, but is unoccupied. Up this river about 20 miles or so is where Buzz Holmstrom killed himself last winter.[31]

Spot a spring on left and stop at Mile 29. While there getting a drink a truck rolls up disgorging some youngsters, belonging to the driver JOE EPSON. He's a friendly chap, full of information. His two little girls, 11 and 8, are dying to get a ride, so we take them aboard to ride awhile, to be picked up below by Joe.

CAPTAIN JOHN CREEK. A good ferry is here, with large ranch on right. We land the girls on the left next to the road, then row across to a big sandbar. During the night we get a hail, and Pres crosses over to see who it is. Some boys from a paper and the radio station. They've met Doris and have brought us mail. This we all read by flashlight. Earlier in evening Pauline, Bruce and I rob a corn patch and was it good! Also jumped a rattlesnake near camp. People here very pleasant but just a bit on the reserved side. Irv uses the phone to get his wife Rebecca.

AUGUST 1

First thing Pres goes over to get our mailbringers of last night. They prove to be: BILL WATTS, GEORGE SHREVE, MIKE MITCHELL. All connected with Lewiston radio station. They want stories and pics too. We try to oblige them, are soon once again embarked. The boys will meets us in Lewiston, if not before. It is reiterated that we will come in on schedule at 2:00 PM on August 2nd!

MILE 21. The redoubtable Howard found there were to be pictographs seen here so we go up to see them. There are some very good ones.

LUNCH. Left. MILE 16 I think. Anyhow it was damn hot, and we found a big weeping willow tree to eat and loaf under. Pauline fell into an occupied beaver den! They could hear the squeal in Lewiston!

Placer mine on left. We visit the folks here, and were just shoving off when here comes a plane we had been looking for. A Stinson[32] with Doris, Porter Ward, and Rebecca Reynolds. They do a wing-over and it's a thrill to watch. They zoom low and drop us mail, weinies, etc. Are we thrilled! We gather things up (they landed the sack not ten feet from a boat right at edge of river) and shove off.

ASOTIN, WASHINGTON. MILE 8. Immediately upon arriving most of us hit for town. Irv Reynolds and I hop a ride on a truck and get to the Malted Milk center and telephone first. Irv gets Rebecca, and she says she'll get Doris and drive out. Whole gang shows up, and the run on malts is really something. Where we first pulled in is no good for camping, so the fellows plan to drop downstream to the mouth of Asotin Creek, and Mile 6 to tie up for the night. Irv and I go on into Lewiston to check on the morrow's reception etc. Some big steaks help!

AUGUST 2

First thing in the morning I drop in at the Clarkston flying field and rent from Virgil Baldwin the manager a Piper J3. I go flitting for an hour and look the country over.

And thence back to ASOTIN. A big reception is awaiting us at Lewiston, and we're due to arrive at 2:00 PM!

The camp I find was a bit rugged at mouth of ASOTIN CREEK. Kind of a garbage dump slough. We clean up, shave etc., get more malts and kill time until just after noon. We shove off!

We first pull in at Mile 1, attracted by a small crowd, including the mayor. Main party at Mile 2/3, so we shove on down, arriving at 2:05 PM. Quite a welcoming committee. Police will watch boats, so we head for hotels.

In the evening a banquet is held for us, we're presented plaques as token of membership in the "ONE WAY CLUB."

AUGUST 3

We fiddle around and get the boats loaded ready for the trip back south. We visit at PAYETTE LAKE again, then on to CAMBRIDGE where we're met by Jack Fletcher, Jack Rottier etc. and commence the trek for the point of embarkation on the Snake.

Anyhow, we ran *ALL THE RAPIDS*. With one more or less open boat at that. One thing sure, the technique and boats heretofore used in Idaho are certainly haywire.

Snake River,
August 4 to August 17, 1946

Upon completion of the SALMON RIVER trip, we immediately commenced preparations for the next jaunt—Hells Canyon. I was a bit dubious about the quality of the rapids, having been led to believe that it would be a very tame trip. Little did I know! Arrangements were finally made to meet at WEISER, Idaho, it being our plan to embark at Huntington.

August 4

Leaving town was quite a chore as loading of boats and equipment is always tiresome. But we finally made it! With Doris and Sandra and Joan in the station wagon, pulling the trailer with the WEN loaded on the MYSTERY CANYON, we led the way, followed by Bruce and Pres, with Kent driving the recon car. Got to Payette Lake that night, and Doris and I stayed at the Carey Nixons. We received even more discouraging reports on the slowness of the water in the Huntington region, so decided upon going to BROWNLEES FERRY! Had a grand time trying out water skiing.

August 5

Arrived at CAMBRIDGE before noon, and everyone got after us to take a short cut route to BROWNLEES FERRY over a mountain road that would cut off many miles. Before leaving town we contracted to give a show in Cambridge that night. Away we went! It's some road, the last ten miles being a tortuous winding steeply graded affair that tried our equipment to the utmost. We left Pres to watch the boat in the company of a very hospitable tender of a nearby ranch house. Rest of us returned to Cambridge, where a very appreciative and receptive audience witnessed our show. The party was a great success despite the fact that none of us knew how to run the borrowed 16mm sound projector! To bed—and glad to be there!

August 6

Drove back to LEWISTON, arriving lateish.

August 7

We made arrangements for car and trailer storage, got our reservations confirmed for the Clarkston-Boise flight. Shortly after lunch took farewell of the family and Rebecca Reynolds, and our DC3 took off with Bruce, Kent, and I. Had a swell trip to BOISE and enjoyed the scenery no end. The Hells Canyon was very impressive from the air, and one or two sections looked like there might be a bit of rough water.

Landed in BOISE to be greeted by a new passenger member, genial George Fletcher[33] and his father. We were whisked over to the Fletcher home where we were surprised to meet our old friend of the RUBY RAPIDS, JACK ROTTIER. Immediately loaded into JACK ROTTIER's car, George,

Departure from Brownlee Ferry, Snake River

Bruce, Kent and I, and away we went. Got to WEISER, but could find little
or no trace of our river party! Word had been sent, but hardly received of
our change of embarkation points! We left word at the hotel and pushed on
to BAKER, OREGON. Finally got dinner, a room—and to bed!

AUGUST 8

One way or another we learn this morning that the word has gone out, and
that the whole party will be on hand at BROWNLEES FERRY.[34] Away we go!
Pick up some bread and eggs at NEW BRIDGE. Drive on over a quite good
road to BROWNLEES FERRY. Everyone is across the river awaiting us. Pres
rows on to our side to take us over. What a day! Back at NEW BRIDGE we
were given to understand that we had a very hard, dangerous trip ahead,
and would see some tremendous rapids. I had received this information
with my tongue in my cheek. The view here of the river certainly didn't
suggest any power or bad rapids. But that's a river—deceptively smooth—a
sudden change of pace, and you're really into it. Crossing to the east side
we found our whole party, plus a collection of local farmers and ranchers.
Pres was in fine shape. I met the blond Ferris Dodge,[35] and her cheerful,
story telling dad, Harry Washington Dodge. We had a bit of a shakedown
of the collective Dodge luggage, loaded the boats under the ever present
strain of a take-off.

1:00 PM. SHOVE OFF! *Mile 148 from Lewiston*
River running 9,770 second feet.

#1   WEN—Nevills, Neill Wilson, George Fletcher
#2   MYSTERY CANYON—Pres Walker, Maradel MARSTON, Loel
      Marston, Bruce Wilson
#3   MEXICAN HAT II—Kent Frost, Ferris Dodge, Harry Dodge
#4   JOAN—Doctor Marston, Margaret Marston, Howard Welty
      (Cowboy)

We were directly past the riffle at BROWNLEES CREEK, and the
river, to seemed to have some good potential power in it. Anyhow, it was
wonderful to be on the way—particularly so in that we were all going to see
some new country, some new river, for the first time.

SALT CREEK. Just riffles so far. Not too bad a traveling, as we're
making around 3½ MPH.

Entrance to OXBOW BEND. Here is where the old railroad tunnel
caved in a few years back, causing abandonment of the railroad. Present
"highway" follows, in the main, on the old roadbed of the railroad.

CAMP. Right hand side. Mouth of beautiful creek. INDIAN CREEK.
Fishermen attack it with glee—but poor results. Sand is a bit scarce, and
what there is of it is a greasy sort of mica-like sand very much different than
that on the San Juan and Colorado. Anyhow, we've made it to here at MILE
132 in good shape, with a resulting 15½ miles for the day. Not bad for an
afternoon.

AUGUST 9
Up real early, and off to a 6:40 AM START!

Today should see us entering the famed HELLS CANYON, so we're
all eager to be on our way.

HOMESTEAD, OREGON. Mile 126. Stopping here we send off
some mail, have a nice visit with the local gentry, and are again warned of
real big rapids to come. I hear now, for the first time, about a new rapid:
KINNEY CREEK! I laugh it off—another rapid! We meet a Chas. A. Cole,
old time steamboat river man, and quite a character. My offer for him to
ride in the WEN to KINNEY CREEK RAPID is accepted with alacrity. He
seems definitely impressed with the quality of our boats after going a short
ways.

KEARNS RAPIDS. Another joke. Yet I feel a bit creepy about these joke
rapids, because I know it never fails—just when the "jokes" are funniest, is
when you run into something that whittles you down to size!

BALLARDS LANDING. Old ferryboat crossing.

MILE 121. Cars are beginning to drive by and watch us. They seem to
be headed down to the KINNEY CREEK. We smile.

Mile 120. CAREY NIXON joins the parade!

MILE 117. Oh oh! Ahead comes a threatening roar. *This* is not the tumbling yap yap yap of an overgrown riffle—but the power filled bark of a bigtime rapid. CHURCH IS OUT! Water is getting glassy smooth. Ahead the river disappears—showing nothing but occasional high tossing waves.

KINNEY CREEK RAPID. MILE 115. Stop right. It's a toughy.

WEN off into rapid—Jack Rottier has caught up with us again. Made it fine, though quite a ride.

MH OK. JOAN OK. Pres in MYSTERY CANYON gets too much water aboard near foot of rapid, and as he approaches shore at bottom right boat practically swamps. We have a hectic time getting it dried out. We lose our supply of fruit juices. But just the same, the boat didn't do too badly for water that violent.

On from KINNEY CREEK! This begins to look a bit more like HELLS CANYON should look. The river is now packing a good wallop. We are on 9,800 feet of water today.

DOYLE CREEK. Mildly mean, and we're taking no chances after seeing the roughness of KINNEY!

SQUAW CREEK. This is another of the fabled bad ones. Doesn't look too tough, though it requires a tricky maneuver involving going way over to the right side, then switching back across towards the bottom.

WEN off OK. MEXICAN HAT II OK. MYSTERY CANYON OK. JOAN OK. Into the boats and on again. The watchers on the banks keep pace with their cars. It's quite a road.

Oh oh. Comes now a roar that has a very devilish authority to it. There's a syncopated pounding rhythm to it that sounds like a very big time rapid. We had heard of BUCK CREEK—and shrugged it off too!

BUCK CREEK.[36] Land right. CAMP. In and amongst the rocks. A preliminary, brief survey really whizzers me. It looks like we might even have to line, though I have a tentative channel selected. But a merry dinner despite our woes. The Dodges fit into the river picture real smoothly and prove real good campers. To bed.

AUGUST 10

An early breakfast and I start surveying and re-surveying the rapid. It's bad. We toss in sticks and logs to see the effect of the turbulent water. It's far from reassuring to see fifteen foot by 8" logs disappear from sight, only to shoot up into the air a distance below. It's rough! In fact more than a mite coarse!

The decision to run is made, and I walk back to the WEN feeling like the cares of the World are hanging on my shoulders. I don't like this one, and I sort of feel like the lamb being led to slaughter, though my judgement tells me I will run it alright. River is running 9,800 second feet again today. At least it's stable.

WEN is off—and at bottom OK. A thriller! MEXICAN HAT II through in good shape. MYSTERY CANYON rears and bucks—Pres goes off seat,

Buck Creek Rapid, Snake River, Preston Walker in trouble

into the river, swims ahead and catches boat, climbs in, takes up oars, and works the heavy water-laden boat to shore on the left below. Kent and I were out for the rescue, and for a few seconds it looked like there'd have to be one! Then the Doctor through in good shape in the JOAN.

We are all in the boats and leaving BUCK CREEK behind. I will never forget this rapid, and I think the rest of the party will have a vivid recollection for quite some time!

SAWPIT CREEK RAPID. Another big namer. Quite rough but a good channel to follow. I run it with Ferris in the WEN. Her first real rapid. George Fletcher rides with Kent in the MEXICAN HAT II. Howard Welty with the Doc in the JOAN. Pres comes through solo. 12:30 PM everybody in and on from SAWPIT.

EAGLE BAR. Old Red Ledge Mine buildings.[37] We make a hard and toilsome trek up a steep cliff side to the buildings above—and no one is there! Do find some swell grapes. Eat lunch, and take a nap. This morning Margaret Marston had left us at BUCK CREEK to go with Jack Rottier to file his story back at Homestead. We expect them soon. I write Doris a letter to send out with Jack. This is the final and definite end of the road. Canyon gets more rugged ahead. Jack shows up, also another car with a party. Have a lot of fun getting picture taken with a very reluctant maiden. We all are photographed on a point of rock nearby, overlooking the river.

There comes a time! We shove off, to finally explore the innermost secrets of the famed HELLS CANYON without signposts, passersby etc. to keep us informed!

STEAMBOAT CREEK. Left. CAMP. A really very swell beach. Most welcome after a long, hard, tired, hot day. This river has a sort of tawny color, and packs the punch that a silty river can deliver.[38] All out fishing. Doc kills a rattlesnake. We find an old homestead, and also some good apple trees. The apples are utilized as applesauce to fill in the gap for the lacking grapefruit juice in the morning.

AUGUST 11

Up fairly early, but the Cowboy was even earlier, and he has the mate to Doc's rattler secured in a sack close by. After breakfast we have a long session of amusement with the snake. These snakes in this country are green in color. I muster the courage to pick the snake up by the tail—pass it over to Ferris—and she holds it! [Find] Harry in bed and put the live rattler on his bed and get a good picture of Harry departing in a hurry. The Cowboy lets the snake crawl all over his feet, and gives us some really good dope on the actions of snakes. We try out the time honored theory of a snake dying real fast in the sun—but this is a tough one, and after interminable waiting he's dispatched with a rock.[39] I *did* see a snake die in the sun, down in Cataract Canyon in 1938.

Time to move on to richer pastures. This brushy side stream here was poor fishing. Time is not too important as we seem to be gaining on our schedule.

DEEP CREEK. This one has quite a reputation for trout, so we plan to linger awhile. A lot of fishing goes on, but with very poor results. Season is wrong, and we're spoiled by the fabulous fishing on the Salmon. LUNCH.

We leave from DEEP CREEK. At least it was a nice place to loaf.

HELLS CREEK. We run wide open, but the name etc. had us jittery over this one. The view back at Deadman's Creek looking up it from Deep Creek was certainly the outstanding view of HELLS CANYON as we found out later on. It really was a thrilling sight and a magnificent piece of scenery.

MILE 101. No name, but a very rough and complicated rapid. TROUBLE! WEN off at 3:05 PM. Make it fine, though it's a tricky wollaper. Have to do some really sharp maneuvering. MEXICAN HAT II OK. Comes the Doctor in the JOAN, and we get one of the real thrills of the trip as he misjudges the current pull and is swept into the rocks, onto one, off, onto another—off! He makes it on down with a close brush with the undertaker! I decide to run the MYSTERY CANYON through myself, but take a different course. OK.

We leave the scene of near disaster![40]

CACHE CREEK. Left. CAMP. Kind of nice camp. The Doc rows across the river and works his way up to Granite Creek. Returns with very few

Checking out a big rapid

fish, but *did* discover an old homesteaders orchard—so brings more apples to camp. Today marks highest water of the trip on SNAKE. 9,980 second feet.

AUGUST 12
Break camp at 8:05 AM.

CACHE CREEK RAPID. Look it over, then I run through with George as passenger. OK. Comes then Neill Wilson as boatman in the MEXICAN HAT II. Good job! On a bet with Bruce I ride through with Pres in the MYSTERY CANYON, riding the stern deck standing up. I make $.52. Doc and Margaret in the JOAN.

We sail on from CACHE CREEK. I let George take over the oars for some first hand experience at rapid running.

George knocks one off at MILE 99 in good style.

MILE 98. George again, does alright.

MILE 96. George still at oars.

Another SQUAW CREEK! I take over the oars.

OOOPS! MILE 94. And very rough. Neill, George and I run through OK. Then I go back and bring the MYSTERY CANYON through with the Marston twins and Bruce in it. Then comes Ferris riding with Kent. Doc solo.

We're off. At least we're getting some thrills out of this trip!

BILLS CREEK. Nice ride.

RUSH CREEK. Watch out for this one. Was a bit too cocky in picking the channel on this baby, or at least didn't reduce all possible hazards quite enough, and Neill on deck, George riding cockpit, found us booming out in middle of the river towards our selected channel alongside a big rock in midstream. We got to the selected point alright, and dropped down into a really tough big hole like a flash.[41] A tense moment or so ensued while the question of rolling over or not loomed up big. Neill almost overboard. Whew! We landed alright below on left, but with the wind somewhat reduced in our sails. I selected a more conservative, though quite tricky channel, and ran through the MEXICAN HAT II myself. Then went back and got the JOAN, and, followed closely by Pres in the MYSTERY CANYON, came through again in good shape. At least the rapid shared honors with me!

So, we get the HELL out of this spot! Never saw so many spiders as there are here amongst the rocks.

Stop a few minutes at Mile 90 to investigate what we think might be ranch owned by Kyle McGrady. No dice.

SHEEP CREEK. Right. Lunch. We take this to be KYLE MCGRADY'S RANCH as there is a sort of boat landing. Beautiful stream here on right. We rassle up some lunch, follow a trail across a field to a real house in amongst the trees. Fruit trees around. Pinned to the back door of the house is a note, to Mrs. Lenora Wilson. Signed by the H. Petris. They tell her to walk down the river trail and they will row across to meet her. We are much puzzled. Finally decide Mrs. Jones looks after the place for Kyle—and forget the whole thing in exploring the kitchen and deciding upon big batches of hot cakes, covered with home made jam as a much to be desired delicacy. All I can say is that everyone ate and ate. Fooled around a bit more—finding less evidence to support the McGrady ownership theory—more another party. We leave a note, citing our plunderings (3 jam, 3 fruit), and finally, still yawning and stuffed to the brim, we shove off.[42]

SAND CREEK. *SURPRISE!* We see recently constructed buildings in considerable number—a real camp! A flash of a woman stepping into a cabin. As we land a pleasant chap who introduces himself as Henri Petri, proprietor of HELLS CANYON LODGE,[43] greets us! We disembark and go up to the very modern-like lodge living room and learn more of the project, which is a *dude ranch* supplied by Kyle McGrady!

A cordial welcome is also given to us by Henri's wife, Alice. Although they prevail upon us to stay overnight, we are urged to make a few more miles. We learn that the Petri's are going to walk some four miles downstream to a ranch house to do some phoning, so we ask them to join us. They do. Alice in the WEN, Henri in the MEXICAN HAT II. As we shove their dog swims out and clambers aboard—also their pet deer! The deer is put ashore, only to swim out again. So we decide to haul the deer along.

CAMP. Left. Nice bar. Mouth of TEMPERANCE CREEK. 15½ fine miles for the day. Our big water is now behind us. There is but the relatively open sections ahead, with not too exciting rapids. George Fletcher calls LEWISTON, then, after dinner, Alice, Ferris, Maradel, Loel and I—also Bruce, go back a ways to the cliffs where we spotted an old mine tunnel. BATS! much squealing etc. ensues as we venture to the hindmost depths some five hundred feet back. Lot of fun. Returning to camp, we all sit around and talk—Ferris and I until lateish. About 9,830 of water today. It's falling off a bit.

AUGUST 13

7:50 AM and we say farewells and shove off.

PITTSBURG LANDING. The Cowboy wants to stop here, but we sort of drift on before sure identification is made. Open section here. well tended ranches—a road.[44]

MILE 56. A nice dropping rapid which George and Bruce run.

WHITEHORSE RAPID. Get quite a thrill here, as the late afternoon light creates illusion of terrific drop. Navigation is difficult, and we tumble around and about in the biggish waves in a manner to thrill anyone. We're all very tired and anxious to camp. We're looking for a campsite now.

CAMP. On left, just above mouth of IMNAHA RIVER. Camp is welcome, and though it's a poor spot for a camp we make out pretty well. One thing about this Idaho run, we have learned to make camp just about anywhere. Fishing is tried, but is not too good. After dinner, Ferris, Bruce, Twins, Pres and I go up IMNAHA RIVER a ways to old mine tunnel. Follow it to end where it comes out on the main river above camp. Try another tunnel, but it's short. Doesn't take too long of this precarious, pathfinding, snake hunting trip to find us all most tired. We made 29 miles today. Quite a run!

AUGUST 14

Up early as usual. Am tired. Really too much river this year, though it's been a lot of fun. But I've really felt the strain of these last two trips, particularly as the alcohol problem was more than a mild worry. Never again!

Leave. IMNAHA. The rapid is quite a go-getter. I let George take the oars, while a do a bit of kibitzing on the side.[45]

SALMON RIVER! George piloted us thus far. We land on right in order to leave off some of the gang who will climb to a cliff above and get a good junction shot. We plan on rowing across and working up the Salmon a mite, then at a signal boom on out. The contrast of the tawny Snake and the crystal clear-like Salmon is something!

We're off! Bruce gets a bit tangled up with the oars, but we make a noble stagger at a good entrance. We land below a ways, back again on the left side of the river. The photographers rejoin us and we're off.

There's good water on left at CHERRY CREEK, MILE 46.

MILE 45. Site of last trips camp, first night on the Snake.

(Standing, left to right) Maradel Marston, Kent Frost, Ferris Dodge, Howard Welty; (seated, left to right) Norm Nevills, Preston Walker, unidentified, Loel Marston, unidentified, Harry Dodge, Otis Marston, unidentified, Margaret Marston

CHINA GARDEN CREEK. M & M ranch. We are glad to see again our hospitable hostess of last trip's stop here, Mrs. Lois Tippett. I call Irving Reynolds, and give him dope on our progress.

Approaching the GRAND RONDE RIVER I get terribly annoyed at the Doctor booming ahead. As I try to catch up he puts on the steam, and I only just to catch him as we come into the Grande Ronde River. I really blow my whistle, and am sorry about as fast—though the whistle blowing *was* justified in a way—that is, if blowing the whistle *ever is* justified.[46] We expect to meet our friend of last trip, Joe Eprun here. Neill and Bruce are going to leave us here this evening and head posthaste for California. We hate to see them go.

GRANDE RONDE RIVER. Left. CAMP. A house nearby, but the phone doesn't work. Joe Eprun shows up with his youngsters, and after some debating he crosses by ferry and drives right to our camp. Damn regretful goodbyes are said to Neill and Bruce. They both of kind of spirit sustainers in a party. A gloom seems to have settled on the party. Dinner gets over—this is anticlimactic. To bed.

[. . .] the SALMON RIVER was kicking in with around 6,000 feet when we passed it. Thus, we arrive in LEWISTON on about 15,000!

AUGUST 15
Break camp and we're off!

LIMEKILN RAPID. The steamboat boys talked about this.

CAPTAIN JOHN CREEK. We look at the boat built by the folks here. Also telephone Irv. This is MILE 23. Quite a ranch. A ferry in operating condition. What a camp we had here last trip!

The folks come down to see us off.

Margaret gets in with us and rides to next stopping point. It's good to get a visit with her. She wants to write trip up.

On right, at sandbar at MILE 21. Stop here to get a landing picture. Margaret returns to JOAN. We've decided upon eating lunch as we drift along, so as to get into ASOTIN early. It's hot!

Just below mouth of TEN MILE CREEK on left. Visit awhile with Wallace Johnson and brother and wives. They are operating a placer mine here. It was this same spot at almost same time that last trip the airplane came over and dropped us mail etc.

We first try to make camp up at MILE 7½, but there's dead animal close by, so we go on. The Doctor, Margaret, and the Cowboy leave us here to spend evening across the river at a Mr. Chapman's house.

MILE 6, mouth ASOTIN CREEK. ASOTIN, WASHINGTON. Frankly this is a hell of a place to camp, but we're not due in LEWISTON until 2:00 PM tomorrow!

George, Harry, and I grab a bus for LEWISTON, and boom into the Lewis and Clark for a big steak dinner. George calls friends. We got out to an auto camp and spend the night. Next morning a friend of George's comes and gets us to go to breakfast.

AUGUST 16
This morning I go to the CLARKSTON airport and rent a Piper Cub and boom down over the boats. Give 'em a good buzzing by amateur standards!

ARRIVE MCGRADY LANDING, LEWISTON. We're greeted here by quite a delegation, and again are presented with certificates citing our accomplishment. We have run all rapids for first time in small boats. These are first women to make the trip. A party and radio broadcast this evening. To bed!

AUGUST 17
Load boats, say goodbye all around, then Ferris, Harry, Kent and I take off for Boise. First night we stay at good old RIGGINS again. Next day we stop enroute and visit NIXONS. On to Boise. Next day we put on broadcast—meet with Jack Rottier—see Don Smith—*THE RIVER TRIP IS OVER!*

[Nevills Notes On Snake River Journal][47]

TRIP:

SNAKE RIVER. From Brownlees Ferry to Lewiston, Idaho.

148 MILES. 115 RAPIDS AND RIFFLES. KINNEY CREEK, SQUAW CREEK, and BUCK CREEK are really tough rapids.

AUGUST 8 to AUGUST 18.

Average 6,500 second feet of water on Snake above SALMON RIVER.

We appear definitely to be the first boats, smaller than a steamboat, to *run* all the rapids of HELLS CANYON.

We seem to have taken the first women on through.

OUR BOATS:

#1. The WEN. Pilot boat. Veteran of 4 Grand Canyon runs, 3 Cataract Canyon runs. 1 Green River run. Piloted by Norm Nevills, with Neill C. Wilson of Burlingame, and George Fletcher of Boise, as passengers.

#2. MEXICAN HAT II. Veteran of '41 and '42 Grand Canyon runs. Piloted by Kent Frost of Monticello, Utah. Ferris and Harry Dodge of San Francisco as passengers.

#3. JOAN. Veteran of 3 Grand Canyon runs. Piloted by Doctor Marston of Berkeley, California, with his wife Margaret, and Howard O. Welty (COWBOY) of Oakland Technical Highschool, as passengers.

#4. MYSTERY CANYON. San Juan Type Boat. Piloted by Pres Walker of Grand Junction, Colorado, with Maradel and Loel Marston, twin daughters of the Doc's, and Bruce Wilson, son of Neill, as passengers.

We did not take on any supplies for the 9 day run other than those we started with.

Wonder of wonders, it didn't rain on this trip!

The water was a fairly good stage, though we could have used a bit more on the real toughy—BUCK CREEK! The river, in Hells Canyon is not to be underestimated. It is rough and powerful. Though the waves are not especially high, compared to the Colorado, yet they have a very real viciousness to them. In real high stages the whirlpools would be very dangerous.

Rattlesnakes are very plentiful, and care needs to be exercised at all times. It's a good, smart, safe idea to camp on the sand.

Just drifting, you average from 3½ to 5 ½ MPH.

IT'S A SWELL TRIP!

Green River,
June 16 to July 5, 1947
Grand Canyon,
July 10 to August 5, 1947

By 1947, Nevills Expedition river trips had taken on a modern form, with a length and style that commercial outfitters still follow. Nevills' San Juan trips were a week long, and by this time, cost $200 for the trip. The longer trips on the Green and Colorado were about two to three weeks. The 1940 trip was just too long; as noted by David Lavender, Doris and Barry Goldwater argued that "three thousand dollars for a summer of working like a dog and broiling like a weenie" was not likely to attract very many guests. Nevills admitted that a lengthy, two-month trip was just too much, not only for the passengers but for the crew and equipment. River running is hard work; downtime is needed to repair equipment damaged during the trip and recruit crews worn out by not only running the boats and doing all the camp chores, but babysitting the passengers. All of the passengers on the 1940 trip, as well as Doris in her published account, complained of the length of the voyage. In 1946, when Nevills went to Idaho after a full season on the San Juan, he wrote, tellingly, that he had had "too much river." In response to a request for a trip that went from the source of the Green to the Gulf of California, Nevills wrote: "I do not recommend taking the whole run of the Green River and the Colorado River in one shot. Its too long a trip, and is much more enjoyed and appreciated when its done a section at a time. It's far better to do a few weeks of it, and end the trip with your appetite whetted for more, than to do it all, become tired of the long grind, and not have anything to look forward to the next year."[1] In his Grand journal for 1947—again after a full season on the San Juan—Nevills wrote: "I feel glad to rest after the rugged series of unbroken river miles of the last two months."

So for the 1947 season, he decided to go back and revisit the Green River, which he had not been on since 1940, but only to float the scenic reach from Green River, Wyoming, to Jensen, Utah. As always, Nevills chose the high water season; the river peaked that year on July 13 at 17,100 cfs, which made for exciting rides. Unfortunately for the crew and passengers, the falling water also meant it was the peak of the mosquito season. Some things hadn't changed: the ranches, the mosquitoes, and the cold weather. But what was noticeably different was Nevills's confidence in his abilities and his boats. The 1947 Grand Canyon trip was also the first time he had been there since the start of World War II, save for a quick run down to Badger Rapid in 1944 for an article that appeared in Life magazine. So despite his weariness, Nevills was eager to get back to the Grand Canyon, even then recognized as the ne plus ultra of western whitewater boating.

Again, it was great water by his standards, with the river at 38,300 cfs on the day they launched. By this time Nevills was charging over $2,000 for a three-week trip, a price that would be considered standard by the 1990s but was quite a sum at the time. His clients, therefore, were usually from the upper end of the social scale—the wealthy and adventurous—or else those who were in a position to provide publicity, such as Randall Henderson, the editor and publisher of Desert Magazine.

But Nevills had a new passion on which to expend his bountiful energies: flying. Throughout his journals he records sightings of airplanes, and it's obvious that he was attracted to the glamour of flight. During the war he gave in to his urge to soar and learned to fly at Drapela Flying Service in Grand Junction, Colorado. His reason was that the roads around Mexican Hat were so atrocious—all but impassable after even a brief rain—and he needed a better way to get around for his trips and in case of emergency. But one can't help but glean from his writing that the little-boy thrill of soaring and flying close to the ground, performing perilous flights under bridges, and what he always called "flitting" was an equally powerful motivator. Just after the Idaho trip Nevills bought a Piper J3, a small agile taildragger, and began work on his own airstrip north of Mexican Hat, which he finished by the end of 1946. From this time on, as revealed in his journals and correspondence, flying is obviously just as important to him as river running. And Nevills—that most cautious of boatmen who would study a rapid for hours and even then sometimes decide to line—turned out to be a daredevil pilot. From the first, he was known for buzzing close to the ground to impress his passengers, for flying under Navajo Bridge near Lees Ferry, and for making landings and takeoffs at primitive, remote airstrips all around the canyon country.

By the summer of 1947, he had already had one wreck, when he tried to land his airplane on a flat patch of ground east of Mexican Hat, with the wife of a local prospector as his passenger. As he told it, while in the air he was struck by a desperate need to urinate, and since he had the passenger along couldn't just go through a hole in the floor of the airplane as he usually did, so he tried to land. In doing so he stood the Piper up on its nose, destroying the propeller. After a frantic search by Eddie Drapela and Pres Walker, he was found. A new prop was flown in, repairs made, and he flew out unharmed.

Not content with the small engine in the original Piper J3, that year he had it "souped up" with a change to a more powerful 115 hp engine, a ram air scoop, and a variable-pitch propeller. He commented in several letters that it now flew like a "Spitfire." He had finished his airstrip at Mexican Hat, built a hanger and other shop buildings, and registered the plane with the FAA and other flying agencies. The Piper was a great convenience for the Nevills family, since Mexican Hat was so isolated and the roads so poor (the roads into the area weren't paved until the late 1950s). But his family and friends were concerned by his daring style in the air, and by the fact that he spent so much time in his airplane that he even neglected old friends. In February 1948, Pres Walker commented in a letter to Otis Marston: "Norm was up last week end . . . I don't know whether he is sore or just so wrapped up in that damned airplane that he hasn't time for anything else. Frankly, if he keeps flying and souping it up, I think he is going to be wrapped up permanently in it."[2] It was to prove a fateful prophecy.

JUNE 16

Leave Mexican Hat around 1:00 PM. Kent Frost[3] and Dave Morris[4] go ahead to Monticello in the Recon car pulling the JOAN and the MH. Doris, Rosalind Johnson,[5] our daughter Joan and I are in the station wagon pulling the WEN. We all get into Moab on the lateish side and stay there.

JUNE 17

All arrive in Price, Utah fairly early. We find that the generator on the recon car is burned out. This all takes time. Elect to go on to Salt Lake to get a generator, and anyhow, going up through Vernal to Green River, Wyoming doesn't seem practical as there is pavement all the way this other route. We run into a place in Salt Lake—Feltes Auto Parts, that exchanges a generator—we eat dinner and take off. Soon run into heavy showers. Try several places along the line to get cabins or hotel rooms but no luck. Finally, at Evanston, Wyoming, I arrange for Kent and Dave to sleep in a corridor of the city bastille. The girls and I drive on another 69 miles to *LITTLE AMERICA,* and there by rare good fortune, at 1:00 AM find one unoccupied cabin! One double bed, so Ros and Joan sleep in their bags on the floor. We all sleep *soundly!* Up fairly early, yet Kent and Dave arrive before we have breakfast.

GREEN RIVER,
JUNE 18 TO JULY 5, 1947

JUNE 18

We are in Green River, Wyoming by 9:30 AM. Check on our hotel rooms, then go down and put the boats in the river at Expedition Island. I see my old friend Adrian Reynolds, and his son A.K. Reynolds.[6] Back and have lunch, then we drive over to Rock Springs, where I rent a plane and take off for a hop.

JUNE 19

Everyone has arrived. Doris, Kent, and I, with Ros, go over to Rock Springs, and I take them all flying. Doris and I fly over to Green River and land on a strip on top of the bluff overlooking the boats. Storms heavily in afternoon. This evening we decide that if it's raining heavily in the morning to postpone our takeoff. I am a guest at the Lion's Club.

JUNE 20

We are at the boats in the rain about 9:30 AM. Large group from town on hand. I announce that we will postpone takeoff for one day—but that we will sail rain or storm or what have you the next day.

JUNE 21

Getting much local interest in trip, also outside papers are carrying stories. This is my second trip from right here, the last being June 20, 1940. 10:00 AM. It's drizzling—but we embark. Good sized crowd. We get toots of whistles, waves, sirens, etc. Cold.

WEN: Norman D. Nevills, Joan Nevills, Rosalind Johnson, Al Milotte[7]

MH: Kent Frost, Maradel Marston, Loel Marston, Willie Taylor[8]

JOAN: Doc Marston,[9] Shirley Marston,[10] Garth Marston, Adrian Reynolds

Last night, or rather this morning, I separated further dealings with Dave Morris my other boatman. He was to have stayed and watched the boats for an hour last night, but took off and left them. Prowlers got a carton of cigarettes. This morning I hire Garth to come in at Lees Ferry to take over the new boat: SANDRA.[11]

Elevation here at takeoff is 6060. We will drop down to 4720 at Jensen, losing 1340' in our 205 miles ahead.

MILE 381. HARSHA RANCH. Up to here we were suffering very acutely from the cold rain. Looking for a place to get shelter we spotted this ranch. Landing on right we wander back across a muddy field and discover a small far from neat, children filled house. But it's warm and out of the rain. We ferry the boats a bit further downstream so as to be closer to the house. Eat lunch here and keep a sharp eye on the weather. Middle afternoon shows a little let-up, and we are only too eager to get from out of our cramped quarters.

MILE 377. LOGAN RANCH. We glide right on by. My memories of this terribly rundown, filthy appearing ranch is borne out, and it would be desperate straits that would compel a stop here![12]

MILE 372. Island on right. CAMP. We land here *cold*, wet, hungry and tired. Everything is wet, but one of those miracles of the out of doors is performed—a fire is made, bed spots located, and dinner soon cooking. It rains very lightly a few times during the night, but we all get a good nights' sleep. Thanks to a big signal tarp brought [for] me by Ros Johnson, Joan and I have a dry bed.

JUNE 22

Skies are a bit clearer, but it's quite cold.

MILE 366. Its very cold and we're all uncomfortable.

MILE 365½. Land right. We pull in here to build a fire. Kent sees a buck, promptly wings it, so its brought to the fire, skinned, quartered and loaded into the boats. Fresh meat! We are jubilant. Skies are clearing a bit more and looks like it won't be so cold now. The fire has warmed us through.

MILE 357. Kent shoots two Canadian geese with the .22 rifle. Gets them right through the head.

MILE 351. HOLMES RANCH.[13] Stopped here in '40. Mrs. Holmes takes a keen interest in all the river parties. Mr. Holmes has died since we were here last, but Mrs. Holmes carries on alone, with occasional help from nephews etc. We bring in our lunch. After lunch, Doc has decided to go back to Green River in order to look for his camera which he believes he left at the Harsha Ranch. This he will do by catching the stage tomorrow morning downstream a ways and just back from river on right. He will then stage it down to Manila, thence through Linwood[14] and to river where we'll camp tomorrow. All ride a horse, principally Joan. I get a mean cut on my left palm from baling wire on reins! Generally enjoy ourselves loafing around. Have the [deer] with dressing, cooked by Mrs. Holmes, for dinner. Al and I sleep in the bunkhouse on the bed, Willie, Doc, and Adrian on the floor. Adrian will go as far as Sheep Creek or possibly Hideout Flat, where his folks will come get him.

June 23

After breakfast, Mrs. Holmes gets out a decrepit Model A Ford, we push it a ways, then drive Doc the odd mile to where a hand cable car crosses the river. I ferry Doc across the river. Garth and Adrian try out a boat that Mrs. Holmes has tied up here, and they have a fearful time getting back and forth across the river. On way back to ranch I note a wonderful landing field in a horse pasture. It is about ¼ mile south and east of the main house. Soon collect our equipment, thank Mrs. Holmes for her grand hospitality, and take off with the best looking weather we've seen so far.

We can see much snow on the mountains ahead! Much of it is fresh. The river is much higher than normal for this time of year, and it seems to be rising as a result of these heavy, unseasonable rains.

MILE 350¼. Cable crossing is here that Mrs. Holmes uses.

MILE 349. See two deer on island just below here.

MILE 346. See a doe and buck swimming in river. Quite a sight. Al gets pics.

MILE 343. Make out old abandoned ranch on right.

MILE 341. DEER.

MILE 341. Old house on left.

MILE 339. Old house on right.

MILE 338. FERRY CROSSING.

MILE 337. Buildings on left. UPPER MARSH CREEK.

MILE 335. Ferry crossing indicated here on map, but there very definitely is absolutely no sign of a ferry, approach road or anything else. We check this very closely.

LUNCH left. Sheep camp is back upstream on this same side a ways. No shade here, but its grassy and looks to be tick free. Really beautiful day. River really booming. Garth is running the JOAN.

MILE 321½. UTAH-WYOMING STATE LINE! It's hard to tell just where the line is here, but Al and I do some trick calculating, sighting, etc., and establish to our own satisfaction the crossing point.

MILE 319. SMITH FERRY.[15] CAMP. *MOSQUITOES!!!* Up to now we haven't been bothered by mosquitoes, but here they are! In droves! River is swollen with floods, and recent rains seem to have brought out the mosquitoes. There's a USGS measuring cable here and we all ride back and forth. A car with people from Linwood drives in to visit. We scatter far and wide rustling up firewood. A fence post or so helps out. Dinner is barely being served when the Doc drives in with a truck. He joins us. No sign of his camera at Harsha Ranch. Roads all washed out. He has Adrian, later on boat down to the island at Mile 365½ where he thinks he may have left the camera. (Incidentally, upon arrival at Vernal we find the camera still in the station wagon where it was left when unloading it at GREEN RIVER, WYOMING!) Have a delicious steak dinner from the venison. It is marvelously tender. After sundown mosquitoes drift off, and we all have a grand night's sleep.

June 24

Very clear this morning. Not a cloud as yet to be seen. River may be falling a bit.

MILE 318. ENTRANCE TO FLAMING GORGE. No wind this time as in 1940!

MILE 315. Rapid here leveled over by the high water. We are all terribly impressed by the unusual beauty of this, Horseshoe Canyon. Not alone is the change so great from the barren canyons above here, but this canyon is outstanding.

MILE 309. SHEEP CREEK. We intended to camp here originally but it looks most uninviting. Mosquitoes are thick, and Sheep Creek is running high with a muddy red water. Adrian leaves his bed roll here, expecting his folks in later in day. Later tomorrow we return to find that someone, probably in a jeep, has driven to here and stolen his bedroll! We leave here deciding to go to the camp ground below. It's clouding up again. More rain in the offing!

MILE 308. Our first rapid, opposite BEEHIVE POINT. It's *mild.*

MILE 307. HIDEOUT FLAT CAMP GROUND, on the right. Road down Sheep Creek ends here. There are camp stoves, hydrants (that don't work), etc. Also quite a few mosquitoes. The river is dropping a bit. It's trying to rain. After lunch we walk up the road a ways. Find tree across road which we try to burn up so as to clear the road. Not too successful. Returning back towards camp Adrian recalls that a trail leaves here, goes downriver 3½ miles to EAGLE CREEK, thence another 3½ miles up to GREEN LAKES. We decide upon this walk, hiring a car to get us the 35 miles by road back to here tomorrow. At 2:30 PM, Joan, Willie, Doc, Adrian and I set out. It's a beautiful hike and well worth the effort. We arrive at Green Lakes Lodge[16] about dark, tired, cool and hungry. A big trout dinner, and good bed makes the venture worthwhile. It snowed up here at the lodge two days ago, so no wonder it's cold. Country is all soaked up with water.

JUNE 25

Breakfast not too early. We arrange for one of the owners here, for $10 to drive us down this afternoon in his weapons carrier to the boats. Wash, wander around, and otherwise spend a pleasant morning. We eat a very hearty lunch. I HAVE SOME *HAMBURGER STEAK*.[17]

Roads are terribly muddy, but away we go. Find Adrian's mother, brother, and brother-in-law in the ditch a ways up from the river in Sheep Creek. Adrian leaves us to ride back to his folks with the weapons carrier.

A good dinner—to bed. River has dropped considerably.

JUNE 26

River has dropped still more during the night. Game of charades played last night.

I don't feel any too wonderful this morning, stomach seems a bit upset.

MILE 305. CARTER CREEK. Al and Doc get out here to walk on downstream a ways in order to get a picture of the boats coming down the canyon. We give them lots of time to get set.

MILE 304. EAGLE CREEK. Pick up Al and Doc. Trail here to top.

MILE 298. SKULL CANYON AND CREEK. Latter has water, but no place to camp. Mouth of canyon dismal sort of place loaded with mosquitoes. We are making camp as we are right on schedule to here.

MILE 298. ISLAND. No mosquitoes here, but lots of ants. Not much in way of shelter, but we want to get where the mosquitoes won't eat us up. I feel kind of lousy. So does Joan and Doc. (We later learn that Adrian gets sick on way home too.) I eat lunch against my better judgement—including SALMON—and get a couple of really rough vomiting sessions. Later a sort of diarrhea. Try to sleep rest of afternoon. Don't eat dinner, and when night comes Al loans me his air mattress. Joan and Doc feel a bit better.

JUNE 27

I feel pretty rocky this morning and decide against eating.

MILE 294½. Kent shoots baby deer, but too small to eat. It looked to be larger than it was, and everyone, including Kent, is sorry.

MILE 292. ASHLEY FALLS. At first glance this looks to be a roughy for everything including lining. We see where the USGS party lined and portaged on the LEFT, also, DON HARRIS tried to run on the left and UPSET.[18] He didn't hold onto his boat, but let it go, and they didn't recover it until an eddy clear down at Mile 272—OLD BRIDGEPORT. He lost all three oars and had to go back to Rock Springs with a rancher to get oars. Kent and I go across the river in the WEN to look it over. Left side is no good. I have trouble getting around as am rather weak and not sure footed. Easy lining job, and Kent and I slip right down, then boom right across to left side below. Then Kent, Garth, Doc and I return with the MH2 and the JOAN. Garth and Kent line more or less alright, but after taking off Kent gets sucked into a hole that gives he and Garth quite an experience. I feel too miserable to line, doesn't look too tough to run, so with the Doctor on deck, I run the JOAN right on through ASHLEY FALLS! Nothing to it.

MILE 291. Mining outfit on right. Saw this too in '40.

MILE 290. All rapids but ASHLEY FALLS, to here very simple to run.

MILE 288½. Big stream of clear water coming in on right.

MILE 282. LITTLE DAVENPORT CREEK. As we approach here we see a man, wife and two children and a horse on the bank. We pull in and find they have been spending the day fishing. The young fellow has a ranch up the canyon about a half mile, and since the war has been developing the place. He proves to be the brother of the young chap, who, with his father, Mr. Burton, met us in 1940 a ways below here. We visit, make camp. They eat with us. Mosquitoes are very bad. I feel better and eat some dinner. Some of us go up to the ranch, and are barely settled when Mr. Burton and one of his sons come in! They left their truck five miles out and walked in to here. Quite a coincidence. These folks address: Mr. and Mrs. Earl Burton, Linwood, Utah. The father is Orson Burton.[19] Back to camp, where we all have a grand nights sleep.

June 28

River is still dropping, and shows a two foot drop from recent flood.

MILE 278. RED CREEK RAPID.[20] Quite a toughy in a way. Has a rather complicated channel, which we climb hill above to better study. I pick a rocky, complicated channel, which requires some lightening of passengers to run. Must watch this one—the waves actually look bigger and the water much rougher than it is when viewing from up on the hill. WEN off, with Ros and Joan Nevills as passengers. MH2 with LOEL and WILLIE, JOAN with Garth and Shirley as passengers.

MILE 275. A small boulder-constructed diversion dam, with takeoff on the left.

MILE 274. ALLEN RANCH (formerly Jarvie's). Number of people here on left bank, and we go up to the ranch house where Mrs. William Allen and her three children, 6,9, and 11 greet us. She wants data on the Calvert School. (Doris sends it to her later.) Mrs. Allen presents us with 4 doz. eggs, and a lot of radishes. Have a nice visit.

MILE 272. LUNCH. No shade, but it's cloudy and the wind is blowing a bit. We stopped first across the river at Old Bridgeport but the mosquitoes were too thick for us. My stomach still touchy, but I put away some lunch.

MILE 270. LEFT. TAYLOR RANCH. We get a somewhat lukewarm reception here. Same as '40. The elder Mr. Taylor, who lived across the river below here died last year, Mrs. Taylor moved to Rock Springs. This younger couple a queer sort of silent customers. Mr. Taylor is going in his pickup to oil town of Clay Basin, and I wangle a ride for Doc, Willie, Garth and Shirley. Rest of us loaf around the ranch until bored to distraction, then decide to take off and camp over at the other Taylor place across the river. We get permission to move into the smaller house.

MILE 268. CAMP Right. TAYLOR RANCH. Raining. Quite a walk over to the ranch house and the mosquitoes are really tough. Shelter behind screens is most welcome. At 6:00 PM, Doc and rest come in the JOAN. Have a good dinner, then make beds around the house on the floor. A cable crossing is here.

JUNE 29

SHOVE OFF. Still plenty of clouds around, though beautiful morning.

MILE 266. Entering SWALLOW CANYON.

Wonderful action on part of the swallows. Get many good pics. This is a really great sight.

MILE 261. COLORADO STATE LINE.

MILE 260. Rickety, high suspension bridge that could handle cars if one wanted a thrill.[21] (On way home I talked with Al Christensen at Hole in Rock eating place, and he told me that when he was with CCC he drove across this bridge a number of times.) Just below here on left Al gets some swell pics of the swallows in action again.

11:00 AM. Mile 256½. Wind is blowing hard. Downstream and cold. At least it's blowing the right direction for us, though where it blows towards a bank it's hard work to keep the boats from being driven ashore.

MILE 253. LUNCH. And it's really blowing. It makes serving lunch hard to say the least, but we make out.

MILE 248. CAMP. We spot the schoolhouse[22] back from the river, but the trees and sloughs between us and mainland make for a very difficult landing. We finally pull in and tie up, Kent and I going to search out a trail. We find one, and, combating the thickets [sic] hordes of mosquitoes we've seen yet we walk some half mile to the schoolhouse and the adjacent building that must have served as the teachers headquarters. We decide upon camping here, and equipment, beds, etc. are all brought up—including water. We cook in the small building, but sleep on the well polished hardwood floor of the school house. After dinner we put on an impromptu entertainment and all have a fine time. Storm holds off, and evening finds the mosquitoes all gone, so a fine nights rest is had by all.

JUNE 30

Day dawns clear. I seem to have an upset stomach again so I pass up breakfast. We get to boats as fast as possible and thus miss some of the mosquitoes.

MILE 243. Entrance to LODORE CANYON.

Nevills party, Green River, 1947: (back row, left to right) Otis Marston, Willie Taylor, Loel Marston, Shirley Marston, Rosalind Johnson, Maradel Marston, Garth Marston; (front row) Al Milotte, Norman Nevills, Joan Nevills, Kent Frost

MILE 238¼. Am keeping close check on position through here so as to not go booming over DISASTER FALLS by mistake. We want pics of the run.

MILE 237. UPPER DISASTER FALLS. Land on left and work over the course. Not too tricky a channel, but distance to run requires a lot of channel to memorize. Cameras set, and we are running with the other two boats following right behind me. WEN, Joan Nevills, MH2, Maradel Marston, JOAN, Shirley Marston. I go through in the WEN right on the button where I picked the channel. Doc gets sucked in on main channel and overtakes and passes me. MH2 picks up water in first drop, lands, bails out, and then comes on through.

MILE 236½. HEAD OF LOWER DISASTER FALLS. This is obviously an easy one to run at this stage so we'll take it on with all passengers aboard. Stomach not so good so am passing up lunch too. Feel a bit weak, but we're making camp down at foot of Triplet Falls, and I'll hang on that long alright.

MILE 236. FOOT of LOWER DISASTER FALLS. All boats through OK.

MILE 234.[23] Glance over this one, then decide for Garth to try it. WEN with Joan and Ros. Kent with one passenger, Garth with Willie. WEN lands at bottom OK, but Kent and Garth can't make pull to shore so go on to land below on right. I end up with 5 passengers aboard and have a good ride to below where we join rest.

MILE 233. I run this one with Rosalind as passenger; Kent and Garth come through solo. They do fairly well, though aren't right on beam.

MILE 232½. TRIPLET FALLS. Really rough on top. I announce no passengers, and that the other two boats are to follow me through. Am missing the fun I should be having as am so tired and weak I can hardly pull an oar. Am substituting skill for strength. Going up to boats I find Joan waiting there, so I load her into the WEN, and off we all go. Both Kent and Garth are solo.

MILE 232. CAMP. Foot of TRIPLET FALLS on left. A beautiful camp which we rig up in style from many drift planks laying around. Everyone goes in swimming. I feel much better after eating. Spend a very pleasant evening, most of gang playing charades, I catch up on a mystery novel I found along the way.

JULY 1

Beautiful day. River raised and lowered 4' during the night. Old boat is still here that was wrecked a good many years ago.[24]

MILE 231. HELLS HALF MILE RAPID. A first class tough deal. The water at no place is unrunnable, but we're sure to ship *some* water on the first drop, and that would mean trouble in dodging the many rocks below. It can be done alright, but is not practical. Government party of Don Harris stupidly portaged the hard way across river on left. It is easy to portage here for 70 yards. At 8:30 AM a Cessna with JACK TURNER of Vernal and ELMA MILOTTE circles and circles overhead. At first I think it's Mandy Campbell.[25]

We start portage by pulling WEN out, unloading, and then carrying the WEN on a partially build *[sic]* up and cleared trail for 70 yards. It's not too hard a job, but when all three boats and their equipment is at river's edge again we're very glad.[26] We eat lunch, then with Joan with me in the WEN, I shove off and run on right to foot of rapid in cove below. I lightly tap one rock enroute. Other boats hit a bit more and often, but we all get there alright. Upon landing, as an experiment for a place to loaf on, I take three of the air inflated belt type preservers and rig up an air mattress. It proves most comfortable to my surprise and I decide upon this type of bed from now on.

MILE 231. Everyone at the bottom of HELLS HALF MILE and SHOVE OFF.

MILE 228. ALCOVE BROOK. Land here and find that there's fine water just a ways up the canyon. At mouth, and for 100 yards or so in canyon water disappears under the gravel. It's a beautiful camp. Kent spotted two deer just above camp, and he and Joan go stalking them. Return much later, but no luck. Have a swell dinner, and my stomach is back to normal. This has been our second perfectly clear and beautifully warm day of the trip. Looks like the weather man finally has taken pity on us. *THIS IS A CAMP SITE TO REMEMBER.*

JULY 2

A very clear morning.

MILE 225¼. On right chase two fawns and a doe in order to try to get them to swim river for pictures. Much beating of brush, and get land shots of them, but they don't take to water.

MILE 225. YAMPA RIVER.

MILE 224. PAT'S HOLE. This is where I spent evening talking with Buzz Holmstrom in '40. Floating up here we spy Mr. Chew[27] and son downstream a ways fishing. They come up and take us over to Mrs. Chew and children where they are about to mow hay. We visit there a while, then Mrs. Chew drives us all up in the truck to their modernized comfortable ranch. Two miles to ranch. We visit wind cave on way back. Have a very fine dinner as guests of Chews. Mr. Chew and I make a trade! After getting home I mail him my 30-30 Savage, which in turn he sends me a brand new 30-30 Winchester Model '94 carbine. Repairing back to the river, Mr. and Mrs. Chew take the MH2 and two of their girls and go for a ride. First time they have ever been in a boat together! Chew pulls a mighty good oar. We wave goodbye and take off.

MILE 218. JONES HOLE CREEK. This is where we should have made camp as the fishing is unusually fine here. NEXT TRIP STOP HERE.[28]

MILE 217. SAGE CREEK. Good camp here, also water, but no fishing. We see a beaver at work across the river. Some old mine tunnels here, so after dinner we go up and prowl around in them. They are not very extensive, but we have a lot of fun. Beautiful night and we all sleep well.

JULY 3

Al makes pictures of the Twins getting dressed and other similar shots. Al is indefatigable in shooting pictures.

MILE 212. RUPLE RANCH.[29] (Joel Evans). What a thrill! Sticking out from the right bank is a stick with a flag on it, so like 1940. We spot Joel Evans too, also Elma Milotte. It's grand to see Joel, and we're all pleased to see Elma. We go over to the ranch house and Joel gets horse saddled for everyone to ride. Joan is in her glory. Yesterday she rode clear from Chew's ranch back to the river. She is really developing into quite a rider. Joel makes up a batch of sourdough bread, and do we eat! And watermelon. It's a grand visit. We hate to leave, but we want to get some miles under us yet today.

SHOVE OFF. Elma comes over into the WEN, and will ride from here on to JENSEN with us. Rosalind goes into the MH2, Willie Taylor goes to JOAN.

MILE 207. We're entering SPLIT MOUNTAIN CANYON—it's trying to rain—and I'm rarin' to run rapids!

MILE 201. We've been pouring on the coal!!

MILE 199. *WE'RE THROUGH SPLIT MOUNTAIN!* See a man, his wife and two children at camping spot by cave on right, so we pull in to say hello and warm up by their fire. Mr. and Mrs. Raymond Rueter, Western Springs, Illinois. We visit a while, then decide to drop on down to the ranch of the brother of Mr. Ruple up at Pat's Hole. We want to get to Dinosaur Monument early tomorrow.

MILE 197. CUB CREEK (CHEW RANCH)[30] Left. Stormy and not too inviting here. We go up to ranch house and find young Chew and his wife at home, but about to drive to Jensen. I think it wise to go on to Jensen then Vernal in order to get the cars and trailers ready to pick up the boats tomorrow in order to save time. So, Joan, Shirley, Garth and I go into town. Chews take us to Vernal and we take them to dinner. Joan and I use Elma's room, Shirley and Garth get fixed up. We check with Mrs. Bus Hatch who has taken care of our cars, and thence to bed!

July 4

Up to an early start. Joan and I in the station wagon, Shirley and Garth in the recon car. On edge of town I see an airfield, so girls stay with recon [car] on highway, and Garth and I rent an Aeronca, and away we go! We boom up the river, locate the boats at MILE 196, and take three first rate passes at them.

We land at Vernal, then drive to Jensen where we park the recon car and the trailers, thence on to Dinosaur Monument where our party has already arrived.

MILE 188. DINOSAUR NATIONAL MONUMENT. We are given a most hospitable welcome here and shown a very interesting trip. It's a highlight of the trip. Kent's wife shows up with her brother. Violet rides on to Jensen with us.

SHOVE OFF from Dinosaur Monument. Joan and Al go overland in the station wagon with Al, who is going to get shore shots. They will join us below.

Pres and Becky,[31] flown by Jimmie Rigg, buzz us in a Super Cruiser.

12:45 PM MILE 182. THIS IS IT! JENSEN, UTAH. Quite a crowd is on bank and bridge to welcome us. Pres and Becky are there. Ethel Rae Zuefelt. Many others. Pics are taken, and we then grab off lunch at a little lunch stand. Then to loading boats—it's hot!

Finally accomplished and we all go into Vernal. Directly though it's 4:00 PM, and we go out to see Pres, Becky and Jimmie take off. Back to Vernal again and first thing we know it's time to eat.

Most farewells are said this evening as we're getting an early start.

July 5

Up for a really early start. Doc, Ros, Joan, Garth and I in the station wagon. Kent and Violet in the recon car.

Kent, Violet, Doc, and Garth stay overnight in Monticello.

Rosalind, Joan and I drive on through to Mexican Hat, arriving about 11:00 PM. We're tired—but terribly pleased with having most successfully completed a trip that was made under most trying conditions. It was a grand group, and certainly equivalent to anything that would arise.

GRAND CANYON,
JULY 10 TO AUGUST 5, 1947

JULY 10

Most all details being caught up with at Mexican Hat, boats all loaded, food and supplies assembled and checked, start is made from Mexican Hat. Doris, Sandra, Dock and I lead off with the station wagon trailing the trailer carrying the JOAN and the WEN. We are followed by Ros and Garth in a Chevrolet sedan with a trailer carrying the new cataract boat the SANDRA.[32] Kent and his wife drive the army recon car pulling the MEXICAN HAT II.

Uneventful and trouble free passage is made to Marble Canyon. Our plans to unload the boats that same day are thrown out of gear by a plea of Al Milotte for pictures the next morning of the boats being trailered down to Lees Ferry proper. It rather spoils our plans but we accede.

JULY 11

Up early and accompanied by movie shots we eventually get the boats down to the boat "landing" at Lees Ferry. Load one trailer on another, and hustle back to Marble Canyon. Doris, in the car with El and Al Millotte and Sandra shift over to the recon car. We rendezvous at Cameron, finding they don't serve lunches! Al and El go on. Doris and Sandra shift over to the recon car. We make the South Rim about 1:30 PM. Get a brief look from the Hopi Tower, then contact Lem Garrison, asst. supt. Meet other of the Park Service personnel, including Perry Brown. Hasty arrangements are made for storing of the trailer, recon car, and food supplies. Dock and Ros are met at Bright Angel Lodge. All of us together arrange with Scotty for a flight from the Rim back to Marble Canyon. I am much annoyed to put it mildly at this rushing and haste, where we had planned on a bit of visiting with friends. Arriving at the airport, driven out by Mr Wright, manager of Bright Angel Lodge, we form quite a company to fill up the ancient but amazingly sturdy and reliable old Ford Trimotor. Captain Wolf, our pilot introduces his wife—who proves to be the former Jean Conrath, veteran of a San Juan river trip back in 1940. The flight is one I will never forget. It gave an unforgettable picture of Grand and Marble Canyon, culminating in a perfect landing at Marble Canyon—largest plane ever to land there. Greeting us upon landing were our whole party, supplemented by Dr. and Mrs. Harold Bryant of the South Rim. Fairly early to bed as the next day would see us embarked.

JULY 12

An assortment of cars got us all to Lees Ferry. The WEN, MEXICAN HAT II and JOAN were already in the water tied up, leaving the SANDRA yet to be christened and launched. With cameras ready, we halted, anticipating the arrival of Barry Goldwater, who had just flown over in his new Navion.

With Barry's arrival we persuaded and after substituting a bottle supplied by Marjory Farquhar for an unbreakable bottle, got the SANDRA duly christened and in the water. Stowing of luggage went ahead smoothly and with good dispatch. Our scheduled start for 10:00 AM was abandoned in favor of taking off when ready—sooooo—we're off! My trip #5.[33]

SHOVE OFF. River had held up rather high. This is highest stage I've ever left on.

1938—34000, 1940—3000, 1941—25900, 1942—19400, 1947—37000.

I am terribly eager to feel out Soap Creek and Badger to get a picture of what this stage of water will mean to us.

WEN   Norman D. Nevills, Doris Nevills, Al Milotte, Randall Henderson.[34]

MEXICAN HAT II   Kent Frost, boatman, Pauline Saylor,[35] Barry Goldwater.

SANDRA   Garth Marston, boatman, Elma Millotte, Marjory Farquhar

JOAN   Dock Marston, boatman, Margaret Marston, Francis Farquhar.[36]

Quite a crowd upon the [Navajo] bridge.

Pause briefly on right for Barry and I to touch off a drift fire.

BADGER CREEK RAPID Mile 8. I look Badger over briefly and find it's an open clear channel presenting almost no problems. I shove off in the WEN with Barry Goldwater as a passenger. We have a fast wonderful ride. To insure Barry getting soaked, near the foot I dip up a bailing can and let him have it! Kent comes through in the MEXICAN HAT II solo. I go back and bring Doris through in the SANDRA. Then Garth brings the JOAN through with Pauline Saylor as a passenger.

Bill Soffley came to here with the passengers in the SANDRA. We also run into two fishermen, one a former newspaperman. Doris, Barry and Bill say farewell and start the trek up the trail to the rim above. We set about having lunch. Water temperature is 72°, and the air-shade is 96°. We are now ready to settle down to the regular and serious routine of regular traveling for the descent of the canyon. The first day is always a hard one.

SOAP CREEK RAPID. MILE 11. Soap Creek is rough but not difficult. Good ride by slipping just a shade on the right side of the tongue. WEN off with Randall as passenger. Others OK, though no passengers aboard. Dock can't pull out of the main current and lands below. We all have a fine ride and the ice is broken for relaxing and running the river.

CAMP. On left at MILE 12. Nice spot. Randall leaves note in cairn on ledge just down from little canyon. It's been a full exciting day, so we aren't long in getting settled for a good night's sleep.

JULY 13

At 6:00 AM it's overcast, and temperature is 84°. The usual heat of the canyon is absent which we're grateful for, though absence of the sun is serious for pics.

MILE 14. SHEER WALL RAPID. Very easy to run.

MILE 17. HOUSE ROCK RAPID. Very easy to run, and we drop right through. The water is turbulent and full of whirls at bottom of all these rapids. I expect more of a rapid at this stage, but the high water has leveled it over.

MILE 20. NORTH CANYON RAPID. This is a meany. The first drop is very easy to handle, but below the river piles into the right wall, and to get over to the left is hard to do. WEN off with Margaret at 9:40 AM. Perfect. Kent in MEXICAN HAT II gets thrown out of control and has a zippy ride. Garth and Dock come through very well. It's a very tough overland walk but all make it OK.

MILE 25. TWENTY FIVE MILE RAPID. This is a touchy one at any stage of water. At this high stage the big trouble lies at the bottom where there's a peculiar mixup of turbulent water. I don't like its looks at the bottom. This will be a solo run all the way through. [All boats] OK. We elect having lunch here. It's still overcast and the temperature is 96°.

MILE 32. VASEY'S PARADISE. CAMP. The last seven miles into here have had very violent and turbulent water at the foot of all the rapids and even the riffles. Eddies, boils and whirlpools. This high stage of water makes camp right at waterfalls impossible, so we pull into cove just above falls. There's a small freshwater spring here, but an overland rope maneuvering expedition is formed to fill canteens out of the big flow. Dock is first let down on a rope, then Francis. Much fun and amusement out of this excursion—plus plenty of fresh water.

Garth lies down as a tooth that appears to be ulcerated is giving him plenty of fun. This is a swell camp. After dinner, Marjory, Pauline, Ros, Al, Kent, and I go up to explore the big cave where I found the Stanton note in 1940. We have a lot of fun exploring, crawling around and poking into odd corners. I leave a note typed by Randall, pinned to the wall in the same place with the same stick as the Stanton note.[37] At the mouth of the cave we find Garth's flashlight which he left there when 16 years old on the 1942 trip. Back to camp, to bed, well pleased with a day marked by much fun, thrills and excitement.

JULY 14

High fleecy clouds this morning. Looks to be a beautiful day. Garth takes off and climbs up to check on cave mouth above, but finds no tunnels leading off. They have probably caved in. Kent, Dock, Al, Elma, Ros, Marjory and Francis go up to just above Paradise Canyon to see the skeleton of a man we found in '40.[38] Rest of us just loaf. I feel glad to rest after the rugged series of unbroken river miles of the last two months.

Nevills party in Grand Canyon: (left to right) Randall Henderson, Francis
Farquhar, Norman Nevills, Elma Milotte, Al Milotte, Garth Marston (hidden),
Pauline Saylor, Marjory Farquhar, Kent Frost, Margaret Marston, Otis Marston,
unidentified

MILE 33. REDWALL CAVERN. LUNCH. A beautiful and impressive
cave. We find a rattlesnake (sidewinder) and get many pics. The snake is left
unharmed to pursue his lonely life in the cave.

MILE 43. PRESIDENT HARDING RAPID. Land left. I in WEN with
Rosalind as passenger slip down the left side for easy run. MEXICAN HAT
II, JOAN with Garth as boatman, then Francis brings through the SANDRA,
all OK. Not hard to run, but requires a bit of finessing.

MILE 52. NANCOWEEP. CAMP. Same old spot just downstream
from mouth of main Nancoweep. Evidence of '42 camp at catclaw tree.
Showered a couple of times on us this afternoon up' around the Bridge of
Sighs section. Arrive with heavy overcast which clears at 9:00 PM. Clouds
up a bit and get weak shower during the night. As camp is being prepared
we amuse ourselves diverting the flow of Nancoweep creek in direction of
camp. Evening is ended up with a game of charades. Garth pulls a song title
out of the bag with 17 words in title!

JULY 15

Day starts out a bit overcast, but clears by 9:00 AM. Most of party take off and
climb up to the cliff ruins back of camp. I employ myself in rigging a shelter
for both possible rains and certain sun. River seems to be at about the same
stage. We all just loaf around, sleep, read, talk, walk, etc. In the evening it's
pleasantly cool, and touch off a great drift pile upstream aways.

JULY 17

SHOVE OFF. Temperature 74°. Marjory and Francis are both riding with
the Dock today, so Margaret goes over with Garth.

MILE 56. KWAGUNT CREEK RAPID. Incidentally the water here is very good to drink. The rapid is very rough, can be fun without looking over, though the takeoff is a bit confusing. I take Marjory in the WEN, the others come through solo, with Garth running the JOAN and Francis the SANDRA.

MILE 61. LITTLE COLORADO RIVER. Barely landed to go around corner and look at Little Colorado when Pauline jumped a 3' rattlesnake. As vicious a snake as I've ever seen. Lots of fight in him. Finally killed him. Surprise! On all previous trips the Little Colorado has had a dirty, murky red water flowing in it, but this time there was a good 100 second-feet of BRIGHT BLUE! The water was a bluer blue than the famed Havasu. Very hot here and no shade to be found. So I elect to drop on downstream for lunch and shade.

MILE 65. LAVA CANYON RAPID—TANNER MINE. LUNCH AND CAMP. We eat lunch under a tree at Joe[39] Tanner's old camp. 102° in the shade. Some of us went back in the old Tanner mine. I find it has caved quite a bit since 1942. Kent and I got the old caps from the mine, took 15 sticks of powder from a box lying nearby and with a brush fire sent up quite an explosion. This we followed by setting off the whole remaining box. It really boomed! Powder was dated: June 1925.[40] Everyone hunted and found shade for rest of afternoon. Pauline and I stayed in entrance of mine tunnel. Between 1:20 PM and 7:20 PM river drops 3" in about a 100 yard section. Build a small signal fire at night. We exchange light blinks with Hopi Watchtower, but as usual, neither party seems to interpret the message sent by the other!

JULY 17

River drops another 1" during the night. Dock catches three catfish which he has for breakfast. We decide upon rowing across the river to explore another mine tunnel that we see over there.

MILE 65. OLD MINE TUNNEL[41] just above LAVA CANYON. Upon entering we find dynamite (Oct. 1928), magazines (1928), miscellaneous tools, pack equipment, some food, much medical supplies. I take some of these, together with two cow bells. Women fuss about setting off the dynamite, so we leave that for a future trip. Passengers are now back to their original seats. At 8:50 AM there were beautiful clouds and a few drops of rain.

MILE 68. TANNER TRAIL. Mildly warm, gradually getting very hot. Rig up a good camp, improvise shelters. At night we build a great "C" shaped drift fire to signal the Rim. Usual blinkings of light are exchanged with many wild guesses at their possible meanings! Two heavy gripes are expressed in the afternoon at this layover. It is obvious that this leg of the trip should be done in six days instead of the present seven. A trip like this more than brings out the full characteristics in people. I leave a cache of food here for next year. It is under conglomerate ledge, 100' downstream from a dark red sandstone ledge. Cache [is]: 1 can matches, 1# coffee, 2 cans milk, 1 can cooked rice, 1 can hash, 2 cans spaghetti and meat balls, 1 can ravioli, 3 string beans, 3 pork and beans, 2 soup, 3 salmon, 3 TREAT.

JULY 18

Everyone up early and rarin' to go in anticipation of the thrilling ride in store of us this last 21 miles into Bright Angel. Days dawns clear and bright. Sun not quite over rim.

MILE 72. UNKAR CREEK. Back at Mile 71 we saw a buck deer on the left shore. We land here and find Unkar at this stage not too tough. We touch off a great drift pile here, then all clamber on board and off! Run on right.

MILE 75 RAPID. Easy to run, just land to check for sure on the tongue takeoff.

MILE 76. HANCE RAPID. Very rough and tricky. Requires some fast maneuvering. WEN off with Elma as passenger, run on left. Just after we shoved off I advised El again on just how rugged a run this was. She said "Maybe I had better not go!" This as the current really grabbed us! But she really enjoyed the ride, and we went thru right on the button. Kent got off beam a bit, picked up 6" of water and nearly upset. Garth in SANDRA fine. Dock too far into main current and had to land quite a ways below. It was a real rapid and lots of fun.

MILE 78. SOCKDOLOGER RAPID. We land as usual on left, and I am surprised to find this stage of water the smoothest for Sockdologer that I have yet seen. We want to leave Al behind for pictures, so I take Elma in with me. All come through right on the button with a swell time had by all!

MILE 81. GRAPEVINE RAPID. Much tougher takeoff than Sockdologer, and generally rougher all the way thru. All at bottom at good shape.

CLEAR CREEK. Very heavy water here and is a lively rapid.

Zoroaster Rapid just another rapid.

BRIGHT ANGEL. DORIS AND JOAN NEVILLS meet us on the beach, followed by Mr. Eden (NPS) and others. We waste little time at the boats, get some pics, then head up to Phantom Ranch. Mr. and Mrs Malone welcome us to the ranch. Clean up, and then a good dinner!

JULY 19

Loaded food in the boats. Checked over the equipment. Pauline and Rosalind went up the trail. We were sorry to see them go.[42] Rest of day relaxing.

JULY 20

Farquhars took off up the North Rim trail. Also the Garrisons for the South Rim. Went over to Pipe Spring with Doris and Joan and saw them off on their mules at 11:00 AM. I repaired back to my cabin and spent rest of day writing out postcards. Late afternoon, Joe Desloge Sr., Joe Jr., Anne and Zoe Desloge,[43] and Marie Saalfrank arrived. Swell to see them. Talked over final details, phoned Doris and talked to Sandra. To bed a bit lateish.

JULY 21

A good breakfast. Malones loaded us with fresh peaches, also went down to see us off. I borrowed a pencil from the relieving USGS engineer, Clifford T. Jenkins, to be mailed to him at end of trip. He was most helpful in getting us river dope, also letting us cache supplies at the govt. cabin. River has been up and down, and this morning found us leaving on 24,250 second feet.

SHOVE OFF.

WEN—Nevills-Henderson-Milotte.

MEXICAN HAT II—Frost, Joe Desloge Jr., Marie Saalfrank

SANDRA—Garth Marston-Anne and Zoe Desloge

JOAN—Dock Marston, Margaret Marston, Joe Desloge Sr.

MILE 90. HORN CREEK. About as usual. Not hard, but requires sharp timing. Run on left of big center hole. WEN off, Zoe as passenger. Then MEXICAN HAT II, SANDRA, JOAN all without passengers. Good fun and makes good pictures.

MILE 93. GRANITE FALLS. (Monument Creek). No rough stuff from Horn Creek to here—but damn me if the main channel with the big waves against the walls aren't tough! I study and study, study and restudy, but finally give up running my usual channel. I elect to run down the middle, skirting a few holes. It is a very tricky but good course. Requires high water to run here. We all go thru solo, and all make a good run. This has been a painfully long delay, but I wanted to make sure that there wasn't a way to run the big waves for the picture. The water directly below the big waves is a treacherous a bunch of boils, eddies, etc. as we were to see on the trip.

MILE 95. HERMIT FALLS. LUNCH. CAMP. We first set about having lunch, which had been long postponed as a result of the long stop at Granite Falls. At 4:00 PM brought MEXICAN HAT II to head, unloaded, and lined to bottom of first drop. Ran on down and hauled up on rocks because of the bad shore surge. At 5:00 PM we had JOAN unloaded, and suddenly I decided to run, ably urged on my Joe, Sr., so Joe and I shoved off. SOME RIDE! We dropped off the tongue to the left, but still got held in on the big waves a bit. They were 12 to 15 feet high. Made it fine though. I was deadly tired after we made shore. Then Garth brought the SANDRA thru in fine style, with me then returning and running the WEN through. At 6:05 PM all boats were at bottom equipment carried down, boats well up out of water—and TIRED! So at last we ran Hermit in high water![44] To bed and glad of it. An exchange of signals went on with the rim again!

JULY 22

MILE 96. BOUCHER RAPID. A soft touch, and we take off with all hands for a fine splashy ride. At first I had this one confused with another rapid that *is* tricky.

Zoe and Anne are swimming, as we come down on CRYSTAL RAPIDS, Anne comes over into the WEN, Zoe goes into the MEXICAN HAT II, JoJo into the SANDRA.

MILE 98. CRYSTAL RAPIDS. Wide open!

MILE 106. SERPENTINE RAPID. Rough and a fine ride. Wide open!

MILE 108. BASS CABLE. Been a marvelous, wet ride to here. We land on the left side directly under the cable and go up for an inspection tour. The "A" frames are in bad shape and it would not be safe to go out on the cable. The pulling mechanism is all shot to pieces. A cross could be affected by hand over hand with some degree of safety. We pass up any thoughts of a ride!

Mile 108½. SHINUMO CREEK right. We have lunch in the little shallow cave, then Dock goes out to check on trout. Fishing for over two miles discloses no trout. Water is not too cold, and if there are trout in this stream they must be up towards the North Rim. Everyone goes swimming but me. I picked up a sinus headache from swimming at Phantom Ranch, so go to sleep and soak up heat. River turns a bright red in the afternoon but doesn't seem to raise any. Skies almost clear. Dock reports 4" suckers and 2" minnows at a point up to 2½ miles from the river. Tries to rain late at night, but doesn't make it.

JULY 23

MILE 110. CABLE CROSSING. A high thin dangerous, worn out looking outfit.

MILE 112. WALTHENBERG RAPID. Very rough and turbulent water. Al goes over into MEXICAN HAT II for pics, Joe Jr. into WEN. A good rough, but successful ride.

MILE 116. ELVES CHASM. LUNCH. We sign the register back up under the cliff then have a good lunch. From here Al is with Dock, Joe Jr., on the oars of the WEN until real rough water.

MILE 125. FOSSIL RAPIDS. Norm back on oars. Entering granite.

MILE 128. 128 MILE RAPID. At foot here eddy slaps us into wall on the left and its touch and go. "Cheating" the rough water is born out as a good idea in this baby!

MILE 129. SPECTER RAPID. These have been very rough to here, though not too tricky to run.

MILE 130. BEDROCK RAPID. As usual a toughy in high water. We walk all the passengers, and it *is* a miserable walk. All boats through in good shape, though eddy at bottom is mean. Big barge lost by Bureau of Reclamation is resting on big rock in middle of river. It has a few planks and oil drums that have kept it afloat to here. End is clear stove in.

MILE 131. Arrive DEUBENDORF RAPID. Very rough, bit late for pics, but looks like a good ride. Decide to run a couple of boats through yet today. I take Margaret with me in the WEN and shove off. A *wonderful* ride. Back to head of rapid. I bring the MEXICAN HAT II thru then, with Kent in the bow, and JoJo on deck. Another wingding!

We make camp at bottom just below the good water coming in from Stone Creek. We want to do a good job here as token to Julius Stone who is reported near death.

July 24
JOJO SWIMS THRU DEUBENDORF!

Then Garth in the SANDRA, with Zoe and Anne.

THENNN Joe Jr. and Dock with no preservers, Zoe with a preserver, Garth on an airmattress, swim through the main channel! Conditions are ideal in all respects, and in very easily changed circumstances could be most dangerous.

All boats at bottom, loaded, and off.

MILE 133. Waves very rough, and got hit just right to take 6" water.

MILE 133¾. TAPEATS CREEK. Dock takes right off to fish. Rest rig up shelters, have lunch. Hot disagreeable wind blows all afternoon. We all sleep, read, swim, etc. Dinner is lateish, and Dock comes in at last minute with a swell catch of about a dozen fine rainbow trout. They are most delicious. This is a poor camp to spend a full day as shade is too hard to find. Fishing is best early morning or late afternoon. Best luck is really almost to mouth of creek where it dumps into the river. They bite on anything.

July 25
MILE 136. DEER CREEK FALLS. Landing, we found no light for pictures so decided to wait a while. I initiated the idea of getting under the falls. It's hard punching, icy like water. Garth, JoJo, Joe Sr. and the Dock went under. At last minute I backed out, remembering two days ago with my sinus. Dock was first out. Kent and I led off to explore the top of the falls by working up the left side which is easy.[45] Garth followed, then Dock. The falls comes about an eighth of a mile thru a fifty foot, narrow, crevasse like gorge, which in turn lets out from an amazing, fairly level tree filled valley. In the gorge a very narrow trail, at one place laid up with rocks by cliff dwellers, gives access from the valley to the river. I believe this place will be a good shot on another trip to lay over a day to explore. Light showed little promise for being good for at least another hour, so on we go.

MILE 137. Cliff ruins on left.

MILE 138. Just a riffle, but in '40 Doris thrown from boat here.

MILE 139. FISHTAIL CANYON. Not much more than riffle. Cheat on right.

MILE 143. KANAB CREEK. LUNCH. Just up canyon right we get some anemic shade under a tamarisk tree. Water in creek murky, muddy and foul. Run the rapid on left tongue, bearing back to middle. Nice long splashy ride. Don't eat lunch here again. GO DOWN TO MILE 147.

MILE 147. WATER. Nice flow from cliff on right. Beautiful spot, good place to eat lunch.

MILE 149. UPSET RAPID. Well! A roughy, and almost impossible to walk around. So we run. Bad hole half way down. Try to get right. Margaret into WEN, Al into JOAN so as to be the last for pics. We hardly get splashed. MEXICAN HAT II gets a hard blow from water in hole. SANDRA medium. JOAN thru fairly dry. Swell ride.

MILE 156. HAVASU CANYON. CAMP. Tricky to get in. Stay close to left wall on approach then duck in quick at mouth of canyon. We arrive too late for pictures. Row right on up canyon to foot of first falls, about ⅛ mile. We anchor boats on right, then ferry across to left where camp is made. Nice spot. Margaret rode on to here from Upset Rapid. Have some rainbows that Dock caught this morning before leaving Tapeats. They're really good. To bed.

July 26

Up early, but are hanging around for light. In meantime we find a place to jump the canyon at mouth of river so get some pics there. It's about 40' from cliff to water. JoJo makes a trick jump from near here into shallow water and I'll bet his arches still hurt!

SHOVE OFF. The Doc is behind as he's still getting pictures.

MILE 162. No sign of the Doc.

MILE 164 CANYON. Wide open. Easy steal to right. Joe Jr. has been on oars from foot of Havasu Rapid to head of this one. All thru OK.

MILE 166. CATARACT CANYON. LUNCH. A Fair place to eat, tho no water here. JOE. JR. Takes on oars again from here.

MILE 171. GATEWAY RAPIDS. Few rocks, bit rough, easy to run.

MILE 174. RED SLIDE CANYON. JOE JR. On oars to here.

MILE 179. LAVA FALLS. CAMP. Left. Very hot when we first land so sit around in what shade can be found and speculate on possible arrival of John Riffey, ranger from the TUWEEP STATION of the Grand Canyon National Monument. Zoe and I row across the river to get shade. Dinner is called. We row back and start eating. JOHN RIFFEY[46] IS SPOTTED! He's walking downstream on other side. I hasten across and get him. We provide another plate. He gives Al and I messages from our wives. Doris and children made it safely to Santa Cruz, so I breathe a sigh of relief. Have looked over the rapid enough to decide on a lining job. Portaging is impractical. Bad current into wall at bottom makes running far too dangerous. The "experts" have a channel picked, but certain features not apparent to untrained eyes make this still a lining job!

July 27

Start lining. John Riffey and Kent on the upstream bow rope, JoJo near me ready to assist, Garth on the stern line. It's damn hard work. Equipment is carried to foot of big drop, then loaded in and ferried down below to cove. We make fast time, tho held up a bit for light for pictures. Lining proceeds very smoothly, and at 11:20 AM all boats are in cove at MILE 179½.

LUNCH. All equipment loaded back in, but we're tired, so coffee and lunch hit the spot. Leaving here I take John Riffey aboard in bow of WEN. All and Randall on deck. We boom off, get caught in reverse wave or hole in rapid against wall just below,[47] and fill clear up to gun'ls with water! Try to bail out, but my foot is in the bailing bucket. We make a precarious way over to the right shore, bail out, none the worse for wear. This has happened but once before to me, and that in 1940 up at Mile 138. We send mail and messages out with John Riffey, and say farewells. We plan on a get together this fall and a raft ride from here to WHITMORE WASH.

ON FROM MILE 180. Our last of the biggest rapids is behind us. At Lava Falls sent definite word out confirming that we would arrive on head of Lake Mead right on schedule.

MILE 187. I spot a green boat with orange trim on the right shore and think it is the Rohmer[48] one man life boat. Upon inspection it proves to be a not too well weathered rowboat evidently left there by fishermen who have probably come down Whitmore Wash.

MILE 188. WHITMORE WASH. CAMP. No water here. [But the wash has grown up with trees and bushes since '42, making passageway up the canyon really tough]. We camp just up from mouth of wash—makes a good camp. [Some of us work up the canyon searching out better shade].[49] Clouds up, and a few drops of rain fall just at bedtime, but it lasts but a few minutes.

JULY 28
SHOVE OFF. Joe Jr. moves in with the Doctor to take over the oars, and Joe Sr. gets over into the MEXICAN HAT II.

MILE 191. Camped here in '41.

MILE 198. PARASHONT WASH. Here, as at Whitmore, there's a good trail in from the back country. We stop to look at the old cache under the ledge, but see no sign of anyone having been here in a long time. Left note in can under ledge.

SPRING CANYON. CAMP. Current been slow to here, so have been dabbling the oars a bit to make a bit of time. Day has been clear, but remarkably cool out on the water. We eat lunch in "shade" of tamarisk trees, then prowl around for shade. THIS is the canyon overgrown with bushes etc. since '42. Its a good night camp, but very poor to spend day at. Plenty of good water here.

JULY 29
SHOVE OFF.

MILE 205. 205 MILE RAPID. Joe Jr. still with Doc. And this *is* a surprise here. Tho I just look over from boat and run wide open, this rapid has some really heavy water, and is quite an eye opener to start day with.

Randall
Henderson

MILE 209. GRANITE PARK. Mildly rough but easy channel. Doesn't look so hot for landing a plane here. Back at SPRING CANYON it looked much better, or even WHITMORE.

MILE 209. A crude shelter is seen on the right bank.

MILE 213 LEFT. A cove and willow tree make this out to be a very wonderful camping spot. No water, but could fill canteens above at Spring Canyon.

MILE 215. Doc's boat saw mother mountain lion and cub on left here.

MILE 215. THREE SPRINGS CANYON. No sign of water, or even mouth of canyon here. Looks like there might have been a slide, as I remember seeing water from the boat here on one of the trips. Could land above and walk into the springs, but I don't see much point in it.

MILE 217. TWO HUNDRED AND SEVENTEEN MILE RAPID. This is a rough and a bit tricky piece of water. I have selected it as a trial horse for "dub" day, tho with some misgivings as at this stage there is some really mean water piling into the wall if a fellow miscalculates his pull out off the tongue to the left. I take Joe Sr. as passenger, then JOAN, piloted by JoJo, OK. SANDRA, piloted by Randall, very perfect run. I expected him to have trouble, but instead he came thru with unbelievably perfect timing! MEXICAN HAT II, piloted by AL, OK. THIS IS ENTRANCE TO LOWER GRANITE GORGE.

LUNCH. Bottom of 217 on left. Nice cove with lots of shade. However the shade is only good at this time of year up to about 1:00 PM.

MILE 225. DIAMOND CREEK. CAMP. Well, this is trip 5 to here. Barely are landed than we go up to perform the solemn rites of the initiatory degree into the ROYAL ORDER OF COLORADO RIVER RATS. Where it is some ways looks like a mild touch of horseplay, it really has a most significant meaning. There are but four initiates, as there are but four who have made the full run from Lees Ferry. In order of initiation: ALL MILOTTE—RANDALL HENDERSON—MARGARET MARSTON—KENT FROST. Shortly after a terrific wind comes up that whips water off the river up to 75' on the adjacent cliffs! Showers a bit too. This all quiets down by dinnertime. After dinner we play charades. VERY COLD drinking water can be gotten upstream a ways from the springs bubbling out of the bank about 200 yards above Diamond Creek. About where we usually tie the boats. NO flies. We have seen few if any pests, flies or insects. I associate this fact with the fact that we have seen no sheep, burros, etc. Usually this camp is a fright for flies.

JULY 30

OUR LAST DAY ON THE RIVER. You get a funny feeling on this morning—at least I do. The accomplishment of having run the Grand Canyon is assured. We are about to check that fact up, so behind me lies one of my really outstanding adventures. I don't want to think that I will never be doing this again, so right here and now I secretly set my next trip! This has been a very swell party—each trip gets smoother and smoother. This will never be a "milk run," it will always be a trip filled with unexpected thrills, surprises, some hardships, and above all, a feeling of having pitted oneself against dangerous and trying conditions—and winning out.[50] I feel relieved to almost be there—and sorry—the worry and responsibility of keeping the boats and personnel out of real danger is quite a job.

SHOVE OFF. Cloudy and pleasantly cool this morning. River is brightish red.

MILE 230. TRAVERTINE FALLS. No rough or tricky rapids to here. Just a lot of fun in nice splashy rapids.

MILE 231. MILDLY ROUGH.

MILE 232. 232 MILE RAPID. Watch this one—VICIOUS!

MILE 236. GNEISS CANYON. *LAKE MEAD!* Funny, I always *feel* the lake under me. This is it. We're off the Colorado River.

MILE 238. Old survey camp on left. Cable overhead. One we ate at in '42.

MILE 239. SEPARATION CANYON. Good current to here. We go up for group pictures at the plaque. It's hot. Thence up Separation a few hundred yards on right to get shade under some trees to eat lunch. Not a

Nevills party on Lake Mead: (left to right) Al Milotte, Garth Marston, Kent Frost, Joe Desloge, Jr., Anne Desloge, Marie Saalfrank, Otis Marston, Norman Nevills, Zoe Desloge, Joe Desloge, Sr.

good spot to loaf during day or hunt shade in. Floor of canyon is regular quagmire. Although my original itinerary called for staying overnight here, I want to slip on down to Spencer Canyon so as to have a better start on the meeting of the big tow boat tomorrow.

MILE 243. It has cooled off and gotten cloudy. I have been rowing to supplement the current. Al now takes over the oars.

MILE 246. SPENCER CANYON. Al on oars to here. We pull in but it being cool etc., I am talked into going on down the lake a ways, so on we go. I take over the oars again.

MILE 248. SURPRISE CANYON. Randall and Al rigged a sail, so I steered with the oars and we've really batted right along.

MILE 252. REFERENCE POINT CREEK. THIS IS AS FAR AS MY MAP GOES.[51] The lake is still very shallow, and it becomes increasingly clear that the big boats can't get up this far. Lake is muddy, and there's still around a three mile current. On we go!

We row in 30 minute heats. I figure we average 5 MPH.

POINT UNKNOWN. Camp on right. Have to row across lake for wood. But it's a swell camp. I can't cease to be amazed at the great bars covered with tamarisks that are all over the lake. The lake appears to be 20–25 feet below high level mark. Garth and JOJO swim across lake and back.

JULY 31

I think that this is about Mile 260. We hope to find Emery Falls around any corner now.

We are getting fed up with rowing. Just now we spot a trail leading up to some caves.

We determine that across in cove on the left is Emory Falls. I feel that the distance in doesn't justify going there and head for shade below. Right here is where we lose the last of the river current. We go on a bit further and it becomes clear that to spend several hours waiting we should have plenty of shade and water, so we signal other boats in and we turn back.

EMORY FALLS. The lake is raised and cove cleaned out so a big boat even can go right up under the falls. We prepare lunch, keeping an alert ear for the sound of approaching motors. Then a siesta. By 1:00 PM, however, both Kent and I are getting tired of this waiting around, so we decide to go on down the lake and maybe hustle the boats up. We advise the others, and further leave word that they are to wait no longer than 4:00 PM, and if by then that no boats have shown up they are to start out.

Kent on oars, we leave Emery Falls.

I take over the oars—a heavy tail wind comes up and Kent holds up a tarp for sail—AND WE MAKE TIME!

Can see PIERCES FERRY—and we cross into the clear water.

We pull into cove just down lake from landing by mistake. We go up to look around, and almost by accident see occupied dwelling over in the next cove. Arriving there afoot we meet one BILL GREEN, who works for Bureau of Reclamation, Weather Bureau, etc., in collecting data at this point. He greets us grandly, and has us in to dinner. Then we drive up to overlook the lake, and rounding the point comes our fleet of boats! Returning to the dock, Bill and I set out in a rowboat with an outboard motor to meet our party. Kent in the meantime ferries the WEN around the point into the main landing cove. We tow our party in—they too did quite a bit of sailing to here.

Landing, we repair to Bill's, and dinner ensues. Hearing a motor, Bill and I go down to meet a private cruiser that has newsman and photographer aboard that came to see us. They told us that the Park boat went on to Emory Falls to spend the night, and the Tours boat was last seen down the lake, and probably would spend the night way below. Get lots of pics, then the newsman took off in Bill Green's car to drive into Boulder City to get the story and pics out. We finally all rolled out on the beach—to bed!

AUGUST 1

We have learned that Mountain Standard Time now prevails in all of Arizona, and that at HOOVER DAM we change, on Nevada side, to PST.

Up at daylight, and the three fellows from the cruiser–JAY PORTER, BILL RUSSELL, RAY PAYNE—join us in breakfast. Bill Green got back at around daylight. Then Garth, Joe Sr., Kent and I climb aboard the cruiser and run the seven miles over to Emery Falls and find the Park Service *et al* just getting up. They are most surprised to see us! They don't look for us *until* today! The message received from Lava Falls said we would be 24 hours late!

I am pleased to meet my old friend Ray Poyser, also Bill Belknap.[52] Also aboard are:

Gordon Baldwin, Park Naturalist
Don Ashbaugh, reporter, Las Vegas Review Journal
Mavin Carter, reporter, Boulder City News
Paul McDermitt, president of Las Vegas Chamber of Commerce.
Harry Meyers, official photographer, Region III, National Park Service.

The thot *[sic]* prevails that the Tours boat, "BETTY D," has broken down and is laying below by the Grand Wash Cliffs. We go on to Pierces Ferry. Arriving there, we are soon treated to a Republic Seabee[53] coming in. They pick up pics and soon take off again. The fast cruiser leaves. Garth goes down in the fast cruiser with Jay Porter and his friends. Rest of river party elects to stay with the boats.

Farewells are said to the hospitable Bill Green and with the boats in tow, away we go. Next to Park Boat #1, in order of two is SANDRA, JOAN, MEXICAN HAT II, WEN, and then the emergency rowboat of the Park Service.

No sign is seen of the Tours boat. We then accept the fact that it may have gone by up the lake while we were all at Pierces Ferry and watching the amphibian.

At noon we pull into a sandy beach at Greggs Basin and eat and swim.

Nice cool trip down lake and the time passes pleasantly. I was handed a letter from Doris which was good to get.

ARRIVE boat docks! Greeted there by friends and relatives. The recon car and trailers are there—I go up to Lake Mead lodge to get the station wagon. I have to take one trailer clear into Boulder City to get air in the tires. By fast works of Garth, JOJO, Kent and myself we are all loaded and up to Lake Mead Lodge by 7:00 PM PST. All have dinner together—grand time.

After dinner, until late I talk with Mr. D.E. Morrison of TOURS, Inc.

First, tho, our dinner is hurried so we can make a deadline of 8:30 P.M. for a special tour of Hoover Dam. Then over to the ball park where we are introduced at a sort of outdoor benefit, ballgame etc., going on. Then back to Lodge, where my late conversation with Mr. Morrison takes place.

AUGUST 2

Desloges are awaiting plane confirmations for South Rim. Randall takes off. I say goodbye to the Milottes. Margaret and Garth and Doc have gone to see

Garth off on plane for Calif.

We go into Boulder City and gas up. We're off! I lead the way in the station wagon pulling the WEN and JOAN. Kent and his wife follow in recon car pulling the SANDRA and MH2nd.

LUNCH at Kingman. Been really cool all morning.

During afternoon run thru several showers. One, as hard a rain as I've ever seen. A reflection of the widely scattered showers is seen by the Desloges passing us in a chartered station wagon, storms evidently grounding flights.

Outside of Kingman, I am intrigued by the countless rows of parked army planes, so, at a close by private field I rent an Aeronca and fly myself over and around the planes. It's an impressive sight.[54]

We eat dinner at Seligman, then on to Williams. Just where the road turns off into the south rim we pull to one side and lay out our beds for the night.

AUGUST 3

Eat breakfast at a little place up the road. Stop in to see the Bill Browns who used to run the MARBLE CANYON LODGE.

Arrive at South Rim. Short visit with the Desloges just before they leave on their way to California.

Nice visit with Lem Garrison, Mr. and Mrs. Bryant. I get to see and borrow a copy of the August issue of National Geographic which has the story in first section of my San Juan River trip.[55]

Visit and see Emery Kolbs show.

Dinner or lunch at Bright Angel Lodge.

Arrive Cameron about 3:00 PM. Recon car has developed a bad engine knock. I decide it will make Mexican Hat if driver never goes over 20 MPH! And what shape the roads are in! You can hardly drive over 10–15 MPH on the roads anywhere anyhow.

At 10:00 PM, just past Kayenta, we pull in and go to sleep.

AUGUST 4

Up bright and early, make coffee and eat some brown bread. Arrive Mexican Hat about 9:30 AM. Boats are unloaded, equipment stowed away. Kent and his wife leave. I prepare and pack for my start in the morning.

AUGUST 5

Rained terrifically during night—all washes are running. I leave Mexican Hat enroute for Santa Cruz, California. It takes me exactly 8 hours to make the 27 miles to Bluff![56]

And so ends another trip through the Grand Canyon. And begins plans for the next trip.

Grand Canyon,
July 11 to August 5, 1948

By 1948, Nevills was perched atop the river running world, and he knew it. He was about to embark on his sixth trip through the Grand Canyon, a number that was unprecedented at the time. He was well aware that he had taken over one-third of the magical "First Hundred" to go through the Canyon, and he was thus assured of a place in river-running history. The 1948 journal—for which the original, penciled notebook has been lost—is indicative of this awareness. Even more than the typed transcriptions of his 1946 and 1947 journals, it is more polished—obviously written for posterity, not just a day-to-day account.

And Nevills had good reason to feel proud: his San Juan trips were consistently booked, and he was turning away requests to go on his Grand Canyon trips. For the first time, he was actually making good money at his chosen career, and he had no competitors to speak of.

The 1948 trip—on a medium water stage of 18,600 cfs—would amply demonstrate that he was at the top of his game. For this run he had a new boatman, Frank Wright, who was loyal, competent, and best of all, not likely to be a contender for the spotlight that Nevills so loved, for Wright was another of those rare individuals in Colorado River history who had no axes to grind, and about whom it is impossible to hear a cross word.

With the 1948 trip, Nevills also gained a new friend: Frank Masland, a wealthy and influential carpet manufacturer from Pennsylvania, who would support him with passengers for his trips, and even help him with funding as needed. Masland's friendship would persevere even in the face of tragedy.

Yet all was not well on all fronts. Some entries in the journal indicate a testiness, a lack of patience with certain members and crew that had not surfaced before. At home, his children, Sandra and Joan, were doing well, but Joan had reached the limits of homeschooling, and they were forced to send her to a boarding school in Utah. It was heart-rending for the close-knit family.

On his rise to the top of the river-running community, Nevills had made not only friends but some enemies. While people like Rosalind Johnson, Frank Masland, Randall Henderson, and Joe Desloge loved Nevills's style and trips, others felt that he was autocratic, imperious, and rigid in his methods, and that his trips had grown stale and lacked variety. Some of those who had worked for him for a while were tired of constantly repairing trailers and equipment made from the junkyards of the

Southwest and claimed that Nevills often made them carry more than their share of supplies and passengers. He completely rejected any suggestion that he make changes to his boats. Worst of all was his lost friendship with Otis Marston, which by this time had changed to an active enmity. 1948 was the last trip that either Otis or Garth Marston would make with Nevills. Marston's hostility, like Masland's friendship, would outlast the life of Norman Nevills.

During 1948 Nevills continued to concentrate on his new love: his airplane. Gaylord Staveley wrote: "The airplane, like the cataract boat, had become an extension of Norm. He loved what a plane could do, where it could put him."[1]

Like many pilots, he always wanted a bigger and better and more powerful airplane. Not content with the Piper J3—even with the upgrades he had put into it the year before—Nevills had traded in the J3 for a Piper Super Cruiser, which was delivered at the end of the 1947 river season. The Super Cruiser was a much more powerful airplane, with more horsepower, a two-way radio, and a two-passenger back seat. He named it Cherry II, after his pet name for Doris. Not only was it sheer fun, it was good for business. No longer did passengers or guests at the Lodge have to make their way on busses and in the back of mail trucks to Mexican Hat; now Nevills could "boom over" and pick them up in Grand Junction or Kayenta, Arizona, and he could visit family and friends as far away as California.

And it was not all "flitting," as Nevills called flying; he flew Christmas presents to isolated communities on the Navajo Reservation, and volunteered to take the sick to hospitals to spare them the agonizing rides on the horrible dirt roads of the area. But at the same time, his devil-may-care attitude toward take-offs and landings, his love of stunts like flying under the Navajo Bridge, and even simple things like being careless about straining his fuel through an old chamois, caused great concern among his friends and family. An old saying about flying goes: "There are old pilots and bold pilots, but there are no old, bold pilots." Norman Nevills was a bold pilot.

GRAND CANYON,
JULY 11 TO AUGUST 4, 1948

1948 marked the 79th year since the first party made the trip thru the Grand Canyon, from Lees Ferry to Hoover Dam. During these years a very few, a very fortunate few of us have had the thrill of seeing the Grand Canyon by boat. Since my first trip ten years ago, in 1938, I have made, with this present trip, six trips thru the Grand Canyon. During these trips we have been responsible for conducting thru the Canyon 34 of the total 100 people who have completed the traverse.[2] So it seems that another milestone in the history of the Canyon has been passed. The canyon has lost none of its glamour, the rapids have lost none of their thrill, their danger—the food still has sand—but it's only inevitable that with so many trips by boat that one gets a knowledge of the Canyon that changes the trip from an uncertain exploratory trip to a trip planned to function on an easily met schedule.

I have already at one time or another expressed my many views relative to the psychology of fast water boating. So I just want to acknowledge again here my very real appreciation to all persons who have run any river anywhere with me, their trust and reliance in my leadership—their support made this all possible.

The "rating" for a trip by boat thru Grand Canyon is based on the traverse of the Grand Canyon from Lees Ferry to Hoover Dam. As a matter of record and interest I am listing below here, year by year those whom I have taken thru.

1938 Elzada Clover, Lois Jotter, Bill Gibson, Loren Bell, Del Reid, Norm Nevills
1940 Doris Nevills, Mildred Baker, Hugh Cutler, Barry Goldwater, C[harles] Larabee, John Southworth
1941 Agnes Albert, Weldon Heald, Bill Schukraft, Zee Grant
1942 Otis "Doc" Marston, Garth Marston, Neill Wilson, Bruce Wilson, Ed Olsen, Ed Hudson, Wayne McConkie, Pres Walker
1947 Al Milotte, Randall Henderson, Kent Frost, Margaret Marston
1948 Rosalind Johnson, Frank Masland, Lucille Hiser, Wayne Hiser, Moulty Fulmer, Frank Wright

Who's who—and where:

BOATMEN: WEN—Norman D. Nevills; MH2—Frank Wright;[3] JOAN—(of course) Otis "Doc" Marston;[4] SANDRA-Garthwaite Marston
THRU PASSENGERS: Frank Masland;[5] Moulty Fulmer;[6] Lucille and Wayne Hiser[7]
LEES FERRY TO BRIGHT ANGEL: Florence and Bestor Robinson[8]
BRIGHT ANGEL TO HOOVER DAM: Nancy Streator; Rosalind Johnson; Howard Welty; John Doerr

JULY 11

This morning we get up secure in the thot that the big cataract boats are already down at Lees Ferry awaiting us. During the last two of the seven San Juan trips this year we hauled down the cataract boats to Lees Ferry, thus precluding any possibility of a last minute delay. Doris, Garth Marston and I are about to leave when my friend Jimmie Rigg[9] of Pioneer Aviation shows up in the Stinson owned and piloted by Andy Watts, Andy's wife, and Frank Hall, all of Grand Junction. They came down to bring Jimmie, who will take my Cruiser out for a working over. We decide on the spot that Doris and I will fly to Lees Ferry in the Cruiser, followed by the Stinson (only the Stinson passed us up!). Garth and Lamar Wright will come overland in the Chevrolet Suburban with additional food supplies. We arrive on schedule and find many of the party already arrived. In the afternoon we launch

Launch of 1948 Nevills Expedition Grand Canyon trip, Lee's Ferry

the boats with the able assistance of two Bureau of Reclamation men, Jim Jordan and Rod Sanderson.[10] Jim used to hold the outboard world's speed record. Took us all for a ride in a Navy storm boat. Some ride and a beautiful display of skillful handling. The river party crew was composed of Frank Masland, Moulty Fulmer, Cowboy Welty and myself. In the evening the whole party assembles for a sort of farewell dinner. Spirits are high and nothing but keen anticipation flavors the outlook of everyone. Takeoffs are so hard, yet everyone is full of zip and rarin' to go.

JULY 12

Shortly after breakfast the last member of our crew arrives in a Piper Cub. Frank Wright. Doc and I borrow the Cub and fly once under Navajo Bridge. We then all repair to the cars and drive down to Lees Ferry. Stowing of luggage commences, the boats are bailed out, and the new nylon hawsers attached. I make a hasty selection of passenger distribution,[11] and we're soon loaded.

WEN: Norman D. Nevills, Florence Robinson, Wayne Hiser
SANDRA: Garth Marston, Lucille Hiser, Moulty Fulmer
MH2:   Frank Wright, Frank Masland, Howard Welty
JOAN: Doc Marston, Bestor Robinson

Cowboy Welty will ride as far as Badger Creek rapid. There we expect the Bureau of Reclamation boat to come down and see us run Badger, and then take Cowboy back upstream with them.

It's a beautiful day, the water is a bit low, only 18,000 second feet, but it has a fairish current. We are glad to be all assembled and on our way.

NAVAJO BRIDGE. Quite a few spectators up on top. We call back and forth. It's a very real thrill to look way up at the almost spiderlike span of the beautifully arched bridge. Too, it means we are really on our way down into Marble Canyon and the rapids ahead.

BADGER CREEK RAPID and Lunch. Mile 8. Coming around a bend we hear the familiar roar of Badger Creek Rapid. After all of the relative quiet water above, plus it's being our first major rapid, there's a tense thrill that fills us all, and we're impatient to get a good look at our first real barrier to the lower canyon. Landing, I find that this lowish stage of water doesn't hurt us here at all—it's a clean cut straight shot channel. I decide the first runs should be solo to test the boat balance and the actual punch of the water. 11:20 AM, shove off in the WEN. Right on course, uneventful but a lot of fun. Garth next in the SANDRA. OK. Frank next in the MH2. The signals fail to get the results, and Frank clips the big right hand center hole. A real thrill ride. I glance up to see the Reclamation boat pulling in with Mrs. Jordan aboard too. I have Doc take Rod Sanderson aboard for the final ride. I do the signalling but again there's a mixup, and Doc and Rod take on the right hand hole—another below, and have one wild and wooly ride. But other than a good soaking and a lot of fun no damage is done. The river always is looking for an opportunity to drive home the point that caution and care is needed at all times!

After lunch we elect to cut any siesta time short and take off for our old friend the Soap Creek Rapid. Final farewells are said, the Jordans, Cowboy and Rod Sanderson take off from the head of Badger, and we repair to our boats and shove off again.

Mile 11. SOAP CREEK RAPID. A fine roar greets our ears—and it's pretty rough. Not a bad channel, tho and easy to pick. I take Bestor as a passenger. Swell ride. Garth comes thru with Frank Masland. OK. Frank [Wright] solo. OK. Doc solo. OK. With the running of Soap Creek we are finally in the groove and somehow adjusted to rapid running. We now are eager and keen to try out the big fellows below. The enthusiasm has been absorbed by the passengers and they too are ready for more. We intend to break the precedent of many years and camp tonight further down than usual. The WEN and the JOAN are leaking quite a bit and require constant bailing. For next season am going to see that they both have a real working over.

Mile 14. SHEER WALL RAPID. A swell ride and easy to run.

Mile 17. HOUSE ROCK RAPID. Clear skies make it safe to camp right in the mouth of House Rock Canyon.[12] Not a bad camp tho a bit short on wood. We're all pleasantly tired and ready for bed. Been a fine day and everyone happy.

JULY 13
Good night's sleep. Everyone eager to be on the way. Not a bad channel here, so we're going thru passengers and all.

Mile 18. BOULDER NARROWS. Top of rock appears to be at the 100,000 second foot stage. This would be a dangerous place with that much water.

Mile 20. NORTH CANYON RAPID. We're rolling! Looked this one over from boat and we all piled thru in fine shape. Fine ride.

Mile 25. TWENTY-FIVE MILE RAPID. We take all passengers thru here, but one boat at a time. Drop off tongue to left.

Mile 26. TWENTY-SEVEN MILE RAPID. Run right thru, but the WEN gets water within 6" of the gunnel. Swell ride.

Between Miles 28 and 29 a hummingbird showed up and proceeded to land on everyone's hats, shoulders, etc., boat by boat. Utterly unafraid. The bird landed on Florence's hat and proceeded to peck on the straw.

Mile 29. TWENTY-NINE MILE RAPID. Loads of fun. Run along right wall.

Mile 32. VASEY'S PARADISE. CAMP. At this stage of water you can reach spring easily along the ledge from the big cavern above the spring. Island in center of river is about 3' out of water. Spring temperature is 61° After lunch all but Garth and I go over to see the dead man, and to explore the old limestone cave. Garth and I try a bit of climbing but finally relax on the sand and talk. A most pleasant lazy afternoon. This is a beautiful spot to loaf in. Fairly early to bed. Grand night for sleeping, and we all do a good job of it.

JULY 14

The party is in its stride. Both in camping efficiency and for adjusting to one another and have a good time.

Mile 33. REDWALL CAVERN. No sign of the rattlesnake we saw and left unharmed here last year. Get group picture.

Mile 35. BRIDGE OF SIGHS. Right. Land just below and Moulty and Garth and I climb up in cavern below and work up inside. With climbing ropes could go up and thru into the Bridge of Sighs. Roll a lot of big rocks down into the river. Difficult landing here.

Mile 40¼. Left. DWB. Initiation of the Driftwood Burners. Initiatory degree given all members. A really unusual and spectacular fire results from considerable resinous wood. Florence and Bestor Robinson, Lucille and Wayne Hiser, Moulty Fulmer, Frank Masland, and Frank Wright receive their degrees.[13]

Mile 40⅔.[14] Right. Fair sized canyon here. LUNCH. It is not on the map we finally determine. It should be added in another printing. We go up a short ways to get shade, then Bestor, Doc and I go on up the canyon to explore. We clamber over numerous huge rocks, shortly coming to a series of beautiful springs with an abundant growth of maidenhair fern. Good water. Other members have a siesta. On way back to the boats another drift pile is taken care of by the DWBs.

Mile 41. Center arch of ROYAL ARCHES. I see buck deer.

Mile 43. PRESIDENT HARDING RAPID. Wide open. We slip around the big rock to the *right*. Be careful, as higher stages make left more desirable. All OK.

Mile 47. SADDLE CANYON. We're drifting about 3½ miles per hour thru here.

CAMP. Mile 52. NANCOWEEP CREEK. As per usual, tired or no, we hurry over and start a diversion project in Nancoweep which results in the water flowing over close to our usual camp site by the big catclaw tree. We have a nice collection of planks to rig up the kitchen. Fearing we will get flooded out, I divert a bit of the water above camp. Next morning there's a regular canyon through the sand!

JULY 15

Camp at NANCOWEEP. This morning all but Frank, Garth, and I go up to see and photograph the ruins. After lunch Bestor, Doc, Moulty, Frank W. and I go over to Little Nancoweep and start up the canyon. We take the main fork to the left and finally get up into an area of vegetation, ferns, and pools of water—all in the shade. Even can swim. The climb on out to the top from here would be very difficult and require climbing equipment. Bestor and I scale around the head of the canyon a bit, but without ropes it's not safe to get too far up. All relaxing by a pool when Bestor rolls a big rock into the pool, causing immediate waking up reactions—but fast! After dinner we have a game of charades, accompanied by a great fire of driftwood. The fire lights up the whole area and is really beautiful. River seems to have been dropping all the way down, but does show changes in color that suggest local showers are occurring at different points on the watershed.

JULY 16

Mile 56. KWAGUNT RAPID. At this stage rough, rocky and tricky. We run wide open and have a lot of fun—but watch this one! Good drinking water here. Good stream.

Mile 59. SIXTY MILE RAPID. Easy and fun. Were here at 10:10 [A.M.] last year!

Mile 61. LITTLE COLORADO RIVER. At first checking it appears that the Little Colorado is a muddy turgid red, but Doc finds the clear blue water about ¼ mile above. It's a brighter blue than Havasu. We all go in swimming and have a grand time. Some of us swim down towards boats a part of the way back.

Lunch and dinner. Mile 65. LAVA CANYON. We eat lunch in the North mine tunnel. Doc takes off for an exploratory trip up Lava Canyon. The rest of us row across the river and go up and into the old Tanner Mine. We find the rate of cave-ins progressing fast even from last year. It is becoming dangerous. Return to mouth of tunnel and thence back across the river. Am awakened from nap by Frank who is worried about Doc. Frank, Garth and I set out to look for him. Reach some foul salt water. Further on Garth elects to return. Shortly beyond we find good water. Garth joins us for drink, then goes back. Frank and I walk fast on up canyon. After 1 hour 45 min. from boats we stop for "war talk." Just then Doc hoves into sight. He has seen a lot of deer, also the probable means of access to the North Rim. We return to find dinner prepared. Eat hurriedly, climb into the boats. and in the failing evening light run LAVA CANYON RAPID, and proceed thru the soft early evening shadows down to our designated camp at TANNER TRAIL. A most beautiful evening.

TANNER TRAIL. We land, start a large drift pile afire, and begin to receive flashlight blinks. They are unintelligible, as are ours to those on the Rim signalling. The blinking keeps up for a long time but we finally give up. Talk for some time—joke about the big run tomorrow—and it's a dilly! After others have long gone to sleep Bestor and I sit and talk. Really enjoy our talk, and the setting is out of this world.

JULY 17

River has continued its drop. Going to be choppy in lower canyons.

Mile 72. UNKAR CREEK RAPID. We land here and look over, then first boat, the WEN, takes off in exactly same time to the minute as last year! I take Florence and Wayne with me, other boats watch, then they in turn come on thru passengers and all. A bit tricky and some sharp water at the bottom. We restrain manfully from having a DWB meeting in the area of the great drift pile here, but—1949?! A good ride and all arrive bottom OK.

Mile 75. SEVENTY-FIVE MILE RAPID. Good idea to check the channel each time here. We do so, then right on thru, all in a row. Bit rough but OK.

Mile 76. HANCE RAPID. Well, the lower stage of water doesn't improve this baby. We need to take the same left, meandering channel as we do in the higher water, yet the rocks and holes are quite a bit more complicated. Others thru OK tho the trusty WEN acting a bit as tho knowing the channel made it thru a bit smoother. Water below here plenty rough itself and after loading up again and going on we get quite some ride. All thru solo on Hance.

Mile 78. SOCKDOLOGER RAPID. Hance had me prepared for a bit of a rough channel ahead, and Sock certainly presents the toughest looking takeoff at this stage that I've ever seen yet. Requires some tricky maneuvering right at the start. Bestor works his way quite a long ways down along the left side and reports that even in this stage of water it would be possible to go down alongside—but difficult. WEN off with Florence and Frank Masland. A marvelous ride, a thrill.

It is my firm conviction that no one has ever really lived until he or she has had a first view of Sockdologer—looked down into that fury of water, knowing he has to go thru it in the boat—taking off, poising on the brink, then with what seems like express train speed literally hurled down into the lashing wave. It's fearful—quickly changing into a perfectly thrilling exhilaration. 'Nuf said.

Mile 81. GRAPEVINE RAPID. Wowsy dowse! All that can be said about Sockdologer can be said about this one—and plenty more! This one has a *really* confused takeoff. Looking at this one I wonder why I ever elected to lead parties into this sort of thing—but know the answer at the same time! It's a frightfully tough looking proposition, and even when we have the channel selected I feel a bit squeamish. But—1:50 PM. Everything snugged down on the WEN. Florence Robinson and Frank Masland are aboard— we're off! It's a thriller, but we slide thru in wonderful style. The rest of the boats, one by one show up. All make it OK! We're ready for lunch.

LUNCH. Mile 82. Left. BOULDER CREEK. Good shade. Have stopped here before.

Mile 84. CLEAR CREEK. A very rough number. Watch it. Land above rapid on right and it's possible to get into Clear Creek. Do it in '49.

Mile 84⅔. ZOROASTER RAPID. Rough as the dickens. In fact all these numbers through here are a fine, equipment-, man-testing thrilling ride!

Mile 87. BRIGHT ANGEL CREEK. On the bank is Doris, Nancy Streator,[15] Rosalind Johnson.[16] Together with some Park men, a few others. Our usual almost formation-like approach is somewhat marred by Garth trailing in quite a ways behind in the SANDRA. But it's grand to touch shore and know we've successfully run the upper part of the canyon. A big job lies ahead restocking supplies. Two weeks and some of the roughest water in the Canyon lies ahead—but we've run some pretty heavy water already and feel confident. We wish the river would stop dropping. It's down today already to about 12,500 second feet. We all head for the swimming pool at Phantom Ranch. We meet our very fine hosts at Phantom, the Malones. Dinner is a fine and gala occasion—followed my much fun and more swimming after dinner. I have been told that our new member of the party, John Doerr,[17] Chief Naturalist of the NPS, is a very big man in size as well as position. How heavy? My boatmen are turning in a very fine job, the boats are behaving beautifully, so I guess everything will work out fine.

July 18

Day spent in loafing and relaxing. John Doerr gets in. After much ribbing etc. I finally learn he only hits scales at 194. I put him on a diet anyhow, and we all have a lot of fun—at both John's and my expense. Poor Nancy got a fine set of blisters coming down the trail so she gets in for a bit of joshing too.

July 19

Doris is off up Bright Angel trail. I see her over to River House. Back to the boats where Frank and Garth have sorted food. Partially stow cans, but it's time for lunch. After lunch Frank and I get some of the supplies we had at the USGS cabin and add to our stock. Everything appears in order and we are set for the morning. A good time at dinner. Nancy takes all of John's food, but at last minute John appropriates her plate.—and so it goes! We all were sorry to see the Robinsons leave. They took off up the trail sometime during the night. The farewells are the hardest part of these trips. Cowboy Welty[18] gets in with his customary enthusiasm, so our final party grouping is all set and we are ready to go in the morning.

JULY 20

If any failing spirits are present they are well concealed. We are given breakfast a bit early in order to give us a better start. We find the river has dropped down to 11,200 second feet, but stormy areas suggest a possible rise. After all I have been thru on 3,000 so we aren't hurt too bad!

Sailing order:

WEN	Norm, Nance, John
MH2	Frank, Ros, Frank (Fisheyes)[19]
SANDRA	Garth, Lucille, Moulty
JOAN	Doc, Cowboy, Wayne

Shove off. We've heavily loaded but everything is running well. The waves are sharp and vicious, and do throw lots of water at us. We bail.

Mile 90. HORN CREEK RAPID. And here we hit another toughy. Our customary left hand channel isn't practicable, and the right hand is a bit of a thriller. We have lots of water ahead, I give orders for solo runs, but decide to take Nancy with me in the WEN. We shove off—and it's a thrill ride! Make it fine. Others thru solo in good form.

Mile 93. GRANITE FALLS RAPID. One place to run, and that's on the right down thru the big waves. They're a bit mean and have some hard punching curls. This will have to be solo, all the way thru. It's some ride. Land below in my usual cove, with plenty of water in the boat. Others thru in good shape, tho all get a good drubbing in the waves and a good workout getting to shore below. It's a difficult walk around this one and is accomplished tho by everyone in good style. It's a very real thrill to get this rapid "under the belt" as it has a lot of potential dynamite.

Mile 95. HERMIT FALLS RAPID. LUNCH. My first cursory glance as we land affirms it can be run tho how am not sure. We go have with lunch, then study the situation a bit. Not too easy, but finally work out a deal to slide thru. All make it fine, tho Frank gets clipped by one wave and is momentarily out of control. This was solo run.

Mile 96. CAMP. BOUCHER RAPID. Camp at head on left. Very little wood, quite a ways up creek to water. Good camp tho, and anchorage is good, which is important as Hermit at foot is very rough. Ros breaks out some South American MATE, similar to tea, and we all enjoy it a lot. A perfectly beautiful night.

July 21

Running Boucher Rapid. Normally we just boom thru this one, but this stage of water renders it a bit more than tricky. Presages rough going in some of our old friends below. Nance and I go off in WEN.[20] OK. Then Garth and Ros in MH2. Rest thru solo. All OK, but wet!

Mile 99. TUNA CREEK. These thru here have been wonderful sport. Water is fast, tricky, and lots of fun. We bail plenty. We had a thot to stop at Tuna Creek, but the famous DOG LEG section[21] ahead is too much to resist so we boom on down. What a ride!

MILE 100. On right. Thru various sources, news accounts, etc., we had all learned of the famous descent by parachute of three army men from a C-54,[22] some four years previously. It was on the Tonto Rim above us. After four days they were spotted, lots of supplies dropped, including a radio, eventually rescued by an overland party from the North Rim. We feel it will be fun to try to locate the camp and also get a great view from the Tonto if we climb out here. We also want to try to find the radio and surprise Harold Bryant with it. Our "search party" resolves itself into: Nancy Streator, Rosalind Johnson, Doc Marston, and myself. We set out about 10:15 AM, go up a ways in the canyon at Mile 99⅔ just upstream a ways, but find it pretty precipitous. Returning to the river we go on upstream a ways to where a long steep slope of talus appears to give access to the rim. It's getting a bit hot, but away we go. Ros and Doc take one route, Nance and I another. Nancy's feet have five blisters to start with so it appears that haste will be most undesirable! We expect to pick up water in Tuna Creek after reaching the rim. About ⅘ of way up, tired, thirsty—Ros and Doc ahead a ways find one of the supply chutes. Mattress, shoes, etc. etc. Broken quart of OLD OVERHOLT, and a quart canteen of water. Might be four years old, but the water tasted like nectar.[23] Reaching the rim we park the girls in the shade and Doc and I scour the ¾ mile square mesa top, soon finding the fliers camp and the cache they left. Radio in good shape. Other stuff, canteens, blankets, etc. many first aid kits, much the worse for weathering, and rats. We get a couple of Very pistols. I go down to get the girls and awake them by shooting off a parachute flare! We gather up our loads and start down. I find I have greatly overestimated my carrying capacity, and end up caching everything but the radio itself, minus the speaker, aerial, etc. Will get it in '49. Ros and Doc go ahead. I instruct Doc to take the party on down to camp at first feasible spot downstream, as where the boats now are there's little or no place to camp. Nance and I finally struggle on down—and flop in the river! The water tasted rather good! Making our way to camp we find Fisheyes and John Doerr [a]waiting us.[24] By now it's getting darkish, and I don't care to risk running any rough water with so much load. We consume gallons of tea, find perches for the night—and sleep!

JULY 22

Nance, Frank, John, and I hurriedly stow our gear and take off down the river.

Mile 101. On right. We find the main party on a fine beach. We get in in time to participate in some breakfast. It's good to get all assembled again. This rapid here, SAPPHIRE CANYON RAPID has a tricky channel. Several holes complicate the picture. But boats are soon packed and we shove off.

WEN shoves off. Rest of boats down, bialed *[sic]* out–and we're off.

Mile 106. SERPENTINE RAPID. Look over briefly, then WEN off. All passengers [ride]. Marvelous ride. We're going to town t his morning.

Mile 108. SHINUMO CREEK. LUNCH. Good shade in the cove. Everyone in swimming. I sleep the soundest I have almost in years.

Mile 112. WALTHENBERG RAPID. Well! I expected this to be a bit rough—and it really is. Very tricky takeoff and course to follow. I don't like the looks of this one. My judgement says OK, so I end up with Nance in the WEN, and we shove off. Make it fine tho quite a thrill ride. Garth smacks the ledge on the left. Frank can't drop into the secondary channel and whizzes thru the hole just off center. Makes it fine. I send John Doerr (Little John) thru with Doc. They boom thru the hole too and have a fine rousing ride. What a day!

Mile 116. ELVES CHASM. CAMP. Like old times. Make out a pretty good camp. All are tired and go to bed early. This has been a day to be long remembered.

JULY 23

Had a good night here at Elves Chasm, tho sand drifted a bit. This morning we go up and sign the register, go up to the falls a few hundred yards up the canyon, then climb into our water ponies and take off.

Mile 118. Right. Bit cloudy and wind blowing. Land here to perform the sacred and ancient rites of inducting Nance and John into the order of the DWBs. Both pass the requisite test and are accepted. The sign of the match is flourishing! John shows an especial ability and most acceptable enthusiasms in his displays of pyromaniasm! We have enjoyed the change from the Granite Gorge, tho are sort of anxious to try out our next session with it below.

Mile 123. FORSTER RAPID. Passengers have been having a whirl at the oars. Ros takes on Forester Rapid—stepping into some really big waves. Does fine.[25]

Mile 129. SPECTER CHASM. Good spot for lunch. It takes a Brunton Compass operated by John to definitely establish our position. We dropped down thru such a collection of fast—lots of fun—drops that I lost position. Thus we are quite close to Bedrock.

Mile 130. BEDROCK RAPID. Stormy and windy. At this stage it proves to be easy to walk around, and the current is a very tricky proposition in its drive to the big rock. Takes some fast dropping off the tongue. Nance and I shove off in the WEN, make it fine, then land and clamber up on the big rock in center of river. Find a wonderful natural pool filled with warm water. Moulty and Garth get in uncomfortable close to the big rock. Frank clips the big rock. Doc clips big rock and springs hole in JOAN. This rapid is a deceptive fellow. Seems like it's always good for a thrill. Starts a hard rain, so Nance and I take off and go across to the other boats, and join all but Ros in huddling under granite ledges. Ros wanders around and soaks up the rain. We are disappointed in not having any waterfalls following up the rain.

Mile 131. DUEBENDORFF RAPID. A technique job. Main channel drives into big holes, so we elect to run just right of center, in and about several rocks. WEN off, solo. Flirting with dynamite with this one, yet I get disgusted beating the rapid out of its fun so much. I go back to run the MH2 thru, and beckon Lucille Hiser over to join me. We come thru right on the money again, and do our best in lower end to have a ride. Not bad. I ride standing on deck. Garth thru solo in SANDRA OK. I go back up and ride thru with Doc in the JOAN standing on the deck with a stirrup rope. Lots of fun. My first real ride with Doc. OK.

Mile 133. TAPEATS CREEK. CAMP. Watch this one dropping thru wide open. I took this one on running into the sun and was just barely able to get the correct channel selected at the last moment. A slipup here could make it a bit rough.

In evening and morning Doc catches about 11 rainbows, John 2. They are really delicious. Most bathe, but it's too rugged for me in Tapeats Creek so I bathe in the river. Nance elicits a lot of whistles when she shows up in a spotless shorts ensemble! The rain at Bedrock gave way to a beautifully clear evening. Once during the night a bank of clouds goes over but it clears again. We set off a couple of the Very flares—they are quite a sight.

July 24

A very wonderful rainbow trout breakfast.

MILE 136. CAMP. DEER CREEK FALLS. Enchanted Canyon.[26] This is where the contest comes off for standing under the falls—the first out buying malts for rest of contestants at Boulder. Nance, Doc and I seem to be the only exploratory minded, so we make the climb to way above the falls and then follow the chasm rim back some several hundred yards to where the valley opens up. It is spectacular beyond description. In deference to blisters, Doc goes on solo to check the water source, while Nance and I loaf in the shade of a big cottonwood tree. Close by the creek comes rushing by, in and thru little pools and grottoes covered with maidenhair fern, and another fern with a strange and wondrous rust color. We merely have to twist and lean over to get a drink of this fine water. Directly below us the water cascades down thru a series of pools, until it reaches the bottom of the gorge proper. There, it rushes on to the mouth of the chasm, shooting out into space to form Deer Creek falls. This is such a restful and beautiful place. Birds seem to be the only things to assure us that this is not some ShangRiLa in another World. It's easy to talk—then drift off into sleep. We are awakened by Docs return with a report of the canyon. He's carrying some board he found a ways above us, thus indicating that in the past some prospector—who knows who—came this way. The left fork above has water gushing right up from the stream bed, whereas the right fork ends in a wall from which, like Vasey's Paradise the water is discharged from the wall. We feel this has been a migration route of the ancient cliffdwellers. The fact is supported by a ruin just below that is at a point that would be fordable in real low water.

Evening is spent in song, stories, and the Yogi appears to tell us all of the origin of the canyon.[27] Another Very flare is set off. A beauty. Goodnight.

July 25
Almost forgot. John seems to have lost the main contest on the malts. Garth and I put on a secondary contest which of course I promptly lost. I still owe him a malt. Will repay him in Berkeley, where the malts are 5¢ cheaper!

Mile 138. DORIS RAPID. Just a bit choppy, tho here in 1940 Doris and John Southworth both fell out of the boat.

On this stretch going down to KANAB CREEK we stop once to settle argument of river width. Rock throwing establishes an average channel of about 100 yards in width.

Too, along here are much amused in the WEN when a dragon fly alights on the gunnel and whenever I would put my finger up towards his right foot, he'd raise the right foot and apparently shake hands. He'd never fail!

Mile 143. KANAB CREEK RAPID. This is a long one. For a change we try running without looking over first. Works fine and we have a wonderful ride. Have to be just a bit sharp at first as there's quite a few holes. It's lots of sport to run as it goes on and on and on.

UPSET RAPID. LUNCH (at foot). This is a solo job. I run both the WEN and the MH2. Thru OK. Garth and Doc OK. Bad eddy at foot and I have plenty of trouble getting off after lunch.

Mile 152. Nance has taken over the oars and she puts us thru this rapid in good style.

Just above Havasu Canyon we all stop, with exception of Doc, to pick up some wood for our camp at Havasu. We plan to camp on the ledge, and past experience has shown it to be free of driftwood!

CAMP. HAVASU CANYON. Mile 156. We hurry up to take advantage of the last sun on the falls back up a ways from the river. Get a few pictures but the light soon fades. The water has a trifle murky cast occasioned by recent showers, yet it is still a beautiful place. To avoid the overland tour, Nance, Moulty and I swim down the canyon to the river to get back to the boats. The rock ledges are hot and next morning we hear of several sleepless nights. In future it is well to be remembered that the lower ledges closer to the boats are most desirable. But it's a wonderful setting—and the moon fills the canyon during the night to make it seem even more unreal.[28]

JULY 26

This makes seven days on the river since Bright Angel. Time really has wings. It seems like yesterday since we took off.

Between miles 162 to 164¼ was staged the great running battle of 1948. The WEN was first attacked, the fight in full swing (full swing of a water bucket) raged on. Nance handled the oars of the WEN, executing skillful flanking maneuvers, and all were well soaked. The greatest tragedy occurred when Wayne Hiser had his glasses knocked off, and had to complete the trip without a correction for distant viewing. We dropped down over our old friend 164½ MILE RAPID and sailed on.

Mile 171. STAIRWAY CANYON. LUNCH. John and Doc go up canyon and finally find a sort of pool. Rest of us relax. The war of the morning continues—this time Lucille directs a deadly fire of pebbles at Nance while she—sleeps.[29] It is hot. Feels good to get out on the water and travel.

In the rapid we run directly below here, Loper and Harris upset in '39. How, we wonder for it's anything but a rapid of severity.[30]

CAMP. Mile 179. LAVA FALLS. We land and find it not too hot. Lining is indicated as the two possible places to run are too much a matter of chance. By dinner time we have carried all the equipment, more or less, down to the foot of the falls where the boats can pick it up. We look and look for John Riffey, but he doesn't show up. After dinner, Garth, Frank and I go across the river to look over the main channel. What a hole! Running here would be impractical. Been a good day, and everyone retires early.

JULY 27

Garth, Doc and I get up extra early and have a light bite, then start lining the Mexican Hat 2nd. This is done from 5:55 AM to 6:30 AM. Really fast! Then the WEN in 30 minutes. JOAN a bit less—and the SANDRA in *15 MINUTES!* This has been the fastest most efficient lining operation I have ever participated in. Boats are soon reloaded and we are ready to go.

LUNCH. Mile 188. WHITMORE WASH. We take to the tamarisks here for shade.

Wind against us. Bit overcast. Have to dabble oars a bit to make time.

Mile 193. Left. The aluminum landing barge that got away at Lees Ferry in 1947, first landed that same year at BEDROCK RAPID, this year in the real high water has been carried down and wedged in here on the left. I doubt if anything will move the barge from now on. Seven steel drums are still attached, but not well, and even with this buoyancy the barge is certainly too well anchored to move.[31] We shall see.

PARASHONT WASH. CAMP. Turns out to be a very nice camp. Beautiful night again. Nance and Garth put the hex on Frank W. and his shaving, but Frank still doesn't nick his throat. I believe this would be a good place to bring in food supplies, and may do so in '49.

JULY 28

Mile 205. 205 MILE RAPID. Run this wide open, but what a ride! Rather than dodge, we boom right thru a largish hole ⅔ of way down. WET! Water hits us hard and I have trouble clearing my head. Nance comes out of it gasping and throwing dirty looks in my direction. All thru fine shape. Must watch this one—it's real sport but can be dangerous.

Mile 209. GRANITE PARK. A good ride. Steal a bit on the left.

Nance takes the oars again to Fall Canyon. Runs a couple of good ones.

Mile 211. FALL CANYON. Sharp drop and rough and tough. Watch it.

Mile 213. Left. Cove with willow tree. Spotted it last year. Beaver have almost ruined the willow tree, but we get some good ledge shade for lunch.

Mile 217. 217 MILE RAPID. This *is* a surprise. I expected this to be a first class son of a gun, but instead it's a nice riding set-up. We first go over and check evidence that unquestionably shows that Doc Marston, Ed Hudson—Sr. and Jr.—with Willie Taylor, made an upriver run to this point.[32] We see their note, also a cache of gas. They did this without any lining, which pales into insignificance any other so called upriver "runs." This party did it with power—not ropes. We declare this "dubs" day—so Nance and I lead thru in the WEN, followed by Moulty Fulmer. He does fine. Then John Doerr does a swell job of running the MH2 thru. Rosalind comes thru in the JOAN, does fine, tho is knocked off the seat. makes a good recovery and lands as we planned. We are going to have another "dubs day" on the run from Diamond Creek to head of Lake Mead.

Mile 219½. Right. Garth in lead spots a two man life raft at the 100,000 second foot level. It appears to be the famous Roemer raft.[33] Initials RUO on front in water-proof tape. All conditions being considered I feel that this raft has probably been lost by some sportsman in the Spring of this year.

Mile 220. Right. Here is where Aleson hauled and dragged his boat up the river to. Too, this is where Doc and Ed Hudson effected repairs to their boat this spring when they were here on 70,000 [cfs]. John Doerr finds a shirt which we think must have been one of the upriver party—gives it to me, and I in turn find it fits Nance so give it to her. Been having a good zippy ride to here. Plenty of rocks showing up. Current is fast and vicious at times. We have been getting by well, tho. so far. Only wide open rock impact was made by Garth when he rammed the SANDRA into a rock head

on just above Deer Creek Falls, breaking the portage bar and springing the transom.

Mile 223. 224 MILE RAPID. Rough fast and fun. Tricky tho. So watch it.

Mile 226. DIAMOND CREEK. CAMP. 27¾ miles today. They were a bit hard earned. Current slow and the wind blew. Nance and John did more than their share of relieving me at the oars. We find the spring water here cool and good. The creek is fine bathing. Establish a good camp and are settled down to a 24 hour layover. To bed to bed says sleepy head.

JULY 29

We all get up early. After breakfast we loaf around and relax in the shade. An impulse to climb starts me up the north face of the south point of Diamond Creek cliff. It is a bit difficult, and am rather glad to finally reach the top.[34] The descent is easy. I then sort of rinse or wash out shirts, sheets, etc. Lunch. Initiation into the Royal and Honorable Society of River Rats is then conducted. This initiation marks the 100th different person to have made the traverse of Grand Canyon from Lees Ferry to and beyond Diamond Creek. Our inductees number: Rosalind Johnson, Lucille and Wayne Hiser, Frank Masland, Moulty Fulmer, Frank Wright. Nance and I take the WEN and row across and up the river to shade side of the canyon and relax under a great willow tree. No flies bugs or ants. Back for dinner. Games stunts etc. are in order. Charades. Baths. And night finds us all pleasantly relaxed from a most interesting day.

Nancy Streator, John Doerr, Norman Nevills, unidentified

JULY 30

This is the day we somehow look forward to, yet really dread too. It's our last day on the river. By noon or before we will be on Lake Mead. One of the greatest adventures any one can have any time is about to be in the past. We want to see it accomplished, but we hate to give up our fun, our comradeship—living in a setting that has been reserved for a very chosen few.

SHOVE OFF. Diamond Creek Rapid is fun, and the water below begins to really get interesting. Fast sharp, plunging drops keeps us constantly alert and very wet. We glory in it, for not far below the river trip is ended.

Be sure to stop at TRAVERTINE CANYON at mile 229 in 1949. Good water and waterfalls.

TRAVERTINE FALLS. Mile 230. River is colored a sort of tawny grey this morning. We later find that it's about 8,000 feet here this morning, thus we have been on a falling stage clear from Lees Ferry. It if hadn't been for local storms we would [have] probably been on even way lower water. Falls here are nice, but the urge to run rapids is uppermost in our minds. The dubs day running seems to go by the board, tho I had Fisheyes warming up ready for a solo run. When the fever to run rapids gets you its hard to stop for other things!

Mile 232. 232 MILE RAPIDS. A zippy fast tricky fine to run number!

Mile 235. BRIDGE CANYON. We're getting close.

Meeting the tow boats, Lake Mead, 1948

GNEISS CANYON. LAKE MEAD. Arrived to the minute at the same time as a year ago today. The river part is now over. Now, on to Hoover Dam.

Left. Mile 238. Bureau [of] Reclamation Camp. LUNCH. We prowl around, rig up a table and chairs to have our lunch on. Then a siesta. Frank W. and I repair to the former supt.'s cabin, sleep on springs and mattress. Smoke and a rumbling hiss awakes us. We dash out to apparently find the cabin afire. I shout "We can save it!" Then for some reason hustle back to get my red hat, come out and with the aid of a long iron rod punch pull and beat at the fire—putting it out—and effecting the laugh it causes—because Doc set the fire! Time's a-wasting.[35]

Mile 239. SEPARATION CANYON. Pictures of the group in the usual tradition obtained with us around the plaque. Very very hot here. A relief to get into the water, and on down the lake. Directly after taking off Nance takes off from the WEN and goes back to the MH2, leaving John and I to our own resources. We row.

Mile 246. SPENCER CANYON. CAMP. Little or no current to here. Quite a trip up the canyon in and thru brush and trees to where the water is clear. Lower end of stream down to mouth is very murky owing to mud deposits. After dinner most everyone takes off to sleep. It's hot. The wind blows. Bugs. Nance and Ros talk with the Cowboy. I am terribly restless

Shirley Marston
and Garth Marston

and sleep seems impossible. It's a let down in more ways than one that's bothering me. Finally I rouse up Frank W. and we row across the Lake to a damp dust-free bar. Quite a time getting over in the dark as an angling current hits us. But finally to sleep.

JULY 31

7:30 AM we take off. I soon conceive the idea of tie the boats end for end and then one man doing the rowing. I start at 8:00, row 'til nine. Garth rows 9:00-10:00. Frank W., 10:00-11:00. Doc takes over at 11:00 and ends about noon on a place on the left that develops some fine shade. A long siesta, then we start out again, this time each boat apart. Nance is on the oars when Doc pulls ahead. I take this as a suggestion to make better time. We do! Nance, John and I keep the oars flailing until sundown, at which time we reach Emery Falls. Get water then row around into a cove and with the aid of a rope establish camp up on a ledge. Nice place, really, wood and everything. Everyone but Ros, Garth, Nance and I are bushed. Garth finally gives up, not followed too long by rest of us. Frank W. and I have a cozy nest on a bunch of rocks in the bed of the wash—but it turns out to be swell place to sleep—and tonight I could sleep on the tines of a pitchfork and like it!

Lake Mead, end of 1948 Grand Canyon trip: (left to right) Moulty Fulmer, Frank
Wright, Rosalind Johnson, John Doerr, Nancy Streator, Norman Nevills, Frank
Masland, Howard Welty, Garth Marston, Otis Marston, Lucille Hiser, Wayne Hiser

AUGUST 1

Breakfast over, dishes done, have just climbed into the boats—and here's the
Park boat! Much excitement. Pictures. Greetings. Water fights. Confusion.
Ice cream. Food. Cigars.

A third boat with Supt. Bagley and others misses us and continues up
lake. But here is the HAE DAE too, which takes us in tow.[36] Doris Nevills,
Frank Streator, Shirley Marston. Our family welcomers. Ray Poyser and Bill
Belknap who have met me on all six of my trips. Supt. Christensen. Act.
Supt. Yeager. Bill Russel. Don Ashbaugh.[37]

And on our way. We stop at noon for lunch and swimming at Temple
Bar, I believe it was. Then on. Ice water. Cokes. Talk. Relax. Boulder City
dock. More friends and relatives. Dinner—to bed.

AUGUST 2

Boats loaded on the trailers in the morning. Able assistance of the Boulder
dock crew made it a short and easy job. Then a hurried lunch and a great
thrill awaited us all. Supt. Christensen took us down to the powerhouse
via the big overhead tramway. And *that* was an experience never to be
forgotten.[38]

At night we had a banquet and the "little flies"[39] had their final meal together. I feel this trip was one of the most successful to ever to thru the Canyon. To those on the trip, those that stayed home "pitching," to those making our arrival so pleasant—thank you.

AUGUST 3
Doris and I clear to Tuba City. Frank to South Rim. We left radio with Lon Garrison. Cowboy rode to South Rim with us.

AUGUST 4
To Mexican Hat by 3:00 PM. Joan and I unloaded and stowed the two boats. Midnight, Frank, his brother and wife arrive with news that trailer axle breaking, complicated by terrific washout made them leave WEN, JOAN at or near Kayenta.

AUGUST 5
Frank, Joan and I go with another trailer out across the mud, lake beds, washouts, rains, etc. etc. etc. to rescue the boats. In by dark, to Mexican Hat.

And now, goodbye to Grand Canyon until 1949.

Green River,
June 19 to July 3, 1949
Grand Canyon,
July 12 to July 31, 1949

No diary, original or transcribed, exists in the Nevills papers for the 1949 Green River and Grand Canyon trips. There is little doubt that Nevills kept one, for he was a persistent journal keeper; but he obviously had no time to transcribe it before his tragic death, just weeks after he returned from the Grand Canyon. Despite searches, no trace of the original has been found. It could have disappeared in the turbulent period immediately after he was killed or it could have ended up in the vast collection of documents compiled by Otis Marston. But in the interest of continuity and to bring closure to his river career, the editor drew upon other diaries that were kept during those trips to give a synopsis of the trips. The sources are: the diary of P.T. Reilly, and to supplement the Grand Canyon trip that year, a diary kept by Frank Masland. Both Reilly and Masland were observant and perceptive diary keepers. Reilly, an engineer by vocation, viewed the personalities and events of the trip with a precise, detailed, and at times acerbic, eye. Masland, who had been on the 1948 Grand Canyon trip—and was by his own admission already completely under the spell of Nevills and made no apologies to anyone for the fact—likewise kept a detailed account. The P.T. Reilly diary is courtesy of the Cline Library, Special Collections and Archives at Northern Arizona University, while the Masland diary is from the Marriott Library's Special Collections Department at the University of Utah. Additional information was gleaned from newspaper clippings that are also found in the Nevills Papers, as well as from P.T. Reilly's 1986 article in Utah Historical Quarterly, "Norman Nevills: Whitewater Man of the West."

GREEN RIVER,
JUNE 19 TO JULY 3, 1949

The water was high in 1949, perfect for a successful river season. Nevills ran five San Juan trips from May 1 through the first week of June, meaning he barely had time to go home, repack the boats and supplies, and turn

Norman Nevills at Expedition Island, near Green River, Wyoming, receiving commemorative license plates for his boats from the Utah and Wyoming Highway Patrol

around for another trip. The reason for the haste was the 80th anniversary of the launching of the expedition led by John Wesley Powell; ceremonies were planned for Green River, Wyoming, and Nevills's old friend, Adrian Reynolds, made sure that Nevills was included in the plans. In fact, Nevills was already planning a Green River run, but had decided to start at Flaming Gorge, thus cutting off about seventy miles of flat water from the town to the first canyon. The prospect of free publicity, however, was always an attraction to Nevills, and the agenda for the trip was changed accordingly.

The last San Juan trip ended at Lees Ferry on June 12, 1949, and after two days to clean equipment, repack supplies, and do maintenance on the trailers, the crew left from Mexican Hat on June 15. In those days of unpaved roads and less powerful trucks, it took longer to cross the distances in the West, and it wasn't until June 17 that they arrived in Green River, Wyoming. They spent the next day repairing one of the trailers, causing Reilly to lament, "Sure wish our trailers were made from new parts instead of being assembled from junk yards." A new monument to John Wesley Powell had been erected at Expedition Island, a cove on the Green River within the little town, and a program was scheduled for the afternoon of June 19. Representatives of the Utah Highway Patrol and Wyoming Highway Department presented Nevills with special commemorative license plates for his boats, and after speeches by local leaders, the Nevills party repaired to the house of Adrian Reynolds for a buffet dinner.

The next day the party got an early start. The boatmen were all veterans save for one: Nevills in the *Wen*, Jim Rigg in the *Mexican Hat II*, Frank Wright in the *Sandra*, and P.T. Reilly[1]—the only new boatman—in the *Joan*. With a couple of exceptions again, all of the passengers had been on previous trips with Nevills. They were: Nancy Streator, Joe Desloge Sr., Zoe Desloge, Marie Saalfrank, and Ros Johnson. The newcomers were: Barney Desloge,[2] and Arthur, Betty, and John (their son) Compton.[3] Watched by townspeople from the banks, they went downriver just a few miles, watching a herd of wild horses swim the river in front of them, and camped in the Firehole Towers area early in the afternoon. That night, as they were all wondering about the height of the hills that shaded their camp, Arthur Compton, a physicist from Washington University in St. Louis, Missouri, told everyone he could easily determine the height of the hill within three percent. Reilly, who had been a surveyor, knew what Compton was going to do, but the others were doubtful. Using a thorn, a cereal box lid, and a piece of string, Compton made a crude protractor, took two measurements, amazed even Reilly by doing the complicated math in his head, and announced that the hill was 328 feet high.

After a "pleasant night," they were on the river shortly before 8:00 AM. Just after pushing off, they came across some geese swimming the river. "Immediately I had visions of roast goose for supper," wrote Reilly, and after trapping the geese—that couldn't fly because they were moulting—he dove in and finally succeeded in grabbing the largest one. Wringing its neck, they went on and soon made the customary landing to pay their compliments to Mrs. Holmes at the Holmes ranch. After leaving her that afternoon, they saw a great deal of wildlife before they camped; besides more geese, there were deer, beaver, ducks, and muskrats. That night they had no dutch oven so there was no way to roast the goose that Reilly had caught earlier. Wright boiled it, but the results weren't worth the effort; the goose was tough, "but the soup was OK." That night Adrian Reynolds and Barbara Rigg came into their camp, bringing business papers for Jim Rigg to sign. They had searched all along the river until midnight before finding the river party.

After another early start, they floated along through the open reaches of the Green, surrounded by more wildlife. At lunch, Arthur Compton once again displayed his various talents by making a complete set of panpipes out of willow twigs. Camp that night was not so pleasant, as they were pestered by a plague of mosquitoes, which was to be an all-too-frequent occurrence for much of the rest of the trip. The next day they woke up groggy and covered with welts, and were off as soon as the sun was up. Finally, they entered first Flaming Gorge, then swept around the bend into Horseshoe Canyon and Kingfisher Canyon—Reilly lamented about his own and Nevills's lack of knowledge about the geology of the Green River canyons—and camped early at Hideout Flat campground. Nevills, Jim Rigg,

Norman Nevills running Ashley Falls, 1949, with Joe Desloge, passenger

Barney and Zoe Desloge, and John Compton set out for the four-mile hike to the Green Lakes Lodge, where they planned to spend the night. The rest stayed by the river and had a pleasant evening, save for another visitation by mosquitoes.

The hikers were back early, and they entered Red Canyon soon after launching. Here they encountered the first real rapid of the trip: Ashley Falls. After searching in vain for the Ashley inscription, Nevills ran the left side of the rapid successfully. He then walked back up and took the *Sandra* through. Jim Rigg also had a good run, but was chewed out by Nevills for neglecting to wear his life jacket. Nevills was even more upset when Barney Desloge and John Compton swam through the rapid, but Reilly noted that it was "no big deal." They ran on down a few miles and camped at the mouth of Cart Creek, which in just a few years would be the site of the Flaming Gorge Dam. The next day they ran down to Red Creek Rapid at the end of Red Canyon, and learned after running it that Ros Johnson was feeling very sick. She had found ticks on her skin a few days before, and as it turned out, had contracted a case of tick fever. Deciding that she needed to see a doctor, they floated down to the Taylor Ranch in Browns Park, where the rancher agreed to take her to Rock Springs, Wyoming, to get treatment. The mosquitoes in Browns Park were even worse than they had been above the canyons, and all suffered greatly. Reilly commented, "I don't know why anybody ever decided to live in Brown's Park as the mosquitoes

Arthur Compton, Betty Compton, John Compton

are unbelievable. Sometimes they hit us in mid-river tho we usually lose them there. As soon as we shove our bows into the grass they come out in great clouds. I think all the outhouses here have smudge pots and anybody going Indian fashion risks losing a pint of blood." Later that day a strong wind—usually the bane of river runners—was welcomed because it brought relief from the mosquitoes. That night, they camped in a drizzle just above the Gates of Lodore and were surprised to see Adrian Reynolds and his wife come up, bringing Ros Johnson back to the trip. It was a measure of her passion for river running that she returned to the trip after being diagnosed with tick fever, a painful and dangerous ailment. A newspaper article written about the trip was headlined "Green River Expedition Seems To Be Plagued by Old '13 jinx," and it commented on Johnson's illness and Jim Rigg's "business emergency." That night they went to sleep with the Gates of Lodore looming over their camp, promising fast water in the morning.

The next day brought them into the Canyon of Lodore, and rapids were soon encountered. Reilly let Barney Desloge row through upper Disaster Falls, expecting the bigger water to be in the lower part, but he was disappointed and commented that it must have been "sheer stupidity" for Powell to lose a boat in such a minor rapid. The level of the water—about 5,000cfs—was perfect for such easy runs of the big rapids in Lodore, and they passed Triplet Falls with no problems. Camped just below it that night,

Portaging Hell's Half Mile, Green River, 1949

Nevills announced that they would portage Hell's Half Mile the next day. During the arduous portage, Reilly was "cussing with every grunt because it was unnecessary." Camp that night was at the foot of the rapid, and they relaxed that evening with a game of charades. With a short day ahead of them, they lounged in camp for the morning and then made the easy miles down to Echo Park, where to Reilly's dismay, they camped on an island at the mouth of the Yampa River. By this time Reilly was getting disgusted with Nevills because he planned no hikes, so they ended up sitting in camp after short days.

After a late breakfast the next day, they ran down to the mouth of Pool Creek, at the lower end of Echo Park, where the party met the caretaker of the Chew Ranch. Nevills had arranged the night before for a ride to the ranch—about four miles from the river—where they all enjoyed fresh homemade bread and buttermilk. Back on the river, they entered Whirlpool Canyon on double the water they had been on, and within a short time stopped at the mouth of Jones Hole Creek, a popular camping and fishing spot. Despite that stream's reputation, Reilly didn't catch any fish, and they soon were on their way to camp at Sage Creek. There, Reilly asked Nevills why he didn't plan any hikes. Nevills replied that he had to make the trips last to keep his prices up, and felt that most passengers didn't like to hike. After a few miles, they left Whirlpool Canyon the next day and rowed out into the flat water between there and the head of Split Mountain Canyon. Reilly noted that the nine-mile stretch "could be a death march at low water." They stopped at the Ruple Ranch, where Nevills had stopped since his first trip in 1940, and Reilly noted that the cottonwood tree in the yard must be at least 25–30 feet in circumference. Alice Bates, a former passenger on the San Juan, arrived with Joel Evans from Vernal, followed shortly by Doris, Barbara Rigg, and Bob Rigg, Jim's younger brother. The party spent the rest of the break riding horses and enjoying lunch at a table with Evans's family. They were back on the water soon after lunch, with Bates[4] along for the last stretch through Split Mountain Canyon.

Split Mountain, with the greatest fall of any of the canyons of the Green, was wonderful with fun, splashy rapids. Reilly wrote that in Moonshine Rapid—the first one—Arthur Compton "served as a splashboard" on his boat and "took a giant wave which came over the stern when I crashed it. We came out whooping exuberantly." Running through the rest of the canyon, Reilly declared—as generations of boaters were to learn after him—that Split Mountain represents rapid running at its finest. Landing at the foot of the canyon, they met Doris and the Riggs once again, and all save for Ros Johnson went with Jess Lombard, the superintendent of Dinosaur National Monument, for a tour of the world-famous dinosaur quarry. Camp that night was at the foot of Split Mountain Canyon, which is today the location of the boat ramp where Green and Yampa River trips take out.

The next day, Reilly noted that the last dozen miles down to Jensen, Utah, were "flat, quiet, boring," and wished that the trip had ended at their last camp on a "high note instead of this anticlimactic leg." Norman and Doris had gone on ahead in the truck and after a few hours came zooming over the river in a rented airplane. After a muddy landing below the Jensen bridge, the boats were loaded and all went into nearby Vernal. They stayed in the best hotel in town, and that night spoke on the local radio station. Reilly met famed riverman Bus Hatch, "who is more stooped and wrinkled than I expected." Reilly then watched in amazement as Joe Desloge, Sr., wrote Nevills a check for almost $5,000, besides giving each boatman a $20 tip. "A true gentleman and well heeled," he commented.

The next day, July 3, they headed back to Mexican Hat, but heavy rains caused slow going and they didn't reach Blanding, Utah, until late that night. They spent the night on Frank Wright's front lawn "under a broken sky." Nevills's final Green River trip was over.

Grand Canyon,
July 12 to July 31, 1949

The 1949 Nevills Expedition Grand Canyon trip left Lees Ferry on July 12 on more than 43,000 cfs, the highest water Nevills had ever seen in his career. The boatmen and boats were the same as the Green River run, but unlike most Grand Canyon trips, this one was composed of a number of newcomers to the river. First timers that were only going as far as Bright Angel were John and Evie Mull;[5] Josiah Eisaman and his daughter, Anne;[6] Eddie McKee[7] of the National Park Service; Molly Maley;[8] and Nancy Streator, who though only a teenager, was by now a veteran of several Nevills Expedition voyages. The only passengers who signed up for the whole trip were Frank Masland[9] and Bill Hargleroad[10] of Omaha. Because the Paria River was flooding, they couldn't reach Lees Ferry and were forced to bushwhack through the willows to launch their boats. A large crowd of well-wishers from Steator's family, as well as friends of Nevills, were there to see them off.

They were accompanied for the first few days by two powerboats with crews from the Bureau of Reclamation, who were on their way down to the Marble Canyon dam site.[11] The high water caught them all by surprise, and it took all their whitewater skills to safely navigate a river that was full of boils, strong eddies, and whirlpools. Badger Creek was a surprise, and—fulfilling a promise made by Nevills the year before—it was Masland's introduction to rowing a boat in big rapids. Masland wrote, "Was lucky, waves broke right, so a dry ride. Managed to pull out in fair shape. But, oh that feel, that marvelous unexplainable feel when the power of the water takes over as the slide down the tongue starts; the water that seems to say 'I kept quiet so you could row out if you wanted to. You passed up your chance, it's now too late.'" In Soap Creek both Reclamation boats were caught by lateral waves and tossed into the air; one almost came down upside down. When the motor was drowned out, the boatman grabbed a set of oars and rowed the boat the rest of the way through. Camp that night was just below Soap Creek. The next day Masland, who was again at the oars, was stopped by a wave in Sheer Wall Rapid and surfed back down the wave face. "Norm and Frank both said they had never seen a boat slide down a wave upstream," he wrote. Masland was learning to row the hard way: in difficult conditions of high water in a narrow canyon. Even with the master Nevills at the oars, it was tough going. The stretch of canyon is today called the "Roaring Twenties" for the many rapids between Miles 19 and 32, and it took all of Nevills's skill to keep the boat off the walls and out of whirlpools.

After a tight camp at Vasey's Paradise, they made the by-now customary visit to the skeleton near South Canyon, and got on the river. The Bureau of Reclamation camp was just downstream, and Reilly recorded that they stopped to look over the camp and the dam site. "Their pack train met them on the dot and Norm and I climbed out to a point [,] took telescopics [photographs] of the burros by the boats." This was far as the powerboats went, so it was time to say goodbye and continue.

They stopped for lunch at what Masland called "Unknown Canyon." Today it's known as Bert's Canyon. Just a few days before, veteran riverman Bert Loper, had been running 24½ Mile Rapid with young Wayne Nichol; Don Harris and his friend, Jack Brennan, were in another boat. As they approached the rapid, Nichol felt they were on the wrong line, so he turned around and said, "Look to your oars, Bert!" But the 80-year-old Loper was unresponsive and glassy-eyed. Just then the boat overturned. Loper was last seen floating in his life jacket, facing downstream. The boat got away and was found near Mile 41. There were other parties on the river then—an indication that Nevills, had he lived, would have had some competition after all—and Harris, Brennan, and Nichol, along with Howard "Cowboy" Welty, and Harry Aleson and his friends, Louise Fetzner and Ralph Badger pulled the boat above the high water and tied it to a tree. On the rear deck they painted Loper's epitaph.[12] Nevills's party hiked to the boat to pay their respects and take photographs, and they erected a cairn with one of the oars for a monument. All noted that the boat was poorly made with shingle nails and quarter-inch plywood; it was, basically, a disposable boat.

No one wanted to camp near that grim reminder, so they moved down to President Harding Rapid, to the big beach on the left below it. There, Reilly, who had earlier on the Green been wishing for a "snort of something stronger than river water" one cold night, found an "old, battered can of beer. No brand visible. We open it, find it palatable and cool and have a round robin." Camp was enlivened by a "roaring fire," as Masland noted.[13] They made the traditional camp at Nankoweap the next day, and Nevills lit two giant driftwood piles, a first for him. As they were running Kwagunt Rapid the next day, the run was so smooth that Nevills dipped a bail bucket of river water and doused Masland. "Probably the only way he would have gotten wet," Reilly said, but that was not Anne Eisaman's experience. In the *Sandra* with Frank Wright, she was sitting on the stern when a big wave washed her overboard. "Miss Eisaman, a Wellesley College student, was flung from the special cataract boat as it bounced and sped in the rock-strewn waters of the river which has claimed many a veteran boatman," a breathless newspaper article noted. "In an instant, willing hands of the boatmen pulled her back."[14] Wright noted, laconically, that "We hit a hole and Ann floated off but hung onto the ropes." No doubt, all were holding on a little more tightly after that, but since there are no significant rapids after Kwagunt for quite a few miles, they drifted along, stopping for lunch at the Little Colorado River, exploring the old mines near Lava Canyon, and finally camping at the foot of the Tanner Trail. Since it was both the first big rapid day and their last day as a group, ceremonies and rituals were held that night. The ceremony inducted Eddie McKee and Nancy Streator, both of whom had already done the lower part of the canyon, into the order of Colorado River Rats. The ritual consisted of "Norm in his usual nerve shattering style and commensurate effect" describing the horrors of Hance, Sockdologer, and Grapevine, the big rapids they had to run the next day. Afterwards, John Mull read a passage from Masland's book, *By the Rim of Time* that described the same stretch; Masland noted that, "The combination was such that several later admitted a fitful night and difficulty swallowing breakfast."

Even Nevills had reason to be nervous and not only because for the first time, their fire had elicited no response from the Desert View Watchtower. Nevills knew the big rapids ahead—had run them more than any man—but he had never seen them with this much water, and two of his boatmen had never seen the canyon at all. "We started the day with tautness obviously present," Masland wrote, a feeling that any big-water boatmen knows well. Tanner, Unkar, and Seventy-Five Mile Rapids were just warm-ups for the big ones to come, and making a tense situation worse was the heat; it was their first really hot day and all were wilting. Hance just looked too difficult, and after studying it for more than an hour, Nevills reluctantly decided to line it. They let their boats down about four hundred feet, past the worst of the boulders at the top, and then ran on. Everyone was anticipating Sockdologer and they weren't disappointed. "What a sight! Monstrous waves." Reilly said. But Masland, who had seen it the year before when the water was at a more difficult level, was relieved: "Only a short look was required to assure us that Soc was in a kindly mood. The great waves were there. The force and power were present but the tongue was clear cut straight through the center . . . it was a marvelous ride, never could it be finer." Wright noted that when Nevills saw it, he was "jubilant." Although Grapevine did not appear so benevolent, all made it through the last of the big three for the day with no problems. They floated down to Bright Angel with "much singing, calling back and forth, and kidding."

At Bright Angel, they found a large crowd, including Doris and Joan Nevills, Ruth Rigg (Jim's mother), and Susie Reilly. There would have been more people, as a great number of tourists had wanted to see them come in, but the decision to line Hance put the river party behind schedule and the tourists had left. Here the party was to change, with virtually all of the passengers from the upper end hiking out. Saying goodbyes were John and Evie Mull, Edwin McKee, Nancy Streator, and Anne and Josiah Eisaman. Even Bill Hargleroad, who had paid for a full passage, decided that the rapids the day before had been quite enough excitement and joined the departing hikers. As usual, Nevills took a two-day layover at Bright Angel to restock food, rest sore muscles, and regain cohesion as a group. Masland's eye had been bothering him ever since some sand blew into it at Lees Ferry; it was so painful at times that he wondered if he should go on. Hearing this, Joe Eisaman immediately called the hospital on the rim and arranged for medicine recommended earlier by Dr. James Rigg, Jim Rigg's father, to be sent down the next day. The medicine worked, and Masland was able to continue, although the eye hurt for the rest of the trip.

On July 20, it was back on the river. Joining them were twelve-year-old Joan Nevills, Mary Ogden Abbott,[15] R.J. "Bud" and Tro Anspach,[16] and Helen Kendall.[17] Susie Reilly, Doris, and several others rode the boats down to where they could catch the trail back up to the rim, and then it was on to Horn Creek. Passing Horn Creek Rapid with nothing more than a "hard, wet, rough ride," they then ran down to Granite Falls, which they ran after a brief scout from the left bank. Hermit was next, and at the water level they were on, there are enormous roller-coaster waves in the center. Nevills decided that the risk of capsizing was too great, so he decided to line. They accomplished this task with "considerable difficulty but great efficiency," as well they should, for a sour Reilly noted that Nevills had run Hermit only three times out of seven trips. The lining meant another short day, and Nevills knew that people on their first night don't want a long day on the river. Camp was at Boucher Rapid. Masland walked a mile back up the winding canyon to find water, which he decided "had unique flavor; most admirable. Noted burro signs everywhere." When he returned, he and Mary Abbott made a pot of tea, and they found it so tasty that, "Then and there formed the Boucher Tea Company, Limited; limited to one product, Boucher Tea Aroma de la Burro."

The next day they stopped at Tuna Creek to revisit the camp where they had found the gear from the marooned airmen the year before. Norman, Joan, Jim Rigg, and Reilly climbed up and soon found the site. They brought back flares, canteens, army blankets (including one made by a mill that Masland's firm had contracts with), and other souvenirs. Reilly even found the original instructions that had been air-dropped to the stranded airmen.[18] Then it was on to the Gems, a series of rapids that are big and fun at high water levels.[19] All had a great time, Mary Abbott especially: "Mary is thoroughly enjoying them," Masland wrote. "[She] states she has absolutely no sense of fear, probably due to complete confidence in Norm." They camped at Shinumo Creek that night and early the next day, they went only a few miles, stopping at Elves Chasm. They climbed to the pools where Masland, like so many after him, was struck by the beauty of the glistening waterfalls: "Joan swam pool then climbed up in back coming out and standing in a window. A nymph of the falls framed with moss and ferns and with a sun splashed pool at her feet. Not a sight I'll forget." Reilly, too, was impressed with the place, and when the gathering clouds cleared "got some good shots–cheesecake by Tro and Joan." Rain came down and all that could fit repaired into Masland's tent; but it soon passed and they spent a quiet night. At camp that night, Nevills told Masland that he was giving him the *Mexican Hat II* as a gift; Masland was touched and thrilled, and planned to put it on display at his mill in Pennsylvania.[20]

The next day Mary Abbott seemed to be missing. Wright noted "Mary caused some concern by not showing up for breakfast. She was finally found in a nice place, well hidden, and had overslept." They moved on through the rapids of the Middle Granite Gorge—"always bailing and never dry"— and made successful runs of Forester, Specter, the dreaded Bedrock, and Dubendorff, which Reilly called a "dilly with many holes and lateral and explosion waves." Masland agreed: "It was worse than last year with tremendous holes that could not be avoided if run full or heavy. Just a succession of holes, all foam, leading through them. Largest hole in center was an explosion hole. The worst of this type I have seen." They were grateful to camp that night by the beautiful Tapeats Creek. Although Reilly and Masland tried their luck at fishing that night and the next morning, the famous Tapeats trout were not biting.

Another short day brought them to Deer Creek, where all rested, hiked to the canyon above the falls, and enjoyed the beauty of the surroundings; but it was too cool to go under the falls for the usual malted milk bet. Joan Nevills came down with a case of swimmer's ear, but treatment in Masland's tent and a night away from blowing sand put her in good condition the next day. Upset Rapid—a "vicious twister"—let them through in good shape, and they ran on down to Havasu for camp.

The water was high enough that they could row up the twisting mouth of Havasu Canyon, and they camped on the ledges above. They "swam and swam and swam and took pictures," and then lounged in the shade as the day passed. Masland was struck by his fellow passenger, Helen Kendall: "She is utterly indefatigable; as soon as we land noon or nite she is off, up a canyon or over a cliff, exploring. Skin scratched, hair awry, clothes in wild disarray; she doesn't give a hoot but keeps on going, getting a great deal from trip." Unlike the previous year, when he had woken bathed in a pool of sweat, Masland and the others had a good night's sleep. They woke to find the river a deep brown, which Nevills declared indicated a flood from the San Juan River. The river had been falling since they left Bright Angel, but recent storms now brought it back up a little. It made no difference when they camped at Lava Falls the next day. New boatman Reilly was impressed, describing the biggest rapid in the Grand Canyon as "a falling, seething mass with no channel." Lining began at dawn, with Nevills "banging the skillets" to get them all up and going. Wright recorded that the process took "45 mins on first boat, 30 on next 2, and 25 mins on last one." By 9:00 AM, the boats were below the rapid and loaded—ready to go. Fortunately, there were few supplies to carry around the rapid, as they were meeting a resupply party at Whitmore Wash, about ten miles downstream.

When they arrived there, they found several members of the Bundy family, a clan of Mormon ranchers who lived some miles away from the river on the North Rim. Also joining them at the bottom of the Whitmore Trail were Doris Nevills; Barbara Rigg, Jim's wife; his father, Dr. James Rigg; and John Riffey, the park ranger in charge of the area. Celebrating that night, they lit a giant cactus on a lava cliff above their camp, which burned for hours: "a never to be forgotten sight that light that blazed above the stygian wall against the starlit sky." The next day, resupplied and with two new passengers—Doris and Barbara Rigg—they ran various Bundy family members through the little rapid below their camp, and bid them adieu. The high water brought them to their next camp, Spring Canyon—just above 205 Mile Rapid—at noon, but by now they could feel the pull of the end of the trip, only a few days away. The next day, Masland rowed Mile 217 Rapid, with Doris as his passenger, and they had no problems getting down to Diamond Creek, their last camp, where they would stop for the usual layover day.

There was little left to burn at Diamond Creek. The next morning, a huge boulder came loose and crashed right into their camp. Just moments before, the boats had been tied to the boulder, and had they not been moved, it could have been a disaster. The day was spent lounging in the creek, taking photographs, and eating. All but the boatmen started on a hike to some old mines that Nevills claimed was only a mile away, with no climbing or bushwhacking. "Somebody ought to write a song about a Nevills mile," Masland wrote. "At about two miles we hit the underbrush just as trail started to climb; after three miles found good shade and gave up." That night they performed the rites of passage into the Colorado River Rats on Jim Rigg and Reilly, and it was the ladies' turn to make dinner.

July 31 was their last day on the river; they started early and within a few hours had reached Lake Mead. The high water helped them, with current all the way to Pierce Ferry, where they met the tour boat *Hae Dae*, which towed the boats all the way to Boulder Landing. The 1949 Nevills Expedition trip through the Grand Canyon was now history.

It had been a great trip for Norman and Doris Nevills: they got to run part of the canyon together with their daughter, Joan, the water had been high, and there had been no accidents or personal problems. Nevills wasn't planning to run the Grand Canyon in 1950 because he had other plans: The Sierra Club had already signed a contract for a trip on the San Juan, and Disney was interested in making a movie about John Wesley Powell. And then there were other rivers; he might try the Fraser River in Canada or even the Brahamaputra in far-off India. Norman Nevills and Nevills Expedition were at the top of the world, and things couldn't seem better.

Coda,
Monday, September 19, 1949

It was a beautiful late summer day in Mexican Hat. The night before, Doris Nevills received a telegram informing her that an uncle had died in California, and she had asked Norman to fly her to Grand Junction, Colorado, so she could catch a commercial flight to California. Joan Nevills, twelve years old, was away at Wasatch Academy, a private school in Mt. Pleasant, Utah; little Sandra—their other daughter—would stay at home with Mae Nevills, Norman's mother. Sandra walked with them to say goodbye and stood watching as Nevills taxied to the upper end of the dirt strip, brought up the power on his Piper Super Cruiser, and took off as he had so many times before.

As Sandra watched, however, the engine on the plane seemed to sputter, and she saw her father start a turn to the left to come back to the landing strip. But instead of landing, the plane disappeared from sight behind a low hill; there was a sound of a crash and a cloud of smoke rose up into the still air. Terrified, Sandra ran back to the Nevills Lodge, about a quarter-mile away, and told her grandmother "Oh Moe, the plane has crashed and Mother and Daddy are burning!" Thinking to reassure the frightened child, Mrs. Nevills stepped outside, saw the plume of smoke, and knew instantly—to her horror—that it was all too true. Failing to reach the runway, the plane had smashed directly into the face of a low cliff at the end of the airstrip; had they had three feet more altitude, they would have made it. Mrs. Nevills ran to get help from Ray Lyman—a friend of the family—and an oil crew working nearby, but all they could do was watch helplessly as the hot fire from a full load of gas consumed the plane and both bodies.

Someone thought to contact Preston Walker of Grand Junction, Colorado, a long-time friend of Norman Nevills. He immediately flew to Mexican Hat with his wife, Becky, and along with Lawrence Wright and Harry Goulding, retrieved the charred bodies from the wreck. They were taken to Grand Junction while funeral arrangements were made. The memorial held a few days later in Grand Junction was well attended, as Norman and Doris had a wide circle of friends. In December 1949, Jim and Bob Rigg flew the cremated remains of Norman and Doris Nevills—

their ashes mingled in death as they had been inseparable in life—over the canyon country, and scattered them along the San Juan River from Mexican Hat to the lower end of the Grand Canyon.

Almost three years later—in July 1952—friends and family of Norman and Doris gathered at the Navajo Bridge near Lees Ferry, under which Norman had passed so many times and from which Doris always waved goodbye to him. The reason was the dedication of a memorial plaque—commissioned by Frank Masland, who had gone through the Grand Canyon with Nevills in 1948 and 1949, and designed by artist Mary Ogden Abbott, who had also floated the Grand Canyon with Nevills Expedition in 1949, shortly before the Nevillses were killed. The original plaque was made of wood and later cast in bronze. Jim Rigg and Louis Grasso, a stonemason from Grand Junction, erected the plaque in December 1951. Barry Goldwater—by now on his way to a political career—was the master of ceremonies, and the keynote speaker was Howard Pyle, the governor of Arizona. Many others attended: people who had been on the river with Nevills, many of his wide circle of friends and clients, and family members. After the speeches, Joan and Sandra, teary-eyed but brave as their parents would have wanted, unveiled the plaque. It was a bronze cenotaph reading:

> They run the rivers of eternity.
> IN MEMORY OF
> NORMAN D. NEVILLS
> April 9, 1908–September 19, 1949
> and—DORIS—his wife
> March 11, 1914–September 19, 1949
> who sought & ran & mastered
> the wild & secret waters
> San Juan River—Green River
> Colorado River—Grand Canyon
> Salmon River—Snake River
>
> By the river they loved so well
> in the desert that was their
> home, this record is placed by
> The Canyoneers

They run the rivers of eternity

IN MEMORY OF
NORMAN D. NEVILLS
APRIL 9, 1908 – SEPTEMBER 19, 1949
– and – DORIS – his wife –
MARCH 11, 1914 – SEPTEMBER 19, 1949

WHO SOUGHT, & RAN, & MASTERED
THE WILD & SECRET WATERS

SAN JUAN RIVER — GREEN RIVER
COLORADO RIVER – GRAND CANYON
SALMON RIVER ——— SNAKE RIVER

BY THE RIVER THEY LOVED SO WELL
IN THE DESERT THAT WAS THEIR
HOME THIS RECORD IS PLACED BY
The Canyoneers

A Note On The Sources

For all the impact that Norman Nevills had on the history of the Colorado River, sources on him are surprisingly scarce. The most obvious one for this book is the man himself. In 1988, Joan Nevills-Staveley, eldest daughter of Norman and Doris, decided to donate her father's extensive collection of letters, records, files, and photographs to the University of Utah's Marriott Library Special Collections Department. Included in that donation were several small, slim, penciled notebooks that contained his diary entries during several of his early river trips, namely 1938, 1940, 1941, and 1942. Also included were various other journals—including Doris's published account of their 1940 expedition—and Nevills's own typed transcriptions of almost all of his journals, which sometimes differ radically from the daily, on-the-river account in his notebooks.

I was happy to be the person assigned to arrange and describe the Nevills collection and spent almost two years going through every piece of paper. From the start, it was evident that Nevills was, as Joan describes him, a "squirreler," meaning that he saved everything. Included in the collection, besides the notebooks and transcriptions mentioned above, were thousands of letters, receipts, applications for draft deferments, brochures, clippings; in short, a virtually complete record of the last decade of his life in Mexican Hat. The collection is contained in forty archival boxes. The family faced a terrible, heartbreaking tragedy when Norman and Doris were suddenly taken away. But if there is any silver lining in that dark cloud, it was that Norman left such a complete and comprehensive legacy in the form of his unpurged papers. The result is that today's researchers have a perfect window onto the small world of river running in the early, formative years—from the top looking down—onto the premier riverman of his time.

Nevills kept his daily diary in small, spiral-bound notebooks, written almost without exception in pencil. His handwriting was hurried and cramped and can be hard to read. The entries were usually short and to the point. There was little hesitation in him, for a question mark rarely appears in any of his journals. Fortunately, during the long, cold, dark—no electricity—winter nights in Mexican Hat, he sat at his old Underwood manual typewriter and pounded out detailed transcriptions of the daily diaries, and it is these documents that form this book. They were at first a strict word-for-word transcription, but as the years went on, he increasingly expanded on the events of that day—and indeed, embellished them too—while it was still relatively fresh, typing out the notes and adding other thoughts and observations. So instead of Nevills's quick jottings from a pitching boat at the foot of a pounding rapid, we have his those notes plus later reflections on those same events. Yet even though it is not faithful to the primary original, in a way, the typed transcriptions are even more revealing of his character, for with them, he realized that they might someday become his legacy to his family and to history.

No original diaries exist for the years 1946, 1947, 1948, and 1949. Typed versions are in the Nevills papers for all those years save one, and from 1946 on they are increasingly polished and written to be read. For many years it was thought that there was no journal or transcription for the 1949 Green River and Grand Canyon trips. In the course of research at the Huntington Library in 1991, I found no trace of a 1949 diary, either the original or a transcription. However, while there on a Fellowship in 2004, during which I had more time to look, I ran across a handwritten transcription of notes he made on his maps during the 1949 Grand Canyon expedition. This is the only documentation from Nevills himself of the 1949 voyages. Obviously, as he had done with all of his previous journals, he intended to go back and type up his notes during the winter of 1949–50, but the unfortunate events of September 1949 precluded his doing so. No trace of the original nor of those for the previous three years has been found. Nevills's papers were shuffled in the 1950s and 1960s, when an attempt was made to produce a biography, and the family has kept in their possession certain memorabilia, such as Doris's diaries, but those original documents have been lost.

In the interest of readability, I have mildly edited the journals in the following ways: whenever Nevills simply listed the time and location, such as on July 7, 1938, when he wrote: "10:35 A.M. MILE 63¾. 11:00 A.M. MILE 61. 11:20 A.M. MILE 59..." and so on, these have been deleted. He was careful to note the time of arrival and departure at a given location, whether it was for camp, or a lunch stop, or at a rapid. He would note,—for example, on June 25, 1940, in Browns Park— "Stop here a few minutes to stretch. 3:15 P.M.–3:27 P.M." Feeling that these would detract from the narrative unless part of a sentence, these references were deleted. Also, when he listed the passengers and crew at the beginning of each journal, he often put in their full addresses; this information is long out-of-date, and was deleted. I have left intact Nevills's tendency to emphasize a rapid or name by putting it in all capital letters, and I did nothing to correct the tense jumps from past to present and back again, often on the same page. I have also retained Nevills's spellings of certain words. Mileages given in the Green and Colorado River journals are in descending order downriver toward Lees Ferry, Arizona, and then in ascending order below that point. Lees Ferry is the official boundary between the upper and lower basin states of the Colorado River drainage area, and all river mileages are measured to and from that point.

Other than those corrections and deletions, the journals are essentially just how he wrote them. Any errors of fact or interpretation that appear in the annotations, however, can of course be laid at no door but my own.

It must be said at this point that Nevills was often accused—in life and after his death—of exaggeration, of molding facts to suit his stories and his ego, of self-aggrandizement, and of downright lying about his origins, accomplishments, and river career. This would seem to make the journals a poor source for information about the man and his life. But many of these accusations came from enemies that he had made at certain points in his career. Some were the result of his tendency to hog the spotlight. Some were personality clashes brought about by too many days on a low-water river trip. And some were simple jealousy of his place as the preeminent river runner of his time. Nevills, for his own reasons, would exaggerate the speed of the river, the height of the waves, and the danger of the rapids. He said he did this to make people aware of the need for safety and to make them feel better when they were through the rapid. Some people just shrugged this off, but others were offended by his lack of concern for facts and figures. Likewise, he tended to tell wild stories about places they visited, to make up new names so that his passengers could feel they had "discovered" the canyon or arch, and to build a whole mythos around river running. For instance, in camp at the mouth of Forbidding Canyon, where he would lay over for a day to hike to Rainbow Bridge, Nevills would stage a spectacular show by pushing a bonfire off the cliff near the camp, then booming out a wholly fabricated story about Yogi, the River God. Passengers loved this, but again, some of his contemporaries felt that by doing these kinds of stunts, he was making light of the river. Gaylord Staveley, his son-in-law, wrote of him: "Besides being preoccupied with passenger safety, especially on-river, he worked very hard to make every trip a mixture of adventure, exploration, games, tall tales, and stunts."[1]

There was no denying he was a show-off; in calm water, if they came upon a large drifting log, Nevills would climb onto the log and do handstands while the cameras clicked. Onshore, he was famous for climbing cliffs and slopes that others hesitated to try, even if it sometimes got him into trouble, as his hazardous climb of Diamond Peak in 1948 demonstrates. Even though he was terrified of rattlesnakes, if one was found in camp, he would pick it up just to show off. So, while some of these stunts make it into his journals, the basic facts found in them are more than corroborated by information found in letters, journals kept by passengers and boatmen, and later research.

Finally, it must be said in his defense that such tale-telling has a long tradition among those who seek the outdoor life—from the mountain men to the keel-boaters to modern commercial boatmen—of which it could also be said that many of them never let facts get in the way of a good story.

To annotate the journals, I have drawn on a wide variety of resources, from the most primary to the most modern. First and foremost were the letters of Nevills himself; these are, in fact, the bulk of the Nevills Papers. Written on the same manual typewriter that he used to transcribe his journals, Nevills kept not only the original but also carbon copies of virtually all of his replies—a fact almost unheard of in archival research. They are long— up to eight single-spaced pages—detailed, and fascinating. The letters, in fact, give an even clearer impression of the man than his journals do, for they were written spontaneously and mailed: "fire and forget" we might say today. He wrote to potential clients, he wrote to potential sponsors, he wrote to his friends and his family. Obviously, Nevills spent a great deal of time on his correspondence. It was essential if he wanted to maintain his contacts among friends and potential clients; although there were building-to-building telephones in Mexican Hat, there were no outside lines. Indeed, given the volume of correspondence, one cannot help but wonder how much he spent on typewriter ribbons and carbon paper. Many of the quotes and other facts found in the notes come from these letters.

Another source from the Nevills Papers are copies of diaries and journals sent to him by passengers on his trips that are, in some cases, very revealing of how Nevills ran his trips and what kinds of people went on them. During his meteoric career, many local and national publications featured articles about Nevills; he was big news in certain circles and copies of virtually all of these articles are found in the Nevills Papers. They represent publications of all kinds, from the *Green River (Wyoming) Star, Salt Lake Tribune,* and *Deseret News,* to national publications such as *Life, Saturday Evening Post, National Geographic, Desert Magazine, Arizona Highways,* and the *Atlantic Monthly.* Among the authors of the journals and the articles are some of the best-known names in America, such as Barry Goldwater, Wallace Stegner, Randall Henderson, and Ernie Pyle.[2]

From the original writings to the digital world, the next source for annotations was an e-mail list consisting of Colorado River historians, scholars, bibliographers, academics, and recovering boatmen—sometimes in the same person—and others with a wide and deep interest and body of knowledge about the history of running the Colorado River. By a cyber-river and around a virtual campfire, they collectively know more about Colorado River history than just about anyone in the world, and I can never thank them enough for their quick and reasoned answers to many e-mail queries. Cort Conley, historian of Idaho rivers and places, deserves an extra thanks for reading through the 1946 journal and notes, and saving me from the embarrassment that can come to a historian who is writing outside his field. Finally, a special thanks to Earle Spamer, Dr. Al Holland, and Brad Dimock, a close collaborator in this project. I never would have done it without them.

In 1991 I spent a week at the Huntington Library in San Marino, California, an institution with beautiful buildings and grounds, and some of the richest collections of books, art, and archival papers in the world. What can only be described as a posh neighborhood might seem an odd place for a voluminous jumble of materials about river rats, but that's where to find the collection of Otis Reed Marston. Marston set himself up as *the* historian of the Colorado River, and over several decades collected—by fair means and (according to some) foul—diaries, letters, official records, maps, films, photographs, and oral histories; anything and everything that would add to the great, all-encompassing book that he was forever planning to write about those who braved the rapids and canyons of the Colorado and the Green. Alas for history, the book was never published, and the Marston Collection remains essentially unplumbed despite the efforts of several historians, myself included.

For certain annotations in the Nevills journals, I relied on my notes from the Marston Collection made during the 1991 visit and another in 2004, when I returned for a longer stay. Even though I was researching another topic, tidbits about Nevills kept cropping up. No matter what one might say of Marston, he was an indefatigable collector and keeper. Like Nevills, he too was a "squirreler." During that decade-old research, as well as my more recent visit, and through letters and e-mail, the curator of the Marston Collection, William Frank, has been unfailingly helpful and informative. The small world of Colorado River history owes Frank an immense debt for making sense out of the jumbled mess that first came to the Huntington shortly before Dock's death. Other archival sources that contain information about Nevills are the Colorado River collections in Cline Library Special Collections at Northern Arizona University, including the papers of P.T. Reilly, Bill Belknap, Tad Nichols, and the Kolb brothers. The Cline also houses a remarkable series of interviews with former boatmen and river runners, including Joan and Sandra Nevills, and Lois Jotter.

Published sources that mention Norman Nevills, besides the articles mentioned above, are few. He figures prominently in David Lavender's *River Runners of the Grand Canyon*,[3] and was the subject of a slim biography by Nancy Nelson called *Any Time, Any Place, Any River: The Nevills of Mexican Hat*.[4] In 1987, William Cook wrote a brief account of the 1938 voyage called *The Wen, the Botany, and the Mexican Hat: The Adventures of the First Women Through Grand Canyon on the Nevills Expedition*.[5] Additionally, a chapter about their San Juan River trips appeared in *The Inverted Mountains*, edited by Rodericky Peattie.

Both of Norman and Doris's daughters, Joan Nevills-Staveley and Sandra Nevills Reiff, reviewed the manuscript for accuracy, and contributed personal and family information that only they could know. Another good source by someone who knew him well is, "Norman Nevills: Whitewater Man of the West," an article in the spring 1987 issue of *Utah Historical Quarterly* by P.T. Reilly. Reilly was a boatman for Nevills in the late 1940s. In the summer 1993 issue of *Blue Mountain Shadows*, I published an article titled, "'Never Was Anything So Heavenly': Nevills Expedition on the San Juan River." Finally, in the spring 2004 issue of the *Boatman's Quarterly Review*—the official publication of the Grand Canyon River Guides Association—

Gaylord Staveley wrote a lengthy article about Nevills, excerpted from a forthcoming book about the history of river running. Other than that and some tributes published after his death, little else can be found in the literature. It is to correct that lack of information about this fascinating, complex man and his world that the present volume is presented.

Notes

INTRODUCTION

1. Information about Norman Nevills's family and early life comes from autobiographical sketches that he wrote later in life (box 1, folder 4, Nevills Papers, Marriott Library Special Collections Department, University of Utah; from family members; and from Gaylord Staveley's article, "Norman Nevills" in *Boatman's Quarterly Review* 17, no. 1 (spring 2004): 26–43.

2. There is some confusion about the origin of the design of both the cataract boats—which were used almost exclusively on the bigger rivers—and the San Juan boats, which he called "punts." Nevills always claimed that his boat designs came from a craft his father had seen on the Yukon River in Alaska during the Klondike gold rush, but was vague about just which boat was inspired by his father's memories. It seems more likely those Yukon River craft were the progenitors of the San Juan boat, not the cataract boat.

3. Norman Nevills to Dr. Andrew Chamberlain, November 23, 1947, box 6, folder 13, Nevills Papers.

4. Alice Bates, journal, May 1946, box 29, folder 17, Nevills Papers.

5. Evelyn Box, journal, April 1941, box 29, folder 6, Nevills Papers.

6. P. T. Reilly, "Norman Nevills: Whitewater Man of the West," *Utah Historical Quarterly*, v. 55 n. 2, 1987. Reilly's claim that Nevills was a "heavy smoker" is not backed up by any other accounts that mention smoking; Nevills said that he allowed himself only five cigarettes a day. However, Gaylord Staveley also describes Norman as "a chain-smoker who rolled his own cigarettes." (Staveley, "Norman Nevills," 32).

7. Nevills to Vernon Cato, November 23, 1948, box 6, folder 11, Nevills Papers.

8. Although there were others whom Nevills had rubbed the wrong way, the most insidious damage to his reputation came from Otis Marston. Both fit perfectly into the milieu of Colorado River personalities, in that there was little middle ground with either of them: they had admirers and detractors, but few were neutral about either one. In some ways, Marston and Nevills were two of a kind; both men were focused and intense, and both wanted to be the center of attention. It was a volatile mix of ego and Colorado River water, and naturally, it couldn't last. By the end of the 1948 Grand Canyon trip, Nevills decided that he could no longer abide Marston's constant criticism and sarcasm, and simply did not invite him back for the 1949 season. After Nevills's death, Marston brooded for the rest of his life over whatever wrongs he felt Nevills had done to him and concentrated his formidable energies and acid wit on demolishing the reputation that Nevills had so carefully built. Yes, Nevills was vain; yes, he was cocksure; yes, he was imperious. By the end of his life he had become a celebrity, and like all famous men, sometimes he didn't

handle it well. But that doesn't mean that he deserved the kind of character assassination that came to his name after he died.

1938 Journal

1. David Lavender, *River Runners of the Grand Canyon*, (Grand Canyon, AZ: Grand Canyon Natural History Association, 1986), 98.
2. The Crystal Geyser, an artificial geyser created by drilling operations in the 1930s, which still occasionally erupts a few miles downriver from Green River, Utah.
3. Dr. Elzada Clover was a botanist from the University of Michigan; a good portrait of her can be found in David Lavender's *River Runners of the Grand Canyon.*
4. Lois Jotter was a graduate student at the University of Michigan, and was recruited for the trip by Elzada Clover. The 1938 journey was her first and only venture on the wild Colorado until fifty years later, when she accompanied a Bureau of Reclamation old-timers trip through the Grand Canyon.
5. Laphene "Don" Harris. An employee of the US Geological Survey, Harris was the water gauger on the San Juan River in Mexican Hat and rented a bunkhouse from the Nevills family. He went only as far as Lees Ferry before he had to leave the river to report for a new posting in Salt Lake City. Enticed by the river, however, he was never far from it the rest of his life, and for quite a few years owned his own river company, Harris-Brennan River Expeditions. He was also one of the founding members of the Western River Guides Association.
6. Bill Gibson, an artist and industrial designer from San Francisco, who was recruited by Nevills for the trip. This was the only river trip that he did with Nevills.
7. Gene Atkinson. He was a graduate student at the University of Michigan in zoology, and was recruited for the trip by Elzada Clover. Obviously unprepared for the hardships of a trip of this length, he soon became unpopular with just about everyone on the crew. Nevills biographer, Nancy Nelson, calls him "the fly in the trip's ointment."
8. Doris Nevills, Norman's wife.
9. Joan Nevills, eldest daughter of Norman and Doris; the connection between Dan Hayes and his wife to Norman is unknown.
10. Mosquitoes can still be a problem in this stretch of river, even with modern repellents and nylon tents. They are especially bad during the period after the spring rise in the river, when the falling water creates breeding pools.
11. Nevills was nervous on this, his first big trip, and his lectures and orders soon got on everyone's nerves to the point that the trip almost broke up before they entered the Grand Canyon.
12. It's unclear what Nevills is referring to by "350' section."
13. Glen and Bessie Hyde, the famous honeymoon couple, who disappeared in the Grand Canyon in 1928. For more on them, see Brad Dimock's *Sunk Without a Sound: The Tragic Colorado River Honeymoon of Glen and Bessie Hyde* (Flagstaff, AZ: Fretwater Press, 2001).
14. The Clyde Eddy expedition, which ran from Green River, Utah, through the Grand Canyon in 1927. Eddy wrote his own account of the trip, *Down the World's Most Dangerous River* (New York: Frederick A. Stokes, 1929), which remains an unintentionally funny classic of Colorado River literature.
15. This river register is still visible in Labyrinth Canyon.

16.   The only official Yokey name is Yokey Bottom, quite a distance upriver from where Nevills places it. The name derives from "Cap Yokey," a pioneer steamboater on the Green and Colorado Rivers. The area he describes at river Mile 21 is known today as the Turks Head, for a distinctive formation on the right bank. Prehistoric Native Americans once heavily used the area, and there are many ruins, petroglyphs, pottery shards, and flint chippings still to be found here. There have been many attempts to homestead Labyrinth and Stillwater Canyons in historic times, and the cabin and boat Nevills mentions here are probably remnants of some of those efforts.

17.   James Knipmeyer, the authority on historic inscriptions on the Colorado Plateau, says, "According to the mileage on the Belknap river guide they would be about Mile 20.7, left bank, just below the mouth of the second, unnamed, southeast tributary below Soda Springs Canyon. They are on the vertical canyon wall just at the top of the talus. Nevills's transcription is almost correct, the full date actually being "10/19–09." Interestingly, this 1909 inscription was painted over an earlier incised one, which reads: "H. T. YOKEY J. A. ROSS 9/25 1904.""

18.   These inscriptions were actually made by the crew of the early steamer *Major Powell*, which made two round trips from the San Rafael River to Spanish Bottom in 1893.

19.   The *Mexican Hat* was one of the boats built by Nevills and Don Harris in the winter of 1937–38. Harris took it over as his pay for the trip and used it for many years thereafter. He made several modifications to make it run better, and it now resides in the John Wesley Powell Museum of River Running History in Green River, Utah.

20.   The *Botany* was named for Elzada Clover's specialty; as part of the deal with Super Hardboard, the company that supplied the wood for the boats, Nevills turned this boat over to them to use for publicity. Legend has it that it was on display in Omaha, Nebraska, when a big flood came down the river, and after being used in rescue operations, it was lost in the flood.

21.   The *Wen* was Nevills's favorite boat; the name came from the initials of his father, William E. Nevills. After Norman's death, the Nevills family donated it to Grand Canyon National Park, where it remains on display at park headquarters.

22.   These rapids are the infamous Big Drops, which are some of the most difficult whitewater on the Colorado River, especially at the higher water levels that Nevills was running on. Today Lake Powell backs up to just below Big Drop 3, so all of the rapids in Cataract Canyon that Nevills describes from this point are flooded by the reservoir.

23.   Lining involves unloading the boat of all supplies and gear, and then moving the boat along the shore by means of ropes tied fore and aft. It is an exceedingly difficult procedure—dangerous in its own right—and is today rarely done. Nevills's cataract boats weighed about 600 lbs each.

24.   Nevills was a teetotaler, who never drank and didn't approve of passengers or crew members bringing liquor on his trips.

25.   "Cherry" was Norman's pet name for his wife, Doris.

26.   Dark Canyon Rapid—now under Lake Powell—was described by Harry Aleson as "The Biggest Ride in the Cataracts." A long S-curve, it was often lined by early river parties because there was a long sandy beach on one side that made for easy lining.

27. The Pathe-Bray party was a film company that was making an adventure movie about the Colorado River, variously titled "Pride of the Colorado" or "Bride of the Colorado." It was to be a standard potboiler of the time, but by the time the crew reached the Grand Canyon a few months later, the funding had fallen through, the cast and crew were not paid, and the film was never completed. For a good account of this trip, see David Lavender's *River Runners of the Grand Canyon*.

28. Haldane "Buzz" Holmstrom, who had run the Green and Colorado solo the year before, and with Amos Burg, would follow the Nevills party by about two months. Nevills consistently misspelled Holmstrom as "Holstrom," but it's easier just to correct his spelling in the text of the journals. For more on Buzz Holmstrom's career, see *The Doing of the Thing: The Brief, Brilliant Whitewater Career of Haldane "Buzz" Holmstrom* (Flagstaff, AZ: Fretwater Press, 1998) by Brad Dimock, et al.

29. Russell "Doc" Frazier, a member of the 1933 party led by Bus Hatch. For more on this trip, see Roy Webb's *Riverman: The Story of Bus Hatch* (Rock Springs, WY: Labyrinth Publishing, 1989). All of the inscriptions mentioned by Nevills at this, and many other spots, were lost when Lake Powell covered this river register in the 1970s.

30. This inscription is also now covered by Lake Powell.

31. Arth Chaffin, a local man who had recently purchased the rights to run the ferry across the Colorado at Hite. He soon had a ferry going—using an old Model A Ford car for power—and in 1946 was able to convince the state of Utah to open a road from Hanksville, Utah, to Blanding, Utah, that later became Utah Highway 95.

32. The dredge and the camp nearby were left from the Hoskaninni Mining Company, which operated in the area from 1899–1900. The dredge was an enormous affair that had cost over $100,000, but the fine "flour" gold in Glen Canyon proved to be all but irretrievable, and the dredge was abandoned after only two months.

33. The Hole in the Rock Trail was one of the landmarks of Glen Canyon and was an epic of early exploration. Over 200 men, women, and children blasted and dug a route down the cliffs to cross the Colorado River on their way to a Mormon mission in southeastern Utah in 1880; even though the crossing is flooded, visitors can still see the trail by boat.

34. From this point to Lees Ferry, Nevills was on familiar ground, as he had already made several trips down the San Juan River through Glen Canyon.

35. Music Temple was a grotto in Glen Canyon that was known for its acoustics; many river parties stopped here to sing or recite poetry, and enjoy the sounds that resulted. It was flooded by Lake Powell. Nevills mistakenly places it on the wrong side of the river in this entry; it was on river left. Register books that were found in a can in Music Temple were removed as the reservoir rose in the 1960s and later deposited in the Special Collections Department, J. Willard Marriott Library, University of Utah. In them are found not only Norman Nevills's signature, but those of many of his boatmen and passengers.

36. Forbidden Canyon was the landing for the hike to Rainbow Bridge, about seven miles off the river. This was one of the most popular stops in Glen Canyon, and thousands hiked to it before the canyon was flooded by the reservoir. The visitor books that Nevills describes are in the National Park Service's (NPS) Lake Powell National Recreation Area headquarters at Page,

Arizona. The USGS name for this canyon is Forbidding Canyon, but the name Forbidden is often used interchangeably.

37. Nevills knew that they were overdue, but didn't realize how that fact was being received off the river. By this time there were concerns that the boats had been wrecked, and he and his passengers lost. The transport plane they saw was searching for evidence of the party or wreckage. While it could be said that Nevills didn't want to worry his wife and family, it can also be said that free publicity is never to be taken lightly.

38. Crossing of the Fathers was the place where the Dominguez-Escalante party managed to get across the Colorado River on their return to Santa Fe in 1776. Today the area is known as Padre Bay.

39. Lorenzo Hubbell was the owner of the Marble Canyon Lodge, near Lees Ferry, as well as several other trading posts in the area.

40. The Kolb Photo Studio on the south rim of the Grand Canyon, owned by Emery Kolb.

41. Lorin Bell was Ed Kerley's cousin.

42. Don Harris regretted missing the traverse of the Grand Canyon so much that he came back the next year and ran it, with veteran boatman Bert Loper.

43. Del Reed was a prospector, roustabout, and laborer who lived at the time in Mexican Hat, Utah. He worked for Nevills for two more trips, in 1940 and 1941. After that, he moved to Bluff, Utah, married a girl many years younger than himself, and had numerous children. He never worked on the river again. Nevills often spelled his name "Dell Reid" or some variation.

44. H. Elwyn Blake Jr. was a second-generation Colorado River boatman; his father had been among the pioneer steamboaters on the Green and Colorado Rivers around the turn of the 20th century. Blake Jr. served as a boatman for not one, but three USGS river surveys—the San Juan River in 1921, the Green River in 1922, and the Grand Canyon in 1923— and acted as the guide for the 1926 Todd-Page party. He was one of the most experienced river runners of the time, but by this point had retired from the river and was running a print shop in Monticello, Utah. Richard Westwood, a descendant, wrote an excellent biography of Blake called *Rough-Water Man: Elwyn Blake's Colorado River Expeditions* (Reno: University of Nevada Press, 1992).

45. Emery Kolb was another well-known riverman, having made a voyage down the length of the Green and Colorado Rivers with his brother, Ellsworth, in 1911, and having been on several expeditions after that. Edith was Edith Kolb, Emery's daughter, while the Tillotsons were Miner R. Tillotson, the superintendent of Grand Canyon National Park and his wife, Maurie. Ellsworth Kolb chronicled his brother's 1911 trip in the 1914 book, *Through the Grand Canyon from Wyoming to Mexico* (New York: MacMillan).

46. Nevills had asked Bill Gibson and Lois Jotter to repaint the boats, but instead, they hitchhiked to Flagstaff, Arizona.

47. Nevills allowed his enthusiasm to get ahead of his geography in this entry; Hopi Point overlooks Granite Falls, some thirty miles downriver. Desert View Watchtower actually overlooks the confluence of the Little Colorado and the Colorado, the area known as Palisades of the Desert.

48. This rapid would later be renamed Nevills Rapid, in Norman's honor. The idea for the name change came from Frank Masland, who was a passenger with Nevills in 1948 and 1949. The proposal was violently and emotionally opposed by Otis R. Marston, who had never gotten over whatever wrongs he

felt Nevills had done to him. In a letter written to Masland in January 1966, Marston wrote: "You are making a serious error in proposing the application of the name and this action will have effects that you do not recognize. I cannot approve and urge that you withdraw your proposition." Marston went further; he wrote to the Board of Geographic Names—the decision-making body that determines what names will appear on maps of the United States—and stated his objections, but J. O. Kilmartin, the head of the Board, disagreed, replying to Marston that the name change was official: "The board feels that the evidence indicates that Norman Nevills was one of the better known rivermen, and that he was intimately associated with this area for many years. Since the proposal had the approval of the NPS, which has jurisdiction over this portion of the river, the Board felt that the approval of this name was appropriate, and the decision was reaffirmed." The name became official in Decision list 6603, published July 1966.

49.   Named for Captain John Hance, an early Grand Canyon resident who had an asbestos mine on the cliffs above the rapid. It is still considered one of the most difficult of Grand Canyon rapids.

50.   Nevills obviously meant National Park Service in this and subsequent entries.

51.   Two park rangers, Glen Sturdevant and Fred Johnson, were drowned on February 28, 1929, when their small boat was swept into Horn Creek rapid. The only survivor was Chief Ranger Jim Brooks.

52.   Dubendorff Rapid, named for a Seymour Dubendorff, a member of the 1909 Galloway-Stone expedition, is one of the major falls of the middle Grand Canyon. In 1927 Clyde Eddy lost one of his boats there and was forced to abandon it; a picture of the wrecked boat appears in his book. Spellings of the name vary.

53.   This trip actually took place a year later in 1940.

54.   This ceremony became a tradition on Nevills Expedition trips through the Grand Canyon. After Nevills's death, the same tradition held for Mexican Hat Expeditions, and it was later picked up by Georgie White's Share-the-Expense trips. Each inductee was given a small pin in the shape of a rat, and thereafter could count themselves as one of Georgie's Royal River Rats. The origins of it are obscure, but it seems to be similar to the crossing-the-equator ceremony common among sailors.

55.   A "felon" is an infection occurring in a finger or toe, around the nail.

1940 JOURNAL

1.   Del Reed, who had served as a boatman on the last leg of the 1938 trip. See the notes for that journal for more information about him.

2.   Charles Larabee owned a garden shop in Kansas City, Kansas, and apparently met Nevills on a vacation to the Southwest in the summer of 1939. He signed onto the 1940 expedition as the official photographer, and took slides as well as motion pictures. Larabee and Nevills did not get along on the trip or afterwards, and he is one of those people who had strong negative feelings about Nevills. After Nevills's death he replied to Frank Masland's request for a contribution for a memorial to Norman and Doris by saying, "I feel that a great many in passing such a memorial to Norm would break into that old song. 'I'm glad your're [sic] gone you rascal you" (box 124, Marston Collection, Huntington Library, San Marino, CA). He disliked him so much that he funded a competing river company run by Harry Aleson called Larabee and

Aleson Western River Expeditions.

3. Hugh Cutler, a botanist with the Missouri Botanical Gardens in St. Louis. His reasons for coming on the trip were scientific, as he brought along a great deal of plant presses and other equipment for collecting plants.

4. Like many others who lived in such remote locations, Nevills was often forced to build whatever he needed out of parts on hand. Nevills, Hugh Cutler, Ray Lyman, and Charles Larabee built this particular rack out of junk before the trip.

5. Joan and Sandra Nevills remember the name as Jenney Barton, but Hattie is the name in the original journal.

6. Bus Hatch was a contemporary of Nevills, and a well-known river runner who later went on to found Hatch River Expeditions, one of the oldest and best-known river outfitters operating today. The two men were completely different in their views on river running. Nevills was a showman who was painfully aware of publicity and craved the spotlight. Hatch was a contractor who looked on river running as an enjoyable pastime to share with his buddies. It was two of his sons, Don and Ted Hatch, who made Hatch River Expeditions into a viable business.

7. The road from Vernal to Green River, Wyoming, crosses an 8,000-foot pass, and there is often snow on the ground well into summer.

8. Adrian Reynolds was the editor and publisher of the *Green River Star* for many years. He helped Nevills with local arrangements and publicity for several of his trips. His son, A. K. Reynolds, was inspired by his father's friendship with Nevills to start his own river running business in the 1950s. River parties such as Nevills's were big news in the small towns along the river, the occasion for banquets, radio shows, and front page newspaper articles. For this trip, Nevills was presented with license plates for the three states they would traverse and treated to a round of speeches and testimonial dinners.

9. Mildred Baker, a woman of means from Buffalo, New York, was very adventurous and outdoor oriented. Contrary to legend, she did not meet Nevills during his 1938 expedition, but showed up at Rainbow Bridge just after his party had left: "Might I say that we arrived at Rainbow Bridge in the summer of 1938, immediately after your expedition had left, which interested us greatly, as there had been speculation wherever we had been in the vicinity as to what had become of you" (Mildred Baker to Norman Nevills, October 4, 1939, box 5, folder 5, Nevills Papers). At any rate, the idea of being on the 1940 expedition possessed her, for she wrote to Nevills in October 1939, asking about his future trips. During the voyage, she, unfortunately, developed a strong dislike for Norman and sometimes for Doris, complaining in her journal (in the Marston Collection at the Huntington Library, and closed—reportedly because of its vitriol—until her death in 1990) that they came close to starvation, that Nevills was a tyrant, that she worked herself almost to death, and so on. She was another who refused to contribute to the memorial to Norman and Doris erected after their deaths in 1949.

10. John Southworth was a mining engineer from California. In the fall of 1939, he was coming home from a mining trip in the LaSal Mountains of southeastern Utah, when he stopped by Mexican Hat. There he talked to Mae Nevills, and learned of the 1940 trip. He continued toward home and stopped the next day at the Marble Canyon Lodge. There he met Nevills, who was just getting off of a San Juan trip. Nevills and Southworth hit it off, and John signed up for the 1940 trip on the spot.

11.   B. W. Deason was an assayer and chemist from Salt Lake City. With two companions, he went on a San Juan River trip with Nevills in 1939, and from there was persuaded to go on the 1940 expedition. His letters to Nevills are always signed "B. W." and that's how his name appears on his stationery as well, so there is no indication what his full name was. Even after spending time together on two river trips, as well as others by car, Nevills always addressed him as "Mr. Deason."

12.   These two women were B. W. Deason's companions on the 1939 San Juan River trip alluded to in the previous note.

13.   The Eveready Company supplied, as a promotion, the flashlights and batteries.

14.   Ann Rosner was a twenty-seven-year-old school teacher from Chicago. She joined the trip at Green River, Utah, and left at Bright Angel, at the bottom of the Grand Canyon. It's probable that she stayed at the Nevills Lodge during a trip through the desert southwest in the summer of 1939. How she became interested in the 1940 expedition is not indicated in the correspondence.

15.   Elzada Clover; see the 1938 journal for more about her.

16.   Barry Goldwater, who would join the trip at Green River, Utah.

17.   The *Mexican Hat II* was a copy of the original *Mexican Hat*. After Nevills's death, it was used by the successor, Mexican Hat Expeditions, and was eventually donated to the John Wesley Powell Museum in Page, Arizona, where it remains on display.

18.   One of the two new boats built specifically for this trip, the *Joan* was used for the rest of Nevills's career. After his death, it was placed on display in the Utah State Capitol Rotunda. Some years later, the boat was returned to the Nevills family, and is now in the possession of Joan Nevills-Staveley.

19.   The pigeons were homing pigeons, part of a publicity deal between Nevills and the *Salt Lake Tribune-Telegram*. Tissue paper was used for typed copy, and the capsules could also carry a few negatives for photos from the river. Details of the pigeon's care and use are found in box 17, folder 7 of the Nevills Papers. The stories appeared throughout the summer of 1940 in the newspaper, and the story was later serialized in the *Grand Junction (CO) Daily Sentinel* as "Woman Conqueror of the Colorado," in July 1941.

20.   Today, Flaming Gorge Reservoir backs up to within four miles of the town of Green River, so all of the places Nevills describes from here to below Ashley Falls are now underwater.

21.   Doris Nevills commented in "Woman Conqueror of the Colorado": "At 12:50 we land at Logan Ranch for lunch . . . This is the filthiest place I have ever seen. Dogs, goats, pigs and cats all came down to the boats. . . . A dirty woman with two small children comes out to talk. She tells us she caught the wildcat all by herself. How can people be so filthy when soap is so cheap?" (box 28, folder 9, Nevills Papers). But when the Kolb brothers stopped at the Logan Ranch in 1911, they left with a much different impression: "The Logan boys' ranch, for instance, was our first camp; but will be one of the last to be forgotten. The two Logan brothers were sturdy, companionable young men, full of pranks, and of that bubbling, generous humor that flourishes in this Western air." The Kolbs used their blacksmith shop to make some changes to their oarlocks, took photos of the ranch, and in general, called this a "pleasant camp" (Ellsworth Kolb, *Through the Grand Canyon from Wyoming to Mexico*, 12–13).

22.   Blacks Fork, a tributary of the Green River that originates in the Wind River Mountains.

23. As Nevills notes here, the Holmes Ranch was a regular stop for river parties on this stretch of the Green. Accounts of their ranch, photographs, and films are still found in archival collections and books that document this part of the river.

24. The Brennegar Ferry. This section of the Green was wide and open, with room for pastures and accessible water, so there were a great many ranches and farms along the banks. The Brennegar Ferry was only one of a number of crossings, footbridges, and ferries.

25. Flaming Gorge and the canyons below—Horseshoe, Kingfisher, Red Canyons—as well as several other features in this stretch, were all named by John Wesley Powell.

26. For many years the highway from Vernal, Utah, to Manila ran through Sheep Creek Canyon. The canyon is notable for unique geologic formations, big springs that gush from the canyon wall, and outlaw history. In the 1960s, Flaming Gorge Reservoir covered the lower end of the road, and now the modern highway bypasses Sheep Creek. Visitors can still take a detour to view the canyon. The mouth of the canyon is now Sheep Creek Bay.

27. Another Powell name, so-called because of the abundance of swallows in the gray sandstone cliff reminded him of a beehive.

28. Hideout Camp, today a lakeside campground, was for many years the favorite starting point for trips through the canyons of the upper Green River. It was easily accessible by a good road from Vernal, Utah, and very scenic.

29. The river register at Ashley Falls was actually one of the oldest along the entire river. Started by William Ashley, a fur trader, when he floated the Green in 1825, it had been added to since that time by virtually everyone who floated the Green River. The rapid itself was a jumble of huge boulders that had fallen into the river channel. It was widely considered the most difficult rapid on the entire Green River, and was often portaged or lined until the 1950s, shortly before it was inundated by Flaming Gorge Reservoir. Flaming Gorge Dam lies about three miles downstream, just below the mouth of Cart Creek.

30. Red Creek Rapid, about twelve miles below Flaming Gorge Dam, is still considered one of the most difficult on the stretch of river from the dam to Browns Park. Oddly enough, most early river parties dreaded Ashley Falls but made it through with no problems, only to wreck or hang their boats in Red Creek, and it has been the site of at least two deaths. This portion of the river is today a blue-ribbon trout fishery, and heavily used by fisherman and recreational boaters.

31. The Jarvie Ranch was settled around 1900 by John Jarvie, a Scottish immigrant. He opened a store there, ran a ferry, and served as postmaster for the upper end of Browns Park. He was murdered in 1909, after which the ranch was essentially abandoned.

32. Site of a short-lived bridge over the Green in the early years of the 20th century. It was built in the summer and taken out by an ice dam the following winter, and was never replaced.

33. Browns Park has long had a reputation as a haven for outlaws, and was home to the famous Wild Bunch in the 1890s. Even today it is a remote and sparsely inhabited area.

34. The Wade and Curtis cabins, later to be the NPS Lodore Ranger Station.

35. Named by Powell's crewman, Andy Hall, in 1869. The word comes from a poem by British Poet Laureate William Southey, and is the name of a cataract in the Lakes District of England. From Lodore to the end of Split Mountain Canyon, the river runs through Dinosaur National Monument.

36. The rapid is Winnie's Rapid, from a scenic grotto on the west side of the river, named on Powell's 1871 trip for John Steward's daughter. Anthony Backus was actually a furrier from Chicago, who tried to run the Green in his boat *Illinois Girl* in 1936. River parties regularly visited the wrecked boat, until it was taken by high water in 1984.

37. In June 1869, John Wesley Powell's expedition lost one of its boats in this rapid, and the name stuck. For many years, because of an overhanging ledge in the lower part of the rapid, it was routinely portaged by river parties. Changes in the river channel have now made it runnable.

38. Named by Powell for three separate falls in the rapid. As Nevills indicates, the wide beach and abundance of driftwood made this a popular and pleasant camp. Several historic inscriptions are still visible today. The wrecked boat was the *Lota Ve*, one of Bus Hatch's boats; Frank Swain was Bus's cousin, and accompanied him on many river trips in the 1930s. The *Lota Ve*, named after Alt Hatch's daughter, was wrecked in 1936. The remains of the boat were removed by Don Hatch, son of Bus, in the 1980s, and are currently in the possession of the Hatch family. The identity of Clyde Cox is unknown.

39. Another Powell name. When his 1871 party reached this rapid, Powell polled his crew for names. Almon Harris Thompson and Frederick Bishop suggested Boulder Falls; Powell's old army companion John Steward looked at the jumble of rocks and said dryly, "Would Hell's Half Mile suit?" Today, it's the most difficult rapid in Lodore Canyon.

40. Steamboat Rock is a high sandstone fin that marks the confluence of the Yampa River and the Green River. The Yampa is still the Green's largest undammed tributary and sometimes dries up, as Nevills noted in 1940.

41. What Nevills called Pat's Hole is today known as Echo Park, named by Powell for the marvelous echoes that come from Steamboat Rock. Pat Lynch was a hermit who lived in caves in the area around the turn of the 20th century.

42. Buzz Holmstrom was then working for the Bureau of Reclamation at a dam site just around the corner from Echo Park.

43. The Echo Park Dam, proposed by the Bureau of Reclamation as part of the Colorado River Storage Project after World War II. The dam project became the center of a major controversy in the 1950s—which led to its cancellation—and is considered by environmental historians as the birth of the modern, politically active conservation movement. Several good books are available about this controversy.

44. The Ruple Ranch, in Island Park, is one of the oldest in Dinosaur National Monument. Henry and May Ruple settled there in 1883 and lived on the ranch until 1910, when they sold out. Their son, Henry H. (known as "Hod"), who was born on the ranch in 1886, bought it back in 1915 and lived there until he died in 1937. His wife, Lily, later remarried local stockman Joel Evans, and lived there until her death in 1945. Evans died in 1956, at which time the ranch was sold to the Utah Department of Wildlife Resources, which still owns it today. The giant cottonwood tree that Nevills commented on is still there and is described by local residents as the world's largest cottonwood tree. P. T. Reilly, who ran this stretch for Nevills in 1949, estimated its girth at 25 feet.

45. Split Mountain Canyon has the greatest fall of any of the canyons of the Green River—twenty-one feet per mile—and has four named rapids and many smaller ones. Another Powell name.

46. Today the site of a boat ramp for river parties, in Dinosaur National Monument.

47. Bush flagged them down from the side of the river, hoping to get a scoop on the story of the Nevills party. Everyone knew him as "Ace."

48. Nevills means the dinosaur quarry, first discovered in 1908. In 1915 it became the nucleus for the present Dinosaur National Monument, which by the time he was writing, had been expanded to include the canyons of the Green and Yampa Rivers.

49. Frank O'Brien was a reporter for the *Salt Lake Tribune-Telegram*; he set up the pigeon post for the river trip. He and Nevills hit it off right away and became fast friends, as shown by their extensive correspondence in the Nevills Papers. When O'Brien went to work for the Utah Department of Publicity during World War II, the friendship paid dividends in publicity for Nevills's river running business. Bill Eldrige was another friend of Nevills's from Salt Lake City.

50. The fact that the "show was a flop," was the exception. By this time Nevills had gained a reputation as an entertaining speaker and by the end of his life, he was traveling all over the West to give lectures and show films.

51. Sand Wash, once the location of a ferry used by sheepherders, is now the launching site for river trips through Desolation Canyon. There is a boat ramp and Bureau of Land Management ranger station, and often clouds of mosquitoes.

52. In the spring of 1940, Bus Hatch and Buzz Holmstrom were trying to explore all the difficult runs of the rapids in Split Mountain Canyon. Buzz is supposed to have challenged Bus by saying, "Let's take the worst places, Bus!", the result of which was noted by Nevills.

53. This beautiful site—now known as the Rock Creek Ranch—was settled by the Seamountain brothers around 1900. By the time the Nevills party stopped there, the owners would have been the Downard family. The spelling of the name was shortened to Seamount, although variations are often seen in the literature. Although the ranch is no longer active today, there are still buildings, orchards, equipment, and artifacts. It is still a popular stop for river runners, and the orchards still produce fruit.

54. Also known as the Florence Creek Ranch, it was settled by Jim McPherson around 1900 and was known as a stop on the Outlaw Trail, which ran through Desolation Canyon. Today some of the outbuildings survive, but the ranch is on the Uintah-Ouray Indian Reservation, and they discourage visitation.

55. Named for early explorer Lieutenant John Gunnison, who crossed the river near here in 1857 shortly before he and his party were murdered by Indians in central Utah. This was also a crossing on the Old Spanish Trail.

56. Today river parties take out at the foot of Swasey Rapids, just upstream of this low-head dam. Travel over the dam can be dangerous and is not encouraged.

57. Joan Nevills, born October 7, 1936.

58. At the time, Barry Goldwater was a successful merchant from Phoenix, Arizona. The trip through the Grand Canyon was a lifelong ambition for him, but he almost didn't get to go as his mother-in-law objected so strongly. Later, of course, he became a powerful Senator from Arizona and was a candidate for president of the US in 1964. His privately published book about the journey, *Delightful Journey Down the Green and Colorado Rivers* (Tempe: Arizona Historical Foundation, 1970), provides an interesting account of the expedition.

59. Barry Goldwater commented in *Delightful Journey Down the Green and Colorado Rivers* that he and most of the others were saddened by Anne's departure, but

according to Nevills, by the time she left at Bright Angel, she and Mildred Baker were barely on speaking terms.

60.   Dismayed over his inability to complete the 1938 Nevills expedition, Don Harris returned the next year with famed riverman, Bert Loper, and went through the Grand Canyon. It was Loper's, as well as Harris's, first trip through the Grand Canyon.

61.   B. W. Deason left the trip at this point, and rejoined them later at the bottom of the Bright Angel Trail in the Grand Canyon.

62.   See the 1938 journal for more information about Arth Chaffin.

63.   McConkie was a native of Moab, Utah, with a great interest in the outdoors. He would later become a boatman for Nevills Expedition and go on many San Juan River trips. Still later, he became a geology teacher at Moab High School, and continued exploring the deserts around his home for the rest of his life.

64.   "River Riders find Huge Natural Arch," *Salt Lake Tribune-Telegram*, August 3, 1940 (box 35, folder 7, Nevills Papers). Prospectors, explorers, and Indians knew about the bridge—it was Herbert Gregory himself who had given Nevills directions to the location—but it had never been measured or photographed.

65.   South Canyon.

66.   Dr. Russell Frazier first noted the skeleton at South Canyon on the Hatch-Frazier expedition (also known as the "Dusty Dozen") in 1934. By the time Nevills saw it, the skull was missing; yet it was present when the "Dusty Dozen" found it, for they recorded that the skull had long black hair. It's likely that Frazier, a medical doctor, took the skull and kept it, although no trace of it has ever been found. The National Park Service removed the rest of the skeleton in the 1960s.

67.   Frank Dodge was a member of the Birdseye survey of the Grand Canyon; the year was 1923, and the boat was actually wrecked upstream at Cave Spring Canyon.

68.   What had been a practical necessity in 1938 became an institution—the Driftwood Burners Club—with this trip. Membership was gained by lighting one of the many of piles of driftwood along the river with a single match. Some of these were a half-mile long and had been there for centuries, so they produced spectacular conflagrations that burned for days. The explanation given was that the Bureau of Reclamation had asked that river runners burn the driftwood so that it wouldn't end up in the turbines in Lake Mead, but one can't help but suspect there was a little adolescent pyromania involved as well.

69.   Actually Phantom Ranch, about a mile off the river; Bright Angel Lodge is on the south rim, about seven miles and 5,000 feet away.

70.   In December 1966, a major flood down the Crystal Creek drainage turned this into one of the deadliest and most-feared rapids in the Grand Canyon.

71.   Because of the incident described in this entry, the rapid was later named Doris Rapid.

72.   By saying the walk up Havasu Canyon was "gruesome," Nevills is just displaying his sense of puckish humor. In his book *Delightful Journey Down the Green and Colorado Rivers*, Barry Goldwater describes their walk up Havasu Canyon: "As soon as we ate our lunch, Mildred, Hugh, and I started up the canyon in an effort not only to see the large waterfalls but also to reach the settlement nine miles distant where I could telephone my family and buy food. We had not

reckoned, however, with the thick, almost impenetrable undergrowth. Wild grapevines trip one at every step. Heavy thickets of catclaw leave scratches wherever the trees touch you. Loose rock on the ledges prohibits walking on them; in fact, about the only place one can walk and make headway is in the stream" (162). By contrast, Doris describes a relaxing day spent around the lower end of the canyon swimming, talking, and taking photographs with Norman, Charles Larabee, B. W. Deason, and John Southworth.

73. Nevills was off by one year on the reference to Jack Harbin, who ran Lava Falls during the unsuccessful search for Glen and Bessie Hyde in the winter of 1928. Harbin was an employee of the Fred Harvey Company, who was hired by Glen's father to go downriver and search for his missing son. Nevills might be a bit off in his calculations as well, for David Lavender, in *River Runners of the Grand Canyon*, credits George Flavell (1896) and Elias "Hum" Woolley (1903) with runs of Lava Falls. Also, Glen and Bessie Hyde are presumed to have run Lava Falls shortly before disappearing in the lower Grand Canyon. At any rate, Lava Falls has long been considered one of the most dangerous of the Grand Canyon's rapids, and was regularly portaged until the 1950s.

74. Today, Mile 232 Rapid is believed to be where Glen and Bessie Hyde lost their lives in 1928. Contrary to Nevills's view, many river runners still consider it a difficult, and even dangerous, rapid. Modern boatmen sometimes refer to it as "Killer Fang Falls."

75. See note #12.

1941 JOURNAL

1. Alexander "Zee" Grant Jr. was an interesting character. A relative of President Franklin Delano Roosevelt—Grant's grandfather was Franklin Delano, later to become involved in plans to dam the Green and Colorado—Grant was employed in New York City by the Union Pacific Railroad. More importantly, though, he was a pioneer kayaker, in the days when the word was known only to anthropologists and an outdoorsy elite on the eastern seaboard of the US. Starting in the 1930s, he paddled a folding kayak—called a foldboat—to victories in just about every whitewater championship held in the eastern US. In 1939, he came west and paddled his folding kayak through Lodore Canyon down to Jensen, Utah, with two companions. The next year, with Elliott Dubois and Stewart Gardiner—two other foldboat enthusiasts—he was the first to kayak the rapids of the Middle Fork of the Salmon River. So Grant was as much an experienced boater in his way as Nevills was in his, when he wrote to Nevills in January 1941 asking if he could accompany a Nevills Expedition trip. Despite some early misgivings, Nevills agreed, impressed by Grant's sincerity and obvious credentials, and sensing the publicity value of such a trip. In doing so, Nevills pioneered another form of river trip that is common today: the kayak support trip. An account of the trip later appeared in the book *Fabulous Folbot Holidays*, and Grant published his own version called "Cockleshells on the Colorado," in the December 1941 issue of *Appalacia*, the journal of the Appalachian Trail Club. Grant continued to kayak after the 1941 trip and served briefly in the US Naval Reserve during World War II. He kept in touch with Nevills until 1946.

2. The *Escalante* was Grant's custom-made 16½-foot-long foldboat. At the time, most folding kayaks were made in Europe by either Klepper (Germany) or Berget (France); there was one company—Folbot—that had by 1935 moved from London, where it was started in 1933, to Charleston, South Carolina.

It was the Folbot Company that built the *Escalante* to Grant's specifications. For extra stability, sponsons made from New York City bus inner tubes were lashed along the sides, and the interior was taken up with as many brightly-colored beach balls as Grant could stuff into it, providing perfect flotation; the *Escalante*, quite simply, could not sink unless it was torn to pieces. In 1991, the editor attempted to organize a commemorative Grand Canyon trip for the 50th anniversary of this voyage, but Folbot Company president, Phil Cotton, decided not to donate a foldboat to the effort, saying that his boats were not intended for the type of whitewater that Grant ran in 1941, and he didn't want to encourage others to try to repeat the experience.

3. William Jaffray Schukraft was the owner of a firm that manufactured truck bodies in Chicago and an active hiker and camper. In the summer of 1940 he was at Phantom Ranch at the bottom of the Grand Canyon when he heard about the 1940 Nevills expedition. Interested, he wrote to Nevills in February 1941, and with only a few more letters, was signed up for the journey. He confessed that he had no whitewater experience but was active and healthy at thirty-three years old, and, more importantly, was able to pay the fare. Like many other passengers on Nevills's river trips, he remained in touch with Nevills for several years after his trip.

4. Del Reed, on his third—and last—trip as a boatman for Nevills Expedition. It's obvious from Nevills's descriptions of Reed's rowing style in this and previous journals that Reed did not care for running big rapids. On July 15 at Soap Creek, for instance, Nevills notes: "Grand ride. Del slips off to the right and misses the big fellows." And again at North Canyon Rapid the next day: Nevills notes, "Del slides off and misses the fun." In correspondence during World War II, Nevills updates the members of the 1941 trip about Reed, saying that Reed bragged about big prospects in southeastern Utah but they never seemed to play out, and that he had bought a big Buick and was marrying a seventeen-year-old girl from Monticello, Utah. After that, Reed dropped out of sight.

5. The final passenger on the 1941 voyage, Agnes Albert was from San Mateo, California. It's not known how she became involved with the trip, but she was one of the first to sign on and stayed in touch with the Nevills family until after Norman and Doris died in 1949. Agnes was from old pioneer families on both sides, and was an enthusiastic camper and musician. Interestingly, at the time her husband was fighting in the German army in Europe, a fact she asked Nevills to play down in any trip publicity.

6. Weldon Heald met Nevills under Rainbow Bridge in the spring of 1941; it was to be an important encounter for both men. "We talked for ten minutes, exchanged addresses, and went our ways. But I plodded up the trail nursing secret ambitions. Norm's river talk was infectious" (box 29, folder 7, Nevills Papers). At the time, Heald was a forty-year-old architect living in Altadena, California, a member of the Sierra Club, and an experienced mountaineer. His other ambition was to become a freelance writer, and he did publish quite a few articles, scripts for plays, and other writing. A piece about the 1941 trip appeared in *Travel* magazine the next year, and his article, "The Colorado is Still Wild," was published in the *Sierra Club Bulletin* in August 1942. He planned to go down the San Juan with Nevills and others from the 1941 trip in May 1942, but was called up for active service in the army shortly before the trip. He finally made a San Juan trip in 1945, and wrote "Fast Water in the Desert" for the summer 1947 issue of *Appalacia*. Heald also wrote chapters about

Norman and Doris for the book by Roderick Peattie, *The Inverted Mountains: Canyons of the West*, published in 1948 (New York: Vanguard Press).

7. 1941 was a good high water year, with over 20,000 cfs. The Paria River, a minor tributary of the Colorado, was flooding when they arrived and blocked access to the usual launching point, Lees Ferry.

8. Ever the showman, Nevills was known for stunts like these. On his San Juan trips, if he found a big log drifting in the river, he would climb aboard it and do headstands on the log as it floated along.

9. Life jackets were not common this early on the river.

10. In "The Colorado Is Still Wild," by Weldon Heald, he describes the decision to run Soap Creek: "Norm suggested to Zee that perhaps it would be wiser to line the kayak around the rapid, but Zee shook his head. 'They'd all get me if I quit now,' he said, 'I've got to run it.' Without another word he studied the rapid, watched the cataract boats go through, then deliberately shot the kayak down the tongue into the heaviest water . . . He landed below the rapid, upright, with a wide grin on his face. 'Will one of you pull the kayak ashore,' called Zee. 'I don't want to get my feet wet'" (box, 29, folder 12, Nevills Papers).

11. Nevills felt that if you exaggerated the dangers of the rapids to come, it would make them seem less impressive when you actually got to them. Not all of his passengers and crew appreciated his "psychology," however.

12. This entry typifies Nevills's approach to river trips: he was always looking for things for his passengers to do, such as poking around in old mines, starting fires, and setting off dynamite left from old mines. All of these activities would be unthinkable on the river today.

13. Sockdologer Rapid, at Mile 78½ in the Grand Canyon, is one of those that only gets bigger as the water gets higher, due to the narrow channel of the river at this point. The name comes from a Civil War slang term for a knockout blow, and was applied by John Wesley Powell in 1869. Nevills was running it at an ideal level for a thrilling ride.

14. This is unusual because, as mentioned previously, Nevills was usually a teetotaler who did not drink at all.

15. An obvious reference to the tensions that had plagued both the 1938 and 1940 expeditions.

16. Associated Press; by this time Nevills had contacts in the newspaper world and was not afraid to call them to drum up some publicity.

17. Located about eight miles up the North Kaibab Trail, Roaring Springs is the main source of water for the entire Grand Canyon National Park complex. Since the 1960s, a portion of the water from these springs is collected and piped down Bright Angel Creek, where it crosses the river under the lower bridge, and is then carried by pressure halfway up the south side of the Grand Canyon. From there, a pumping station takes it to the south rim. The huge springs are a very impressive sight.

18. Mary Elizabeth Jane Colter designed the swimming pool—along with the rest of the buildings—at Phantom Ranch in the 1920s. It was a naturally appearing pool with a creek falling into it, and was much admired by all who saw it and appreciated its cooling waters after long, hot days in the canyon. After refreshing generations of hikers and river runners, the pool was damaged by the major floods that ravaged Bright Angel Canyon in December 1964, and eventually was declared unsanitary by the National Park Service and removed in the 1970s. Virtually every early traveler comments on how much they enjoyed the pool.

19. Doris was equally sad not to go, and in fact, never again went through the Grand Canyon before she was killed in 1949. In a July 1941 letter to Weldon Heald, Doris wrote, "The scenery just can't be described. Too, there is a spiritual peace one finds in that river canyon that is seldom found elsewhere. Please excuse it if I seem eloquent as to the trip. All I can say is, if I didn't have a three-months old baby I'd again be with Norm" (Doris Nevills to Weldon Heald, July 6, 1941, box 11, folder 13, Nevills Papers).

20. The Bright Angel pack trail, used by tourists taking the mule ride from the south rim to Phantom Ranch, reaches the river at Pipe Spring and runs quite close to the river for about a mile.

21. Modern Grand Canyon river runners call this series of rapids the Jewels— or the Gems—for their names: Crystal, Agate, Turquoise, Sapphire, Ruby, Serpentine, and so on. As Nevills describes them, at higher water levels these rapids are river running at its very finest.

22. Nevills's original, pencilled notebook entry says simply "Kyack [*sic*] thru on right side fine" (box 27, book 9, Nevills Papers).

23. Actually a California kingsnake, *lampropeltus getulus*.

24. Upset Rapid was named by the USGS in 1923 to commemorate a capsize by head boatman, Emery Kolb. A difficult rapid in any stage, it has been the scene of numerous accidents and at least one death, that of Jesse "Shorty" Burton in 1967.

25. The camp on the right near Mile 164 is Tuckup Canyon, just below 164 Mile Canyon, which is on the left.

26. According to the unwritten code of the West, it was all right for travelers to take supplies from camps they found along the trail, and Nevills does this on several occasions. The travelers were expected to either replace the supplies at the same camp, or add to the larder at a different camp, as a way of repaying the loan.

27. The burros—which had been turned loose by prospectors—flourished in the environment of the Grand Canyon and were especially common near Parashaunt and Whitmore Canyons. By the 1960s their presence had become a management problem and the National Park Service removed virtually all of them; today they are seldom, if ever, seen.

28. Nevills's original, pencilled diary ends on July 28, so there is no mention of this premonition. William E. Nevills took his own life, after years of poor health.

29. Aleson was obsessed with the idea of driving a motorboat up the Colorado River through the Grand Canyon, a task that was to occupy him for years but at which he never succeeded. Aleson's problem was always that he could never afford the powerful engines that were required to overcome the stiff currents of the Colorado River—or in Nevills's succinct phrase, "Motor not enough soup." Aleson usually had a small motor in the 20-30 hp range; when the uprun was finally accomplished in 1960—not by Aleson—the party used jetboats with two 185 hp engines! For a good description of Aleson's various attempts, see David Lavender's *River Runners of the Grand Canyon*.

30. Although Nevills agreed to this donation, it was not done until after his death in 1949. A fragment of Powell's 1871 *Nellie Powell* was found at Lees Ferry and is in the possession of the National Park Service, but none of Stanton's boats are in existence today, and it's not certain what Nevills was referring to here. The oldest boat in the collection is one of Julius Stone's Galloway-Stone craft from his 1909 expedition. As far as is known, none of Stanton's boats—used during his railroad surveys in 1889-90—are known to exist.

1942 JOURNAL

1. Neill Wilson to Norman Nevills, June 4, 1942, box 21, folder 7, Nevills Papers.

2. Edwin E. Olsen was a contractor in Pittsburg, Pennsylvania, when he saw an article about Nevills in *Travel West* magazine called "Riverman." Intrigued, he immediately wrote to Nevills and asked about going along on one of his San Juan River trips, which he did in July 1941. On that trip Olsen revealed to Nevills a secret ambition, which was to move to Los Angeles and make his hobby—film making—into his profession. By the time he had signed up for the 1942 Grand Canyon run, he had made the first part of that move. Olsen was already known for his ski movies of Sun Valley and Alta, and during the 1942 trip, Olsen took thousands of feet of film. Then World War II intervened, and though Olsen was not called for military service, his busy schedule kept him from doing anything with the river trip films. After the war, he secured the services of a professional editor and within a year had produced a film called *Facing Your Danger*, which won an Academy Award for short subjects in 1946. Olsen later re-edited the outtakes from *Facing Your Danger* into another short film called *Danger River*. Nevills obtained a copy of this and showed it to every party that assembled at Mexican Hat to take one of his river trips and at venues all over the west. It was an advertising bonanza for Nevills Expedition. A copy of *Danger River* can be found in the Joseph Desloge Collection (A0641), in the Marriott Library Special Collections Department at the University of Utah.

3. Dr. Harold C. Bryant, the superintendent of Grand Canyon National Park, and his wife. At this time the NPS was so small, and Colorado River trips such a novelty, that the superintendent of the park became personally involved.

4. Although his name appears several times in Nevills's journals, just who Harry Franse was remains unclear. He wrote an article in the October 1938 issue of *Arizona Highways* called "Vest Pocket Horses," but the article gives no indication of who he worked for or what his position was. It's likely that he was employed by the Fred Harvey Corporation, who managed the concessions at the south rim.

5. Emery Kolb's daughter, by now married to Park Ranger, Carl Lehnert.

6. Preston Walker was one of Nevills's oldest friends; their correspondence starts in 1933, even before Norman met and married Doris. Preston's father, Walter Walker, was the editor and publisher of the *Grand Junction (CO) Daily Sentinel*, and a pillar of the community; Preston also worked at the newspaper. Nevills provided Walker with tips, gossip, and stories for his newspaper articles, and in return, Preston made sure that the Nevills Lodge and Nevills Expedition were often found in the pages of the newspaper. For years, Nevills attempted to persuade Preston (whom he always called "Pres") to accompany him on a river trip, but it wasn't until the autumn of 1941 that he did so. By then, Preston had unfortunately developed a drinking problem. The trip—of six weeks duration—was ostensibly to explore Glen Canyon and develop camps for Nevills Expedition trips, but was in reality a plan by the elder Walker and Nevills to dry Preston out. The plan more or less succeeded, and by 1942, Preston was ready to accompany Nevills as a boatman on that year's Grand Canyon traverse. Shortly after that river trip, the younger Walker was called up for the military, and served in combat in the Army Air Corps in North

Africa, Sicily, and Italy, which reactivated his drinking. He rowed a boat for Nevills on quite a few more river trips—including the major runs in Idaho in the summer of 1946—and despite any personal problems Preston might have had, the two men remained fast friends. When Norman and Doris were killed in September 1949, it was Preston and his wife, Becky, who retrieved their bodies and made the memorial arrangements. Walker Field in Grand Junction—the main airport—is named for Walter Walker, who was also an early advocate of airline travel and civilian flight. The Nevills Papers contain extensive correspondence between Nevills, and Preston and Walter Walker in box 21, folders 2–6. Preston Walker died of an apparent heart attack at the oars of his boat on the Dolores River in the summer of 1952.

7.   Wayne McConkie of Moab, Utah, who first appeared in the 1940 journal with his father.

8.   Ed Hudson, a pharmacist from Banning, California, heard about Nevills Expedition from the Standard Oil Co. information bureau, and wrote to Nevills in April 1941. By that time, Hudson had his own boat, a light skiff that he had taken down the Colorado from Boulder Dam to Needles, California. He wrote asking if he could bring his boat along on a Nevills trip on the San Juan. He went in May 1942 (but not in his boat), on the same trip as Neill Wilson, and like Wilson, was persuaded on that trip to sign up for the 1942 Grand Canyon run. Hudson seems ill-suited for the active river life, as he was overweight and complained about conditions quite a bit, but after the 1942 trip he developed his own ambition: to run a power boat up and down the Colorado through the Grand Canyon. To this end he hooked up with Otis Marston, whom Lavender later called "The Guru of Gasoline," and made several attempts in the late 1940s. After the debacle of the *Esmerelda II* in 1950, Hudson gave up on the river and thereafter led a more peaceful life. His various river trips are recounted in detail in David Lavender's *River Runners of the Grand Canyon.*

9.   At times Nevills's preoccupation with obtaining film seems obsessive, but he was quick to realize that nothing sold trips better than color films of the action. He seldom missed an opportunity to have cameras and people skilled in their use along on his trips, even giving people who could use a camera a special rate. His concern highlights yet another problem that was growing as American became enmeshed in World War II: color film was a priority material and most of it was earmarked for the armed services.

10. Frank Dodge was one of the least known yet most interesting characters to dwell around the Colorado River. A native of Hawaii, he was like a fish in the water and was one of the few men living at the time to have been all the way through the Grand Canyon twice, having been on the 1923 Birdseye USGS expedition and the 1937 Cal Tech survey, as well as the 1928 Pathe-Bray film trip to Hermit Falls. By 1942 he was having problems with arthritis and had taken a job as the water gauger at Lees Ferry, where he often met Nevills Expedition trips as they came out of Glen Canyon, and just as often had to write letters of apology to Nevills for his drunken behavior. Dodge wrote his own autobiography for the USGS, but it was never published; some information about him is available in David Lavender's *River Runners of the Grand Canyon.*

11. Another indication of war-induced shortages. It wasn't lack of money that prevented civilian travel during World War II; it was lack of oil, gas, and tires.

12. Neill Wilson was an advertising executive from San Francisco, who had been a reporter on the San Francisco waterfront and climbed all the 14,000-foot peaks in the western US. Seeking new adventures, he went on a Nevills Expedition San Juan River trip in May 1942, along with Ed Hudson, who would also be on the Grand Canyon traverse that same year. Like so many others, he was persuaded during that trip to take the longer Grand Canyon trip, which Nevills had planned for later that summer. From his correspondence, it is obvious that Wilson had a very active sense of humor, which shows throughout the 1942 Grand Canyon trip, most notably with "Irene," the stewardess. Even though Wilson and Nevills talked about a book about the 1942 Nevills expedition, it never materialized, although his article "Brother, take the oars!" was re-printed several times. Neill and Bruce were on the 1946 Nevills Expedition trips in Idaho, and in 1964, the elder Wilson wrote a novel about the area called *Deepdown River*. For more on that, see the 1946 notes. For the extensive correspondence between him and Nevills, see box 21, folders 27–28 of the Nevills Papers. His son, Bruce, who also was along on the 1942 Grand Canyon trip, wrote Nevills in 1948 asking for a job as a boatman. Plans were made for him to work for Nevills, but just before he was to start he was drafted and ended up entering the US Marines instead.

13. The Oxford English Dictionary defines "nemesis" as "one that avenges relentlessly or destroys inevitably." Nothing could better describe Otis Reed Marston, who was in every sense of the word Norman Nevills's nemesis. The complicated and anguished relationship between these two intense men cannot be adequately described in a footnote; it would take a book, or more appropriately, a treatise by an expert on psychoses. The two men started off as friends after the 1942 Grand Canyon trip, and for several years Marston helped Nevills with publicity, booking passengers, and rowing a boat on trips. The correspondence between the two men fills an entire box in the Nevills Papers (box 16), and even though Marston's circular, swooping handwriting is hard to decipher, the detailed, personal letters between him and Nevills contain probably the best revelations as to their respective characters. After Nevills died, Marston went on to a long career on the river, becoming known to all as "Dock." As a man of means, he could afford to spend all his time involved with powerboat trips on the Grand Canyon, including the uprun attempts from 1949–60, as well as serving as the technical advisor for the Walt Disney film, *Ten Who Dared*, and many other river-related projects. Marston also appointed himself the historian of the Colorado River, and his voluminous collection at the Huntington Library in San Marino, California, contains probably the world's most comprehensive library of documents, books, films, photographs, and manuscripts about the history of running the Colorado River. For more about Marston, see David Lavender's *River Runners of the Grand Canyon*, which covers his background and life in detail. Garth Marston, Otis's son, later went on to work for Nevills Expedition as a boatman on several Grand Canyon trips; the animosity between the elder Marston and Nevills was apparently not shared by Garth.

14. With this comment, Nevills was foreshadowing a controversy that wracks the boating world today: motors or no motors. Earlier, Doris had commented on negative effects of motors in her published account of the 1940 trip, "Woman Conqueror of the Colorado": "The continual putt-putt of this motor is telling on us. . . . I'd rather flirt with uncertainty than sit in a boat and hear the darn putt-putt hour in and hour out" (August 1, 1940, box 28, folder 9, Nevills Papers).

Norman had no objection to using motors, and in fact, planned on extensive use of outboard motors for a Sierra Club trip that was scheduled for 1950.

15. This passage highlights a problem that can still plague river runners. McConkie was obviously spending too much time watching Nevills and not enough time watching the river. He was an experienced canoeist and must have known how to "read" water, yet he was so concerned with following Nevills's instructions that he missed the correct channel and almost flipped. Later in the trip, when he began to trust his own instincts, his rowing greatly improved and Nevills never had another problem with him.

16. By "#24" Nevills almost certainly means 24½ Mile Rapid, which is still considered a "toughy at all stages." In 1949, two months before Nevills death, Bert Loper had a heart attack while running this rapid and disappeared. His body was found over two decades later. Nevills also sometimes confuses 25 Mile Rapid with 24½ Mile Rapid.

17. See the entry for August 7, 1940.

18. In 1889, Robert Brewster Stanton was the chief engineer for a railroad survey of the Grand Canyon sponsored by the Denver, Colorado Canyon, and Pacific Railroad Company. By the time Stanton reached the cave that Nevills describes, his party had already lost three men to drowning and they were only looking for a way out of the canyon. Stanton's men stashed much of their river equipment in what is now called Stanton's Cave and hiked out the adjacent South Canyon (which Nevills persistently calls Paradise Canyon, after the nearby Vasey's Paradise). They returned in early 1890 and completed the railroad survey, although not without more injuries and problems. The note is now in the Nevills Papers; there is no reason to doubt its authenticity. For more about Stanton and the railroad survey see David Lavender's *River Runners of the Grand Canyon* or Dwight L. Smith and C. Gregory Crampton, eds., *The Colorado River Survey: Robert B. Stanton and the Denver, Colorado Canyon & Pacific Railroad* (Salt Lake City: Howe Brothers, 1987).

19. In this same cave, the 1934 "Dusty Dozen" trip found split-twig figurines of bighorn sheep made of willow that were subsequently recognized as belonging to the oldest-known inhabitants of the Grand Canyon. The figurines, and probably the basketry that Nevills was walking over, have been found to be around 3,500 years old.

20. President Harding Rapid was named by the Birdseye survey party in 1923 to commemorate the death of President Warren G. Harding in August of that year. It consists of a huge block of limestone in the middle of the river, which is why Nevills always refers to it as being harder at high water.

21. It's odd that Nevills so consistently dismisses the mouth of the Little Colorado River as not worth stopping for, but perhaps it's because he passed by in the middle of the summer, when the normally sky-blue water is often muddied by monsoonal floods. Another reason could be that Nevills commented to his daughter, Sandra, that he saw more rattlesnakes at the mouth of the Little Colorado than anywhere else in the canyon. (See the entry for July 17, 1947, for an example of finding rattlesnakes at this location.) Today river parties almost always stop there, and if they are lucky enough to catch it when the only flow is from Blue Springs—about thirteen miles up the canyon—it is truly a magical place in a spectacular setting. The springs and the canyon loom large in the cosmogony of the Hopi Indians, who live east of it. To them, the Little Colorado is the location where all life came from the underground onto the earth.

22. Later, Wayne McConkie swore he "could see gravel at bottom of hole that upset them." A copy of this film and a number of other Nevills Expedition films can be found in the Joseph Desloge Collection (A0641).

23. The Butte Fault crosses the river at this point, and copper and other mineral deposits are exposed. These mines were worked in the early years of the 20th century.

24. Phil and Emma Poquette managed Pearce Ferry, at the lower end of the Grand Canyon, for Grand Canyon-Boulder Dam Tours. Virginia Opie does not appear in the Nevills Papers or other sources.

25. Besides the historic inscriptions nearby, there is still a river runner's register hidden at Elves Chasm.

26. Sometimes known as "Christmas Tree Cave" for the mineral formation at the back of the cave. In the 1980s, the cave was home to a flourishing date palm, no doubt grown from a date pit left by a river runner. The NPS, however, felt that since it was non-native they should destroy it.

27. From the mouth of Kanab Canyon, it is about seventy-five miles to the town of Kanab, Utah. In 1872, upon reaching this point, John Wesley Powell declared, "Well boys, our journey's through," and abandoned the river. It is one of the few places where a well-defined route leads all the way out of the Grand Canyon.

28. Nevills was lucky here, for the mouth of Havasu Canyon is not a good place to be in a rainstorm, as more than one subsequent river runner has found out to their dismay!

29. Actually desert bighorn sheep, *ovis canadensis*, which are native to the area and quite common in the Grand Canyon today.

30. This note is also found in the Nevills Papers.

31. A twin-engine fighter built by Lockheed. Nevills was always conscious of airplanes and fascinated by flight.

32. Today's readers might be shocked by this casual use of a racial slur, but in the context of the times it meant "laggard" or "holding back." Nevills at no time displays any characteristic that would today be labeled "racist."

33. The drillers were testing the rock for the proposed Bridge Canyon Dam. During the controversy over dams in the Grand Canyon in the 1960s, the Bridge Canyon Dam was not as well known as the proposed Marble Canyon Dam farther upstream, but it would have backed up a larger reservoir. The dam was never built and today, little remains of this once-flourishing camp.

34. It turned out later that Olsen, exhausted by the heat, had immediately checked into a hotel room and slept for almost twenty-four hours straight. By the time he woke up everyone was gone, and he headed home alone.

1946 Journal

1. The San Juan boats were also of Nevills's own design, and differed from the larger cataract boats. They were squared-off at each end; fifteen feet long with four feet of beam; and were open, with no covered compartments. He used them primarily on the San Juan River, for which they were well-suited, but the only time they were used on one of his "big trips" were the 1946 Idaho runs. Although several of the fleet of San Juan boats survived, the *Mystery Canyon* was not one of them and its fate is unknown.

2. This was a Dodge one-quarter-ton reconnaissance car that Nevills bought as surplus just after World War II. As soon as the war ended, the armed forces

sold as surplus everything from bombers to cases of beans at pennies on the dollar (although Nevills commented in several letters about the "red tape" involved in buying this vehicle).

3.   Kent Frost of Monticello, Utah. He was a local boy who met the Nevills family in the 1930s and stayed in touch with them for the rest of Norman's life. An adventurous wanderer, he had already been down the Colorado through Glen Canyon as a boy, a tale well-told in his book, *My Canyonlands* (Moab, UT: Canyon Country Publications, 1997). Nevills often asked Frost to be a boatman on San Juan trips, but he was unable to go for one reason or another, until service in the Midwest as a missionary for the LDS Church and later, in World War II in the US Navy interrupted his wanderings in the deserts of southeastern Utah. After the 1946 Idaho trips, he rowed a boat for Nevills Expedition on the Green River and the Grand Canyon in 1947, and the Grand Canyon in 1948, as well as various San Juan trips.

4.   Lucius Moore was a friend of Nevills and the Walker family from Grand Junction, Colorado. He went on a San Juan trip with Nevills Expedition in the fall of 1941, and he and Nevills became good friends. He was planning to do other trips, such as the 1942 Grand Canyon run, but by then had entered the military and served out the war in the US Army. An extensive correspondence between him and the Nevills family can be found in the Nevills Papers, box 15, folders 24–25.

5.   Covey's Little America Hotel in downtown Salt Lake City.

6.   Doris, whose maiden name was Drown, was originally from Oregon, and most of her family still lived there and in California.

7.   Unfortunately, this trip was to give dramatic evidence that Pres Walker's drinking problems had only gotten worse after his service in World War II. Even though he had been drinking to excess before the war, family and friends attributed this worsening of the problem to his service in combat in the Mediterranean theater in World War II, including the landing in North Africa. After this trip, Walker checked himself into a rehabilitation center, and by the time of Nevills's death, was sober. It's a measure of their friendship that Nevills still considered Walker a good friend after the humiliations caused by his drinking on this trip, although he did not work for Nevills Expedition after 1946. For more on him, see the notes for the 1942 Grand Canyon expedition.

8.   June Chamberlain was the owner of a hospital in Santa Rosa, California, and went on a San Juan trip with Nevills Expedition in May 1942 (the same trip that Neill Wilson and Ed Hudson went on). After that trip, she maintained a close correspondence with Nevills, and decided to accompany the 1946 Salmon River run. Chamberlain did not go on the next leg of the Idaho trips through Hells Canyon of the Snake River. She kept in close contact with the family until 1948.

9.   In 1946, Pauline Saylor was a schoolteacher in Covina, California, where she saw an article about Nevills Expedition in the *Saturday Evening Post.* The article awakened a long-held desire to see the country around the Colorado River, so she contacted Nevills and inquired about going on the San Juan. However, the water was so low that year that the San Juan trip she booked had to be cancelled, and he persuaded her to instead sign up for the Salmon River voyage he was planning. She only made the Salmon River portion of the Idaho trip, leaving at Lewiston, Idaho. Saylor finally got to see at least

part of the Grand Canyon, going from Lees Ferry to Bright Angel with Nevills Expedition in 1947.

10.   Margaret Marston, Otis's wife, and their twin daughters, Loel and Maradel. Otis also kept a journal on this trip, a copy of which is found in the Nevills Papers, box 29, folder 19.

11.   Nevills is to meet Bennett again later in the trip. Jack Rottier, a newspaperman from Boise, Idaho, wrote of Bennett in a letter to Nevills later that year: "Last week I returned from a trip into the wilds of the Middle Forks [sic] with A.A. Bennett. He is some boy. At 65 he has retired to the leisure of his ranch after flying all over the west and in Alaska. Did you know that he owned and operated the Alaskan Airways at one time and that he was the guy who found the [dirigible] *Norge* when it was ground[ed] in the arctic?" (Jack Rottier to Norman Nevills, October 2, 1946, box 18, folder 20, Nevills Papers). Bennett had been a bush pilot in Alaska in the 1930s, and after his move to Idaho, his company, Bennett Air Transport, carried mail, passengers, freight, and equipment to isolated mining communities, and had a flying school for bush pilots in Salmon, Idaho. He was one of the most famous backcountry pilots in the West. His ranch was at the mouth of Impassable Canyon on the Middle Fork of the Salmon River.

12.   Few figures are more important in Salmon River history than Don Smith and his father, Clyde. From the 1920s to the present day, generations of Smiths have run the rivers of Idaho. The family deserves their own book, but some good information can be found in John Carrey and Cort Conley, *River of No Return* (Cambridge, ID: Backeddy Books, 1979).

13.   The same father and son who had been on the 1942 Grand Canyon voyage, as well as San Juan trips with Nevills Expedition. Twenty years after this trip, Wilson wrote a novel called *Deepdown River* (New York: Morrow, 1964), which was a fictionalized account of life on the "Big Piney River" in Idaho. The dust jacket for that book noted that, "Neill C. Wilson is just as interesting as his fictional characters—although in a more sophisticated way. He has been a newspaperman and, among other things, covered the San Francisco waterfront, climbed all the 14,000-foot peaks in western America, and has shot a thousand miles of rapids including those of 'The River of No Return' in Idaho."

14.   Howard O. Welty was the principal of the Oakland Technical High School in Oakland, California. He met Nevills when both were involved in the Rainbow Bridge-Monument Valley Expedition in the early 1930s, and even earlier, his children went to the same high school as Nevills in Oakland, California. By 1946 Welty had started making travel films and showing them on the lecture circuit. His Idaho film was titled, *Canyon Trails of the Shoshone*, and was shown with some success for a number of years. Finally, in search of more scenes to film, he signed up for the Bright Angel to Lake Mead leg of the Nevills Expedition trip through the Grand Canyon in 1948, but was dissatisfied with the way Nevills ran his trips, feeling that he did not stop enough for movie-making purposes. In 1949, he ran the Grand Canyon with Harry Aleson and was in the party that discovered Bert Loper's boat after Loper disappeared in 24½ Mile Rapid in July.

15.   Another good example of Nevills's idea of "fun." Old mine adits, or horizontal tunnel shafts, are extremely dangerous and should never be entered.

16.   Otis Marston was neither a medical nor an academic doctor. He himself usually signed his letters as "Dock," not the shorter "Doc," and among other

explanations, said that he got the nickname because he rowed so fast that he was always the first at the dock. Idaho historian Cort Conley related that Marston told him that people on one trip started calling him "Doc," since with his Vandyke beard, he looked like a doctor should look; and he "adopted the "k" so no one would think he was trying to pass himself off as a physician." In their earliest correspondence, Nevills referred to him as "Oty," so it's easy to see why "Dock" was preferable.

17. Since so many people lived along the Salmon River and depended on freight and supplies brought in by boat, it was common practice to try to ease the difficulty of rapids by dynamiting them. Carrey and Conley say in *River of No Return,* "The falls was a serious obstacle to boats until it was repeatedly dynamited" (128).

18. One of many hermits who inhabited the canyons of the Salmon River, Strauss was known as "Andy the Russian." In *River of No Return,* Carrey and Conley note that Strauss "grew great quantities of flowers, and went around naked as Adam. Whenever a boat stopped, the guide would go ahead to let Andy know that he had visitors, so he could pull on a pair of shorts" (134). Otis Marston noted in his journal that Strauss lived on a budget of $15 per year.

19. Howard A. Wilson, known as "Haywire Wilson," was one of the more notable characters on the Main Salmon. Carrey and Conley have a good description of the ranch on Wilson Bar and the history of the Wilson family. They note that the girls the Nevills party surprised—only a portion of the large Wilson family—were "pretty as a heart flush." For more on them, see *River of No Return* (187-189).

20. For a detailed history of Mackay Bar, see *River of No Return* (190-193).

21. Without doubt, a sturgeon—a member of the *Acipenseridae* family—the largest fresh-water fish known today. A five-foot sturgeon is not all that large an example of this leviathan of inland fishes.

22. It's unclear from the journal what "Goopies" meant, and there's no mention of this landing in Marston's journal. One interpretation is cow pies, or droppings from cattle.

23. Jack Rottier was a reporter for the *Idaho Statewide,* a weekly newspaper. He was one of Nevills's many contacts in the newspaper business and wrote several stories about the trip for his paper. For copies of his stories, as well as those of Irvine Reynolds (note #25, below), see the Nevills Papers, box 36, folder 5.

24. Carey Nixon was an attorney from Boise, Idaho. It's unclear how Nevills met him or what their connection was.

25. Like Jack Rottier (see note #23 above), Reynolds followed and reported on the progress of the Nevills Expedition trips, and rode with the trip from Riggins to Lewiston. His stories were wonderful publicity for Nevills's trips. His wife, Rebecca, is also mentioned in the journal. In 1947, Reynolds moved to San Diego, prompting him to write to Nevills saying that he had to "resign as your Idaho press agent" (box 18, folder 9, Nevills Papers).

26. Joan Nevills was, by this time, ten years old, and with her sister, Sandra (five years old), had come up to Idaho with their mother to help bring supplies and passengers in and out for the trips. Joan was able to ride along on parts of this and subsequent Nevills Expedition trips.

27. Otis Marston's journal notes, "Two prospectors visited us. Young and clean shaven, they had been three months studying the language of a small tube that witches gold" (box 29, folder 19, Nevills Papers). A doodlebug, in this case, was a forked rod made of metal (also called a dowsing rod), which the

user held loosely in his hands so that it could point to the presence of minerals or water underground.

28. Both Snowhole and China Rapids can still be run, and are often run upstream by jetboats carrying loads of tourists.

29. According to Idaho historian, Cort Conley, "The One-Way Club was started by the Idaho Scenic Land Assoc. It consisted of a long list of names written on paper and stashed in a jar about 50 feet upslope from the river and on the Main [Salmon River] about 5 miles above its confluence with the Snake. Passengers on trips that went through to Lewiston stopped to sign. Boatmen left their names on a carved wooden sign at the same site." The "one-way" referred to the Main Salmon's being known as "The River of No Return."

30. Another famous name in Idaho river history. In *Snake River of Hells Canyon*, he is called, "the dominant powerboat personality on the river through the Forties" (John Carrey, Cort Conley, and Ace Barton [Cambridge, ID: Backeddy Books], 78). A detailed sketch of him is found in the book on pages 78–80.

31. For a detailed discussion of Holmstrom's suicide, see *The Doing of the Thing: The Brief, Brilliant Whitewater Career of Buzz Holmstrom* (Dimock, 1998, 260–282).

32. A type of small airplane, Stinsons were light, high-wing "taildraggers," capable of taking off and landing on short, rough airstrips. In appearance and function, they are almost identical to the Piper J3 that Nevills would buy later that year.

33. Nevills met George Fletcher of Boise at the Payette Lake home of Carey Nixon, and invited him along on the trip. No correspondence file exists from him in the Nevills Papers. See July 27 entry.

34. Now the site of the Brownlee Dam, built in the 1950s for hydroelectric power. Three dams now flood parts of what Nevills ran in 1946: the Brownlee Dam, the Oxbow Dam, and the Hells Canyon Dam. From where Nevills started at Brownlee Ferry to just above his August 11 camp at Deep Creek, the river canyon has been completely covered by the waters of one or another of these reservoirs. From there down to Lewiston, the river still flows, although there is a low dam below Lewiston that backs up a few miles above the town, but no rapids were flooded. There are no dams on the Salmon River.

35. Unlike virtually everyone else mentioned in Nevills's journals, there is almost no correspondence between him and Ferris Dodge, and none with her father, Harry Dodge. There are two letters in the "D Miscellaneous" file (box 7, folder 18, Nevills Papers) between Ferris Dodge and Nevills; and both her and her father are mentioned in the correspondence between Otis Marston and Nevills (box 16, folders 5–6, Nevills Papers). It can only be surmised that the Dodges were friends of Marston's from San Francisco.

36. Now flooded by the Oxbow Dam, Buck Creek was once one of the most feared rapids in Hells Canyon. Carrey, Conley, and Barton in *Snake River of Hells Canyon* noted: "'Big, Bad, Buck,' was the most awesome rapid on the Snake. Veteran and unperturbable [*sic*] river-runner Don Hatch described it as 'the damnedest thing I ever saw.' The river went off a ledge and there wasn't any way to cheat the rapid at most flows. Many early river parties portaged Buck Creek" (146–147).

37. Idaho Power used the mine buildings here during the construction of the Hells Canyon Dam, which is just downstream. *Snake River of Hells Canyon* has a good description of the mine and its history (Carrey, Conley, and Barton, 148–149).

38. A common belief among river runners to this day is that silt-laden water is heavier and therefore, makes the waves in rapids hit harder. The San Juan and Colorado, where Nevills was used to running, were of course among the siltiest rivers in the world. The steamboat referred to in this entry is the *Shoshone*, a grand craft almost 140-feet-long. A detailed history of this and other steamboats on the Snake can be found in Carrey, Conley, and Barton, 28–67.

39. This casual dispatching of rattlesnakes, described throughout the Nevills journals, would be anathema to most river runners today, not to mention illegal in federally managed lands, but at the time—and indeed still in many parts of the country—rattlesnakes were routinely killed.

40. This rapid, known as Copper Ledge Falls (Carrey, Conley, and Barton, 41) no longer exists. There are no more dams from this point to Lewiston, and whatever Nevills describes from this point on to Lewiston can still be seen. Today jet boat tours roar up and down this stretch.

41. "Rush Creek contains a serious hole at the head of the rapid. There is ample room to avoid it on the right" (Carrey, Conley, and Barton, *Snake River of Hells Canyon*, 212).

42. Another good example of what today would be considered breaking and entering, and petty theft, the party's casual use of a stranger's kitchen and supplies was not looked down upon at the time. The assumption was that at some time in the future you would give supplies to someone else to repay the debt.

43. Like many of the structures Nevills describes, the Hells Canyon Lodge was deliberately burned in the 1960s by the US Forest Service.

44. After the Idaho trip, Nevills tried to interest Howard "Cowboy" Welty in more trips, but Welty was unsatisfied with the journey from a filmmakers' standpoint, saying in a letter written December 1, 1947, that he didn't want to go on another trip if he couldn't determine where to stop and film (box 21, folder 17, Nevills Papers). Pittsburgh Landing is one of the most historic places along the Snake River, with evidence of Native American habitation long before white men settled there.

45. Carrey, Conley, and Barton, in *Snake River of Hells Canyon*, note of Imnaha Rapid on page 342 that, "This innocuous-looking stretch of choppy water sank a jet boat in the spring of 1974. Seven people were aboard without life-jackets and two of them drowned."

46. A facet of Nevills's personality that comes out through his and other people's journals: that he was the one in charge and rarely brooked any disagreements or questions about his decisions. Most passengers didn't mind this, but among his boatmen and some of the passengers, this caused increasing tensions and sometimes, open splits.

47. These notes, appended by Nevills at the end of the 1946 journal, are indicative of what Nevills discusses in much subsequent correspondence. He was greatly impressed by the commercial river running possibilities of the Snake and Salmon, and even waxed eloquent about it in a newspaper interview (box 36, folder 5, Nevills Papers). He immediately began planning a trip on those rivers for October of the following year, but was told by Jack Rottier that the fall was right in the prime hunting season and he was unlikely to find any passengers (box 18, folder 20, Nevills Papers). For one reason or another, he concentrated for the rest of his life on his home rivers—the San Juan and Colorado—and never returned to Idaho. He would be proven correct

long after his death, and today, commercial river running flourishes on the Snake, the Salmon, and their tributaries. Nevills's claim of having taken the first woman in small boats through Hells Canyon is questionable, given the amount of traffic on the Snake River.

1947 JOURNAL

1. Norman Nevills to S.S. England, November 28, 1947, box 8, folder 9, Nevills Papers.

2. Pres Walker to Otis Marston, February 1948, box 241, Marston Collection, Huntington Library.

3. In 1948, Kent Frost started his own river-running company to compete with Nevills, but it was short-lived, and by 1949 he was back to rowing boats for Nevills and occasionally for Nevills's successor, Mexican Hat Expeditions. In later years, he found his niche as a jeep and hiking guide in the canyonlands country. One of his guided hikes was to go down Kanab Creek to the bottom of the Grand Canyon, then back up the river to Deer Creek, and then retrace the route. This was a distance on foot of almost two hundred miles! See notes for 1946 for more about Kent Frost.

4. Dave Morris's brother, Archie, worked for Nevills on the San Juan in 1946. When he was unable to continue, he suggested that his brother, Dave, take over as a boatman. Dave ran several trips with Nevills as a boatman on the San Juan before the 1947 Green River trip.

5. Rosalind Johnson, a "famous horsewoman from Pasadena," first went on a Nevills Expedition San Juan River trip in June 1946, and like Otis Marston, was immediately hooked on river running. Apparently she and Nevills hit it off right away, for from that time on, she wrote frequently to him—sometimes beginning her letters "Dearest Norm"—and received immediate replies. By the time of the 1947 Green River trip, she had already been on other San Juan trips, and was helping Nevills with bookings for trips, obtaining gear and supplies, and even industrial espionage when he asked her to write to Larabee and Aleson Western River Expeditions in 1948 and check out their operations on the sly! At any rate, she and Nevills remained fast friends to the end of his life, their correspondence filling three fat folders (box 13, folders 5–7, Nevills Papers). Johnson's friendship and respect for Nevills continued long after his death. In a 1950 letter to Frank Masland, she wrote: "I can fully echo your statement that Norm gave 'directly and indirectly more than anyone has ever given in sheer enjoyment.' I too view my river experiences as something to which I could always look forward." (Box 102, Marston Collection)

6. The younger Reynolds (whose name was Adrian but was always known as "A. K." to distinguish him from his father) was so impressed with Nevills's cataract boats that he asked for the plans so he could copy them. Nevills—probably flattered and thinking of all the favors Reynolds senior had done for him since 1940—agreed. A. K. and his brother-in-law, Mike Hallacy, made two boats that he used for his company, Reynolds-Hallacy River Expeditions, which ran only on the upper Green through the early 1960s. For more about the elder Reynolds, see the 1940 journal and notes.

7. Al and Elma Milotte were experienced freelance filmmakers who specialized in nature films. In 1946, the Disney Studios contacted Nevills with a request to send some of their photographers on his San Juan and Grand Canyon trips to take footage for a possible movie about John Wesley Powell. After much correspondence and renegotiating of agreements (which included a request

to Nevills that he repaint his boats bright red so they would show up better on film), the Disney Studios suddenly dropped out, but hired Al Milotte to take over their spaces on the Nevills Expedition trips and shoot the footage they needed. The Milottes later made several movies for Disney, two of which won Academy Awards.

8.   Wilson Taylor ran a leather goods store in Berkeley, California, and was a friend of Otis Marston. After the 1947 Green River trip with Nevills, he went on several powerboat trips through the Grand Canyon with Marston, including one where an incident with a rope that became accidentally looped around his neck earned the sobriquet "Willie's Necktie." Despite this, his main claim to fame was dying of a heart attack while on a Grand Canyon river trip with Marston in 1955 and being buried in the Grand Canyon below President Harding Rapid. Brief mentions of him can be found in David Lavender's *River Runners of the Grand Canyon.*

9.   Even though Dock Marston was still working for Nevills, by this point there had been a subtle shift in their relationship. In the correspondence between the two men in the Nevills Papers (box 16), during the winter of 1946–1947 Marston had begun questioning Nevills's statements and methods of running the river, and Nevills's replies had begun to seem almost testy. From this point on, their friendship turned almost to open animosity, and by the end of the 1948 season it had, sadly, grown into a full-blown dislike. After Nevills's death, Marston—for reasons known only to himself—made it his mission to the end of his life to drag the Nevills name through any mud he could find, even to the point of alleging that Nevills's death in a plane crash was actually suicide.

10.   Shirley Marston was Garth's wife.

11.   Unless forced to, as in this situation, Nevills chose the boatmen for the Grand Canyon and Green River with care, usually after they had worked several trips on the San Juan. On that river, if he needed someone to row a boat, it was common for him to choose any likely looking male passenger, and tell them to simply follow him and do what he did on the river. The *Sandra* was the last cataract boat built by Nevills. P. T. Reilly, who worked for Nevills in 1949, made suggestions to Nevills about improving the boats—which were consistently ignored—much to Reilly's chagrin. Reilly counts seventeen boats built to the same cataract design. He later designed and used a boat that was pointed on both ends and claimed that it worked better. Not surprisingly, Marston agreed, writing in 1950: "Norm's boats were never satisfactory and their deterioration finally brot [sic] them to a most dangerous condition." And, "I have come to the conclusion that the Nevills boat leaves much to be desired. It is worthy of note that he has not improved his boat since he built the first one in 1938." Reilly agreed, but in discussing a 1957 run through the Grand Canyon with Mexican Hat Expeditions—which used the same cataract boats as Nevills—passenger Mary Beckwith wrote to Marston: "I do not know what it proves but our "sadirons" as you call them, made the run from Hance to B.A. [Bright Angel] on 105,000 in one hour and five minutes—Pat's [Reilly] pointed ends, one hour and 25 minutes. This to me, indicates that he did a lot of going around in eddies; uncontrollable rowing. IF pointed ends were 'more better' his time should have been under an hour. We waste no motions to speak of, but came on down—yet we did it faster and I THINK with greater ease and control. Either THAT or something happened to Pat that he isn't talking about. Outside of that great cottonwood tree which whirled along with him in Nancoweap rapid. Ah Well, I still don't know" (box 16, Marston

Collection).

12. In his 1940 journal, Nevills noted about their stop here: "DO NOT STOP HERE IN FUTURE" (emphasis in original). See the 1940 journal for more about the Logan Ranch.

13. Virtually every river runner who passed this way stopped at the Holmes Ranch and left a description of the hospitality offered by the Holmes family. For instance, in 1911 the Kolb brothers camped nearby and were invited to dinner, about which Ellsworth commented, "[T]he evening will linger long in our memories." He gives a good description of the ranch in *Through the Grand Canyon from Wyoming to Mexico*, 16–17. See notes for 1940 for Nevills's earlier comments about the ranch.

14. Linwood was a small town on the Green River at the mouth of Henry's Fork. When Flaming Gorge Dam was built, the reservoir covered the site of the town, but not before a long-time resident, Minnie Crouse Rasmussen, burned her house to the ground in defiance of the Bureau of Reclamation.

15. Named for Keith Smith, one of early settlers of the area, and one of the founders of the little town of Linwood.

16. The Green Lakes Lodge is still—as of this writing (2004)—in business.

17. Joan Nevills-Staveley later remembered that while she normally would have jumped at the chance to have a hamburger, for some reason on this occasion she chose trout, which was also on the menu. While the others suffered from food poisoning, she did not.

18. Don Harris, on a survey trip for the USGS in the fall of 1946, pinned one of his boats at Ashley Falls but was able to extricate it. The next year he came back on high water, and capsized as Nevills describes. In a 1990 interview, the unpretentious Harris noted that the 1947 upset was due to "pilot error" (Don Harris, interview #256, Everett L. Cooley Oral History Collection, Marriott Library Special Collections Department, University of Utah).

19. Orson Burton was also the father of Jesse "Shorty" Burton, who became a boatman for Hatch River Expeditions. He later drowned in Upset Rapid in the Grand Canyon, in June 1967.

20. See the notes for the 1940 journal for more about Red Creek Rapid. Unlike the other rapids described to this point, Red Creek can still be run as is about fourteen miles below Flaming Gorge Dam. A recent flood washed in more boulders, making the run even more difficult, so local "vigilantes" dynamited the right side to make a clean run.

21. The famous Swinging Bridge of Browns Park. Still in use, the bridge has a sign that says it is safe for one car or forty sheep. The editor has crossed this bridge a number of times and can testify to the truth of Nevills's assessment of it as "rickety."

22. The Lodore School, which was the scene of several noted events during the days of the outlaws in Browns Park. The building is no longer a school, but still stands and is used for social gatherings.

23. What Nevills calls Mile 234 is Harp Falls, named by the Powell Expedition when the constellation Lyra was seen over the cliff above the rapid. At low water there is no rapid here, but at the high water such as Nevills was on in 1947, there are big waves. The same is true of the rapid Nevills notes at Mile 233.

24. The *Lota Ve*. See 1940 notes for more about this boat. For many years there was an established camp at Triplet Falls, but in the 1980s the Park Service closed it due to overuse. Still, it remains one of the nicest beaches in the Canyon of Lodore.

25.   A friend of Bus Hatch, both of whom Nevills met in 1940. See the 1940 journal for more about Mandy Campbell.

26.   Hell's Half Mile was regularly portaged on the right until the 1960s. Even though it was much easier on the right side, it was still an arduous task at best. For film depicting the same portage in 1949, see the Joseph Desloge Collection (A0641) in the Marriott Library, University of Utah.

27.   The Jack Chew family had a ranch a few miles up Pool Creek, which enters the Green at the lower end of Echo Park (which Nevills calls Pat's Hole) since the early 1900s, and also grew hay in Echo Park. Many early river runners stopped and visited with the Chews. (See Kolb, *Through the Grand Canyon from Wyoming to Mexico*, 72–76 for an account of the Kolb brothers' stay there in 1911.) The family signed the ranch over to the National Park Service in the 1970s, and although the ranch buildings are still there, it is no longer farmed. Today Echo Park is a car camp in Dinosaur National Monument, and a frequent stop for river runners for water, and to stretch their legs amid magnificent scenery. The wind cave that Nevills mentions is less than one-quarter mile from the river, an easy walk, even in wet shoes.

28.   Indeed, Jones Hole today is the site of four established camps for river runners in Dinosaur National Monument, and is still considered a prime fishing spot due to the fish hatchery four miles up Jones Hole Creek.

29.   For more on their 1940 visit, and more on the Ruple Ranch, see the entry for June 28 in the 1940 journal. Some of the original structures still stand, but the ranch is no longer in use.

30.   The lower Chew Ranch, below Split Mountain Canyon, was bought by Doug Chew in 1941 and is still owned and farmed by the Chew family.

31.   Preston and Becky Walker, his wife. See 1940 and 1946 notes for more on Preston Walker, a long-time friend of Nevills. Jim Rigg was another friend of Nevills from Grand Junction, Colorado, as well as a pilot who had taken over Drapela Flying Service in Grand Junction. With his brother Bob, he later became a boatman for Nevills, and after Norman's death in 1949, was one of the partners who took over Nevills Expedition, renaming it Mexican Hat Expeditions.

32.   The last of the Nevills fleet of cataract boats, the *Sandra* languished for many years after Nevills's death, but was recently restored by boatbuilder Andy Hutchinson and Greg Reiff, one of Nevills's grandchildren. It's now in the family's possession.

33.   With five trips through the Grand Canyon, Nevills was by far the most experienced boatman in the Grand Canyon.

34.   Nevills's friendship with Randall Henderson, the peripatetic editor and publisher of *Desert Magazine*, dates back to 1938, when Henderson reported in the magazine on the progress of Nevills's first major expedition. Thereafter, Henderson published many stories about Nevills's river trips and the Mexican Hat Lodge, as part of his focus on the desert southwest. Nevills, in his turn, purchased ads in *Desert Magazine*, and utilized Henderson's press for printing his brochures, so they had both a personal and a business relationship. At the end of World War II, Henderson went on a San Juan trip with Nevills, and like so many others, was convinced during that trip to take the longer Grand Canyon voyage. Henderson wrote feature articles about both of these trips, and the Grand Canyon trip was serialized over four issues. Henderson's loyalty to Nevills extended to refusing to run ads for his competitors until after Norman and Doris were killed, at which time he wrote to Becky Walker, "And

the river trips will go on. It could not end with Norman Nevills." Henderson published several memorials to them in his magazine.

35. See the notes for the 1946 journal for more on Pauline Saylor.

36. Francis and Marjory Farquahr were from San Francisco; he was a long-time member of the Sierra Club, and served as president of the club several times over the years. Both of them were well-known as rock climbers, and she was the first woman to ascend Shiprock in New Mexico. Francis is also known as the first bibliographer of the Colorado River. His 1947 trip gave them a taste for river running, so in 1948 they chartered a San Juan trip with Nevills Expedition, in which Francis wished to row one of Nevills San Juan boats. It turned out, however, that for whatever skills he had as a climber, he "did not have the knack" of rowing a boat, in the words of another passenger on the trip. Not long after they started, he lost control of the boat, which was swept against a wall and capsized. Two women were trapped under the boat, and while no one was lost or even injured, it was scary for all involved. Questioned later about why he had permitted Francis to row a boat, both Norman and Doris "exclaimed in unison, 'But you don't know the pressure that was brought to bear; we just had to let him'" (Margaret Wood, journal, May–June 1948, box 29, folder 34, Nevills Papers).

37. This typed note, headlined, "NORMAN NEVILLS COLORADO RIVER EXPEDITION ****1947," was found by Rod Sanderson in May 1962, and is now in the Nevills Papers (box 29, folder 24). Henderson left similar notes at a number of other places in Grand Canyon, including another found in a can at Stone Creek, below Dubendorff Rapid, which is also in the Nevills Papers.

38. First noted by the "Dusty Dozen" Hatch-Frazier party in 1934. See notes for 1940 for more about the skeleton.

39. The actual name is Seth Tanner, who was Mormon pioneer of the area, one of the settlers in the Little Colorado River mission.

40. More Nevills "fun;" this would cause investigation and arrest today, besides being highly dangerous since dynamite becomes unstable as it ages.

41. The Morning Star Mine opened in 1904.

42. Nevills doesn't mention it, but Elma Milotte also left the trip at this point. Apparently there was some tension between the Milottes and Nevills over their demands for filming stops and other problems, and they didn't go on another Nevills Expedition river trip. After Nevills's death, Elma Milotte was one of those who would not support a memorial for Norman and Doris, adding, "I will say this much. Norm made a fine reputation for himself as a river man and made history by his persuing [sic] the river as a business."

43. Joseph Desloge Sr. was the patriarch of one of the oldest, most established, and wealthiest families in St. Louis, Missouri, and lived on an estate of over 1000 acres of land at the junction of the Missouri and Mississippi Rivers. Although there is no indication of just how he became interested in Nevills Expedition, he probably heard about the trips from Hugh Cutler, a botanist with the Missouri Botanical Gardens who had gone on the long Green-Colorado River expedition in 1940. Desloge and Cutler knew each other from St. Louis, and by 1945, Joseph Sr. and Nevills were corresponding like old friends. In the summer of 1945, Joseph chartered a Nevills Expedition San Juan trip, and from then on, he was both a devoted river runner and supporter of Nevills. He would write checks for passage for his whole family for up to $5,000 without hesitation, and was a great source of supplies, contacts, and even funding for Nevills for the rest of the latter's life. Anne and Zoe Desloge were his

young, adventurous daughters, while Joe Jr.—who is sometimes referred to by Nevills in the journal as "JoJo"—was his son. Marie Saalfrank was Joseph Sr.'s companion and they were later married. In a letter to Adrian Reynolds, Nevills describes the two Desloge daughters: "Miss Anne Desloge who has been on the river before with me was just made queen of the Veiled Prophets Ball in St. Louis. She and her sister are very pretty, and are top-notch swimmers and divers." (box 18, folder 8, Nevills Papers). The Desloge family went on to take several more river trips with Nevills Expedition, and even after Nevills's death continued their river travels with Reynolds-Hallacy Expeditions and with Sanderson River Expeditions. In 2001, the descendants of Joseph Sr. donated a large collection of 16mm color films, depicting river trips both with Nevills and after his death, to the University of Utah. (Desloge Collection, A0641) The correspondence between Nevills and Desloge fill four folders in the Nevills Papers (box 7 folders 7–10), and one of the last letters Nevills ever wrote was to Desloge, dated September 15, 1949, just a few days before Nevills was killed.

44.   Nevills ran Hermit in low water in 1940, but as he notes, it is completely different when the water is high. Hermit at high water is a gigantic roller coaster and while the huge waves can still cause problems, it is considered one of the most "fun" rapids in the Grand Canyon.

45.   This is one of the first mentions of the hike into the hidden grotto above the Deer Creek waterfall and out into the valley beyond. Native Americans, cowboys, and prospectors had long known about the valley of Deer Creek but at the time, river runners seldom hiked up off the river corridor without a reason. Today this hike is a staple of modern Grand Canyon river runners, and at times the mouth of Deer Creek is a veritable parking lot of boats as parties line up to go up into the canyon.

46.   John Riffey was the ranger at Toroweap, a remote outpost on the north side of the Grand Canyon above Lava Falls, for over forty years. He had a small airplane named *Pogo* that he used for patrols over and around the canyon. He was known as a good Samaritan for acts such as bringing the messages to the Nevills party.

47.   Known informally as "Lower Lava," "Little Lava," or "Son of Lava," this rapid immediately below Lava Falls is formed by the river piling up against a cliff on the left side. It has caught more than one boater—overjoyed by a successful run of Lava Falls—by surprise, and even caused some capsizes.

48.   Charles Roemer (Nevills's "Rohmer") was a retired engineer from New York City who dreamed of running the Grand Canyon. He set out from Lees Ferry in October 1946, against the advice of Art Greene, owner of the Marble Canyon Lodge, in a small one-man life raft, with only two loaves of bread, two onions, and five small packages of raisins for provisions. On October 24, he was seen passing Phantom Ranch, but neither he nor his boat were ever seen again and it is presumed that he died in the canyon. More about Roemer can be found in Michael P. Ghiglieri and Thomas M. Myers, *Over the Edge: Death in Grand Canyon* (Flagstaff, AZ: Puma Press, 2001), 156–157.

49.   The sentences enclosed in brackets in this entry were crossed out in pencil on Nevills's typed transcription. The reason is explained in the entry for the next day at Spring Canyon, Mile 204. Nevills had obviously confused the two canyons.

50.   After Nevills's, death, his company became Mexican Hat Expeditions, running cataract boats until 1969. The company later became Canyoneers, Inc., which

has run weekly trips for "the lame, the halt, and the blind"—in Marston's arch phrase—for the last thirty years. Today some 15,000 people per year go down the Grand Canyon.

51. These are US Geological Survey maps of the Green, Colorado, San Juan, Snake, and Salmon Rivers that were cut into sections to fit into a wooden map holder devised by Nevills for use on the river. He also used a homemade scroll map where the sections of maps of the Grand Canyon were pasted onto brown paper to make a continuous scroll. The maps—including the scroll which contains many handwritten notes by Nevills—and the holder are found in box 34 of the Nevills Papers.

52. Bill Belknap would become a well-known figure on the Colorado River in later years. A photographer from Boulder City, Nevada, he got involved with the powerboat runs of Otis Marston and later started his own river-running company specializing in trips with sportyaks. With his son, Buzz, joined later by his daughter, Loie Belknap Evans, he also started producing a series of river guides—maps of the river corridor with notes on the history, geology, natural history and so on—which came to be known as the Belknap guides. There is hardly a modern river runner that does not own and use at least one of the Belknap guides.

53. An amphibious airplane, capable of landing on either land or water.

54. The field at Kingman was one of several where thousands of US Army warplanes were stored after the conflict ended; most ended up as scrap metal.

55. Alfred M. Bailey, "Desert River through Navajoland," *National Geographic* (August 1947).

56. Another good example of why his airplane was such a necessity in Mexican Hat.

1948 Journal

1. Staveley, "Norman Nevills," 42.

2. The list of the "First Hundred" to go through the Grand Canyon has become something of a sacred text among Colorado River historians, with scholars checking and cross-checking the list to make sure someone deserves to be included. The criteria is that the person had to have gone from Lees Ferry through the Grand Canyon to the Grand Wash Cliffs (although not necessarily in one trip), thereby excluding people such as John Wesley Powell's three men who left at Separation Canyon in 1869; or Glen and Bessie Hyde, who apparently only made it as far as Mile 232, and so on. Only a person's first trip was counted, so while Nevills had gone the most number of times, he is only listed for his 1938 trip. As might be expected, this was something that Otis Marston became obsessive over in his later years, even though his own place on the list was assured, for his first trip in 1942. But toward the end of his life, Marston began to wonder if Sandra Nevills—who was a fetus in Doris Nevills's womb in 1940—likewise deserved a place on the list; he wrote to doctors, scientists, and clerics, soliciting their opinions of when a fetus became a person. Sandra's presence on the list would bump either Ed Hudson's son (also known as Ed), or Willie Taylor, or Bestor Robinson (who only went partway with Nevills in 1948 and came back the next year with Marston) from the list. What cannot be gainsaid, at any rate, is the fact that of those one hundred, Nevills took thirty-four—more than one-third—down the river.

3. John Franklin Wright was a local Mormon from Blanding, Utah, a small town near Mexican Hat. He and his wife, Dora, had been the weather recorders

for the US Weather Bureau in Blanding for some years by this point. He started working with Nevills on the San Juan in 1947, and by 1948, Nevills knew he could become a good Grand Canyon boatman. In a 1948 letter to Ros Johnson, Nevills described Wright this way: "He's 100%. He's so honest, reliable and dependable. That plus his loyalty makes him invaluable" (Norman Nevills to Ros Johnson, December 15, 1948, box 13, folder 6, Nevills Papers). After Nevills's death, Wright became one of the partners in Mexican Hat Expeditions, which carried on the Nevills tradition for many years. Still later, he joined the Museum of Northern Arizona surveys of Glen Canyon before that area was flooded by Glen Canyon Dam, and for a time operated the marina and ferry at Wahweap. By the time of his death at an advanced age in 2002, Wright probably knew more about the Glen Canyon region than anyone.

4.   This was Otis Marston's last trip with Nevills Expedition. By this time, notes P. T. Reilly in a 1987 article in *Utah Historical Quarterly*, "Marston refuted [Nevills's] yarns to the passengers, belittled his leadership, and continuously advanced his own status as an authority. Norm did not actually discharge him; he simply did not include him in his plans for 1949" (197). Reilly goes on to claim that Marston was unaware that he had offended Nevills, but this seems disingenuous at best.

5.   Frank Masland was the owner of a successful carpet-manufacturing firm in Carlisle, Pennsylvania, who read the article by Neill Clark in the 1946 *Saturday Evening Post*. It awakened a dream he had held since 1939, when he had seen the Grand Canyon during a stopover on a business trip. Masland was a very successful businessman, besides being a fair-minded and humble man. In the boiling mix of Colorado River personalities, he stands out as one who avoided the ego trips that sometimes seemed to poison the atmosphere. He was a great friend of Nevills, and was one of his staunchest supporters both while Nevills was alive and after his death. It was Masland who organized and helped fund the memorial to Norman and Doris, which still stands near Lees Ferry. In a 1950 letter to Otis Marston, Masland said, "By this time, Doc, you well know that I am not objective. I try to confine that to my business activities. Where the river is concerned, I am definitely subjective, and I have an overgrown tendency to personalize, besides I think a hell of a lot of Norm Nevills and you know it. I don't give a damn about his faults . . ." (box 145, Marston Collection). Masland was also one of the driving forces behind the successful effort to have the rapid at Mile 75 in the Grand Canyon renamed Nevills Rapid. He is represented by two full folders of correspondence, as well as copies of his 1948 and 1949 journals, in the Nevills Papers (box 15, folders 10–11; and box 29, folders 35–36). The correspondence and other materials relating to the memorial, as well as Masland's proposal to name the new reservoir behind Glen Canyon Dam as Lake Nevills are found in box 1 of the Nevills Papers.

6.   Moulton Fulmer, of Muncie, Indiana, read of Nevills Expedition's San Juan trips in a 1942 issue of *Sunset* magazine, and wrote to Mexican Hat right away to inquire about booking a trip. He went in June of that year with his wife, Janice. After that, he was obviously bitten by the river bug, to the point of building his own boat and taking it down the flood-swollen White River in his hometown, with near-disastrous consequences. He wanted to go on more river trips with Nevills, but as with so many others, service in the US Army in World War II intervened, and it was not until the end of the conflict that he

was able to again go down the San Juan with Nevills, this time rowing a boat. In 1947, he came out to the Mexican Hat country and took his own boat down the San Juan, and then ran the Grand Canyon with Nevills Expedition in 1948. After Nevills's death the next year, Fulmer maintained his interest in the Colorado River, and returned for other trips with P. T. Reilly and others.

7.   Wayne and Lucille Hiser of Toledo, Ohio, first heard of Nevills Expedition when they stopped at the Mexican Hat Lodge while on a tour of the southwest in 1947. Shortly after that, they booked a San Juan trip for the spring of that year. Like so many others, Nevills convinced them that they should try the Grand Canyon as well, and kept in touch with them for the next year. By 1948, they were ready to go and insisted on riding with Nevills himself in the *Wen*.

8.   Bestor Robinson was a lawyer from Oakland, California, and a long-time member of the Sierra Club. Described by historian Al Holland as a "rock climbing fanatic," he had been involved in many early climbs in the Yosemite Valley, and would become an environmental activist when the Sierra Club moved in that direction. Another who went with Nevills but didn't particularly care for his style, Robinson did go on other river trips, including the Sierra Club trips in Dinosaur National Monument during the Echo Park Dam controversy in the 1950s. Those trips made Hatch River Expeditions a household name. Had he lived, Nevills and Hatch would, no doubt, have become competitors.

9.   For more about Jim Rigg, see the notes for the 1947 journal.

10. Both Jim Jordan and Rod Sanderson spent quite a bit of time on the river subsequent to this trip. Sanderson worked for the Bureau of Reclamation at the Marble Canyon dam site with his brother, Larry, and later started Sanderson River Expeditions with his son, Jerry. Jordan, likewise a Bureau employee, later became involved in the powerboat trips that thundered back and forth on the river from the late 1940s through the 1950s. The Marble Canyon dam site was active from the end of World War II until a major environmental controversy resulted in the abandonment of the plans for a dam there in the 1960s. The camp was supplied both by boat and by a series of aerial tramways that came down from the rim. There is still a great deal of evidence of the work at the site in the form of test holes, cables, painted lettering, and junk.

11. Nevills always reserved this selection to himself, not to the passengers or other boatmen. It became a source of contention later, when some of his boatmen felt that he always reserved space in his boat for the pretty girls on the trip, while they carried the older passengers, and a greater share of the supplies and gear.

12. Now known as Rider Canyon, named for Roy Rider, who ran the ferry at Lees Ferry in the 1910s. House Rock Valley, to the north of Marble Canyon, is the source of the name. Early Mormon pioneers camped beneath huge boulders there and gave the site the name House Rock.

13. Frank Masland gives a good account of this initiation into the DWB in his *By the Rim of Time* (box 29, folder 35, Nevills Papers, 10–11).

14. This is today known as Buck Farm Canyon.

15. Nancy Streator was a spunky teenager from Salt Lake City; her father, Frank Streator, owned a successful Chevrolet dealership and was involved in the Civil Air Patrol, both reason enough for him to know Nevills. Shortly after World War II, Nancy went on a tour of Navajoland with her Episcopal Church youth group, where she met Father Liebler, a missionary in that area who had been on a Nevills San Juan trip. The idea of a wild river appealed to the

adventurous girl, and she finally talked her father into allowing her to go on the trip. After that, she proceeded to the lower end of the Grand Canyon in 1948, and the Green and upper end of the Grand in 1949. An enjoyable oral history interview with her can be found in the Everett L. Cooley Oral History Collection, (ACCN 814).

16.   For more on Ros Johnson, see the notes for 1947. That year she was on both the Green River trip and the upper end of the Grand Canyon.

17.   John Doerr quickly became known as "Little John." In her journal, Nancy Streator wrote: "'Little John' as we nicknamed him because of his huge build, was the object of much kidding. Norm was sure he weighed 235 lbs and was trying to figure out a scheme for keeping the boat maneuverable in rapids with 'Little John' aboard. He was put on a liquid diet until Norm found out he only weighed 194 lbs., at which time he was allowed to eat again" (box 29, folder 30, Nevills Papers).

18.   For more on Welty, see the notes for the 1946 journal.

19.   Masland explained how he got the name "Fish-Eyes" in *By the Rim of Time*. "It was this day that my companions started calling me 'Fish-Eyes.' It seems the usual way for the person riding the stern of the boat to go through a raid is sitting up, but being blissfully ignorant of the approved technique, I stretched out face down with my head overhanging he stern. Since the boats go through the rapid stern first, I was under water most of the way. . . . After two or three trips in this submerged position, they began talking about the fish-eye view I had of the water, and soon 'Fish-Eyes' was the name" (8).

20.   For the Hisers, the trip changed after Bright Angel. They complained to John Doerr of Nevills's seeming preference for Nancy Streator—in allowing her more rides through the rapids—and also felt that the food was inadequate in variety and amount (box 53, Marston Collection).

21.   Now known as the Esmerelda Elbow, named for a boat wrecked there in 1950 by Ed Hudson, who had run the Grand Canyon with Nevills in 1942.

22.   It was actually a B-24 bomber on a training mission at night. The bomber's engines quit all at once, and three of the crewmen bailed out through the bomb bay. As they floated down, the pilot managed to restart the engines and flew on. The three men were disconcerted to see the lights of small towns disappear as they dropped below the rim. They were rescued after a few days by climbers that came in from the north rim and led them out.

23.   Ros Johnson says of the water in the canteen: "4 yrs. old and rank." She also noted the smashed bottle of whiskey "to our immense disappointment."

24.   Although Nevills makes light of this, Masland and the rest of the crew were very concerned by the long absence. When Nevills, Marston, and the two women did not return, the rest of the party was afraid there had been some accident. It was a bad place to camp, so all the others went on ahead while Masland and Doerr maintained a fire to guide the hikers in. They all ended up sleeping in the rocks above Tuna Creek. Nancy Streator was still suffering from the painful, infected blisters she had gotten walking down the Bright Angel Trail, and Nevills's shoulder was "rubbed raw" by the strap on the heavy radio. Ros Johnson wrote of the trek: "I've never been as near complete & utter exhaustion but the worst was I couldn't walk on my feet." She also says that they floated downriver a short way to a small beach at the head of Turquoise Rapid, where they spent the night.

25.   While Johnson was going on San Juan trips, Nevills had promised to let her row her own boat there, an unprecedented move among river runners of

the time. It's unclear whether she did indeed serve as a boatman, as her handwriting is difficult to decipher. But obviously he had enough confidence in her to let her take a boat through both Forester and Mile 217, neither of which is an inconsequential rapid.

26. The name "Enchanted Canyon" appears on no maps of this area. The valley above the Deer Creek grotto at one time was known as Surprise Valley, a name that has moved to the arid depression between Deer Creek and Tapeats Creek. Enchanted Canyon is indicative of Nevills's tendency to name features off-the-cuff, to impress passengers with the feeling of being pioneers, or because Nevills truly felt he was a pioneer. However, the Deer Creek Valley had long been well known both by Native Americans and early prospectors and surveyors. Some of Nevills's names stuck—especially in Glen Canyon—such as Twilight Canyon and Mystery Canyon. But names in the Grand Canyon were for the most part well-established by the time he came along.

27. A standard feature of his San Juan trips, this is the only time Nevills mentions his telling the story of Yogi, god of the river, on one of his Grand Canyon trips. It was a complete fabrication to impress the tourists, but like many boatmen, Nevills was never one to let facts get in the way of a good story. Alice Bates, a passenger on one of his San Juan trips in 1946, wrote: "Norm told us what caused [the sand waves] and why they were given their name but Norm's stories were many and varied. It was hard to tell where facts ended and fiction began" (box 29, folder 17, Nevills Papers). Above all, Nevills was a showman and many passengers on the San Juan trips recorded their memories of him recounting the tale of Yogi, which he usually did at the layover camp at the mouth of Forbidding Canyon, accompanied by a dramatic fire-fall off the cliff. Randall Henderson wrote: "It seems that Norman has a mythical pal—a follower of the ancient Hindu philosophy of Yoga, and has installed him as a sort of river god in the canyon country, to protect his boats and their human cargoes from the hazards of submerged rocks and rough water. Norman spins a long yarn about how Yogi happened to desert his ancient home in India and adopt the desert of the Southwest as his new abode" (Randall Henderson, "River Trail to Rainbow Bridge," *Desert Magazine* (September 1945): 19). In an exerpt from her May 1946 journal, Alice Bates writes: "Yogi, Nevills's mythical god of the river, was another aspect of his self-created river persona" (box 29, folder 17, Nevills Papers).

28. In John Doerr's diary, he records that the Hisers were upset about the camp at Havasu: "They called attention to situation at Havasu when Norm gave no instructions as to what to do." Neither Nancy Streator nor Frank Masland give any indication as to what the problem was, although Masland does note that it was a hot night, and they spent it on the rock ledges at the mouth of the canyon, waking the next morning in "pools of perspiration" (box 53, Marston Collection).

29. Nancy Streator wrote: "Not only were the rocks uncomfortable, but a lot of them were very small. These pebbles afforded Lucille [Hiser] with enough ammunition to fire at me during the whole hour after lunch."

30. Only Bert Loper flipped, the first time he had ever capsized a boat in over forty years on the river. Legend has it that he righted his boat and climbed back in, looked back up at the rapid, and said, "Kiss my ass!"

31. Nevills was correct. In 1957 there was a giant flood when the Colorado ran over 120,000 cfs, but the barge was still there until the early 1970s, when it was hauled out by Tour West.

32.   See *River Runners of the Grand Canyon* by David Lavender for a good account of these up river attempts.

33.   See the notes for 1947 for more about the missing Charles Roemer. Both Nancy Streator and Frank Masland commented on the speculation that the raft belonged to the ill-fated Roemer, but it was later proven to belong to a Boy Scout troop led by Al Quist, and had been lost in Glen Canyon earlier that year.

34.   This situation was considerably more dangerous than Nevills lets on here, and the others were very concerned. Frank Masland recorded: "Two-thirds of the way up he ran into trouble. He couldn't go up and he couldn't go down, and spent about an hour trying to figure how to get out of there. Everything he touched was loose and came crashing down 300' or 400' to the rocks below. Finally, he made it to the top, and then came down the talus slope, the easy way."

35.   The pyromania evident in all the men taken to extremes: Dock Marston set fire to the bunkhouse tent with Masland and Nevills sleeping inside. Ros Johnson described Marston as being "in rare high spirits today . . ."

36.   Ros Johnson commented about the tow-out across the lake that "The trip down the lake was wonderful—we feasted on the food brought us & stopped in a cove to have lunch & swim—the boats just nosing into the sand—it was so much fun—much dousing & general horse-play. Far from the anti-climax someone warned the lake would be, I found truly that one was 'so full of so much'—I spent most of the six hours of the trip in my always favorite spot on a ship, the prow, joined by Frank & Nance who also appreciate it. The trip is over—I feel above all a great and overwhelming satisfaction & very deep gratitude" (box 13, folder 6, Nevills Papers).

37.   Many of these people had met the Nevills Expedition party the previous year as well.

38.   Indeed, the tramway was an open car with no rails on the sides, which went down a steep cable. Nancy Streator noted that "several of us were frightened stiff," and most sat in the center of the platform and refused to budge.

39.   "Two Little Flies" is the name of a nonsense song made up by Tro Anspach, a passenger on a Nevills San Juan River trip in 1948, and on the next year's Grand Canyon run. Adopted by Nevills, it was added to and modified by many subsequent river parties. Some examples of verses: "Some little flies decided to roam / So they packed their bags and they left their home / Flew right out to Mexican Hat / And signed for trip in nothing flat / [chorus] / You fly right over the rapids rough / And take to the thrills with a huff and a puff / The fly at the oars in the boat in the lead / Is a fly called 'Norm' of a higher breed." And so on, for many verses. The chorus was "Some were black and some were blue / And some had spots on their tra-la-loo / Others had spots on their tra-la-loo / Hi, oh, the Merry O!" For more of the verses, see box 29, folder 39, Nevills Papers.

1949 JOURNAL

1.   P. T. Reilly's real name was Plez Talmadge, so he either went by P. T. or Pat. He was an engineer from North Hollywood, California, and first wrote to Nevills about taking a San Juan trip in 1946. After a couple of false starts, he and his wife, Susie, were able to take a trip in May 1947, and "really had a swell time." Like so many others, Reilly could not get the river and the canyons

out of his mind, and by the next year had signed on to be a boatman on that season's San Juan trips. Since he did so well on those, Nevills asked him to be a boatman on the big trips for the 1949 season, an offer Reilly accepted with alacrity. Two weeks was too long for the showman Nevills and the no-nonsense engineer Reilly, however, and their personalities began to clash, as shown in Reilly's diary. After Nevills's death, Reilly continued his river career, building and designing his own boats, and running them through the Grand Canyon and other places. He is generally credited with being one of the people who helped introduce the dory to river running in the Grand Canyon, along with Martin Litton.

2. For more about the Desloge family, as well as Nancy Streator, see the notes for 1948. Barney Desloge was another son of Joseph Desloge Sr.

3. Arthur H. Compton was a physicist of great renown from the University of Chicago. He won the 1927 Nobel Prize in physics, and had a distinguished academic career. John Compton, himself to become a professor of philosophy, was their youngest son. Oddly, there is no correspondence file with Dr. Compton in the Nevills Papers, so there is no information on how he became interested in Nevills Expedition.

4. Alice Bates went on a Nevills San Juan trip in 1946, and tried to sign up for the 1949 Green River trip, but it had already filled. However, Nevills wrote and offered to take her through Split Mountain as his guest, which she accepted. She wrote a detailed account of the trip called "Drifting Along with the Current," which she sent to Nevills. It can be found in box 29, folder 33 of the Nevills Papers.

5. John and Evie Mull were from Malvern, Pennsylvania. They took a San Juan trip with Nevills in May 1949, and had such a good time that they immediately signed up for the Lees Ferry to Bright Angel section of that year's Grand Canyon trip.

6. Josiah Eisaman was a physician from Pittsburgh, Pennsylvania. Anne was his daughter. Unlike most people on Nevills's Grand Canyon trips, he had not been on the San Juan and signed up directly for the Grand Canyon in early 1949. A great deal of the correspondence between him and Nevills concerns his wife's worries about allowing her daughter to go, but Nevills was able to soothe her fears, and Anne made the trip in good style.

7. Edwin McKee had actually been on the river in the Grand Canyon before Nevills's first trip in 1938. A National Park Service geologist, he accompanied the 1937 Cal Tech-Carnegie Tech scientific party from the Bass Trail in October of that year. McKee came along as Nevills's guest on the first leg of the 1949 Grand Canyon trip, and used the time to make scientific studies and collect geological data. Frank Masland, foreshadowing what would become a trend on river trips in the future (including a specialist to interpret the trip), wrote of McKee: "Eddie added immeasurably through his knowledge and willingness to teach us. I have never known anyone who more thoroughly knew his subject."

8. In 1946, Molly Maley saw the Burton Holmes travelogue film about Nevills's San Juan expeditions, and wrote to Nevills asking about the trips. She went with Nevills in May 1947, and wanted to go on the 1948 Grand Canyon run, but by the time she wrote, it was full. She was able to sign up for the first part of the 1949 trip, and left at Bright Angel. A copy of the Burton Holmes travelogue about Nevills Expedition is in the Norman Nevills Audio-Visual

Collection, A0241.

9.   For more on Frank Masland, see the 1948 notes.

10.   William Hargleroad Jr., of Omaha, Nebraska, is something of a mystery, for there are only two letters from him in the Nevills Papers. By the time he wrote the first one (June 17, 1949), he had already signed up for the 1949 Grand Canyon trip. Even though he had paid full passage, he left at Bright Angel because, according to P. T. Reilly, he "figured the next two weeks on top of the first half would be too rugged." Hargleroad wrote again on August 8, giving no indication of why he left, and indeed, saying, "It is pleasant to be home again but I certainly look back with pleasure on our trip. I don't know of anything I ever have done since I soloed that gave me as much satisfaction. You certainly do know how to run a good expedition and with Doris as the business manager, you make a fine team" (box 12, folder 21, Nevills Papers).

11.   For more on the Marble Canyon dam site, see the notes for 1948.

12.   The story of Loper's end is one of the best known on the river. His body was found almost twenty-five years later, about fifty miles downriver, near Cardenas Creek. After identification, he was removed from his beloved canyon and buried next to his wife, Rachel, in Sandy, Utah. Despite his age and poor health, Loper had insisted on the trip and built the boat as described, probably aware he didn't have long to live. The boat was still there as late as the 1990s, but by today has deteriorated to a pile of wood and nails. A plaque set into a boulder just above it tells his fate.

13.   What made the fire roar even brighter was the addition of two cans of gasoline found in a nearby driftwood pile that Nevills and Jim Rigg poured on the flames. Marston had stashed the gas for one of his upriver runs, and when he found out that Nevills had burned it, he was enraged and blamed Nevills. In 1952, Rigg wrote a long apologetic note to Marston, confessing that it had been he who discovered the gasoline cans and encouraged Nevills to pour it on the flames, with predictable results: "I must confess that the gasoline almost got even with us for the sin we did," he wrote. "I nearly burned my hair and my eyebrows and Norm would have too, except he had just turned to high tail it when it blew." He rather lamely explained the reason for burning the gas: "As a matter of fact the reasoning behind [burning] the gasoline was that you had been unsuccessful in your attempt to run up-stream, the gasoline was there for the run up-stream, and because of your failure, you would never need it again." Despite Rigg's apology, Marston remained upset over the incident for the rest of his life (box 198, Marston Collection).

14.   "Perilous Voyage: Girl Shoots River Rapids," *Citizen-Times* (Hollywood, CA), July 26, 1949.

15.   Mary Ogden Abbott was a woodcarver and sculptor from Sudbury, Massachusetts. After reading Wallace Stegner's article in the *Atlantic Monthly* ("Backroads River," January 1948), she wrote to Nevills and inquired about the trips, and went with him on the San Juan in the summer of 1948. By the next year she was ready for the Grand Canyon, and signed on for the section from Bright Angel to Lake Mead. She fit perfectly into the group; camped at Elves Chasm, Frank Masland recorded seeing her walking along the beach: "Mary just passed, walking down the beach like an old Roman on parade. Many colored bathing suit, great green hat, erect carriage, Mona Lisa slight smile—or grin" (*By the Rim of Time*, box 29, folder 36, Nevills Papers). After the death of Norman and Doris, Masland commissioned her to design the

memorial plaque that was placed near the Navajo Bridge in 1950.

16. R. J. and Tro Anspach lived in New Jersey, where he was "one of about seven million people fighting one another for a few dollars in New York City." However, as he wrote Nevills in August 1947, he had always wanted to live in the West and spent at least a month each year exploring the country. Then Bud, as he was known, saw a notation on a Conoco road map that read, "Scenic boat trip, Mexican Hat to Lee's Ferry," and immediately wrote to sign on for a trip. They went in June 1948, and were quickly persuaded to book part of the 1949 Grand Canyon trip. Tro Anspach was the author of the nonsense song, "Two Little Flies." See the 1948 notes for more about the song.

17. Helen Kendall, from Long Beach, California, read Randall Henderson's article on the Nevills San Juan trips in *Desert Magazine* and immediately wrote to Nevills asking to go along. She described herself thus: "I can swim, sleep on a rock, eat anything, do not mind hardships and can agree with almost anyone." She went on the San Juan in May 1948, and kept a detailed diary which she later sent a copy of to Nevills, where it can be found in box 29, folder 29 of the Nevills Papers. An adventurous woman, she had hiked to the bottom of the Grand Canyon and back in 1926, making the same time as the mule train, so it was not hard for Nevills to convince her to try the Grand Canyon. She went on a number of other river trips in the ensuing years, including trips with Mexican Hat Expeditions and Georgie White's Share-the-Expense Expeditions. She was killed in a traffic accident in Los Angeles in 1961.

18. For Nevills previous visit to the site of their camp, see the 1948 journal and notes.

19. The rapids are Agate, Sapphire, Turquoise, Ruby, and Serpentine. Hence the title, the "Gems"; they are sometimes called the "Jewels."

20. Masland didn't keep the boat, however; after Nevills's death he returned it to the family. For the eventual fate of the *Mexican Hat II*, see the notes for 1940.

A NOTE ON THE SOURCES

1. Gaylord Stavely, "Norman Nevills,"*Boatman's Quarterly Review* 17, no. 1 (spring 2004): 26.

2. Copies of all of these articles can be found in box 38 of the Nevills Papers.

3. David Lavender, *River Runners of the Grand Canyon* (Grand Canyon, AZ: Grand Canyon Natural History Association, 1986).

4. Nancy Nelson, *Any Time, Any Place, Any River: The Nevills of Mexican Hat* (Flagstaff, AZ: Red Lake Books, 1991).

5. William E. Cook, *The Wen, the Botany, and the Mexican Hat: The Adventures of the First Women Through Grand Canyon on the Nevills Expedition* (Orangevale, CA: Callisto Books, 1987).

Index